Hermann Olshausen

Biblical commentary on the Gospels and on the Acts of the Apostles

Adapted expressly for preachers and students

Hermann Olshausen

Biblical commentary on the Gospels and on the Acts of the Apostles
Adapted expressly for preachers and students

ISBN/EAN: 9783337281151

Printed in Europe, USA, Canada, Australia, Japan

Cover: Foto ©Lupo / pixelio.de

More available books at **www.hansebooks.com**

BIBLICAL COMMENTARY

ON

THE GOSPELS,

AND ON

THE ACTS OF THE APOSTLES,

ADAPTED EXPRESSLY FOR PREACHERS AND STUDENTS,

BY HERMANN OLSHAUSEN, D.D.,
PROFESSOR OF THEOLOGY IN THE UNIVERSITY OF ERLANGEN.

TRANSLATED FROM THE GERMAN.

THIRD EDITION.

VOL. I.

EDINBURGH:
T. AND T. CLARK, 38, GEORGE STREET.
LONDON: HAMILTON, ADAMS, AND CO.   DUBLIN: JOHN ROBERTSON.

MDCCCLX.

TABLE OF CONTENTS.

	PAGE
Translator's Preface,	ix
Author's Preface,	xi

INTRODUCTION.

	PAGE
§ 1. On the Origin of the Gospel-Collection,	1
§ 2. On the Character of the Gospel-Collection,	3
§ 3. On the Affinity of the first three Gospels,	6
§ 4. On the Gospel of St. Matthew,	8
§ 5. On the Gospel of St. Mark,	12
§ 6. On the Gospel of St. Luke,	15
§ 7. On the Harmony of the Gospel-History,	17
§ 8. On the Credibility of the Gospel-History,	22
§ 9. Survey of the Literature,	28

FIRST PART.

OF THE BIRTH AND CHILDHOOD OF JESUS CHRIST. Matth. i., ii.; Luke i., ii.

FIRST SECTION.

ST. MATTHEW'S ACCOUNT—Chaps. i., ii.

	PAGE
§ 1. Genealogy of Jesus. Matth. i. 1-17; Luke iii. 23-38,	35
§ 2. The Birth of Jesus. Matth. i. 18-25,	43
§ 3. Visit of the Magi—Flight into Egypt—Murder of the Children—Arrival at Galilee. Matth. ii. 1-23,	56

SECOND SECTION.

ST. LUKE'S ACCOUNT—Chaps. i., ii.

	PAGE
§ 1. Proëmium. Luke i. 1-4,	73
§ 2. Annunciation of the Birth of John the Baptist. Luke i. 5-25,	80
§ 3. Annunciation of the Birth of Jesus. Mary's Visit to Elisabeth. Luke i. 26-56,	91

§ 4. John's Birth and Circumcision. Prophecies of Zacharias concerning him and Christ. Luke i. 57-80,
§ 5. Birth, Circumcision, and Presentation of Jesus in the Temple. Luke ii. 1-40,
§ 6. Jesus converses with the Priests in the Temple. Luke ii. 41-52,

SECOND PART.

OF JOHN THE BAPTIST. CHRIST'S BAPTISM AND TEMPTATION.

Matth. iii. 1—iv. 12; Mark i. 2-13; Luke iii. 1—iv. 13.

§ 1. John's Doctrine and Baptism. Matth. iii. 1-12; Mark i. 2-9; Luke iii. 1-20,
§ 2. The Baptism of Christ. Matth. iii. 13-17; Mark i. 9-11; Luke iii. 21-23; John i. 32-34,
§ 3. Christ's Temptation. Matth. iv. 1-11; Mark i. 11, 12; Luke iv. 1-13,

THIRD PART.

OF CHRIST'S WORKS AND DISCOURSES, PARTICULARLY IN GALILEE.

Matth. iv. 12—xviii. 35; Compared with Mark i. 14—ix. 50; and Luke iv. 14—ix. 50.

§ 1. Jesus appears as a Teacher. Matth. iv. 12-17; Mark i. 14, 15; Luke iv. 14, 15,
§ 2. Jesus chooses Disciples. Matth. iv. 18-22; Mark i. 16-20,
§ 3. Christ's Sermon on the Mount. Matth. iv. 23—vii. 29,
§ 4. Healing of a Leper. Matth. viii. 1-4; Mark i. 40-45; Luke v. 12-16,
§ 5. Healing of the servant of a Centurion. Matth. viii. 5-13; Luke vii. 1-10,
§ 6. Raising of the young Man at Nain. Luke vii. 11-17,
§ 7. Healing of Peter's Mother-in-law. Matth. viii. 14-17; Mark i. 29-34; Luke iv. 31-41,
§ 8. Peter's Draught of Fishes. Luke iv. 42-44; Mark i. 35-39; Luke v. 1-11,
§ 9. Jesus stills the Sea. Matth. viii. 18-27; Mark iv. 35-41; Luke viii. 22-25,
§ 10. Cure of the Gadarene Demoniac. Matth. viii. 28-34; Mark v. 1-20; Luke viii. 26-39,
§ 11. Cure of a Paralytic. Matth. ix. 1-8; Mark v. 21; ii. 1-12; Luke v. 17-26,

ORDER OF THE SECTIONS OF THE GOSPELS IN VOLUME I.

ARRANGED AFTER EACH GOSPEL.

ST. MATTHEW.

	PAGE			PAGE
Chap. i., ii.	35—73	Chap.	viii. 1—4	235—245
,, iii. 1—12	151—158	,,	viii. 5—13	245—251
,, iii. 13—17	158—165	,,	viii. 14—17	254—256
,, iv. 1—11	165—175	,,	viii. 18—27	263—265
,, iv. 12—17	176—179	,,	viii. 28—34	265—282
,, iv. 18—22	179—180	,,	ix. 1—8	282—288
,, iv. 23—7, 29	180—235			

ST. MARK.

	PAGE			PAGE
Chap. i. 1	35	Chap.	i. 35—39	256—263
,, i. 2—8	141—158	,,	i. 40—45	235—245
,, i. 9—11	158—165	,,	ii. 1—12	282—288
,, i. 12—13	165—175	,,	iv. 35—41	263—265
,, i. 14—15	176—179	,,	v. 1—20	265—282
,, i. 16—20	179—180	,,	v. 21	282—288
,, i. 29—34	254—256			

ST. LUKE.

	PAGE			PAGE
Chap. i., ii.	73—136	Chap.	v. 1—11	256—263
,, iii. 1—20	141—158	,,	v. 12—16	235—245
,, iii. 21—23	158—165	,,	v. 17—26	282—288
,, iii 23—28	35—43	,,	vii. 1—10	245—251
,, iv. 1—13	165—176	,,	viii. 11—17	251—254
,, iv. 14, 15	176—179	,,	viii. 22—25	263—265
,, iv. 31—41	254—256	,,	viii. 26—39	265—282
,, iv. 42—44	256—263			

TRANSLATOR'S PREFACE.

THE work, a part of which is here presented to the English reader, has attained such a deserved celebrity in Germany, and is so well known to students of German literature in our own country, that a translation of it cannot but be welcomed by those to whom the original is inaccessible. The portion of Scripture also to which it relates, offers a peculiarly interesting field for study. The difficulties we there meet with have been turned, by the adversaries of the truth, into weapons of attack; and the only successful defence that can be made is derived from a deeper study of these records; and the very circumstance of our possessing more than one narrative of the life and sufferings of our blessed Lord, which, at first sight, might appear to give room for cavil, and afford a vantage ground for the opponents of the Gospel, does, in truth, constitute one of the strongest props of the historical argument for Christianity. But there are other difficulties in the interpretation of the Gospels still greater than these. They are the necessary result of the *form* of this part of God's revelation. These records present to us not an orderly system of truth, but a most impressive picture of the holy life and divine instructions of our Saviour Jesus Christ. They belong to a transition period, when the former things that had decayed and waxed old were "ready to vanish away;" and we see the great principles of the Christian economy, and the grand motives of the Christian life, which had been only obscurely intimated under the old dispensation, now gradually unfolded by the teaching and example of the Son of God, and just ready to assume that matured form, in which it has pleased God to give them to us by the holy Apostles. Hence the Gospel-narratives bear the impress of that period, and the form of revelation in them is less easily reducible to our modes of thought, requiring both depth and spirituality of mind to grasp the principles, as well as judgment to apply them. The author of this Commentary has brought a large measure of these qualifications to bear upon his work, as none can fail to recognize the sincere piety which pervades his investigations into the meaning and spirit of Scripture. It will readily be seen, that the author is by no means a rigid disciple of any school of theology. He evidently does not call Calvin master, which is not surprising in one whose opinions were formed in the communion of the Lutheran Church. This will subject him to the charge of looseness from many, and may induce some, perhaps, to condemn the book altogether, instead of applying the Apostle's injunction: "Prove all things; hold fast that which is good."

To a translator, the work presents some special difficulties, from the very abstract mode of thought and expression with which it abounds. To this tendency in the German mind, the native tongue is as congenial as the English language is unsuited, and a translator must be allowed some liberty in departing from such a literal rendering as would leave the sense obscure, not to say unintelligible. In the present translation, I have endeavoured to give the sense of such passages in a form as much adapted to the English idiom as I could cast them; and though I cannot expect, at all times, to have succeeded, yet I would hope the pains have not been altogether in vain.

A few notes have been added, principally where the authorized English version differs from the translation adopted by OLSHAUSEN, and sometimes where the author's peculiar views required some notice. The latter have been introduced very sparingly, not from want of occasions of difference of opinion, but from the feeling, that many, into whose hands this translation will come, would not sympathize with those differences, and that most readers would themselves notice and weigh them. Great care has been taken to verify the references to Scripture. It will be observed, that there are some to the apocryphal books of the Old Testament. The views of German Theologians respecting these books differ from those usually entertained in this country; but as none of the quotations in this volume is adduced to establish a doctrinal point, I have not scrupled to leave them unaltered. The references to other works have not always been verified, as I had not all the books at hand; but, from the general correctness of those that have been so compared, I expect very few errors will be found.

H. B. CREAK.

AUTHOR'S PREFACE.

THE plan and arrangement of this work, notwithstanding many alterations and additions in the details, remain essentially the same in this new edition of the Commentary, since I think I may take it for granted that, in these points, I have met the wants of our times. I regard it as my chief object to bring out the inward unity of the whole New Testament, and of the Scriptures generally, and, by the interpretation, to introduce the reader to the unity of life and spirit in the Sacred Books. To have been continually noticing interpretations which originate in entirely separate views, as well as to have been constantly opposing unchristian tendencies, would have rendered it impossible to enter into the spirit of the Bible, since in that way the flow of the spirit would necessarily have been interrupted. The exegetical lectures have to supply what is necessary in reference to the enumeration of different interpretations, the refutation of errors, the grammar, archaeology, and history.

Hence it naturally follows, that, in this third edition, such lately published works as Strauss' Life of Jesus, and De Wette's Commentary, (who professes to agree with Strauss in the principles, but would prefer a less extensive application of them, which is, indeed, evidently inconsistent, as Strauss has very justly demonstrated in reply to him, see "*Berliner Jahrbücher*," 1837, No. 1, ff.) could not be noticed by me, inasmuch as there is a difference of principles between their authors and myself. In those passages where that difference was not involved, I have not omitted to notice these works also, but have used them as well as treatises more congenial to my own mind, among which I mention particularly Tholuck's masterpiece of exposition on the Sermon on the Mount, in order, by strict impartiality, to gather with increasing purity the sense of the Word of God. Still it was very rarely that I gained any light from the works of Strauss and De Wette, even as to the externals of Scripture;

while I am greatly indebted to Tholuck's labours in every respect.

Still, as the notorious work of Strauss contains a continued series of attacks on my Commentary, I make use of this opportunity to explain my silence with reference to these attacks. At first, I determined to write a special work on the subject; but the composition of it was prevented by protracted illness. Meanwhile, such a flood of refutations is being poured forth, that I cannot even begin to write down my thoughts, because every moment brings some book or pamphlet, which has already discussed first this point and then the other on which I intended to enlarge. On the other hand, not a single work appeared in favour of Strauss; and even in the few critiques that were somewhat favourable, nothing new whatsoever was brought forward in confirmation of his view. All parties in the theological world are unanimous in the rejection of his work. This being the state of affairs, the danger to theology from Strauss' work may, we hope, be regarded as removed; among the laity, indeed, it will do the more mischief. Of course, science is not to expect thus to be freed from the conflict; for even though the inapplicablity of the mythical interpretation to the New Testament has been evidently demonstrated, yet heroes will soon arise to call our courageous and unprejudiced Strauss a cowardly poltroon, full of superstitious assumptions, because he did not dare to speak out plainly, but only now and then gently hints that Christianity and the books of the New Testament are to him simply the product of unbounded fanaticism, or, to speak more decidedly, of a monstrous deception. As Dr. Paulus at first propounded his natural explanation of the miracles amid loud rejoicing, and now sees it turned to ridicule by Strauss, who stands upon his shoulders, a similar result awaits the latter with his mythical explanation. And unless we are greatly mistaken in reading the signs of the times, Strauss will not need, like his predecessor, to live to be eighty years old, in order to hear with his own ears the derision of his more decided disciples. The members of Antichrist are extending vigorously in the bosom of society, in order soon to appear in their consummation. The pace of the world's history is continually being accelerated. May but the Church of Christ attain more and more to a knowledge of itself, so as to be able to separate itself from all antichristian elements; and may Christian science vigorously guard itself against the dangerous error of supposing that such excrescences of unbelief, as the hypothesis of the mythical character of the New Testament, necessarily belong to the course of its development! Such phenomena, Theology ought to treat purely apologetically,—*i. e.*, in that department which defends the domain of Christian science against attacks from without; in its inward sanctuary such inventions have no place at all.

In an apologetic point of view, I still intend to contribute something towards a refutation of the mythical system, inasmuch as I propose to myself a renewed comprehensive investigation on the genuineness of the Gospels, which Dr. Theile of Leipsic has kindly invited me to do in his work recently published against Strauss. If it be proved that our canonical Gospels are the productions of eye-witnesses of the facts, the applicability of the mythical interpretation of the life of Jesus vanishes most certainly and completely, according to Strauss' own confession. If God grant life and health, I shall proceed to this recasting of my earlier work on the genuineness of the Gospels, immediately after the completion of the printing of the third edition of the second volume.

* * * * *

THE AUTHOR.

August 19, 1837.

PROOF OF THE GENUINENESS

OF THE

'INGS OF THE NEW TESTAMENT:

FOR

INTELLIGENT READERS OF ALL CLASSES

TRANSLATED FROM THE GERMAN

OF

DR. HERMANN OLSHAUSEN,
PROFESSOR OF THEOLOGY IN THE UNIVERSITY OF ERLANGEN,

WITH NOTES, BY

DAVID FOSDICK, Jr.

CONTENTS.

Author's Preface,

Introduction,

CHAP. I.
Of the New Testament in General,

CHAP. II.
Of the Collection of the Gospels,

CHAP. III.
Of the Gospels Individually, and the Acts of the Apostles,

CHAP. IV.
Of the Pauline Epistles,

CHAP. V.
Continuation. Of the Pauline Epistles composed during and after Paul's imprisonment at Rome,

CHAP. VI.
Of the Epistle to the Hebrews,

CHAP. VII.
Of the Catholic Epistles,

CHAP. VIII.
Of the Second Epistle of Peter,

CHAP. IX.
Of the Epistles of James and Jude,

CHAP. X.
Of the Revelation of John,

Conclusion,

AUTHOR'S PREFACE.

SEVEN years ago, when I published my history of the Gospels, it was my earnest desire to show the genuineness of all the books of the New Testament, in a small work, designed for intelligent readers generally. But, urgent as the necessity of such a work appeared to me even then, the execution of my plan has been postponed to the present time; partly because I was hindered from entering upon it by multiplied avocations, and partly because I hoped some one would present himself who was more capable of such an undertaking than I felt myself to be. For I knew but too well how difficult it would be for me to write simply and plainly, so as to become even intelligible to those who are not conversant with investigations of such a description as must be noticed in this work. As, however, no one has yet appeared to present such a work to the Church of Christ, and the necessity of it has meanwhile much increased, nothing remained for me but to surmount my scruples, and execute the work as well as the Lord might permit.

The necessity of such a work will have been evident to every one who has observed how certain positions as to the pretended spuriousness, or at least suspicious character, of the writings of the New Testament (positions which were formerly current only within the circle of the clergy), are now entertained among the common laity. It is easy to imagine the injury which is effected by such foolish opinions. To the audacious opponents of Divine truth, they afford a fine occasion for repelling every attempt to win their assent to it; and well-meaning persons often find in them occasion of doubts and anxiety, which they might be spared, did they only at least receive the antidote at the same time with the poison. Such an antidote, to obviate, or at least lessen, the destructive consequences of the views of many theologians in regard to the biblical books (views which are diffused abroad sometimes indiscreetly, and sometimes with a bad intention), I wish this little work to be considered.

It will, at the same time, be my endeavour to correct the views of many not very clear-sighted though well-meaning persons, who appear to think that all critical investigations of the genuineness or spuriousness of the books of the Bible are, as such, wrong, and take their origin from unbelief. This idea is fundamentally erroneous, and not seldom arises from a religious conceit, to which there is a special liability on the part of persons who, conscious of their own internal religious life, dispense with all enlarged views of the connection of theology with the whole Church of God on earth, and nevertheless are tempted to judge of things beyond the pale of their capacity. It would have been better, therefore, had all such investigations been confined within the circle of theologians; but, as the doubts to which we have referred, have been promulgated among the laity, their refutation must also find a place in general literature.

I should very readily have extended my investigations to the writings of the Old Testament; but have not, in the first place, because the results of researches in regard to the Old Testament are of a less stable character than in regard to the New; and, moreover, because those who are not theologians by profession have far less need of such information in regard to the Old Testament as is here given concerning the New, inasmuch as to Christians the testimony of Christ and his apostles respecting the Old Testament, the canon of which was then completed, affords a much more certain evidence of its Divine origin (and thus of its genuineness), than any historical reasoning could exhibit, especially since, from the paucity of sources of information, the latter could not be so satisfactory as it is in relation to the New Testament. As to unbelievers, it is of much greater consequence to urge the claims of the New Testament upon them than those of the Old, because, so long as they are opposed to the former, they certainly will not admit the latter. In my closing remarks, however, I have endeavoured to designate briefly the right point of view in the determination of critical questions concerning the Old Testament.

To conclude, I pray that the Lord may be pleased graciously to accompany this my book with his blessing, and cause it to serve as an admonition to many a scoffer, and to console and set at ease the minds of such as have been perplexed with doubts.

OLSHAUSEN.

INTRODUCTION.

For fifteen hundred years, the New Testament, as we now possess it, has been generally current in the Christian Church, and constantly used, as well publicly in the churches as likewise in the domestic circles of believers. This fact is admitted by the scholars of modern times unanimously, since it can be shown by the most certain historical proofs. Hence, all investigations concerning the genuineness of the writings of the New Testament, and the manner of its formation, relate only to the first few centuries after the ascension of our Saviour and the death of the apostles. Indeed, it is easily seen that in reality everything must depend on this primitive period; for, after the New Testament was once made up and generally admitted in the Church, it could not be lost. Even before the invention of printing, it was spread abroad in all parts of the Christian world by a multitude of copies, it being more frequently transcribed than all other books together. Hence, even supposing that the New Testament, say by war or devastation, had utterly perished in any country, it would immediately have been introduced again from surrounding ones. Of this, however, there is no example. Even such churches as entirely lost connection with the great Catholic Church, and on that account sank to a very low point, yet faithfully preserved the sacred Scriptures, as is proved by the instance of the Ethiopian Church, in which, on its discovery after the lapse of centuries, the Bible was found still in use.

From the great importance of the New Testament to the Church and the whole civilized world, it was a very natural desire on the part of scholars, to know exactly how this momentous book was formed. On entering upon this inquiry, however, in the perusal of the earliest writers of the Church, accounts were met with which were somewhat difficult of adjustment. It was found that even before the compilation of all the writings of the New Testament into one collection, many fathers of the Church, perfectly well disposed towards Christianity, had doubted the genuineness of particular books of the New Testament. This circumstance naturally arrested attention, and the next inquiry was, what grounds such early fathers might have had for scruples respecting these writings. In considering this question, one thought he had discovered this reason and another that; and it often happened that these reasons were considered weighty enough to justify the ancient doubts as to the genuineness of the books. It was at the Reformation, particularly, that this free investigation of the Bible began to extend widely; and among the Reformers Luther himself was specially remarkable for it. From these inquiries he became fully convinced of the genuineness of most of the writings of the New Testament; but he supposed it necessary to regard some of them, *e. g.* the Epistle of James, and John's Revelation, as spurious. In this opinion he certainly erred, particularly, as is now acknowledged by nearly all scholars, in his rejection of the Epistle of James; but great as was, and still is, his authority in the eyes of many millions of Christians, his belief of the spuriousness of these two books has done no essential harm; they have maintained their place in the New Testament since as before, and the circumstance of his rejecting them has only shown the Church the truth of the old remark, that even God's saints may err.

From this example may be clearly seen, however, the total groundlessness of the fear of those who imagine that such scrutinizing inquiries must be, in and of themselves, prejudicial to the Church. Such examinations of the origin of holy writ, and its individual books, are not only *allowable*, but absolutely *indispensable;* and they will injure the Church no more than gold is injured by being carefully tried in the fire. The Church, like the gold, will but become purer for the test. In the Scriptures, both of the Old and New Testament, the eternal revelation of God reposes in quiet security and brightness. A wonderful Divine ordination has preserved it to us without any essential injury, through a succession of dark ages. It exerts at the present day, upon all minds receptive of its spirit, the same blessed, sanctifying influence which the apostles claimed for it eighteen centuries ago. How, then, can these sacred books suffer from careful historical inquiry respecting their origin? Investigation must rather serve to confirm and fully establish belief in their purity and genuineness. That this is actually the effect of really learned investigations, is apparent, likewise, from the following instance. When the very erudite and truly pious Professor Bengel of Tubingen published his New Testament, with all the various readings which he had been able to discover, many minds were filled with anxiety, thinking that an entirely new Testament would be the result in the end, if all the various readings were hunted up. They thought it would be better to leave things as they were. But mark—although 40,000 various readings were discovered in the ancient MSS., the New Testament was hardly at all altered thereby; for very few readings were of a nature to have any essential bearing upon a doctrine. Most of them consisted of unimportant transpositions, or permutations of synonymous words (such as in English *also* for *and*, &c.); and though some readings were more considerable (as *e. g.* the celebrated passage, 1 John v. 7, "For there are three that bear witness in heaven, the Father, the Word, and the Holy Ghost, and these three are one," which must certainly be regarded as spurious), still they are really of no more consequence. For such is the nature of the Holy Scriptures, that there are always many proof passages for any important doctrine; and hence, although these words are withdrawn from the Bible, their purport is still eternally true, and the doctrine of the Holy Trinity remains at the present time, as before, the doctrine of the Church. Now that all the MSS. have been read and accurately collated, there is no further occasion for fear that somewhere or other something new may be discovered which will thrust the old-loved Bible aside. Moreover, the principles on which scholars determine the right one among different readings of the same passage are so skilfully devised, that it is almost impossible for a false reading to creep in; and, should one individual err in this respect, another immediately steps in and corrects the error.

It certainly is not to be denied that pious persons, who valued God's word, might well, for some time, be anxious at heart; for one biblical book after another was stricken from the list of those which were genuine, and at last we seemed to have none but spurious books in the Bible; though, on the other hand, it remained inexplicable who could have taken pains either to forge so many spurious writings himself, or to make a collection of them after they were forged. And then, what could have been the character of the deceitful author or authors (for, at all events, the books must have been written by somebody), who could compose *such* writings,—writings which for many centuries have consoled millions in calamity and death? It is now seen, however, that the reason why things were so for a time, was, not that men inquired and investigated (for no injury can ever accrue on that account), but that they did not prosecute the investigation with a *right spirit and disposition.* Every one can see that it is not a matter of indifference with what feelings we engage in investigations of this kind, in regard to the sacred books. Suppose a man to see in the books of the New Testament only monuments of antiquity, of just as little or as much value as other ancient writings, to have felt nothing of the saving influence of God's word upon his heart, and on that account to be devoid of love for it; yea, even to feel vexed that others should hold it so dear, and enviously and maliciously study how he might destroy their delight in this treasure—such a man, with his perverse disposition, would rake up any thing and every thing in order to undermine the foundation of the Church. Whether such corrupt motives have really operated in the heart of any inquirer, no man can determine. It is always presumption to take it upon ourselves to judge respecting the internal position or intention of any heart. We may even suppose one who rejects the whole New Testament to possess honesty and sincerity, which want only the necessary light of conviction. But the *possibility* that such motives may affect these investigations, certainly cannot be denied; and that is fully enough for our purpose. If, moreover, we look at the manner in which a Voltaire among the French, and a Bahrdt among the Germans, have treated the sacred books, we find cogent reason to *fear* that *they* did not keep themselves free from such corrupt motives, however heartily we wish that God's judgment may pronounce them pure. This consideration is of importance, however, because we may see from it how all depends on this interior state of mind with which a man commences his undertakings; so that even the noblest enterprise may, by an unholy intention, lead to pernicious results. But, setting entirely aside the possibility that a man may undertake investigations respecting the Scriptures in a positively corrupt state of mind, he may also do much injury therein from *levity and frivolity*. If he is not sufficiently penetrated with a conviction of the great importance of investigations concerning the genuineness of the Sacred Scriptures, if he does not treat the weaknesses of the Church with sufficient tenderness (for she may feel herself wounded in her most sacred interests by the inconsiderate expression of doubts), it may easily happen that, at the first impulse, upon some supposed discovery, this discovery will immediately be blazoned before the world, without having been previously *tested* with soberness and care by all the means within reach. There is little reason to doubt that vanity is commonly at the bottom of this superficial haste; for it is always delightful to what Paul calls the *old man* to be the author of any new and striking opinion. Had all inquirers been able properly to restrain this vain desire to shine, much offence would, without doubt, have been avoided, and many a heart would have escaped considerable suffering.

Still, in what department of life or knowledge have we not many errors to lament? He who knows his own heart aright will therefore forgive learned men, if they have now and then been governed by vanity or other wrong motives. The misuse of a good thing should not abolish its use; and it is still true that all investigations respecting the sacred books, their history, and compilation, are in themselves very useful and necessary, as without them we must be entirely in the dark in regard to their true character. We will only wish that henceforth the God of truth and love may infuse truth and love into the hearts of all inquirers, and then it will not be of any consequence that many books have been *pronounced* spurious; for, fortunately, they do not *become* spurious from the assertions of this or that man, and it is always allowable for another scholar to point out the errors of his predecessor. From this freedom of investigation, the truth will certainly come to light by degrees.

If the thoughts here presented be duly considered, it will be readily seen, that he who has deep love for the word of God need not take it much to heart, that this or that scholar has rejected a particular book. After long investigation, and frequent assertions, that most of the books of the New Testament are spurious, it is nevertheless now agreed among scholars generally, *that all the writings of the New Testament are genuine productions of the apostles.* As to several of them, it is true, precise certainty has not been attained, but it is to be hoped that uniformity will be exhibited soon in regard to these likewise; and, moreover, the difference of opinion in this view concerning several of these books is not so dangerous as it may appear. Concerning the *Epistle to the Hebrews, e. g.,* there is not uniformity of sentiment as yet. Many very estimable divines, with whom I feel myself constrained to coincide in opinion on this point, think that the Epistle was not composed by the Apostle Paul, but by some other very worthy member of the Apostolic Church. It is clear, however, that even though Paul did not write the Epistle, we cannot on this ground regard it as spurious, inasmuch as its author is not mentioned in it. Hence, the only question in relation to it is *who* was its author? and on that point it is hard to decide, from the obscurity of the accounts given by the ancient fathers of the Church. All, however, regard this Epistle as genuine, *i. e.,* it is universally believed that its author composed it without any intention to palm it off as the production of somebody else, for instance the Apostle Paul. Had that been his purpose, he would have taken care that the Epistle should at once be recognised as Paul's production, by assigning his name to it, or in some other way. The case is certainly different as to *the second Epistle of Peter,* against the genuineness of which many doubts are prevalent. In relation to this Epistle, the first inquiry is not *who* was its author? for the apostle Peter is most clearly designated as such, but *whether* Peter was really and truly the author? If the conclusion be that the Epistle cannot be attributed to Peter, then it must be forged or spurious. It has been attacked with more plausibility than any other book of the New Testament; and yet much may be said even in behalf of this Epistle, as we shall see hereafter. We may therefore assert, that by Divine Providence some good has already accrued from the rigorous sifting to which the books of the New Testament have been subjected in our day. True, it did at first seem as if the whole New Testament would, in the course of time, be declared spurious; but when the first heat was over, and sober perspicacity returned, it was seen by inquirers that far the greater part of its books rested on a firmer historical foundation than most works of profane antiquity, which all the world regard as genuine. Hence we may be of good courage in entering on the consideration of the individual books of the New Testament, for the result of critical investigation is by no means so much to be dreaded as is sometimes thought. First, however, we desire to premise something further respecting *the New Testament generally.*

CHAPTER I.

THE NEW TESTAMENT GENERALLY.

THE oldest traces of the existence of the whole New Testament as a settled collection, occur so late as three centuries after the time of the apostles. The particular reason why so long a period elapsed before this body of writings became definitely determined was, that its individual books, which of course existed before the whole collection, were at first circulated in part singly, and in part in smaller collections. For, so long as the apostles were upon earth, and the power of the Spirit from on high was in lively action in every member of the Church, so long there was no sensible necessity of a book to serve as the norm or rule of faith and practice. Whenever any uncertainty arose in regard to either, application was made to one of the apostles, and his advice was taken. The Epistles of the Apostle Paul owe their origin in part to such inquiries. Now some of the apostles lived to a very great age. Peter and Paul, it is true, died under the emperor Nero, (67 A.D.), suffering martyrdom at Rome; but the Evangelist John, who outlived all the rest, was upwards of ninety years of age at his death, which did not happen till the time of the emperor Domitian, at the close of the first century. Hence, in the lifetime of the apostles, though their writings were highly valued, they were naturally not regarded as sacred writings, which were to be the rule of faith; because there was a more immediate guarantee of truth in the living discourse of the apostles and their first companions, as also in the Holy Spirit, which was so powerfully exerting its influence upon the Church. The apostolic writings, therefore, were indeed read in the public assemblies, but not alone, and not regularly. The book for regular public reading was still the Old Testament; and this is always to be understood in the New Testament, when the Holy Scriptures are mentioned. Besides the apostolic writings, however, other profitable books were used for the edification of the Church. In particular, we have still some remains of the writings of immediate disciples of the apostles, commonly called *apostolic fathers*, which were publicly read in the ancient churches. These men all lived in the first century and some time in the second. Among them are Clement, bishop of Rome, Ignatius, bishop of Antioch, Polycarp, bishop of Smyrna, Hermas, who was probably presbyter at Rome, and the well-known Barnabas. The Epistles of Clement and Polycarp, as well as the Book of Hermas, were read with special assiduity in the ancient churches. On account of the great antiquity of these writings, the books of the New Testament are very seldom quoted in them, and much of what coincides with the contents of the New Testament, *e. g.* Christ's sayings, may have been drawn by these apostolic fathers from oral tradition as well as from perusal of the Gospels. Indeed, the former source is perhaps most probable, since Christians certainly did not then read the Gospels so assiduously as they were read in later times, when they could no longer listen to the living discourse of the apostles and their immediate companions. The reason why so few written remains of the immediate disciples of our Lord are now extant, is in part the long lapse of time, which has destroyed many books once current, but in part also that the ancient Christians laboured more than they wrote. The preaching of the gospel, and the regulation of infant churches, consumed so much of their time, that little remained to be employed in composition. Moreover, in the first century it was always as when Paul wrote the following declaration (1 Cor. i. 26): "Not many wise men after the flesh, not many noble were called." For the most part only people of inferior standing joined the Church of Christ; and these had neither the capacity nor the inclination to labour with the pen. In these circumstances, it is undoubtedly true that we find little information concerning the books of the New Testament in the first centuries. That they did, nevertheless, exist in the Church we shall prove hereafter. But it might be expected, then, that although the most ancient Christians do not speak of their sacred writings, still, the heathen writers of Greece and Rome must have done so, considering the multiplicity of their works on all subjects. The heathen writers, however, who were contemporary with the apostles and the Apostolic Church, make no mention of the apostolic writings, because they cared nothing at all about the Christian Church. They considered the Christians as only a sect of the Jews, and despised them as much as they did the latter. They therefore credited the malicious reports which were circulated respecting the Christians, and treated them, accordingly, as the offscouring of humanity. Such is the procedure of Tacitus, a noble Roman, who relates the persecution of the Christians under Nero. Thus, of course, nothing could induce the Greeks and Romans to cultivate acquaintance with the writings of the Christians, particularly as they were distasteful on another account, from their not being clothed in the same elegant language as their productions. It was only when the number of the Christians became so great as to excite apprehension, that they began to pay attention to everything of importance concerning this new sect, and so at last to their sacred books. But it is not till after the middle of the second century that we find examples like that of Celsus, who, in order to confute the Christians, made himself acquainted with their sacred books.

The original condition of the primitive Church, in which less stress was laid on the Scriptures than on the word of the apostles, was not indeed of long continuance. For the mighty outpouring of the Spirit, which, on the day of Pentecost filled the disciples of our Saviour, had hardly been communicated to a considerable number of other minds, and lost its first power, ere erroneous schisms began to prevail in the churches. The germs of these may even be discovered in the writings of the apostles. The first of these party divisions of the ancient Church was that of the *Jewish Christians*. As early as in the Epistle to the Galatians, Paul speaks expressly of persons who desired to bring the Galatian Christians again under the yoke of the law. They wished faith in Christ and his redemption to be regarded as insufficient for salvation, unless circumcision and the observance of the law were added. The great preacher of the Gentiles, however, zealously opposes this restricted idea of Christianity, and shows that the soul must lose Christ, if it seeks to use any other means of salvation. It was the object of the law of Moses to lead by its injunctions to conviction of sin, and thus to a desire for salvation; by its prophecies and types of Christ it was a schoolmaster to guide us to him; but salvation itself could come only from Christ. Still, Paul was by no means of opinion that those who were Jews by birth must not observe the law when they became Christians; he rather favoured their doing so, if the pious customs of their fathers had become dear to them, or if their own weakness, or that of the Jews around them, would be offended by the contrary course. Hence, the apostles who remained in Jerusalem till its destruction, as did Matthew and James, observed the law invariably, and so did Paul likewise, when he was in Jerusalem. But the apostles, as well as their true disciples, were far from being desirous to impose this observance of the law upon the Gentiles also. The milder, and really Christian view of the observance of the law, was constantly entertained by many Jewish Christians in Palestine, who in later times were called *Nazareans*. Many, on the contrary, took the wrong course, which the Apostle Paul reproved in certain individuals in Galatia, and these obtained the name of *Ebionites*. They, however, fell into other heresies, besides their idea of the necessity of circumcision and observance of the law in order to salvation, particularly in regard to the person of Christ. They denied the real divinity of our Lord, and regarded him as a son of Joseph, thus seceding wholly from the true Church of Christ.

In precise contrariety to this *Judaising* division of the Church, others entirely discarded Judaism. The instructions of the Apostle Paul had taken deep hold of their minds, and given them a strong conviction that the gospel went far beyond the formalities of Jewish practice, and would bring all nations under its sway. But from this perfectly correct idea they wandered into an opposition to the Old Testament, which was never felt in the slightest degree by the Apostle Paul. They remarked rightly, that in the Old Testament, the Divine *justice* was most prominently exhibited, in the revelation of a rigorous law; while the New most fully displayed Divine *mercy* in the revelation of forgiving love. But this fact, which was necessary for the education of mankind, since the need of salvation will never be felt until the claims of justice are perceived, was employed by them for the purpose of wholly disuniting the Old Testament from the New, and referring it to a distinct author. This sect are termed *Marcionites*, from Marcion, the man who urged this view to the greatest extreme. In connection with their opposition to Judaism, they also held Gnostic opinions (whence they are commonly ranked with the Gnostics), and these gave a hue to their absurd notion that the God of the Old Testament was different from that of the New. The Old Testament, they thought, presented to view a God of justice without love; the New Testament, one of love without justice; while, in reality, the only true God possesses both attributes in perfection. It is easy to see that in these notions Paganism is mingled with Christianity. The sublime nature of the latter was admitted by the Marcionites; but they could not look upon the other true form of religion, Judaism, as reconcilable with it. Hence, although they no longer revered the numberless gods of the heathen, they imagined the two attributes of God, justice and love, to centre in two distinct divine beings. Besides this ungrounded violence against Judaism, the Marcionites maintained a silly error in regard to Christ's nature, which was the precise opposite of the opinion of the Jewish Christians. The latter denied his divinity, and the Marcionites asserted that he had no true humanity. The humanity of Christ, said they, was only apparent. In their opinion, a purely heavenly vision was presented in the person of Jesus Christ; his life, and all his acts in life, were merely in appearance, designed to exhibit him to men in a human manner.

This idea the Marcionites entertained in common with the *Gnostics*, properly so called, who did indeed judge more correctly than the former, in regard to the mutual relation of Judaism and Christianity, but, on other points, maintained the most grievous errors. The seeds of their doctrine are referred to by the Apostle Paul, *e. g.* in 2 Tim. ii. 17, 18, where he warns against the heresy of Hymeneus and Philetus, who maintained that the resurrection of the dead had already taken place. For, as they denied the true humanity of Christ, they could not, of course, admit the corporeal resurrection of all men; and, therefore, understood it spiritually of the interior vivification of the heart by the spirit of Christ. Undoubtedly, this perversion of doctrine on the part of the Gnostics, is to be referred to their belief in another being besides God. While they regarded God as a pure spirit, the fulness of all good and all beauty, they looked upon matter as another being, the source of everything corporeal and visible, as also of all evil. It was from a mixture of the spiritual and the material that this world originated, and particularly man, who at one time displays so much that is lovely and elevated, at another, so much that is low and base. Thus, the only way to purify and sanctify man was, that he should be gradually freed from every thing material, and, by the divine germs of life within him, be brought back to God. It is easy to imagine what a distorted view of all the doctrines of salvation must be produced by such an idea, since holy writ nowhere countenances the opinion that evil resides in *matter*, but rather expressly refers it to the *will* of the creature, who, by disobedience to the holy will of the Creator, has destroyed in himself, and about him, the harmony which originally prevailed in the whole universe.

In this condition of things, then, when Jewish Christians, Marcionites, and Gnostics, to say nothing of other insignificant sects, were disturbing the unity of the Church, it was seen to be necessary that every effort should be exerted to uphold the purity of the apostolic doctrines. But, as at the time when these sects became very powerful, the apostles were no longer upon earth, no direct appeal could be made to their authority whenever oral tradition was adduced against them, these heretics appealed themselves to pretended communications from the apostles. The Gnostics, in particular, asserted that the deep wisdom which they taught in their schools was communicated by the apostles to only a few; very simple Christian truth alone, they supposed, was only for the multitude. What remained, therefore, since appeal to oral tradition from the apostles was of no avail, but reference to written authority? This could not be altered and falsified like oral language; it was better suited to be a fixed, unchangeable norm and rule of faith, and could therefore be employed with exceeding force and efficiency against all heretics. Thus the time was now come when a sifting and separation of the many professedly Christian writings scattered abroad in the Church was necessary. Moreover, the different sects of heretics had all sorts of forged writings among them, in which their peculiar opinions were presented in the names of celebrated prophets and apostles. Against such writings explicit declaration must be made, in order to preserve the true apostolic doctrine from mixture with erroneous and confused notions. As of course, however, individual fathers of the Church could have but little influence against the established sects of heretics, it was felt to be necessary that real Christians should be more closely and intimately united, and from the endeavour consequently made sprang the so-called *Catholic*, i. e. *Universal Church*. The teachers of the Church, as well as the laity, agreed together in the avowal of certain doctrines, which afterwards formed their creed or so-called *apostolic symbol*, because in them the true apostolic doctrines were stated in opposition to heretics. Thus it became practicable to set firm bounds to the tide of corruption; and thus the various sects were gradually suppressed by the preponderant influence of the universal Church. Still some of them lasted down to the fifth and sixth centuries.

This sifting of the various Christian writings demands a more careful consideration. It has been before remarked that certain edifying productions of estimable Fathers, *e. g.* Clement of Rome, Hermas, and others, were publicly read along with those of the apostles. Still, however profitable the perusal of these writings might be, the bishops of the Catholic Church correctly felt that they could be of no service against heretics, as these would not allow them any weight. Since, however, they commonly acknowledged the writings of the apostles, these and these alone could be appealed to in confutation of them. All such writings, therefore, as were allowed to be the compositions of other authors, were first separated from the rest. If this had not been done, it would have remained uncertain in all subsequent time what books were properly to be regarded as pure sources of apostolic doctrine; and at the time of the Reformation it would not have been so easy to restore the true uncorrupted doctrine of Christ by means of the Scriptures, as it actually was, on account of the circumstance that the genuine Scriptures were possessed in a separate, fixed collection. Now, in the endeavour to gather the genuine apostolic writings together by themselves, some of them were very easily distinguished from the rest as the apostolic productions. These were called universally-admitted writings; in Greek *Homologoumena.* Among these were reckoned the four Gospels of Matthew, Mark, Luke, and John; the Acts of the Apostles; the Epistles of the Apostle Paul to the Romans, Corinthians, Galatians, Ephesians, Philippians, Colossians, and Thessalonians, to Timothy, Titus, and Philemon; and, lastly, two Epistles of John and Peter, viz., only the first and largest of both apostles. Among these writings, it is true, there appear two which were not composed by apostles, *i. e.* by members of the first circle of twelve men which our Lord Jesus gathered about him. [It is to be observed that Paul ranked with these in authority, partly because of his immediate call by the Lord (Acts ix.) and partly on account of his extended and blessed labours in behalf of the Church.] We mean the Gospel of Mark and the work of Luke. We say the *work* of Luke, for Luke's Gospel and his Acts of the Apostles do but make two halves of the same work, as is plain from the commencement of the Acts. There was no scruple on the part of the Catholic Church to class these two works of assistants of the apostles with those really apostolic, because both wrote under the influence and approval of apostles. According to the unanimous account of the most ancient Christian Fathers, Mark wrote under the guidance of Peter, and Luke under that of Paul, so that Mark's was regarded as the Petrine, and Luke's as the Pauline Gospel.

These universally received writings of the apostles were divided into two collections. *First,* the four Gospels by themselves formed a collection called *the Gospel.* For, although this collection contained four narratives of our Lord's life, they were not regarded as different writings, but only as different aspects, or, so to speak, *sides* of one and the same work. Hence an ancient Father of the Church, Irenæus, Bishop of Lyons in France, terms the four Gospels, the one four-formed or four-sided Gospel. The other writings constituted a *second* collection which was termed *the apostle,* or the preaching of the apostle. Probably the name took its rise from the fact, that at first the Epistles of Paul alone were collected together, and he was called the apostle by way of eminence, especially in Europe, on account of his active labours. To this collection of Pauline

Epistles the Acts of the Apostles were added subsequently, because it formed, as it were, an introduction to the Epistles, containing an account of Paul's travels and labours in the vineyard of our Lord. Later still were also added the two larger Epistles of John and Peter.

Besides these generally-admitted writings, there were others, which were indeed regarded by many as apostolic, but as to which some estimable persons entertained doubts, viz., the Second and Third Epistles of John, the Second Epistle of Peter, the Epistles of James and Jude, the Epistle to the Hebrews, and John's Apocalypse. Hence these were termed *disputed writings;* in Greek, *Antilegomena.* About the close of the second or the commencement of the third century, most of the fathers of the Catholic Church became united in believing the genuineness and apostolic origin of all these writings excepting the Epistle to the Hebrews and the Apocalypse. A *third* small collection was now formed of these epistles, and into it were transferred the two larger Epistles of John and Peter, which were at first contained in the *second* collection. Consequently, the third comprised *seven Epistles,* which were called the *seven Catholic, i. e., universally-admitted Epistles,* in contradistinction from the various rejected writings. Out of these collections there now remained, therefore, only the *Epistle to the Hebrews,* and the *Revelation* of John. In regard to the Epistle, as has been already mentioned, no doubt was entertained of its genuineness; the only controversy was, whether Paul was its author or not. At last, the opinion that it was Pauline prevailed, and it was introduced into the collection of Pauline Epistles; though, as the collection was already made up, it was placed at the end, after the small Epistle to Philemon. In the Lutheran version of the Bible, however, the Epistle obtained another place, viz., between the Third Epistle of John and the Epistle of James, for reasons which will be stated hereafter. The whole question, therefore, in regard to the Epistle to the Hebrews, was of little consequence; for, if Paul did not write it, it is certain that the author of it wrote under his guidance (as will be shown more at length in the sequel), and the case is the same with this Epistle as with the Gospels of Mark and Luke. It is otherwise, however, with the history of the *Apocalypse,* which also will be particularly related hereafter. Although it has the oldest and most trustworthy witnesses in its behalf, indeed beyond most of the writings of antiquity, it still early met with numerous assailants, on account of its contents. True, many did not exactly regard it as spurious; they only maintained that it was written, not by John the Evangelist, but by another man of less note, bearing the same name. Others, however, felt such excessive dislike towards the book, that they declared it must have been composed by the worst of heretics. Yet here, too, truth fortunately obtained the victory, and the genuine apostolic character of this elevated production of prophetic inspiration was at last acknowledged. As the three smaller collections were already made up, nothing remained but to place it at the end of them all. This was precisely the position to which the Apocalypse belonged; for, considering the Gospels to be, as it were, the root of the tree of life exhibited in the whole New Testament, and the Epistles as the branches and blossoms, the Apocalypse may be regarded as the fully ripened fruit. It contains a picture of the development of God's Church down to the end of time, and therefore forms the conclusion of the Bible, as properly as Genesis forms its commencement.

In order that the various writings and small collections might be permanently united, the smaller divisions were entirely given up in the fourth century, and henceforward there was but one great collection, containing all the New Testament writings. A decisive decree on this point was issued by a council, held in the year 393, at Hippo, now Bona, in Africa. In itself considered, this union of the smaller collections into a single large one is of no consequence, and hence, too, it is of none that it took place at so late a period; for, as early as during the third century and the commencement of the fourth, there was entire unanimity in regard to all essential questions concerning the books of the New Testament, as the following particular history of them will evince. Still there was this advantage arising from the union of the apostolic writings into one body, viz., that they were in a more safe and determinate form, and might now be placed with the Old Testament, as a complete second part of holy writ.

CHAPTER II.

THE COLLECTION OF THE GOSPELS.

Of the three smaller collections of the writings of the New Testament, which, as we have before stated, were in use in the ancient Church, none can be traced farther back than that of the Gospels. We find so many and so weighty testimonies in its behalf, that it would seem as though Providence designed that this palladium of the Church should be in a special manner secure against all attacks. Not only is it the case that some of the most ancient fathers testify to its existence, as *e. g.*, Tertullian, Clement of Alexandria, Irenaeus, Justin Martyr (all of whom lived in the second century after Christ, and were preceded only by the so-called apostolic fathers); but, moreover, the witnesses in its behalf belonged to all parts of the ancient Church. Tertullian lived in Carthage; Clement in Egypt; Irenaeus was born in Asia Minor, and became bishop of Lyons in France; Justin Martyr was born in Palestine (in Flavia Neapolis, otherwise called Sichem), but taught in Rome. Thus the testimonies in favour of the collection of the Gospels come from all the chief stations in the ancient Church; and this circumstance, of course, supposes its very general diffusion. The greatest number of testimonies, all proceeding from *one* province, would not be of so much weight as these coincident declarations from the most various parts of the world, as to the currency of the Gospels. A circumstance, however, still more important than these testimonies from different parts of the ancient Church is, that not only the members of the Catholic orthodox Church, but the heretics also, were familiar with our Gospels. If it be considered what violent mutual animosity there was between the fathers of the Catholic Church and the heretics; that one party would not adopt or receive anything at all from the other, but was rather disposed to reject it, for the very reason that it came from so detested a quarter: no one can help seeing in the circumstance that both the Catholic Church and the heretics were familiar with the collection of our Gospels, an uncommonly cogent proof of its genuineness and great antiquity. For, had it been formed *after* the rise of these sects, either within the pale of the Catholic Church, or in the midst of this or that party of heretics, it would be wholly inexplicable, how it could have been introduced into these sects, from the Church, or *vice versa*, into the Church from these sects. Thus the collection of our Gospels must at all events have taken place *before* such sects arose; for on no other ground can it be explained how these books, which were generally known and used before open rupture in the Church, should have been admitted as genuine by both parties alike. Now the sects of the Gnostics and Marcionites originated as early as the beginning of the second century; and from this circumstance we are entitled to regard the collection of the Gospels as in existence at a period very near the times of the apostles. Besides the heretics, moreover, we find pagans acquainted with the collection of the Gospels. We refer particularly to Celsus, a violent opponent of Christianity, against whose attacks it was defended by Origen. It is true this man did not live till about two hundred years after the birth of Christ (we do not know the precise period); but it is, notwithstanding, a decisive evidence of the general diffusion and acknowledgement of the Gospels throughout the Church, that they are cited and assailed by pagan opponents as official sources of the Christian doctrines. For, had Celsus been aware that Christians themselves did not acknowledge these writings, it would have been an absurd undertaking to refute the Christians from the contents of the books.

Further, it is a wholly peculiar circumstance in the history of the Gospels, and one which goes a great way to sustain their genuineness, that we nowhere find, in any writer of any part of the ancient world, any indication that only a single one of the four Gospels was in use, or even known to exist separately. *All possessed the entire collection of the Gospels.* It is true there is one writer, Papias, bishop of Hierapolis in Phrygia, concerning whom there is no express statement that he had all the four Gospels. But the manner in which Eusebius speaks respecting him in his Church History is such that there is nothing questionable in this silence. Eusebius adduces from a work of Papias, now not extant, some notices of Matthew and Mark. It is certainly true that nothing is said of Luke and John; but this is, undoubtedly, because the ancient bishop had not made any particular observations on these two Gospels. His silence respecting them is the less an evidence that he was not acquainted with them, as the theatre of the labours of Papias was in the vicinity of Ephesus, where John lived so long, and moreover wrote his Gospel. On this account Papias must necessarily have been acquainted with it. Eusebius, moreover, remarks, in the same place, that Papias was acquainted with the first Epistle of John. How much rather, then, with his Gospel? Thus Eusebius says nothing concerning Luke and John, only because it was a matter of course that Papias was familiar with them, and the latter had not said anything special in regard to their origin. There were, moreover, some heretics who made use of but *one* Gospel, *e. g.*, Marcion used Luke, and the Ebionites Matthew; but they had special reasons for doing so in their doctrinal opinions. They did not, by any means, deny the three other Gospels to be genuine; they only asserted that their authors were not true disciples of our Lord. Marcion held the erroneous notion that all the disciples, with the exception of Paul, still continued *half Jews*. The Jewish Christians maintained that all the disciples, except Matthew, had strayed away *too far from* Judaism, and on that account did not receive their writings. In this state of the case there is clear evidence from their opinions also that the Gospels are genuine, and were in that day generally diffused in the Church. Now, as the collection of our four Gospels existed so very early and so universally, the inquiry occurs, how it could have originated? Shall we say that a particular individual or church may have formed it, and it may then have spread itself everywhere abroad? This supposition seems to be countenanced by the circumstance of the general uniformity as to the order of the four Gospels. A very few MSS. place John next to Matthew, in order that the writings of the apostles may be by themselves. Clearly, however, this transposition arose from the fancy of some copyist, and has no historical foundation. There is still, therefore, positive authority for the universally-received arrangement. The most weighty circumstance against the opinion that the first collection of the Gospels was made in a particular place, and diffused itself abroad from thence, is, that we have no account respecting such a process though we should expect one, from the fact that John lived, and moreover wrote his Gospel, at so late a period. For this reason, had the Evangelist John himself, as some suppose, or any other man of high authority in the Church, formed the collection of the

Gospels, we should, one would think, have had an account of its formation, as it could not have taken place before the end of the first or commencement of the second century, which period borders very closely on that from which we derive so many accounts concerning the Gospels. But this same circumstance, that we read nothing at all respecting a collector of the Gospels, that writers have been left to conjecture in regard to the manner in which the collection of them was made, leads to another view of its formation, which casts the clearest light on the genuineness of the books. It is in the highest degree probable that our Gospels all originated in capital cities of the Roman empire. Matthew probably wrote his in Jerusalem, the centre of Judaism, where also, as appears from the Acts of the Apostles, a large Christian church was early gathered. Mark and Luke undoubtedly wrote in Rome, the political centre of the empire, to which innumerable multitudes of men thronged from all quarters of the world for the transaction of business. In this city, too, a flourishing Christian church was early formed, as is seen from the Epistle of Paul to the Romans, which was written before Peter, or Paul, or any apostle, had visited Rome. Lastly, John wrote at Ephesus, a large and thriving city of Asia Minor. It was the residence of many learned and ingenious heathen. The large church at Ephesus was, according to the Acts, founded by Paul. It was fostered by the labours of John. Now, let it be considered how many thousands must consequently have been most exactly aware who wrote the Gospels, and it will be perceived that these circumstances afford weighty evidence of their genuineness, particularly as *there is not to be found in a single ancient writer the faintest trace of any doubt in regard to it;* for the heretics, who, as we have remarked, disputed the Gospels in part, did not deny their genuineness (they rather fully admitted it), but only their obligatory authority. Now, as very active intercourse was maintained among the Christians of the ancient Church, partly by constant epistolary communications, and partly by frequent personal visits, nothing is more natural than the supposition that the Christians of Jerusalem very soon transmitted the Gospel of Matthew, which was composed in the midst of them, to Rome, Ephesus, Alexandria, and other places, and that, on the other hand, those of Rome and Ephesus also transmitted the writings composed among them to the other churches. In every church there were archives, in which were deposited important documents. Into these archives of the Church the Gospels were put, and as only these four Gospels were composed or vouched for by apostles, the collection of Gospels took its rise, not in this or that place, but in every quarter simultaneously. This statement of the matter is, in the first place, strictly in accordance with the circumstances known to us in regard to the ancient Church, and also the only one capable of explaining satisfactorily the existence of the collection in everybody's hands, while no one knew how and whence it originated. As, further, we find *no other* Gospel but these in general use, it is clearly evident that only these four were of apostolic origin. It is true we find in circulation in individual churches Gospels which appear to have differed from our own, *e. g.* the church of Rhossus in Cilicia, a province of Asia Minor, made use of a Gospel of Peter, and in Alexandria one called the Gospel of the Egyptians was current. It is possible, however, that these two writings were either the same or at least were very nearly allied, and also bore close affinity to our Mark; and in that case their use is as easily accounted for as the use of Matthew and Luke by the Ebionite and Marcionite sects in Recensions somewhat altered from the original.

From this cursory view of the evidence in favour of the genuineness of the Gospels, it cannot but be admitted, that no work can be adduced, out of the whole range of ancient literature, which has so many and so decisive ancient testimonies in its behalf as they. It is therefore, in reality, a mere laboured effort to try to maintain and demonstrate the spuriousness of the Gospels. Since, however, this attempt is made, it may reasonably be inquired—*Whence is derived any occasion for doubt? Is not every thing, without exception, in favour of their genuineness?* We cannot but say, that no thorough, serious-minded scholar, would ever have denied the genuineness of the Gospels, had not the question in regard to their genuineness been conjoined with another investigation of extreme difficulty and intricacy. In the ardent endeavour to get rid of this difficulty, scholars have been seduced into the invention of hypotheses irreconcilable with the genuineness of the Gospels. They should, on the contrary, have set out invariably with the admission of their genuineness, as an irrefragable fact, and then have employed only such modes of solving the difficulty above alluded to as were based on the supposition of their genuineness. The difficulty is this. On a close comparison of the first three Gospels, we discover a very striking coincidence between them. This is exhibited, not merely in the facts and the style, but also in the order of the narration, in the transitions from one narrative to another, and in the use of uncommon expressions, and other things of the same character. Further, the coincidence is interrupted by just as striking a dissimilarity, in such a manner that it is in the highest degree difficult to explain how this coincidence and this dissimilarity, as it is exhibited in the Gospels, can have originated. This is a purely learned investigation, which writers should have quietly prosecuted as such, without allowing it to influence the question respecting the genuineness of the Gospels. Such has been its influence, however, that some scholars suppose a so-called *Protevangelion,* or original Gospel, which the apostles, before they left Jerusalem, and scattered themselves abroad over the whole earth, prepared, in order to serve as a guide to them in their discourses. This writing is supposed to have contained the principal events of the life of our Lord. It was carried into all lands by the apostles. Now, in these different countries, it is said by the defenders of this hypothesis, additions were gradually made to this original Gospel. These were at first short, and thus arose the Gospels of the Jewish Christians, the Marcionites, and others; afterwards they became longer, and in this way, at last, our Gospels were produced. Now, as it cannot be stated by whom these additions were made, this view is really equivalent to making our Gospels spurious, for, according to it, only the little portion of them which existed in the brief original Gospel is of apostolic authority. But, setting aside the fact that the hypothesis must be false, for this very reason, because it opposes the genuineness of the Gospels, which can be demonstrated by historical proof; this theory has been, moreover, of late utterly discarded by learned men on other grounds. In the first place, no ancient Christian writer exhibits any acquaintance with such an original Gospel; and is it conceivable that the knowledge of so remarkable a work should have been totally lost? Then, too, the idea that a guide was composed by the apostles for themselves, in order to preserve unity in doctrine, is not at all suited to the apostolic period. At this period the Holy Spirit operated with its primeval freshness and power. This Spirit, which guided into all truth, was the means of preserving unity among the apostles. Not an individual of those witnesses to the truth needed any external written guide. Besides, this supposition solves the difficulty in question, respecting the coincidence of the Gospels, only in a very meagre and forced manner, while there is a much simpler way of reaching the same result far more satisfactorily. We must suppose more than one source of this characteristic of the first three Gospels. *Sometimes* one Evangelist was certainly made use of by another. This remark is applicable particularly to Mark, who undoubtedly was acquainted with and made use of both Matthew and Luke. *Moreover,* there existed short accounts of particular parts of the Gospel history, such as narratives of particular cases of healing, relations of journeys, and the like. Now, when two Evangelists made use of the same brief account, there naturally resulted a resemblance in their history. Still, as each was independent in his use of these accounts, some variations also occurred. *Finally,* much of the similarity between them arose from oral narrations. It is easy to believe that certain portions of the Evangelical history, *e. g.* particular cures, parables, and discourses of our Lord, were repeated constantly in the very same way, because the form of the narrative imprinted itself with very great exactness on every one's memory. In this manner the songs of Homer and Ossian were long transmitted from mouth to mouth. Uniformity in an oral mode of narration is not sufficient of itself alone to explain the relation between the Gospels, because in prose it is impossible (in poetry it is much easier) to imprint on the memory minute traits and important forms of expression with so much exactness as would be necessary to account for the mutual affinity of the Gospels; and, moreover, could their similarity be thus explained, the variations between them would only stand out in more troublesome relief. But that which cannot be effected by a single hypothesis, can be by that in conjunction with others. And here, perhaps, we may see the true solution of a problem which has so long occupied the attention of theologians. But, whatever opinion be entertained on this point, the investigation of it must always be kept aloof from the question of the genuineness of the Gospels, which should first be established or denied on historical grounds. Thus will the collection of the Gospels be secure from all danger.

CHAPTER III.

THE INDIVIDUAL GOSPELS AND THE ACTS OF THE APOSTLES.

OF the four Gospels, that of Matthew holds the first place in the canon. The author of this first Gospel bore, besides the name of Matthew, that of Levi also (Matt. ix. 9; Mark ii. 14), and was the son of a certain Alpheus, of whom we have no further information. Of the history of Matthew very little is known, in addition to the accounts in the New Testament. After our Saviour called him from his station as receiver of the customs, he followed him with fidelity, and was one of the twelve whom Jesus sent forth to preach. His labours as an apostle, however, seem to have been wholly confined to Palestine; for, what is related of Matthew's travels in foreign countries is very doubtful, resting only on the authority of rather late ecclesiastical writings. But the information respecting him which is of most importance to our purpose, is given with perfect unanimity by the oldest ecclesiastical writers, who declare that Matthew wrote a Gospel. It is true that they likewise subjoin, equally without exception, that Matthew wrote in Hebrew, at Jerusalem, and for believing Jews; and that this account must be correct, we know, from the fact that the Jewish Christians in Palestine, who spoke Hebrew, all made use of a Gospel which they referred to Matthew. This Hebrew Gospel did, indeed, differ from our Greek Gospel of Matthew, for it contained many things wanting in our Gospel; but still, it was in general so exactly like the latter, that a father of the fourth century, the celebrated Jerome, felt himself entitled to treat the Hebrew Gospel expressly as Matthew's. It is a singular circumstance, however, that, while all the fathers of the Church declare Matthew to have written in Hebrew, they all, notwithstanding, make use of the Greek text, as of genuine apostolic origin, without remarking what relation the Hebrew

Matthew bore to our Greek Gospel; for, that the oldest Fathers of the Church did not possess Matthew's Gospel in any other form than that in which we now have it is fully settled. That we have no definite information on this point is undoubtedly owing to accidental causes; but, since it is so, that we have not any certain account, we can only resort to conjecture in regard to the mutual relation of the Greek and Hebrew Matthew. Existing statements and indications, however, enable us to form conjectures which, it is in the highest degree probable, are essentially correct. The idea that some unknown individual translated the Hebrew Gospel of Matthew, and that this translation is our canonical Gospel, is, in the first place, contradicted by the circumstance of the universal diffusion of this same Greek Gospel of Matthew, which makes it absolutely necessary to suppose that the translation was executed by some one of acknowledged influence in the Church, indeed of apostolic authority. In any other case, would not objections to this Gospel have been urged in some quarter or other, particularly in the country where Matthew himself laboured, and where his writings are familiarly known? There is not, however, the slightest trace of any such opposition to it. Besides, our Greek Gospel of Matthew is of such a peculiar character, that it is impossible for us to regard it as a mere version. Does a man who is translating an important work from one language into another, allow himself to make alterations in the book which he is translating, to change the ideas it presents? Something of the kind must be supposed to have been done in the Greek Gospel of Matthew with regard to the Hebrew. This is beyond denial, if it be considered merely, how the quotations from the Old Testament are treated. These do not coincide either with the Hebrew text of the Old Testament, or with the version in common use at the time of the apostles, viz., the Septuagint (which was executed by some learned Jews at Alexandria, several centuries before the birth of Christ); but rather exhibit an independent text of their own. Now, as sometimes the argument is wholly based on this independent character of the text in the citations from the books of the Old Testament, and could not have accorded at all with the Hebrew Gospel of Matthew, it is clear that our Greek Gospel must be something else than a mere version. It is rather an independent work, though closely allied to the Hebrew Gospel of the apostle. Now, since this same work is universally regarded as an apostolic production, and as having been written by Matthew, there is no more simple and effectual mode of solving all the characteristics of the Gospel of Matthew, than to suppose *that Matthew himself, when he had composed the Hebrew Gospel, executed likewise a free translation or new composition of it in the Greek language.* It makes no essential difference, if we suppose that a friend of Matthew wrote the Greek work under his direction and authority; but Matthew's authority must necessarily be supposed to have been the means of the diffusion of the Gospel, as otherwise it is inexplicable that there does not appear the faintest trace of any opposition to it.

No definite *objections* can be made against our supposition that Matthew wrote a Greek Gospel besides his Hebrew one. A single circumstance, however, may appear strange, viz., that Papias, the ancient bishop of Hierapolis in Phrygia, whom we have before mentioned, a man who was conversant with persons that had themselves seen and heard our Lord, informs us that every one endeavoured to translate the Hebrew Gospel of Matthew as well as he was able. Thus, according to this passage, our universally-received Greek transformation of the Hebrew Gospel was not commonly known in Phrygia, so that persons who did not very well understand Hebrew made use, as well as they could, of the Hebrew Gospel. But the circumstance, that the Greek Gospel of Matthew was not yet current in the immediate vicinity of Papias, is no proof at all that it was not yet in existence. For, as Matthew's work was already diffused throughout the Church, in the Hebrew language, and the Greek Gospel of Matthew corresponded with the Hebrew in every essential point, it was very natural that the Greek Gospel should be circulated in a more dilatory manner; and by some accident it is probable, it was particularly tardy in reaching Phrygia. As, however, in the west generally, very few understood Hebrew, when the Greek Gospel of Matthew was once procured, that only was circulated there, and thus the Hebrew Gospel was completely lost in Europe. In Palestine alone, as the Hebrew was better understood, the Gospel in that language continued in use, though it was encumbered with divers foreign additions by the Jewish Christians.

Thus the genuineness of the Gospel of Matthew is fully confirmed on historical grounds, aside from its position in the collection of the Gospels. Recent investigators have raised doubts in regard to its genuineness from *internal* considerations. They say, in particular, that if the statements of Matthew, in the character of eye-witness (for he was one of the twelve apostles), be compared with the descriptions of Mark, who does not write as an eye-witness, it will be evident that the advantage is on the side of the latter. Everything which Mark narrates is represented in so graphic a manner that it is plain he derived his accounts from eye-witnesses; while the narrative of Matthew, whom we are to regard as himself an eye-witness in respect to most of his relations, is dry, and without the least vivacity. This remark is perfectly correct. Comparison of a few passages will at once show how much more minute and graphic are Mark's descriptions than those of Luke. This is particularly the case as to the accounts of cures. In these Mark frequently describes the circumstances of the sick person before and after the cure, in so lively a manner as to make us imagine the scene really before us; while Matthew, on the contrary, describes the occurrence only in very general terms. Let a comparison be made in this view between the following accounts which Matthew and Mark give of the same occurrences:—

MATTH. viii. 28-34.	MARK v. 1-19.
"And when he was come to the other side, into the country of the Gergesenes, there met him two possessed with devils, coming out of the tombs, exceeding fierce, so that no man might pass by that way. And behold they cried out, saying," &c.	"And they came over unto the other side of the sea, into the country of the Gadarenes. (This is another reading for Gergesenes.) And when he was come out of the ship, immediately there met him out of the tombs a man with an unclean spirit, who had his dwelling among the tombs; *and no man could bind him, no, not with chains, because that he had been often bound with fetters and chains, and the chains had been plucked asunder by him, and the fetters broken in pieces; neither could any man tame him. And always, night and day, he was in the mountains, and in the tombs, crying, and cutting himself with stones. But when he saw Jesus afar off, he ran and worshipped him, and cried with a loud voice, and said,*" &c.
Respecting their cure, Matthew merely says (ver. 32):—"And he said unto them, Go. And when they were come	Respecting his cure, Mark says (ver. 13 and onward):—"And forthwith Jesus gave them leave. And the un-

out they went into the herd of swine, and behold the whole herd of swine," &c.	clean spirits went out and entered into the swine," &c. "And they (that were in the city and in the country) went out to see what it was that was done. And they come to Jesus, and see him that was possessed with the devil, and had the legion, *sitting, and clothed, and in his right mind:* and they were afraid."
ix. 18-26.	v. 21-43.
20. "And behold a woman, which was diseased with an issue of blood twelve years, came behind him, and plucked the hem of his garment."	25. "And a certain woman, which had an issue of blood twelve years, *and had suffered many things of many physicians, and had spent all that she had, and was nothing bettered, but rather grew worse,* when she had heard of Jesus, came in the press behind, and touched his garment." Moreover, the whole account contained in verses 29-33 is in Mark only.
xiv. 1-12.	vi. 14-20.
Account of the execution of John the Baptist by Herod.	The whole narrative is given in Mark with much more minuteness and vivacity.

Such a difference in the style of narration runs throughout Matthew and Mark; and it cannot well be denied that at first view there is something surprising in it. But careful examination of the object of the two Gospels plainly shews whence this different manner of narration in Matthew and Mark takes its rise, and thus does away with all the inferences which have been deduced therefrom in opposition to the apostolic origin of Matthew. The reason why Mark describes the outward relations of our Lord's life in so vivid and graphic a manner is, that it was his *special design* to portray *Christ's performance of the outward functions of his office.* Hence, all which related to that, he details very carefully; while whatever did not pertain thereto he either entirely omits, as, *e. g.,* the history of the childhood of Jesus, or communicates very briefly, as, *e. g.,* many of our Lord's larger discourses. Matthew, on the contrary, makes it *his* chief object to communicate our *Lord's discourses.* He commonly makes use of events only as points of support for the discourses; to which he, like John, directs special attention. If it be considered, moreover, that the graphic nature of style is, in great part, owing to peculiar talent, such as is not bestowed alike on all men, and such as was by no means requisite in every one of the apostles, there remains not a shadow of reason, why the want of vivacity, which is certainly exhibited in Matthew's Gospel, should become a motive for denying its genuineness. In truth, moreover, there is no period at which a forgery of the Gospel in Matthew's name is even conceivable. For it is demonstrable from the book itself that it must have been composed a few years before the destruction of Jerusalem, and hence about sixty-six years after the birth of Christ. Now we find Matthew in use in the Church before the close of the same century, at a time when John the Evangelist had but just died, and many disciples of the apostles were living and labouring in all parts of the world. How was it possible, in such circumstances, to introduce a work forged in the name of Matthew into so general currency, that not the very slightest opposition should ever have been raised against it?

From what has been said it will have been inferred, that the genuineness of Mark is not at all disputed. His graphic, lively manner has even been made to afford occasion for assailing the genuineness of Matthew. Nor, in truth, was there in ancient times the least opposition to Mark's Gospel. It was known to Papias of Hierapolis, *i. e.*, as early as the close of the first century, and there is an unbroken chain of evidence in its favour since that time. It is true, Mark's work was, in all probability, written at Rome, at that time the capital of the known world, and therefore a fixed and sure tradition as to the author of the work might be formed at once, and would easily diffuse itself everywhere abroad. Still, however, there is one thing which appears very remarkable in regard to the rapid diffusion and reception of Mark, viz., that it was a production whose author was not an apostle. John Mark, frequently called Mark only, was the son of a certain Mary who had a house in Jerusalem, (Acts xii. 12.) Mark himself, as we are told in the Acts (xii. 25; xiii. 5; xv. 36, seq.), at first accompanied the apostle Paul in his travels for the dissemination of Christianity. He afterwards attached himself to his kinsman Barnabas. At a later period, however, we find him again in Paul's company, (2 Tim. iv. 11.) According to the fathers, he was, also, for a considerable time, closely connected with Peter, and was interpreter to the latter when he preached among the Greeks. He invariably, however, occupied a dependent situation, and on this account it is impossible that his name alone should have procured his Gospel an introduction into the Church. But, as has been already mentioned, Mark did not write without apostolic authority. *On the contrary, he was under the direction of the apostle Peter.* This is stated by the entire series of church fathers during the second and third centuries, with perfect unanimity in the main; and the statement is corroborated by the case of Luke, which was exactly similar. On this account, the Gospel of Mark was considered as originating with Peter, and such individuals as were particularly attached to this apostle used Mark in preference to all others. Unfortunately, however, we have no minute accounts as to this matter, and hence do not know whether these individuals corrupted the Gospel of Mark, as the Jewish Christians did that of Matthew, or not. It is possible, however, that the so-called *Gospel of the Egyptians* was a corruption of Mark, though the fragments we have of it are not sufficient to enable us to form a certain opinion on this point.

As to *Luke*, we have more clear and certain evidence in this respect. We know that that sect which carried the sentiments of Paul to an erroneous extreme, the *Marcionites*, used only the Gospel of Luke, although Marcion was very well acquainted with the other Gospels, and regarded them as genuine. They had, however, altered Luke in conformity with their opinions, and thus formed, as it were, a new Gospel out of it, which, notwithstanding, still retained much resemblance to the original. The reason why the Marcionites selected Luke was, that this Gospel was written under the direction of the apostle Paul, who alone, in their opinion, was a genuine apostle of our Lord. Luke, as we know from the Acts of the Apostles, had travelled about with the apostle Paul for a long time, and, in particular, had also accompanied him to Rome. This is clear from the final chapters of the Acts of the Apostles. Connecting this fact with the conclusion of the work, it is perfectly evident when the Evangelist finished it. According to the last chapter, Paul was two years in confinement at Rome. Here Luke breaks off, without mentioning the issue of his trial. Had this been concluded, should we not, of course, have had an account of the emperor's decision respecting the great apostle of the Gentiles? It can be made very probable, by circumstances deduced from another quarter, that Paul was liberated from his first imprisonment at Rome, and did not suffer as a martyr, till he had been a second time placed in bonds. Luke, however, abruptly breaks off in the midst of his narrative. Now, as the Acts of the Apostles are only the second part of Luke's work, the Gospel being the first (compare Luke i. 1, with Acts i. 1), the latter cannot have been written subsequently; and probably when Paul's death was apprehended, Luke wrote down the accounts he had received from him, or through him, in order to secure them to posterity. Then the apostle, who was still living, attested the purity and accuracy of the work, and from Rome, the great central point of the religious, as well as the political world, it speedily made its way into the churches, in every province of the vast Roman empire. Thus, it was not Luke's name which procured for this Gospel its currency in the Church, *but the authority of the Apostle Paul.* Without this, the work of Luke, with its two divisions, the Gospel and the Acts, would have been the less likely to obtain general credit, because it purports to be a mere private production, addressed to a certain *Theophilus.* It is, indeed, very probable, that this Theophilus was a man of note, who was either already a member of the Church, or at least well-disposed towards it; but still he was only a private man, whose name could have no weight with the whole Church. He had, probably, already perused divers accounts concerning Christ, and the formation of the primitive Churches, which, however, were not duly authentic and certain; and, for this reason, Luke determined to compose for his use an authoritative history of the important events in our Lord's life, and of the foundation of the Churches. (Comp. Luke i. 1-4.) Under these circumstances, it is not astonishing that, in the primitive Church, there was no opposition either to Luke's Gospel, or his Acts of the Apostles.* The many and close relations of the writer, together with the apostolic authority in his behalf, were such evidence in favour of the work, that not a single valid suspicion could arise respecting its genuineness.

Lastly, The circumstances in regard to the Gospel of John are particularly calculated to place its genuineness beyond dis-

---

* So far as the Acts of the Apostles speaks of the circumstances of Paul, it has a perfect correspondence with Paul's Epistles, as the latter have with the former. See this fact more fully developed in the *fourth chapter* of this treatise.

pute; for John the Evangelist lived much longer than any of the other apostles. So far as we know, none of the others were alive after the destruction of Jerusalem by Titus, the Roman emperor, in the year 70 A.D. John, however, survived it nearly thirty years, dying about the close of the first century, under the reign of the emperor Domitian. Hence, many Christians who had heard of our Lord's farewell words to him (John xxi. 22, 23), believed that John would not die, an idea which the Evangelist himself declares erroneous. This beloved disciple of our Lord, during the latter part of his life, as we know from testimonies on which perfect reliance may be placed, lived at Ephesus, in Asia Minor, where the apostle Paul had founded a flourishing Church. The importance of this Church, about the year 64 or 75 A.D., is evinced by Paul's Epistle to the Ephesians; and subsequently it was very much enlarged. It was in this subsequent period that John wrote his Gospel. This is clear, *first*, from a comparison of the Gospel with the Revelation. This last work was written by John, at an earlier period, before the destruction of Jerusalem. John's style in this prophetic composition is not so thoroughly easy as we find it at a later period in the Gospel, which he must have written after longer intercourse with native Greeks. *Again*, John plainly had the three other Gospels before him when he wrote; for he omits all which they had described with sufficient minuteness, *e. g.*, the institution of the holy supper, and only relates that which was new respecting the life of his Lord and Master. Hence, these must have been already composed, and also so generally diffused, that John could presume them universally known in the Church. *Moreover*, the persons to whom John's work has special reference, viz. certain Gnostics, did not obtain importance till Jerusalem was destroyed, and most of the apostles had left this world. Now, if we duly consider all these circumstances, it will be even more incredible in regard to John's Gospel than any other, that it should have been forged in his name. From his being the sole surviving apostle, innumerable eyes were upon him and his movements. He lived and laboured in one of the chief cities of the known world, in which was a large church, and the vicinity of which was wholly peopled with Christians. We have an epistle of Pliny, a distinguished Roman officer of that region, written only a few years after the death of John the Evangelist, in which he describes the vast increase of the Christians in Asia Minor, and lays before the emperor Trajan (the successor of the emperor in whose reign John's death took place) measures for preventing the further extension of their tenets. Now, how was it possible that, in this state of things, a work could be forged in John's name; or, supposing even that one might have been (though history says nothing of any such imposition under the name of John),* how is it conceivable that no opposition should have been made thereto, when many thousands were acquainted with John, and must have known exactly what he wrote, and what he did not? *Of such opposition, however, there is nowhere the slightest trace.* Not merely all teachers of the orthodox Church, in all parts of the wide Roman empire, but also all heretics of the most various sects, make use of the work as a sacred valuable legacy, bequeathed to the Church by the beloved disciple; and the few heretics who make no use of it, as *e. g.* Marcion, still evince acquaintance with it, and regard it as a genuine work of John's, but are impudent enough to deny that John himself had a correct knowledge of the Gospel, because he was too much of a Jew. Whether, as was the case with the other Gospels, John's also was corrupted by the heretics, who felt that they were specially aimed at in it, is uncertain. The Gnostics, with the exception of Marcion (who, however, as has been already mentioned, is only improperly reckoned among the Gnostics), made most frequent use of John, as in their opinion specially favouring their spiritual ideas. We do not learn, however, that there existed in ancient times any Gospel of John, corrupted by the Gnostics, as Luke's Gospel was mutilated by Marcion. In modern times, it is true, a Gospel of John thus disfigured has come to public knowledge; but the alterations in it originated at a late period in the middle ages.

The doubts respecting the genuineness of John's Gospel which have, nevertheless, been proposed in recent times, took their rise, like those in regard to Matthew, solely from its *internal*

---

* There does exist in MS., it is true, a second apocalypse under John's name; but this production appears to belong to a much later period. There is also an apostolic history of older date, in which, however, John is only mentioned along with others; it is not ascribed to him.

character. When once doubts were thus occasioned, endeavours were made to sustain them on historical grounds likewise. These, however, are of little weight,* from the firmness of the foundation on which the Gospel rests. It was with John much as with Matthew, in regard to those characteristics which excited doubt of the genuineness of the book. It was correctly remarked, that John gives a different representation of our Lord from that presented by the first three Evangelists. In his Gospel, Christ's actions and discourses appear, as it were, transfigured and spiritualised, while, in the other Evangelists they appear in a costume more or less Jewish and national. Now, as it is not conceivable, it is said, that the same person should be so differently represented, and John, the beloved disciple of our Lord, would certainly not have portrayed his Master as other than he really was, while the description of the actions of Jesus (who appeared as a Jew, among Jews, and in behalf of Jews), given in the accounts of the first three Evangelists, is much more conformable to probability, the Gospel which bears John's name must be of later origin. But here, as in regard to Matthew, it may be observed, that from a perfectly correct remark, false conclusions have been deduced. It is indeed true that John exhibits the Saviour in a far more spiritual and glorified character than the first three Evangelists; but this proves nothing, except that John was the most spiritual of the Evangelists. The same individual may be regarded and described very differently by different persons. Of this truth we have a remarkable example in a great character of Grecian antiquity. Socrates is presented to our view, in his actions and discourses, by two of his confidential pupils, Xenophon and Plato. And, how entirely different is the description given of him by these two writers! In fact, these biographers may be said to sustain very much such a mutual relation as that of John and the first Evangelists. While Xenophon paid attention principally to the external acts of Socrates, Plato describes his spiritual characteristics. Now, if it were possible to represent a common human being of eminence in two very different lights, without doing

---

* The most weighty opponent of the genuineness of John, has given the excellent example of publicly acknowledging that he has become convinced of the genuineness of this jewel of the Church, and retracts his doubts. May this example find numerous imitators!

violence to truth, how much rather might it be so in regard to one who was greater than Solomon, or than Socrates and his biographers? He who lived a purely heavenly life on earth, and spake words of eternal truth, could not but be very variously described, according to the characteristics of the human soul which received the rays of light proceeding from him. Each soul reflected his image according to its own profundity and compass, and yet each might be right. It was for this reason that more than one Gospel was included in the collection of the Sacred writings, since only the presentation of different portraitures together could prevent a partial view of our Saviour's character. As it is only from connexion of the accounts of Xenophon and Plato that we can obtain a complete picture of Socrates, so we cannot comprehend the life of our Lord, which affords so many different aspects, without uniting the peculiar traits scattered in all the four Gospels into one general portraiture. With all the difference of representation observable in the Evangelists, there are still resemblances and affinities enough to make it evident that they all had the same great personage in view. As John relates narratives of cures exactly like those in Matthew, Mark, and Luke, so the Gospels of the latter contain passages which, in elevation, depth, and richness of thought, are not inferior to our Lord's discourses in John, and indeed resemble them in phraseology. Among these is the lofty and astonishingly beautiful passage, Matth. xi. 25-30—" I thank thee, O Father, Lord of heaven and earth, because thou hast hid these things from the wise and prudent, and hast revealed them unto babes. Even so, Father, for so it seemed good in thy sight. All things are delivered unto me of my Father; and no man knoweth the Son but the Father; neither knoweth any man the Father save the Son, and he to whomsoever the Son will reveal him. Come unto me, all ye that labour and are heavy laden, and I will give you rest. Take my yoke upon you and learn of me; for I am meek and lowly in heart, and ye shall find rest unto your souls. For my yoke is easy, and my burden is light." He from whose mouth such language proceeded might certainly be represented in such an aspect as John has given to Jesus, if the description were undertaken by one in some measure capable of appreciating a character of this nature; and that John was thus capable is sufficiently clear from his Epistles.

If, therefore, we look at the Gospels as a collection, or consider each separately, we cannot but say that they are more strongly accredited and sustained by external and internal proofs than any other work of antiquity. *Few* writings have such ancient testimonies in their favour, reaching back to the time of the authors; *none* have so many of them, so totally distinct, so corroborative of each other. While, then, the chief argument in behalf of the Scriptures generally, and of the Gospels in particular, is the *witness of the Holy Spirit*, perceived in his heart by every believer as he peruses the Scriptures (a point on which we shall enlarge at the close of our treatise); still, the possibility of proving on historical grounds the genuineness and primitive character of the Gospels, is a great additional cause of gratitude, inasmuch as it removes occasions of distrust, particularly from weak and doubting minds, and affords motives for the confirmation of their faith.

CHAPTER IV.

THE PAULINE EPISTLES.

ALONG with the collection of the Gospels, there existed at an early period of the Church, as was related above,* a collection of Paul's Epistles called the Apostle. In the lives of Irenæus, Tertullian, and Clement of Alexandria, who were all acquainted with and used it, this collection contained thirteen Epistles, viz., the Epistle to the Romans, two to the Corinthians, those to the Galatians, Ephesians, Philippians, and Colossians, two to the Thessalonians, two to Timothy, and those to Titus and Philemon. The Epistle to the Hebrews was not inserted in this collection, because opinions were not united as to its origin. (See Chap. vi. below.) Half-a-century before the time of the fathers just mentioned, we find a collection of the Pauline Epistles in the

---

* Comp. Chap. i.

hands of Marcion, that extravagant reverer of the apostle Paul. He was born in Asia Minor, where, as is well known, the apostle Paul had long lived and laboured, and was highly reverenced. Thence Marcion went to Rome, carrying with him the collection of Pauline Epistles which he had made use of in Asia. This, however, contained but ten Epistles; there were wanting the three commonly termed *pastoral* letters, viz. the two to Timothy, and that to Titus; called *pastoral* letters, because in them Paul gives directions to spiritual pastors in regard to the suitable performance of their official duties. The small Epistle to Philemon was known to him, because it stood in close connection with the Epistle to the Colossians; but the three pastoral letters seem to have been diffused but slowly, as independent private productions, and hence, also, not to have been inserted in the original collection. How the collection of the Pauline Epistles, in the form in which we now have it, originated, is unknown, and has not yet been satisfactorily accounted for by any conjecture.* For the supposition that, like the collection of the Gospels, it originated in different places at once, merely by the gradual transmission thither of the Epistles of Paul as fast as they were composed, is forbidden by the circumstance that, as can be proved, they are not arranged in the order of their composition. The collection cannot, however, have been accidentally formed; for it is clear that a certain plan has been followed. At the beginning are placed the Epistles to the Romans and Corinthians, distinguished by their length and internal importance; then follows a letter to several churches in a whole province, the Epistle to the Galatians; then the smaller Epistles to churches in particular cities, to the Ephesians, Philippians, Colossians, and Thessalonians; lastly, come the Epistles to private persons. Moreover, had the collection of them been left to accident, sometimes one arrangement would have been adopted and sometimes another, which is not the case, the order having been the same that we now observe, as far back as the second century.

---

* We find very few traces of a different arrangement of the Epistles of Paul; a different one, however, is followed in an old catalogue of the books of the New Testament, probably pertaining to the Church at Rome. It is called *Muratori's* Catalogue, from an Italian abbot of that name, who discovered the MSS. which contained it.

As, therefore, the order of the Epistles was evidently the work of design, and its general reception throughout the Church indicates that it proceeded from some authoritative source, the most reasonable supposition is, that the apostle Paul himself made the collection. During the second imprisonment at Rome, to which, as we shall see hereafter, it is highly probable that the apostle was subjected, he may have collected together the ten Epistles, as being the principal ones of a doctrinal nature which he had as yet written, in order to bequeath them as a legacy to the Church. It was in this original form that Marcion possessed the collection.* After the collection was made up, near the close of his life, Paul wrote the three pastoral letters, which were afterwards added to the original collection, and naturally placed last. By accident, Marcion had not become acquainted with these letters, and therefore retained the most ancient form of the collection of Paul's Epistles. A very weighty testimony in favour of this view is presented in the second Epistle of the apostle Peter, who, at near the conclusion of his letters, says: "And account that the long-suffering of our Lord is salvation; even as our beloved brother Paul, also, according to the wisdom given unto him, *hath written unto you; as also in all* (his) *Epistles, speaking in them of these things;* in which are some things hard to be understood, which they that are unlearned and unstable wrest," &c. (2 Pet. iii. 15, 16). According to the first Epistle of Peter (i. 1, comp. 2 Pet. iii. 1), Peter wrote to the Christians in Pontus, Galatia, and other provinces of Asia Minor, to which also Paul's Epistles to the Galatians, Ephesians, and Colossians, are directed. Peter, therefore, might presume that his readers were acquainted with these. The expression *all* (his) *Epistles*, however, clearly indicates a collection of Epistles. Otherwise, there is something of indefiniteness in it. Paul, no doubt, wrote more Epistles during his life than we now possess. But most of his Epistles were not exactly adapted for general diffusion. The expression, *all* (his) *Epistles*, must

---

* According to the account of Epiphanius, it is true, the order of the ten Epistles in Marcion's Canon was different from that in ours, viz. Galatians, Corinthians, Romans, Thessalonians, Ephesians, Colossians, Philemon, and Philippians. If this statement be credited, it must be allowed that Marcion's collection originated independently of ours.

therefore have reference to a collection of the apostle's letters, which could be read through. If it be also considered that Peter was in Paul's company in Rome, and that consequently he would naturally have had acquaintance with the collection of his Epistles, it will be plain that this passage is hardly intelligible, except on the supposition that a collection of Paul's Epistles was already in existence.* It is true the genuineness of the second Epistle of Peter is now disputed, and certainly much that is of an imposing nature can be alleged against it. Still, however, all that can be said does not, I am convinced, demonstrate its spuriousness, while there is certainly much evidence of its genuineness. At any rate, this mention of a collection of Paul's Epistles should not be urged against the genuineness of the second Epistle of Peter, as all acknowledge that nothing certain is known in regard to the formation of this collection. But on these points we will speak more at large hereafter.

If it be admitted, however, that Paul himself made the collection of his Epistles, or at least caused it to be made at Rome, under his direction, we have then an explanation of the fact, that in regard to the genuineness of this collection, as in regard to that of the Gospels, *not the slightest doubt was ever expressed.* Members of the Catholic Church in all parts of the world, as also of the various sects, make use of the collection and of the individual Epistles, without allowing themselves to intimate the smallest doubt in regard to them. Now, this undeniable fact is wholly irreconcilable with the supposition that all or any Epistles in the collection are spurious. Indeed, the first supposition, that all the Epistles of Paul are spurious, has never been

---

* Some may think that too much is inferred by the author from Peter's expression; and, indeed, it must be admitted, that to say that Peter's language is hardly intelligible, except on the supposition of an existing collection of Paul's Epistles, is somewhat extravagant. Our English translation, by inserting the word *his* in the phraseology of Peter, has somewhat modified the sense of the original, and weakened the force of Olshausen's remarks. The Greek expression is, ἐν πάσαις ταῖς ἐπιστολαῖς, i.e. perhaps in all *the* Epistles. Now, though it would give an intelligible sense to these words to suppose that Peter meant to make his observation concerning Paul's Epistles generally, of which he presumed some might, and some might not, have come to the knowledge of those to whom he wrote; still, it can hardly be disputed, that his phraseology becomes much more natural, if we suppose a current collection of the Epistles.—T.

maintained, and never can be, except in despite of all history. But even the idea that one or two spurious, forged Epistles may have obtained a place in the collection, is hardly to be reconciled with the universal acknowledgment of all the Epistles in the Church of ancient times. Consider only, how universally Paul was known in the early Church! From Spain (which in all probability he visited), he had travelled about through Italy and all Greece to the remotest countries of Asia Minor, Syria, and Arabia; he had resided for years in some of the large cities of the then known world, in Rome, Corinth, Thessalonica, Ephesus, Antioch, Cæsarea, Jerusalem; he had everywhere founded numerous churches, and maintained the most active intercourse with them. How, then, when he was so well known, could a work be forged in his name, with any prospect of its being generally acknowledged? The impossibility of this occurrence is the more evident, from the fact that all Paul's Epistles are addressed to important churches, or to persons living in well-known places. If those who received the Epistles were not always designated, then it might be supposed that some spurious ones obtained general circulation. No one, perhaps, could then say with certainty, whether Paul wrote such a particular Epistle or not; for it is not conceivable that Paul should at once have told everybody he knew how many Epistles he had written; and thus one might be personally acquainted with Paul, and still be deceived by an artfully-contrived Epistle. But take the case as it is. Were the Epistle to the Ephesians, against which, as we shall see, objections have been raised, really spurious, forged in Paul's name, we readily admit that it might have been received as genuine in the whole Church beside, for it is as like Paul's Epistles as one egg is like another; but could it have been acknowledged as genuine in Ephesus itself, and the Asiatic churches connected with the Ephesians? Can we suppose that the Ephesians had so little regard for the great founder of their Church, that they did not even know whether their beloved preacher had or had not written them a letter while in bonds? And can they have been so totally wanting in sensibility to friendship and love, as not to preserve the apostle's communication, when every man, at all susceptible of emotions of friendship, is anxious to preserve what has been traced by a beloved hand? It is hence plain, that a spurious

Epistle to the Ephesians, must have been known in Ephesus as what it really was, a forged production; and it is impossible to suppose, that if the Epistle had been disputed by any considerable church, and particularly by the very one to which it purported to have been sent, the opposition should have been so completely suppressed. The declaration of the Ephesian Church, that they had received no such Epistle, that they had not the original in their archives, would have been sufficient to destroy its credit.

To this it is added, that all the Epistles of Paul go beyond general expressions, such as may be easily invented; that they exhibit a definite concrete * purport, which has reference to the particular wants of each church, and its manifestations as to Christian life. Such representations of actual facts, in regard to the ancient churches, can have proceeded only from immediate contact with them, and consequently certify us of the genuineness of the Pauline Epistles. With all that is of a special nature, however, in each particular Epistle of Paul, there is observable, in all together, a uniformity of style, and a unity in doctrinal ideas, which wholly prevent suspicion respecting the genuineness of the epistolary collection. For the usual reason of forging writings in the name of another is, that the forger wishes to give currency to a favourite idea under some celebrated name. In no Epistle, however, is there any prominent idea which is remote from the circle of Pauline doctrine, and seems to be a foreign idea clothed with the costume of Paul's style. We rather find everywhere the same main thoughts which actuated the life of Paul, running through the entire collection, and giving their stamp to the whole.

The principal evidence, however, of the genuineness of the Pauline Epistles, regarded in a historical light, is the circumstance that we can assign to the Epistles their exact places in the life of the apostle Paul by following the Acts of the Apostles. Thus are they most fully and firmly bound one to

---

* This term, in the sense in which it is here used, is borrowed from logic. In that science, it is known, abstract and concrete terms are contra-distinguished. An abstract term is one signifying some attribute, without reference to any particular subject; a concrete term designates both the attribute and the subject to which it belongs.—T.

another, and all to the Acts of the Apostles. This arrangement of the individual Epistles, in accordance with the thread of Paul's life, is effected in such a manner as to show, in chronological order, the occasions of their composition, and their strict relations to his known movements.

Paul, the great apostle of the Gentiles, who, as is well known, was at first named Saul, was a native Jew of the tribe of Benjamin, and was born in Tarsus in Cilicia. In order to perfect himself in the knowledge of the law of his native country, he early betook himself to Jerusalem, where he was taught by the celebrated Gamaliel. His zeal for the hereditary observances of his countrymen, caused him to persecute the Christians, as soon as he obtained knowledge of them, with all the vehemence of his fiery nature. At the death of *Stephen*, the first Christian martyr, he was busy keeping the clothes of his murderers while they stoned him. (Acts vii. 57 seq.) From Jerusalem Paul betook himself to Damascus, to stir up the Jews there also against the Christians; but the Lord Jesus appeared to him before the city in his Divine glory, and shewed him who it was that he persecuted. (Acts ix. 22-26.) As Paul had not persecuted the Christians from intentional wickedness, or from carnal selfishness, contrary to his interior conviction, but rather with the honest idea that he was thereby doing God service, the Divine light which enlightened his dark mind by this vision at once produced an entire change in his feelings. With the same ardent zeal for truth and right, which he had manifested in persecuting the Gospel, he now defended it; though his zeal was indeed purified and made holier by the Spirit of the Lord. After a season of quiet reflection and repose, such as he needed to perceive the greatness of that internal change which he had undergone, and the depth of the new principle of life within him, Paul began to make known the conviction he had just obtained. It was in Antioch (about 44 A.D.) that Paul began formally to preach; and he taught in this city, along with Barnabas, a whole year. After a journey to Jerusalem, whither he carried money that had been collected for the poor in that city, the elders of the Church at Antioch designated him as a messenger to the Gentiles; and he, with Barnabas, set out on *the first missionary expedition*, about 45 A.D. It extended no farther than the neighbouring countries of Asia Minor. Paul travelled through Cyprus to Perga in Pamphylia, and Antioch in Pisidia, and returned through Lystra, Derbe, and Attalia, by sea to Antioch. Consequently, on his first missionary enterprise, the Apostle did not visit any of the cities or provinces to which he wrote epistles. On his return to Antioch, he found that some strict Jewish Christians had come thither from Jerusalem, and excited dissensions. Paul had begun to preach the Gospel to the Gentiles, and in such a way as to dispense with the observance of the Mosaic law as a necessary duty. Many Jewish Christians could not rise to the level of this evangelical freedom in regard to the external law. Even Peter at first adhered so strenuously to the forms of Jewish practice, that nothing but a vision could bring him to see that, under the New Testament, the Mosaic law, in regard to meats, had lost its external importance. (Acts x. 11 seq.) In order to come to a fixed decision on this important point, the Church at Antioch determined that Paul and Barnabas, with several companions, should proceed to Jerusalem, to present this question before the apostles. They there declared what God had wrought by them among the Gentiles; Peter testified the same in regard to his labours; and James, the brother of our Lord, shewed that it was foretold, in the prophecies of Scripture, that the Gentiles likewise should be called into the Church of God. On these grounds, the apostles, with the elders, and all the Church at Jerusalem, determined to send deputies to Antioch with Paul and Barnabas, and communicated their judgment in a letter carried by them to the Church at Antioch. This important transaction at Jerusalem, which publicly announced the character of Christianity as an universal religion, is called the *Council of the Apostles.* It was held about the year 52 A.D. The decision of this apostolic body was of the utmost consequence to the apostle Paul, as, in his subsequent labours, he had to contend constantly with narrow-minded Jewish Christians, who wished to impose the Mosaic law upon the Gentiles also, as essential to salvation. Against these Paul now advanced, not only his own personal influence, but the authority of all the apostles. This, at least, was effected thereby, that the supporters of the ceremonial law and its perpetual validity, were compelled to secede from the universal Apostolic Church, and form themselves into a distinct sect. It is true, however, that their opposition to the apostle Paul was continued with extreme obstinacy; and we find in his Epistles numberless allusions to the persecutions which he encountered at their hand.

Soon after the apostolic council (53 A.D.) Paul undertook his *second* great journey. He separated from Barnabas, who united with his kinsman Mark in preaching the Gospel. Paul took Silas as his companion instead of Barnabas. He directed his course first to the churches founded on his previous journey; and thence onward to *Galatia*, and to Troas, on the western coast of Asia Minor. Thence the Lord conducted him, by a vision in a dream, into Macedonia, where he founded the Church of *Philippi*; and then went to *Thessalonica*. (Acts x. 10 seq.; xvii. 1 seq.) Unfortunately, Paul could remain only about three weeks in the latter city, for, as he met with much success among the proselytes that had connected themselves with the Jewish synagogues, there arose an uproar against him among the Jews, who actually compelled him to leave the city, and flee to Berœa. (Acts xvii. 10.) As, however, the Jews in this place likewise vented their rage against the apostle of our Lord, Paul betook himself to Athens, where also some hearts were warmed by the fire of his preaching. He next proceeded onward to Corinth. Here, in one of the great cities of antiquity, where luxury and debauchery had reached their highest pitch, but where, on that very account, a strong desire for salvation was readily excited, Paul laboured with remarkable success for more than a year and a half. He found there a Jewish family from Rome, Aquila and his wife Priscilla, celebrated in the history of the ancient Church. As Aquila pursued the same craft with Paul, the latter lived and wrought with him, and besides discoursed in the house of a certain Justus. From hence Paul wrote the first Epistles among those still preserved to us, viz., the two Epistles to the Thessalonians. Now, if we compare the tenor of the Epistles with the situation of the Apostle, and their relation to the Church at Thessalonica, we shall find them throughout conformable to the circumstances. As Paul was unable to preach in Thessalonica more than three weeks, he must naturally have been very anxious respecting the fate of those who believed in that city; he feared that they might again fall away on account of the persecutions which threatened them. Hence, his apprehensions had already induced him, as soon as he arrived at Athens, to send Timothy from thence to Thessalonica, in order to learn what was really the condition of the Church. Timothy rejoined him at Corinth: and his mind being set at rest by the information which Timothy communicated, he wrote the first Epistle, for the purpose of confirming and establishing the Thessalonians in the faith to which they had so faithfully adhered. (Acts xvii. 15; xviii. 5; 1 Thess. iii. 2, 5, 6.) It is a circumstance entirely consonant with what we must suppose to have been the situation of the Christians in Thessalonica, that they did not rightly comprehend the doctrine of our Lord's resurrection. This would naturally be the case from the shortness of the period during which they enjoyed the Apostle's instructions. (1 Thess. iv. 13 seq.) They feared that those believers who might die before the coming of our Lord, would be shut out from the joys attendant on the Messiah's reign upon earth. The apostle, however, sets them right in regard to their fear, showing them that there would be a twofold resurrection. Those who had fallen asleep in faith respecting the Saviour, would not rest till the general resurrection, but would be raised up at the coming of Christ, and would behold the Lord with those who were alive. The same subject also soon afterward caused the apostle Paul to write the *second Epistle* to the Christians at Thessalonica, also from Corinth. The explanation of Paul had indeed quieted the apprehension of the believers of that city in regard to those of their number who met with an early death; but some expressions used by Paul in his first Epistle (particularly 1 Thess. iv. 17), together with false rumours respecting his view of the proximity of our Lord's coming, had led some susceptible minds to the idea that this important event not only *might*, but *must*, take place very soon. Thus they openly designated the period of our Lord's return, in total contrariety to Paul's meaning, who did indeed, with them, hope and earnestly desire that our Lord might come in their time, and by no means stated expressly that he would not do so, since that would have been a negative determination of the point; but maintained the *possibility* that he would, and founded thereon, after the example of Christ himself, an exhortation to constant watchfulness. In order, therefore, to moderate the excessive disposition of the Christians at Thessalonica to look upon this great event as *necessarily* about to take place in their own time, Paul presented to view certain things which must all take place before it. From the consideration of these points, it could not but be evident to the Thessalonians, that this event could not take place so suddenly as they anticipated, and thus their excited minds would probably be quieted. In these respects, as regards the state of things at that time, the two Epistles possess entire and undeniable historical keeping; and we shall not err widely from the truth if we assign their composition to the years 54 and 55 of the Christian era.

From Corinth the apostle Paul now returned to Antioch, whence he had been sent. (Acts xviii. 22.) Without, however, remaining long at rest, he, in the following year (57 A.D.), entered upon his *third missionary tour*, going first to Galatia again, where he had preached on his second tour, and then to the wealthy and celebrated city of *Ephesus*, where he abode more than two years. From this city, Paul wrote first to the *Galatians*, and subsequently to the *Corinthians*. The Epistle to the Galatians was occasioned by those same Jewish Christians, of whom we have before remarked that they constantly strove to cast hindrances in the way of Paul's operations. The Galatian churches, which Paul on his second visit to Galatia (Gal. iv. 13) had found walking in the true faith, had been misled by these men in regard to the requirements of religion. Through the idea that the observance of the Jewish ceremonial law was essential to salvation, the Galatian Christians were led to regard circumcision, the solemnisation of the Sabbath and of the Jewish feasts, and other ordinances of the Old Testament, which the New Testament valued only from their spiritual signification, as of worth in an external view, and in this way suffered themselves to lose sight of the interior life of faith. The object of the Apostle, therefore, in his Epistle, was to develop thoroughly to the Galatians the relation between the law and the Gospel, and to show that, in the spiritual freedom conferred by the latter, the external rites of the former might, indeed, be observed, but that they must be observed in a higher manner, *i. e.*, spiritually. Previously, however, he makes some remarks respecting himself personally. For, as the Jewish Christians presumed to dispute Paul's apostolic authority, he found himself compelled to vindicate it by a historical account of himself. He states (i. 12 seq.), that he did not receive his Gospel from man, but immediately from God; that at first he had persecuted the Church of God, but that God, who had called him from his mother's womb, had been pleased to reveal his Son in him, that he might preach him to the heathen, through the Gospel. This evidently refers to the event of our Lord's appearance to Paul, near Damascus, on which occasion the Lord said to him, "I am Jesus whom thou persecutest. But rise, and stand upon thy feet; for I have appeared unto thee for this purpose, to make thee a minister and a witness both of these things which thou hast seen, and of those things in the which I will appear unto thee; delivering thee from the people and from the Gentiles, unto whom now I send thee, to open their eyes, and to turn them from darkness to light, and from the power of Satan unto God, that they may receive forgiveness of sins, and inheritance among them which are sanctified by faith that is in me." (Acts xxvi. 15-18.) This reference to so peculiar occurrences in Paul's life exhibits a sufficient security for the genuineness of this Epistle; and, in connection with its entire contents, as also with its style, has sufficed to place it for ever beyond suspicion.

An occasion equally sad in respect to the apostle gave rise to the *first Epistle to the Corinthians*, which was likewise written from Ephesus. Before the first of the Epistles which are in our possession, Paul had written another to Corinth (1 Cor. v. 9), which, however, has perished. We have, indeed, a *pretended* Epistle of Paul to the Corinthians, which claims to be this lost Epistle, but a slight examination is sufficient to manifest its spuriousness. Moreover, this Epistle of Paul was regarded as lost by all Christian antiquity. This first Epistle, as is shown by 1 Cor. v. 1-9, was occasioned by the circumstance, that an individual in the Corinthian church had matrimonial intercourse with his mother-in-law, the wife of his deceased father. Paul pointed out to the Church the necessity of excluding from among them him who sustained this incestuous relation, that he might be awakened to penitence. To this Epistle of Paul, the Corinthian Christians replied in such a way, as to show plainly that they misunderstood some parts of it, particularly what Paul had said respecting the avoidance of lasciviousness. These misapprehensions are corrected by Paul in the *first* of the two Epistles which have been preserved to us. He likewise speaks in this same letter of another important circumstance in regard to the Corinthian Church, which presents considerable coincidence with the situation of the Christians in Galatia. It is that some of the Jewish Christians, who had excited dissensions among the believers there, had come to Corinth also. True, some had remained faithful to Paul; but others appealed, in contradiction of his authority, to Peter (Cephas), although he agreed perfectly with Paul in his views respecting the law. They probably objected to the apostle Paul, as did the Jewish Christians in Galatia, that he had not, like Peter, known our Lord personally. Besides these two parties, Paul mentions two others (1 Cor. i. 12), the distinctive characteristics of which, however, are uncertain. There were, therefore, divisions in the Corinthian Church, and from these had proceeded manifold disorders. Paul's first Epistle is occupied with the reconciliation of the former, and the removal of the latter.

Our first Epistle to the Corinthians comprises such an abundance of peculiar circumstances entirely conformable with the situation of the Church in its earliest days, that we cannot for a moment suppose it possible that it is a forgery. Moreover, particular facts mentioned in it coincide most exactly with the events of Paul's life, as known from the Acts of the Apostles. Thus, according to Acts xix. 22, he sent away his two companions, Timothy and Erastus, from Ephesus, a short time before he himself left the city; and, according to 1 Cor. iv. 17, likewise, he had despatched Timothy to the Corinthians. According to the same passage in the Acts, Paul purposed soon to leave Ephesus, and travel through Achaia (this was the Greek province in which Corinth was situated) to Jerusalem, and the same thing is indicated by 1 Cor. xvi. 5. Thus, all circumstances unite to give a sure historical basis to the Epistle. As its composition must be placed a little before Paul's departure from Ephesus, it was probably written about 59 A.D., while the Epistle to the Galatians may have been written about the year 58 A.D.

Before the apostle Paul left Ephesus, then, he sent Titus with a special commission to Corinth. He hoped to be able to wait for him in Ephesus, in order to receive an account of the troubled state of affairs in the Corinthian Church, and of the reception which his Epistle encountered. But a sudden uproar, created by Demetrius the silversmith (Acts xix. 24 seq.), who saw himself injured in respect to the gains which he derived from the sale of small silver models of the celebrated temple of Diana at Ephesus, compelled him to leave the city earlier than he wished. In Macedonia, however, whither Paul immediately betook himself, he again met with Titus, who then informed him particularly of the condition of the Church at Corinth, and the impression which his Epistle had produced. This account induced the apostle to write the *Second Epistle to the Corinthians,* from Macedonia. The contents of this other Epistle, which was written a few months after the first, bear so close a relation to the contents of the first, that the identity of the author is, thereby alone, made sufficiently evident. In the second chapter, *e. g.,* we find mention again of the incestuous person, whom Paul had enjoined it upon the Church to exclude from communion with them. As he had now been excommunicated, Paul speaks in his behalf, that he might not sink into utter despondency (2 Cor. ii. 7.) Of most importance, however, are the particular expressions in regard to those Jewish Christians who desolated the Corinthian Church, as well as others. Titus had informed the apostle with what an arrogant disposition they had received his letter. Against these, therefore, he expresses himself with the utmost severity, while he treats those who remain faithful to the truth, with suavity and great kindness. In rebuking the perversity of these Judaizers, he feels it necessary to speak of himself; for these proud sectaries not only rejected the apostolic authority of Paul, but also sought, by their calumnies, to deprive him of the honour of being the most successful labourer in our Lord's vineyard. With noble plainness, therefore, Paul boasts of all that the Lord had done for him and through him; and the further removed this plainness was from false humility, and the less he avoided giving ground for the imputation of *appearing* arrogant and self-conceited, the more likely was his account of himself to make an impression upon all his opponents. We do not know definitely what effect this Epistle produced upon the state of things at Corinth; but, from the subsequent flourishing condition of the Corinthian Church, we may with great probability infer that Paul's Epistle contributed essentially to the annihilation of divisions. At all events, the Epistle is so completely Pauline, and harmonises so exactly with all known historical circumstances, that its genuineness has never been contested either in ancient or modern times.

What was not effected by the Epistle of Paul to the Church of Corinth, was undoubtedly accomplished by the apostle's personal presence in this metropolis. For, from Macedonia Paul went to Achaia (Acts xx. 3), and abode there three months. The greater part of this time he certainly spent in Corinth, and from thence he wrote the *Epistle to the Romans*, shortly before his departure from Corinth for Jerusalem, in order to carry a collection of alms for the poor of that city (Acts xxiv. 17 seq.; Rom. xv. 25, 26). This important Epistle (viz., that to the Romans) bears the stamp of a genuine apostolic letter so completely, in both thought and language, that neither ancient nor modern times have advanced a single doubt as to its origin. The particular doctrine which Paul presented to view more frequently and more prominently than any other apostle, viz., that man is saved by faith in him who was crucified and rose again, and not by the works of the law, either ceremonial or moral, forms the central topic of the Epistle to the Romans; and, moreover, all the historical allusions which occur in it are entirely suitable to the circumstances under which it was written. Paul, *e. g.*, according to this Epistle (Rom. i. 12, 15; xxiii. seq.), had not yet been in Rome when he wrote it; and this agrees exactly with the statement of the apostle in Acts xix. 21. The many persons whom he salutes at the end of the Epistle, he became acquainted with from his numerous travels in Asia Minor and Greece; for, as there was a general conflux to Rome from all quarters, and also a general dispersion thence, it being the centre of the world, there was no city in which Romans did not reside, or of whose inhabitants many were not constrained by circumstances to journey to Rome, or to establish themselves there as residents. On account of this importance of the city of Rome, which must necessarily have been communicated to the Church in that place, there is sufficient proof of the genuineness of this Epistle, in the single circumstance that this Church, in which Paul afterwards abode some years, never contradicted the universal opinion that Paul wrote this Epistle to them, but rather rejoiced in being honoured with such an apostolic communication.

Hitherto we have seen the celebrated apostle of the Gentiles constantly labouring with freedom and boldness; but his departure from Corinth brought upon him a long and cruel imprisonment. For Paul immediately returned from Corinth to Macedonia, embarked there at Philippi (Acts xx. 3 seq.) and sailed along the coasts of Asia Minor. At Miletus he called to him the elders of the Church of Ephesus (Acts xx. 17 seq.), and took pathetic leave of them; for he was persuaded that he should never again see these beloved brethren (xx. 38). About the year 60 A.D., the apostle arrived at Jerusalem, having passed through Cæsarea; but was there immediately arrested (Acts xxii.), and carried back to Cæsarea. (Acts xxiii. 31 seq.) Here he was indeed examined by the proconsul Felix; but, as he could not pronounce sentence against him, and hesitated to release him, Paul remained two years in captivity. At the end of that time, there came another proconsul, Porcius Festus, to Cæsarea. He commenced the examination anew, but when the apostle, as a Roman citizen, appealed to Cæsar, he sent him to Rome. This was about 62 A.D. On the voyage thither, Paul, together with the Roman soldiers who accompanied him, suffered shipwreck, and they were compelled to pass the winter on the island of Malta. Paul did not, therefore, arrive at Rome before the commencement of the following year, and was there again kept as a prisoner for two years, *i. e.*, till 65 A.D., before his case was decided. Still his confinement at Rome was not so strict as that at Cæsarea. He was permitted to hire a dwelling in the city, to go about, speak, and write as he pleased; only, he was always accompanied by a soldier. Luke alone details all these events in the last chapters of the Acts, with very great minuteness. From Paul's Epistles we learn nothing respecting this period; for Paul seems not to have written at all from Cæsarea. Probably the strict durance in which he was held did not permit any communication by writing. In the providence of God, this long confinement may have served to acquaint Paul with himself, with the depths of his own interior being. For the manner of life which Paul led, and was obliged to lead, the perpetual bustle of travel, his constant efforts in regard to others, might have injured him by dissipation of his thoughts, and might, so to speak, have exhausted the fulness of his spirit, had he not possessed some quiet seasons in which, while his attention was turned wholly upon himself, he might be spiritually replenished and invigorated for future seasons of intense outward exertion.

But from the other of the two places where Paul was compelled to remain a prisoner for a long period, *i. e.* Rome, he certainly wrote several Epistles, viz., *the Epistles to the Ephesians, Philippians, Colossians, and Philemon.* Still, although in these Epistles mention is made of some historical particulars, he supposes the occurrences in regard to himself to be generally known among the Christians of the churches in Macedonia and Asia Minor, and therefore does not enter into details respecting them. Unfortunately, Luke closed his book of Acts at the point when Paul had lived two years as a prisoner at Rome; and therefore, in further designating the historical connection of Paul's Epistles, we are not able to state the circumstances of time and place with so much precision and certainty as hitherto. This circumstance, likewise, explains how, in such a state of things, the remaining Epistles of Paul afford more room to doubt of their genuineness than was the case in regard to those which, we see, well and easily fall into the history of Paul as related in the Acts. We shall therefore devote separate consideration to these Epistles.

CHAPTER V.

CONTINUATION.—OF THE PAULINE EPISTLES COMPOSED DURING AND AFTER PAUL'S IMPRISONMENT AT ROME.

Of the Epistles composed by Paul during his imprisonment at Rome, the Epistles to the *Philippians, Colossians,* and *Philemon,* can be easily shown, with sufficient certainty, to be genuine writings of the apostle. First, as to the Epistle to the *Philippians,* Paul clearly represents himself therein, not only as a prisoner, but also as a prisoner at Rome; for he speaks of the barracks occupied by the imperial guards (the Prætorium: Luther translates the word by *Richt-haus,* or hall of justice, Phil. i. 13), into which the fame of his imprisonment had extended itself. Probably Paul had won over to the gospel the soldiers set to guard him, to whom he was wont to preach, and, through these, others in the camp may have been converted. Even the imperial palace itself is mentioned by Paul (Phil. iv. 22), as having been already penetrated by the seeds of the Word of God. These clear allusions leave not the slightest doubt that the Epistle was written from Rome. Nor can any doubt remain as to the question, whether it was really written to the inhabitants of the Macedonian city *Philippi*. For, according to Acts xvi. 12 seq., the Apostle's labours in this city had been particularly blessed. The Lord at once opened the heart of Lydia, so that she believed the preaching of Paul. An unfortunate occurrence respecting a damsel possessed with a spirit of divination, which the apostle expelled, constrained him to leave the city. The church at Philippi, however, always preserved a particular attachment to the apostle Paul, and his acknowledgment of this fact runs through the whole of his letter to them. The apostle calls them his brethren dearly beloved and longed for, his joy and crown (Phil. iv. 1), and thanks the Philippian Christians that they so faithfully had respect to his bodily necessities (Phil. iv. 15, 16). These characteristics are decisive in favour of the genuineness of the Epistle, which, moreover, has not been contested either in ancient or modern times.

The case is the same in regard to the *Epistle to the Colossians*. This church was not founded by Paul in person; as he himself indicates in Col. ii. 1. He had, indeed, been in Phrygia, but had not visited the city of Colosse on his journey through this province of Asia Minor. Paul nevertheless wrote to them, as also to the Romans, in part from universal Christian love, which called upon him to acknowledge the members of every church of Christ as brethren, and in part from the special reason, that the Gospel had been carried to Colosse by disciples of his, particularly *Epaphras*. The immediate occasion of his Epistle, however, was, that heretics threatened to draw away the church from the true faith. These individuals were not of the ordinary Judaizing class; along with much that was Jewish, they had some Gnostic characteristics. Now Phrygia is the precise spot where, from the earliest times downward, we find a prevalent tendency to a fantastic apprehension of religion. Thus the circumstance that, according to Paul's representation, men of this stamp had gained influence in Colosse, suits perfectly well with what we know of that city. Nor is it otherwise than very natural, that few particular allusions occur in the Epistle, as he was not personally known to the church. He, however, mentions his imprisonment, and sends salutations also from some persons of their acquaintance who were in his vicinity, among others from Aristarchus (Col. iv. 10), who, as we learn from the Acts, had come to Rome with Paul and Luke (xxvii. 1.) The latter companion of Paul likewise salutes the believers in Phrygia (iv. 14.) Of individuals themselves resident in Colosse, he saluted especially *Archippus* (iv. 17), who occupied some ministry in the church. Concerning this man, as also concerning *Onesimus*, whom Paul mentions (Col. iv. 9), we gain more particular information from the Epistle to Philemon. In this Epistle to the Colossians, likewise, everything harmonises so exactly with Paul's circumstances in general, and his relation to the church which he addressed in particular, that no one has ever been led to question its genuineness, either in ancient or modern days.

With the same entire unanimity has the genuineness of Paul's *Epistle to Philemon* likewise been always admitted. This delightful little Epistle so clearly exhibits all the characteristics of the great apostle, and is so utterly free from everything which would make it probable that any person could have a motive in forging it, that no one would ever entertain the idea of denying that Paul was its author. Philemon, to whom the Epistle is addressed, probably lived in Colosse, for that Archippus, who held an office in the church at Colosse, appears here as his son, and Appia as his wife (Phil. v. 2). Probably Philemon was an opulent man; for he had so spacious a house, that it accommodated the assemblies of believers. Paul wrote this Epistle, likewise, in confinement (v. 13), and sends salutations from all those who, according to the Acts and the Epistle to the Colossians, were in his vicinity (v. 23, 24.) Onesimus, who had fled from the relation of bondage which he had sustained towards Philemon in Colosse, Paul sends back to his master, whom he informs that his slave had been led by him to obey the Gospel, so that Philemon is to receive back again as a brother him whom he had lost as a slave. The whole of this small Epistle comprises, indeed, no important doctrinal contents; but it is an exhibition of interior, deep feeling, and delicate regard to circumstances on the part of the apostle, and, as such, has always been very dear and valuable to the Church.

In regard to the *Epistle to the Ephesians*, however, the case is totally different from what it is in regard to the three other Epistles sent from Rome. There are so many remarkable circumstances in relation to this Epistle, that we can easily comprehend how its genuineness has been often brought in question. Still, all the doubts which may have been excited are completely removed on a closer examination, so that it can by no means be denied that the Epistle was written by the apostle, even if its actual destination to Ephesus cannot be established.

If it be considered that Paul, as we saw above in the historical account of the apostle's life, was twice in Ephesus, and that once he even resided there for about three years, it must certainly appear very strange that, in an Epistle to this church, of the elders of which Paul had taken leave in so pathetic a manner (Acts xx. 17), there should be found no salutations. In writing to the Romans, Paul, though he had never been at Rome, sent salutations to so many persons, that their names fill an entire chapter, while in this Epistle not a single person is greeted. Moreover, there are no personal and confidential allusions in any part of the Epistle. Paul appears only in the general relation of a Christian teacher and a friend to his readers. There is certainly something extremely strange in this character of the Epistle, particularly, moreover, as that which we should especially expect to find in the Epistle, viz., allusion to heretics, against which Paul had so expressly warned the Ephesian elders, is entirely wanting. (Acts xx. 29 seq.)

The difficulties are increased when we know what was the case originally concerning the address to the readers of the Epistle (Eph. i. 1). Instead of "Paul, an apostle of Jesus Christ, by the will of God, to the saints which are at *Ephesus*," as it stands in most copies, Marcion, in his MS., read: "to the saints at *Laodicea.*" In other MSS. there was no name at all, neither Ephesus, nor Laodicea; and in these the inscription or the Epistle ran thus: "Paul, an apostle of Jesus Christ, by the will of God, to the saints which dwell at ———." Instead of the name was a vacant space, which, however, was often neglected by the copyists, who thus perplexed the matter still further.

In addition to all this, if the Epistle to the Ephesians be compared with that to the Colossians, we shall find the same fundamental thought, and often even the same train of ideas, only the first is more minute and expanded, while in the Epistle to the Colossians the thoughts are more concisely and briefly presented. On account of this relative character, it has been declared that the Epistle to the Ephesians is probably only an enlargement of the Epistle to the Colossians, made with a special design by some other hand. But though for a moment such supposition might not appear altogether unfounded, its plausibility is completely dissipated when the peculiar character of the Epistle is made apparent by a right and thorough notion of its origin. The Epistle to the Ephesians is undoubtedly what is termed a circular letter, directed not to a single church, but to many at once. In such a letter, therefore, there could be no personal allusions, because what might interest one circle of readers might be unintelligible to another. In this Epistle, therefore, Paul adheres exclusively to generalities, and touches only on such topics as would be of interest to all members of the churches for whom the Epistle was intended. Now, on the supposition that Ephesus and Laodicea were of the number of those churches for which the Epistle was intended, nothing is more easy of explanation than the fact, that the name of the former was in the inscription of some MSS., and the name of the latter in that of others. The messenger who carried the apostolic letter may have taken several copies with him, in which the space for the name of the place was not filled out, and remained thus until they were delivered, when the name of the church which received any particular one was added to it. The diffusion of the Epistle abroad was mainly from the capital city Ephesus; and hence the name Ephesus got into the inscription of most of the MSS. Marcion, however, came into possession of a transcript from the copy which was delivered at Laodicea, and for this reason he read Laodicea instead of Ephesus in the inscription. In some copies, there may have been a total neglect to fill up the spaces left vacant for the names; and in this way some MSS. got into circulation in which no city was designated.

It is seen how satisfactorily and completely, on this single supposition, that the Epistle to the Ephesians was a circular letter, our difficulties disappear at once. It is true, the striking resemblance of the Epistle to that to the Colossians still remains; and in recent times the greatest stress has been laid on this very point. Both Epistles have essentially the same contents, only the Epistle to the Ephesians is more full and minute, as has been already remarked. But let it be considered that the two Epistles were written, not only about the same time, but under entirely similar circumstances. Is it then to be wondered at, that there is a striking similarity in contents and arrangement? What purpose could there have been in forging or counterfeiting an Epistle, in which the fraudulent author said the same things which were contained in a genuine Epistle of the man to whom he wished that his production should be ascribed? It is, therefore, clear that there is nothing in this resemblance of the Epistle to the Ephesians to that of the Colossians, which can justify us in inferring the spuriousness of either. For, whether we suppose that the longest (that to the Ephesians), was written first, and that Paul afterwards repeated the same thoughts in the shortest (that to the Colossians); or *vice versa*, that he wrote the shortest first, and afterwards felt himself called upon to state the same ideas more at length in the other, there is not the least harm done by their similarity to each other, particularly as the Epistle to the Ephesians contains many ideas wholly peculiar to the apostle Paul, which are wanting in the Epistle to the Colossians, and this, too, in his own phraseology and style.

It is to be observed, further, that Paul, in his Epistle to the Colossians, mentions a letter to the Church at Laodicea, and charges the former to communicate their Epistle to the believers in Laodicea, and, in return, to request the Epistle addressed to them. Now, because, as we have seen, Marcion regarded the Epistle to the Ephesians as having been directed to the Laodiceans, it has been supposed that our Epistle to the Ephesians was the one meant by Paul. But, plausible as this may appear at first sight, it is still improbable, on a closer examination, that it is correct; for, first, the great similarity between the two Epistles makes against it, as this must evidently have rendered their mutual transfer of less consequence. Then, too, it is not common to direct special salutations to be given to those to whom we write ourselves at the same time, which is done by Paul in relation to the Laodiceans, in his letter to the Colossians (*passim*). Moreover, our Epistle to the Ephesians, as a circular letter, could not well be designated by the name, Epistle to the Laodiceans. Thus, it is far more probable that this letter was a separate one, which has been lost to us.

As early as the time of Jerome, there existed a separate Epistle to the Laodiceans, different from that to the Ephesians. But the father just mentioned, remarks, that all, without exception, reject it. It is probable, therefore, that, on account of the passage, Col. iv. 15, 16, some one had forged an Epistle to the Laodiceans, just as was the case, as we have before stated, with the first Epistle to the Corinthians, which was lost.

There remain, therefore, only the three Epistles of the apostle, which are usually comprehended under the title of *Pastoral Letters*, viz., the two to Timothy, and that to Titus. They are all three occupied with a consideration of the duties of a pastor of the Church of Christ, and on account of this common purport, are classed under the general designation which we have mentioned. In a close investigation of the contents and the historical allusions of these Epistles, there arise very many difficulties, on which account they have become subject to doubt beyond all the other Pauline Epistles. Ancient tradition is certainly wholly in favour of their genuineness, as in relation to the Epistle to the Ephesians; for the circumstance that Marcion did not have them in his canon, is not regarded as important, even by opponents of the Epistles, who are at all impartial. It was undoubtedly only through accident that these Epistles remained unknown to him, and to his native city, Sinope, upon the Black Sea; for had he possessed historical reasons against its reception, they could not have been so completely lost at a later period. We may here see, in fact, a very important evidence in behalf of the genuineness of these Epistles; for Timothy lived when Paul wrote to him, not in a distant, unknown place, but in Ephesus, one of the chief cities frequented by the Christians of the ancient Church. The scene of the labours of Titus was the isle of Crete, which also, on account of its vicinity to Corinth, and to other important churches, maintained lively intercourse with the churches generally. Now, how Epistles, directed to persons labouring in places of so much note, and holding so high a rank, as being assistants of the apostle, could gain the reputation of being genuine throughout the whole ancient Church, when they were really forged in the name of the apostle, is indeed difficult of comprehension, as so many must have been able to expose the deception. Supposing, therefore, that, on a close investigation of the contents of the Epistle, there should appear much that is strange, it must be considered as losing a great deal of its influence in relation to the question of the genuineness of the Epistles, from the fact that this is so firmly established by the tradition of the Church.

Another circumstance to be premised, which is very much in favour of their genuineness, is, that in all the three epistles there occurs a multitude of personal and particular allusions. Now, it is clear that an impostor, who was palming off his own epistles as another's, (for such is the language which we must use concerning the author of these three compositions, if they are not the work of Paul himself, since he expressly names himself as the author, besides indicating the fact in a manner not to be mistaken,) would avoid as much as possible all special circumstances, because he would be too likely to betray himself in touching upon them, since particulars cannot be very minutely known to a stranger. Moreover, a forgery generally wants that graphic exactness which is exhibited so manifestly in writings that spring out of actually existing circumstances. Hence every unprejudiced person would, in the outset, think it very unlikely that a writing was forged in which there occurred such special allusions as we find in 1 Tim. v. 23, where Paul says to Timothy, "Drink no longer water, but use a little wine for thy stomach's sake, and thine often infirmities." Of the same nature, also, is a passage in the second Epistle to Timothy, (2 Tim. iv. 13,) in which the apostle complains that he had, through forgetfulness, left his cloak, some books, and parchments with a friend, and desires Timothy to take care of them. Plainly, such things are not forged; for to what end should any one give himself the useless trouble to invent such insignificant matters, if they did not actually happen, since they could not do either any harm or any good? In the same Epistle (2 Tim. iv. 20, 21) Paul sends salutations from many individuals, and gives various information respecting persons of their mutual acquaintance. "Erastus abode at Corinth," says Paul, "but Trophimus have I left at Miletus sick;" and he invites Timothy himself to come to him before winter. If any person invented all this, we must at least call him extremely inconsiderate, for he ought not certainly to have mentioned such noted cities, since the Christians who dwelt in them could learn, without any great difficulty, whether any one of the name of Trophimus was ever at Miletus with the apostle, and was left there by him sick, and whether Erastus abode at Corinth. The same is true of the Epistle to Titus, as one may be convinced by examining Titus iii. 12.

Still, let us look at the reasons which are advanced *against* the genuineness of these Epistles. Certain investigators have thought that there was in all three of them something not only in the phraseology, but in the style altogether, which cannot but be regarded as unlike Paul. The weakness of such statements, however, may be clearly inferred from the fact that another investigator, of no less acuteness, supposes the second Epistle to Timothy and the one to Titus to be really genuine Epistles of Paul, while the first to Timothy is spurious, and imitated from the other two. This second investigator, therefore, founds his argument for the spuriousness of the first of the three Epistles on the genuineness of the two others, thus overthrowing, by his own reasoning, the position of the former investigators in regard to the necessity of supposing them all spurious. The historical difficulties, however, which are discerned on close examination of the Epistles, are of more consequence. It is from these properly that all attacks upon these pastoral letters have originated, and in these they find their excuse, only writers ought not to have so manifestly confounded *difficulties* with *positive arguments against the genuineness of a writing*.

As to the *First* Epistle to Timothy, the principal difficulty is, to point out a period in Paul's life exactly coinciding with the statement which the apostle makes at the outset (i. 3). He says that when he went to Macedonia he left Timothy at Ephesus, to protect the true faith and thwart heretics in that city. Now we know, indeed, that when Demetrius the silversmith drove Paul from Ephesus, he went to Macedonia; but it is impossible that he should then have left Timothy behind at Ephesus, since he sent him before himself to Macedonia with Erastus. Thus, when

Paul wrote his second Epistle to the Corinthians from Macedonia, Timothy was with him. (Comp. Acts xix. 22 ; 2 Cor. i. 1). Moreover, we are informed of no other journey of Paul from Ephesus to Macedonia, when he left Timothy behind in the city to watch over the Church; and hence arises a difficulty in assigning this Epistle its proper place in Paul's life.

There are similar circumstances respecting the *Second* Epistle. This Epistle, too, is directed to Timothy at Ephesus. Paul clearly writes from Rome. (Comp. 2 Tim. iv. 16, 17, with 2 Tim. i. 16, 18; iv. 19). He was in bonds (i. 16), and was expecting a new examination of his cause. Now, he invites Timothy to come to him, and requests him to make haste and come before winter (iv. 13, 21). But, according to Col. i. 1: Philemon, ver. 1, and Phil. i. 1, Timothy, at the time of Paul's imprisonment at Rome, as related by Luke in the Acts, was in Paul's company; and hence it seems impossible that Paul could have written to him at Ephesus. It is true Paul's imprisonment at Rome lasted two years, and it might be supposed that Timothy was for some time with him, and for some time away during his imprisonment; but there are other circumstances which make it very improbable that the Second Epistle to Timothy was written during the same imprisonment in which the Epistles to the Ephesians, Colossians, and Philippians were composed. According to 2 Tim. iv. 18, Paul had left at Troas, a cloak, books, and parchments, which Timothy was to bring with him when he came to Paul (v. 21). Now, before Paul's imprisonment at Rome, which lasted two years, he was also two years in Cæsarea. We should, therefore, be compelled to suppose that he had left these things behind at Troas, four years before. But certainly it is probable that Paul would have made some other disposition of them in the meantime, if they were of any consequence to him. But, even if we may suppose that Paul would send for clothing and books which had lain at Troas for years, it is out of the question that he should say in relation to a journey made four years before: "Erastus abode at Corinth, but Trophimus have I left at Miletus sick." (2 Tim. iv. 20). Miletus was in the vicinity of Ephesus, at a distance from Rome, where Paul was writing. Now, if Paul had not been in Miletus for four years, it is wholly impossible that he should have mentioned the illness of one whom he had left be hind at Miletus so long a time before, because his case must long since have been decided. Similar difficulties present themselves, likewise, on a close examination of the *Epistle to Titus*. For Paul writes in this Epistle (i. 4, 5; iii. 12), that he himself had been in the island of Crete, and had left Titus there behind him for the same purpose which caused him to leave Timothy in Ephesus; and states that he intended to spend the winter in Nicopolis, whither he directs Titus to come and meet him. Now, it is true, Paul, according to the Acts (xxvii. 8), was once in Crete, but it was as a prisoner, and on a voyage. In these circumstances, therefore, he could not accomplish much; nor could he leave Titus behind, as on his voyage Titus was nowhere in his neighbourhood. Nothing is told us in any part of the New Testament history as to Paul's residence in Nicopolis, and it is the more difficult to come to any assurance respecting it, from the fact that there were so many cities of that name. Thus, this Epistle, likewise, cannot be assigned to its place in Paul's history, and therefore it is perfectly true, that there are difficulties incident to an examination of these pastoral letters; but, as we have before observed, difficulties are not equivalent to positive arguments against their genuineness. It is true they would be, were we so exactly and minutely acquainted with the history of the apostle Paul, that such a difficulty in assigning an epistle its place among the circumstances of his life would be the same as an impossibility. If, for example, we knew with certainty that the apostle Paul never resided in any city by the name of Nicopolis, we should be obliged to consider the Epistle to Titus, which purports to have been written from some place called Nicopolis, as spurious and forged.

But this is so far from being the case, that in those Epistles of Paul, which are admitted to be genuine, very many occurrences are noticed, of which we have no further information. A remarkable instance of this kind is the well-known passage, 2 Cor. xi. 23 seq., in which Paul states, that he had five times received of the Jews forty stripes save one, thrice being beaten with rods, once stoned, thrice suffered shipwreck, &c., &c. Of very few of these sufferings of Paul do we know the particulars. How much, therefore, of what took place in his life may remain unknown to us. It is to be remembered, too, that the brief general statements given by Luke in the Acts extend over long periods in the apostle's life. At Corinth, Ephesus, Cæsarea, and Rome, Paul abode for years. Now, as slight journeys abroad are, it is well known, commonly comprehended by historians in a residence at any particular place for a long period, may not this have been frequently the case in Luke's history? Many have thought this probable, and have therefore supposed short journeys from this or that place, and in this way have attempted to find some situation in Paul's life, which should appear suitable for the composition of one or another of the pastoral letters. We will not trouble our readers, however, with an enumeration of these different views, which, nevertheless, show that it is not *impossible* to designate some situation in which Paul might have written these Epistles. We choose rather to confine ourselves to the development of an important supposition by which a suitable period of time is obtained for all the three Epistles together, and their relation to each other is determined. This supposition is, that Paul was set at liberty from the first imprisonment at Rome, related by Luke (which had lasted two years when Luke finished his Book of Acts), performed important missionary tours afterward, and was at last *imprisoned a second time at Rome*, and at this time died there a martyr's death. It is very evident that, if we can in this way gain space of time for another journey to Asia and Crete, it will be easy to imagine the situations which gave rise to the first Epistle to Timothy, and that to Titus. The second Epistle to Timothy must then have been written in Rome itself during the second imprisonment, and any remarkable expressions which it contains are then perfectly intelligible, if it be supposed that Paul wrote the Epistle after his arrival at Rome from Asia Minor. The only question is, whether this supposition, that Paul was a second time imprisoned at Rome, is a mere hypothesis, or can be sustained by any historical evidence. Were it a mere conjecture, it must be admitted it would be of little importance.

There are not wanting, however, some historical facts of such a nature as to confirm the supposition. First, we find it current among the fathers of the fourth century. It is true, they do not expressly present historical grounds for their opinion; they seem rather to have inferred a second imprisonment at Rome from the second Epistle to Timothy. But, that they at once assumed a second imprisonment, when they might have hit upon other modes of explanation, seems to indicate a tradition, however obscure, in regard to the fact of its having occurred. Moreover, we are told by a very ancient writer of the Roman Church, the apostolic father, Clemens Romanus, that Paul went to the farthest west. This must mean Spain. In the Epistle to the Romans (chap. xv.) Paul expresses a strong desire to visit that country. This he cannot have done before his first imprisonment; it is not at all improbable, therefore, that he may afterwards have journeyed to this country, the most western region of the then known world.

Whatever may be thought of this supposition, so much is clear—the difficulties which the attentive reader meets with in the Epistles, are no arguments against their genuineness. Indeed everything essential is in their favour. The internal similarity of the Epistles, however, makes it probable that they were composed about the same time, and the idea that they were written during the second imprisonment, of which we have spoken, accords very well with this supposition.

CHAPTER VI.

OF THE EPISTLE TO THE HEBREWS.

OF the investigations of learned men respecting the genuineness of the writings of the New Testament, we have hitherto been able to give a very favourable account; but the case seems now to be different, in considering the investigations respecting the Epistle to the Hebrews. For, he who has been accustomed to reckon this Epistle among those of Pauline origin (the Lutheran version, such as it now is, expressly attributing it to this apostle, although Luther himself, as will be shown presently, held a different opinion), may be surprised at hearing that the latest, extremely thorough and generally impartial, investigations respecting this important Epistle, determine that Paul was not its author.* We have before remarked, that the genuineness of the Epistle to the Hebrews is not at all in question: the only inquiry is, who was its author. For he has neither named nor designated himself throughout the Epistle. Thus, even though Paul should not be considered the author, it does not follow that the Epistle is a forged or spurious one.

Now, that the case of this Epistle must be peculiar, is clear from the fact, that it was not admitted into the midst of the other Pauline Epistles. In the Greek Testament it does indeed come directly after the Epistle to Philemon, and thus by the side of the collection of Paul's Epistles (though Luther has placed it after the Epistles of Peter and John); but it is clear that this large and important Epistle would have been placed among the other large Epistles of the same apostle to whole churches, perhaps after the Epistles to the Corinthians, had it been originally regarded as a production of the apostle to the Gentiles.† Consequently, its position after the Epistle to Philemon, the smallest and most inconsiderable of Paul's private letters, shows plainly, that it was not generally reckoned as one of the Pauline Epistles, until after the collection of them was completed. However, all this is, of course, of an incidental nature; there are far more important reasons, which make it improbable that Paul was the author of the Epistle to the Hebrews; and to the consideration of these we will now direct our attention.

The *form* of the Epistle is, it is seen, entirely different from that of Paul's letters. He opens each of his Epistles, not only with his name and the title of his sacred office, but also with an apostolic salutation: "Grace be with you, and peace, from God our Father, and our Lord Jesus Christ." Nothing of this kind

---

* But see Professor Stuart's discussion of this point in his masterly Commentary upon the Epistle. See also an able discussion of it in a work published at London in 1830, entitled "Biblical Notes and Dissertations," written by Joseph John Gurney, an Englishman, member of the Society of Friends. Mr. Gurney's dissertation was republished in the Biblical Repository for July 1832 (Vol. II. p. 409.)—Tr.

† According to Epiphanius, a church-father of the fourth century, some MSS. placed the Epistle to the Hebrews *before the Epistles to Timothy;* probably only because it seemed to some copyists improper that an Epistle to a whole church should stand after Epistles to private individuals.

is to be seen at the commencement of the Epistle to the Hebrews. It begins like a treatise (which indeed many have been inclined to suppose it to be), without any reference to its readers: "God, who at sundry times, and in divers manners, spake in times past unto the fathers by the prophets," &c. The conclusion bears more resemblance to Paul's Epistles; for it contains a salutation, such as those of the apostle, and announces a visit to the readers of the Epistle on the part of the author in company with Timothy. The writer sends a salutation on the part of the brethren *from* Italy; from whence it has been erroneously inferred that the Epistle was written in Italy, whereas the phraseology indicates exactly the contrary.* For the author would not have employed such an expression unless he was writing *out of* Italy in a place whither brethren had arrived *from* that country. The Epistle contains no particular salutations from one individual to another; but this is not strange, as it is addressed to so many. For the *Hebrews*, to whom the Epistle was written, were the Jewish Christians who lived in Palestine. Their benefit was intended by the entire contents of this profound Epistle. It analyzes thoroughly the relation of the Old Testament to the New.

Nevertheless, it may be said, no great stress ought to be laid upon the external *form* of the Epistle; Paul might for once have deviated from his usual custom. But the *historical evidence* is very decisive in regard to this Epistle. For, in the western Church, and particularly the Roman, the Epistle to the Hebrews was not at all acknowledged as Paul's production until some time in the fourth century. It was through Augustine's means, who died so late as 430 A.D., that it first became common to ascribe it to Paul; and even this father of the Church sometimes speaks doubtfully of the Epistle, as do other fathers

---

* The original Greek reads, οἱ ἀπὸ τῆς Ἰταλίας, which is translated in our English version "they of Italy." Olshausen considers it necessary to translate ἀπό *from*, making the whole expression to mean, *those who had come from Italy to some place where Paul was writing.* Consultation of a good Greek lexicon will cause any one to doubt whether there is any such necessity as Olshausen supposes. See, for example, in Passow, under the word ἀπό, such expressions as, αἷμα ἀπὸ Τρώων, the blood of the Trojans, οἱ ἀπὸ Πλάτωνος, they of Plato's party, &c.—Tr.

after his time. Plainly this is very remarkable. For, if it be considered how well known Paul was, and how deeply loved at Rome, and that he was twice imprisoned there for years, it will be evident that it must have been known in that city whether Paul was its author or not. Thus the testimony of the Roman Church is of the highest importance in the question under examination. Now, it is observable, that Clement of Rome, an immediate disciple of Paul, makes very ample use of the Epistle to the Hebrews, and even introduces long passages of it into his own Epistle to the Corinthians. This is indeed a very decisive proof of the high antiquity of the Epistle; but Clement does not mention the author of the writing from which he quoted, and therefore the use he has made of it has no farther influence in regard to the question, who was its author. Still, he must certainly have liked the Epistle, and esteemed it very highly; otherwise he would not have been induced to embellish his own Epistle with large passages from it, which are interwoven with his train of thought, as though they were original.

That in the West there was general uncertainty in regard to the author of the Epistle, is shown by the circumstance, that an African father of the Church, Tertullian, names Barnabas as its author. Others, especially some orientals, ascribed it to Luke, and some to the before-mentioned Clement, though unfortunately without good reason. There was no uniform tradition in the West in regard to its authorship; it was, from conjecture alone, ascribed to various individuals.

The case was totally different with the Greek Church in the East. The predominant opinion with this was that Paul was the author. It was the celebrated fathers of the Alexandria Church especially, together with the Syrians, who made great use of the Epistle to the Hebrews, and referred it to the apostle Paul. The old Syriac version contains it in its canon. This circumstance is not to be overlooked, particularly as the Epistle is directed to the Christians in Palestine, from whom, of course, it might very easily come into the hands of the neighbouring Syrians and Egyptians. Historical testimony, however, in favour of any Epistle, must be sought for mainly in the place where it was composed, and that to which it was addressed. One of these furnishes evidence against the Pauline origin of the Epistle, and the other in its favour; a circumstance which, as we shall see hereafter, is of no slight consequence in an inquiry respecting the canonical authority of the Epistle.

Although the Greek, and especially the Alexandrian fathers, were favourably disposed towards the Epistle to the Hebrews, the learned among them admitted the great difference between it and the other Epistles of Paul. They explained this difference by supposing that Paul wrote the Epistle in Hebrew, and Luke translated it into Greek. This Evangelist was fixed upon as the translator, because, as was thought, a resemblance was discovered between his style and that of the Epistle. The supposition, however, is not at all probable; for the style of the Epistle to the Hebrews is so peculiarly Greek, that it cannot have been translated from the Hebrew. We may see, merely from the conjecture thus presented, that inquiring minds, in perusing the Epistle, came to doubt whether it was really Pauline in its character, even where it was commonly considered as a Pauline production.

Hence it was that our Luther, when he studied the Scriptures in a critical manner, renewed the doubts respecting the Pauline origin of the Epistle to the Hebrews, after it had been regarded throughout the middle ages as the apostle Paul's production. He writes on this point as follows:—" As yet, we have mentioned only the principal indubitably genuine books of the New Testament. The four following books, however,[*] have in times past held a different rank. And first, that the Epistle to the Hebrews is not St. Paul's, nor any apostle's, is proved by the tenor of verse 3 of chap. ii. : 'How shall we escape if we neglect so great salvation, which at first began to be spoken by the Lord, and was confirmed unto us by them that heard him.' It is clear that he speaks of the apostles as though he were a disciple, to whom this salvation had come from the apostles, perhaps long after." (See Walch's Ed. Luther's Works, Th. xiv. p. 146). The passage to which Luther refers is indeed remarkable, and has been employed by scholars of a more recent day to prove that Paul cannot have been the author of the Epistle. For we know

---

[*] He means, besides the Epistle to the Hebrews, the Epistles of James and Jude, and the Revelation of John.

that he always maintained strongly (particularly in the outset to the Epistle to the Galatians), in opposition to his Jewish adversaries, who presumed to dispute his apostolic commission and authority, that he had received everything from the immediate revelation of God. How, then, is it conceivable, that in Heb. ii. 3, he should have represented himself as a disciple of the apostles; and this in an Epistle to Jewish Christians, before whom it was specially important for him to appear as a real apostle of our Lord? This circumstance, moreover, that the Epistle to the Hebrews was written to Jewish Christians, deprives of all probability that interpretation of the passage according to which Paul speaks merely out of courtesy, as though he himself was a disciple of the apostles, which in reality was the case only with his readers. For then Paul would have expressed himself in a manner very liable to be misapprehended; and that this should have happened when his relation to the Jewish Christians was so peculiar, is extremely improbable. Luther, with his free, bold disposition, which did indeed sometimes carry him beyond the limits of truth in his critical investigations, did not content himself with merely disputing the Pauline origin of the Epistle; he even ventured to institute conjectures respecting its author. He regarded the celebrated Apollos as its author; the same of whom mention is made in the Acts. In truth, this supposition possesses extreme probability, and has, therefore, of all the hypotheses respecting the author of the Epistle, recommended itself most even to recent investigators. The book of Acts describes this man as having precisely that character of mind which the author of this Epistle must have had, to judge from its contents. He is stated (Acts xviii. 24), to have been by birth an Alexandrian, an eloquent man, and mighty in the Scriptures. Now, the author of the Epistle to the Hebrews shows himself to have been thoroughly acquainted with the Old Testament, and eloquently maintains the deep and sublime ideas which it presents. According to the same passage, he constantly overcame the Jews in conversation with them, and proved publicly, by means of the Scriptures, that Jesus was the Christ. Undoubtedly, in these disputes he made use of just such forcible expositions of the Old Testament, as those of which we find so many in the Epistle to the Hebrews, and which were very commonly employed by the Alexandrians in particular. The idea that Titus, or Luke, or Clement, might have been the author of the Epistle to the Hebrews, is untenable, for this reason, if there were no other, that these men were Gentiles by birth, and the author declares himself a native Jew. There would be more reason for fixing upon Silas or Silvanus, who were, as we know, Paul's companions, or, likewise, upon Barnabas. For the last we have even one historical evidence, as we have already remarked. A father of the Church, Tertullian, expressly ascribes the Epistle to Barnabas. But, as we have an Epistle written by this assistant of the apostles, we are able to see from it with perfect certainty that he cannot be author of the Epistle to the Hebrews. His whole manner of writing and thinking is different from the course of ideas in this production. It is true there is nothing so decisive against Silas; but, too, there is nothing definite *in his favour*. His peculiar character of mind is nowhere described, as the character of Apollos is in the Acts of the Apostles.

The idea, therefore, that Silas was the author of the Epistle, is a wholly unsupported conjecture. It is true, too, it is merely a conjecture that Apollos wrote it; but it is a conjecture more probable than could be required or wished in respect to opinions of any other nature than those in question.

But though we could assign the name of the author, it would be of little consequence in our investigation. It is sufficient that we cannot suppose Paul to have been the author.

Here, however, arises the very difficult question, what we are to think of the *canonical authority* of the Epistle if its author was not an apostle? for the primitive Church would not receive the writings of any but these into the collection of Sacred books; and those who rejected the Epistle to the Hebrews, e. g. the Roman Church, did it for the very reason that they could not admit Paul to have been its author. *Must we then reject the Epistle to the Hebrews, or at least esteem it less highly than the other writings of the New Testament, because it was not written by Paul?* This inquiry merits the more careful consideration, because the contents of the Epistle are of a very profound and important nature to the Church generally, and the evangelical Church in particular. For the sacred doctrine of the high priesthood of our Lord and Saviour Jesus Christ is, in this very Epistle to the Hebrews, treated of more at length, and more thoroughly, than in any other book of the New Testament.

Hence the circumstance that the Epistle is not from the pen of the apostle Paul might give rise to inferences against the validity of the doctrine which this Epistle in particular inculcates.

It must certainly be admitted that the ruling idea in the formation of the canon was to admit only apostolic productions. For although Mark and Luke, whose writings were acknowledged by the whole Church, were not apostles, they were in intimate connexion with Peter and Paul, and their works were therefore regarded as properly the productions of those apostles. And this principle was perfectly correct. Though it must be allowed that the Holy Spirit might exert its power on others besides the apostles, and might enable them to compose excellent productions, still it was wise in the ancient Church to restrict the canon of the Holy Scriptures, which was to serve as the *norm* or *rule* of faith and practice, for the complete development of the kingdom of God, exclusively to apostolic writings. For the apostles, as most immediately connected with our Saviour, had received into their souls, in the greatest abundance and purity, the spirit of truth which flowed forth from him. The more distant the relation which individuals sustained to our Lord, the feebler the influence of the Spirit from above upon them, and the more easily might their acts be affected by other influences. It was therefore necessary that the Church should admit as the norm of faith only such writings as sprang from the most lively and purest operation of the Holy Spirit, as it was manifested in the apostles. Otherwise there would have been ground for fear, lest errors, perhaps indeed of a slight character, might have crept in, and then been continued from generation to generation in the Holy Scriptures, and propagated as of sacred authority. It was such thoughts undoubtedly which induced some learned men to distinguish the Epistle to the Hebrews and certain other books of the New Testament, which were not adopted with perfect unanimity by the primitive Church, from those which were properly canonical and universally acknowledged, denominating the former *deuterocanonical*. They probably regarded it as possible that some error had crept into these books, notwithstanding the excellence of their contents generally; and, in order to obviate the influence of such errors, they were desirous of introducing an external separation of these writings from those which were decidedly apostolical. But, with regard to the Epistle to the Hebrews, we must say that this separation appears totally unfounded. Probable as it certainly is that Paul did not compose the Epistle, it is still certain that its author wrote it under the influence of Paul, and an influence indeed which exhibits itself still more definitely than that of the same apostle over the writings of Luke, or of Peter over the Gospel of Mark. This position is sustained by history, as well as by the contents of the Epistle, in the most decisive manner.

On the score of history, in the first place, we cannot, except on the supposition that Paul had an essential share in the composition of the Epistle to the Hebrews, explain the remarkable circumstance that the entire oriental church attributed it to the apostle. This view continued to prevail in the East, even after it was very well known that the western churches, particularly that of Rome, held a different opinion. The tradition that Paul was the author of the Epistle to the Hebrews cannot have rested on mere conjecture, since there was in fact much in the Epistle itself which constrained learned men, who in the main shared the prevalent opinion respecting the author of the Epistle to resort to expedients for the purpose of upholding the general idea that Paul wrote the Epistle, and at the same time of solving the difficulties which this supposition involved. Such an expedient, for example, was the idea of which we have before spoken, that Paul might have written the Epistle in Hebrew, so that we have only a translation of it. Let it be considered, too, that this opinion of the Pauline origin of the Epistle prevailed in the very countries to which its original readers belonged; and then no one will doubt that the only mode of explaining it is, to suppose Paul to have cooperated in the composition of the Epistle, and the first readers of it to have been aware of the fact, and on this account to have referred the Epistle to Paul himself.

To this is to be added the character of the Epistle itself. For, although the ancient observation, that the style of the Epistle is not Pauline, is perfectly well founded, still the tenor of the ideas bears a resemblance, which is not to be mistaken, to the writings of the great apostle of the Gentiles. If we merely keep in mind that the Epistle to the Hebrews was addressed to Jewish Christians, while the other Pauline Epistles were all of them* written to churches, the majority of whose members were Gentiles, we shall not discover the least thing in the Epistle which could not have proceeded from the mind of Paul. Indeed, the main doctrine of the great apostle, that in the death of Jesus an offering of reconciliation was made for the whole world—that with and through it all the ceremonial observances of the Old Testament first obtained their fulfilment as types of what was to come—forms the central point of the Epistle to the Hebrews. If it be further considered that there was always a certain distance of demeanour between the apostle Paul and the Jewish Christians, even the best of them, it will be very easy to understand why Paul did not write to them himself; and still it must have been his heart's desire to exhibit clearly and in suitable detail his views in regard to the law and its relation to Christianity, which were of a profound nature, and drawn directly from the genuine spirit of the Gospel. What more obvious mode of presenting these to the Hebrews, than through the medium of a disciple or faithful friend, who, like Apollos, had a correct apprehension of this relation between the old and new covenant.

Supposing this to have been the state of the case, all the circumstances in regard to the Epistle are explained. In the West it was known that Paul did not write the Epistle. On this account the western Church denied that he was the author, without being able, however, to designate any other individual as the author. In the East, on the other hand, it was known that he had an influence in the composition of the Epistle; and, moreover, his spirit and his ideas were recognised in it. In the East, therefore, it was used; in the West less. In our days, we may impartially admit that Paul was not the writer of the Epistle, and still maintain its perfect canonical authority, since the apostle certainly exerted an essential influence over its composition.

Thus, though this Epistle belongs to the class of those which

---

* Though the expression is thus general in the original, of course only those Epistles which are directed to churches can be here referred to. The phraseology is exceptionable, as some of Paul's letters are not directed to churches at all, but to individuals.—TR.

have not the unanimous voice of Christian antiquity in favour of their apostolic origin, still it can be shown that this want of agreement did not arise from any really suspicious state of things, but was occasioned merely by the peculiar circumstance under which it was composed.

CHAPTER VII.

OF THE CATHOLIC EPISTLES.

It has already been observed, in the first chapter, that in early times the third collection of the writings of the New Testament was termed that of *the seven Catholic Epistles*. The Greek word *Catholic* means *general*, in opposition to *particular*. Now, as the Church general, in opposition to individual heretical parties, was termed Catholic, so the same expression was used to denote those writings which, as universally acknowledged and used, it was designed to distinguish from those which were current only in particular circles.

The fact that those writings which, in addition to the collections called the Gospel and the Apostle, were acknowledged to be genuine and apostolical, were thus united into one separate collection, produced this advantage, that it became thus more difficult ever to confound them with the many apocryphal writings which were spread abroad in the ancient Church. In regard to the origin of this third collection, however, there is an obscurity which can never be entirely dissipated. At the end of the third and commencement of the fourth century, the collection of the seven Catholic Epistles first appears in history; but who formed it, and where it originated, we do not know. It is impossible, however, that it should have been *accidentally* formed, as the position of the Epistles is too peculiar for us to suppose this. The Epistle of James, which was by no means unanimously regarded as apostolic, holds the first place in the collection, while the first Epistle of Peter, and the first of John, which have always been regarded as of apostolic authority, come afterward. This very order of the seven Epistles, however, suggests to us, by the way, a probable supposition as to the place *where* the collection of these Catholic Epistles must have originated. James, the author of the Epistle of James in the canon, nowhere possessed a higher reputation than in Palestine and Syria; for he was a brother, *i. e.*, according to the Hebrew mode of speaking, a cousin of our Lord, and, at the same time, bishop of the Church at Jerusalem, and head of the Jewish Christians, as we shall presently show more at length. In the same countries Peter was held in high estimation, as the one among our Lord's apostles to whom, in particular, was committed the preaching of the Gospel among the Jews. It is probable, therefore, that the collection of the Catholic Epistles originated in Palestine or Syria; and, out of veneration for the brother of our Lord, and the first bishop of Jerusalem, the author of the collection gave to the Epistle of James the first place, and put those of Peter next. The Epistles of John had less interest for him, on account of his Judaising sentiments, and the Epistle of Jude he placed at the very end. The supposition we have made finds confirmation in the fact, that a father of the Palestinian Church, Eusebius, bishop of Cæsarea, gives us the first certain account of the existence of a collection of the seven Catholic Epistles.

From the various character of the writings classed together in the collection, we may see clearly its late origin; for it has already been mentioned above (chap. i.), that the first Epistles of John, and that of Peter, were originally, as being very ancient, and universally admitted writings, connected with *the Apostle* so called, *i. e.*, the collection of the Pauline Epistles. At a later period, in order to leave these latter by themselves, the two Epistles were taken from the collection of Pauline writings, and classed with the five other apostolic Epistles. These last, however, belonged to the number of those which were universally admitted in primitive times, and thus Antilegomena and Homologoumena were introduced into one and the same collection. Still, there arose from this procedure one advantage, viz., that the Epistles of the same author were, as was proper, brought together. Luther, with his excellent tact, correctly felt that the collection of the Catholic Epistles unsuitably confounded writings which were universally admitted with those which were not, and therefore placed the Epistles of Peter and John immediately after those of Paul, and then at the end, after the Epistle to the Hebrews, the letters of James and Jude, and the Revelation of John. Still, this did not wholly do away with the impropriety, as the second Epistle of Peter also had been disputed with special zeal. Had he, however, placed this Epistle likewise at the end of the New Testament, along with the other Antilegomena, he must have disturbed too much the old accustomed arrangement. He left it, therefore, and also the two smaller Epistles of John, in connection with the first and main Epistle of the two apostles. It is to be considered, too, that the bearing of the arrangement of the New Testament books upon our critical inquiries is of but secondary consideration; the main point is their internal character, and, in reference to this, no fault can be found with the original arrangement.

In regard, therefore, to the Catholic Epistles generally, little further can be said. Of the Epistles individually, we will consider first the *three Epistles of John*. As to the first, and main Epistle, it, like the Gospel of John, was always regarded by the ancient Church as the production of the evangelist of that name. In modern times, it is true, doubts have been started in relation to the Gospel. But the principal writer by whom they have been suggested, has himself since retracted them. Indeed it was nothing but the very striking similarity, in style and ideas, between the Gospel and the first Epistle of John, which made it necessary, almost whether one would or no, to extend the opposition against the Gospel to the Epistle likewise; for one cannot but suppose them both to have had the same author, from their resemblance in every peculiar characteristic. If, therefore, the Epistle were admitted to have been written by the Evangelist John, the Gospel also could not but be attributed to him. But though there may have been a somewhat plausible reason for disputing the Gospel, in the idea that the Saviour is represented by John very differently from the exhibition of him in the other Gospels, in regard to the Epistle, there is no reason which possesses the slightest plausibility for disputing it. On the supposition that it is spurious, the error of the whole ancient Church in referring it, without contradiction, to the Evangelist John, would be completely inexplicable, especially if we carefully compare the history of the Epistle with that of the Evangelist. John, as we have before remarked, lived the longest of all the apostles, viz., till sometime in the reign of Domitian, and he resided at Ephesus, in Asia Minor. From no country within the limits of the Church, therefore, could we expect to receive more accurate accounts, in regard to the writings of the beloved disciple of our Lord, than from those of Asia Minor. Now, it is from these very countries that we receive the most ancient testimonies in behalf of the existence and genuineness of the Epistle. Instead of mentioning all, I will name but two of these testimonies, which, however, are so decisive, that we can perfectly well dispense with all the rest. The first is presented by Papias, bishop of Hierapolis, in Phrygia, whom we have already mentioned. This man lived, as has been before said, at the end of the first century and beginning of the second, in the immediate vicinity of Ephesus, where the Evangelist John laboured so long and so successfully. He knew not only the Evangelist John, but other immediate disciples of our Lord, who were probably of the number of the seventy, particularly a certain Aristion, and another John, surnamed the Presbyter. Now, is it to be supposed that such a man, who had at his command so many means of arriving at certainty respecting John's writings, could possibly be deceived in regard to them? We must, indeed, renounce all historical testimony, if we deny this witness the capacity to speak in behalf of the genuineness of the Epistle of John.

The second testimony, however, is of equal importance. One of the apostolic fathers, Polycarp, bishop of Smyrna, in Asia Minor, makes use of the first Epistle of John, in the same way as Papias, as though it was admitted to be a genuine production of the Evangelist. Now, Polycarp lived till after the middle of the second century, and, at the age of eighty-six, died a martyr's death in the flames. He had not merely become acquainted with John in the neighbouring city of Ephesus, but had even heard him preach the way of salvation, and was his faithful disciple. The testimony of such a man, therefore, is likewise above all cavil, and is especially confirmed by the fact, that there never has been, in later times, any general opinion against its genuineness, either in the Catholic Church, or among the adherents to any particular sect. Against this weight of historical evidence, therefore, nothing can be effected by the mere conjectures of modern times; and at present all theologians are perfectly agreed in the acknowledgment of this precious relic of the beloved disciple of Jesus, his first Epistle.

If, in regard to the *second and third Epistles* of John, such perfect agreement of the ancient Church in recognising their genuineness cannot be asserted, the reason of this lies entirely in a circumstance which also occasioned the tardy insertion of the pastoral letters to Timothy and Titus in the collection of Pauline Epistles, viz., that they are directed to private persons, and, moreover, are of no very great extent, or very important contents, and thus awakened less interest in their diffusion.

The *second Epistle* of John is addressed to a Christian lady and her family; the *third* to a Christian friend named Gaius. Of the private circumstances of these two persons we know nothing but what is indicated in the letters. Now, although certainly these two smaller Epistles afford no important information respecting the Gospel, or the history of the ancient Church, still, as estimable legacies of the disciple who lay in Jesus's bosom, they deserve a place in the canon as much as Paul's Epistle to Philemon. The oldest fathers of the Church express no doubt in regard to the two Epistles. Only at a later period do we find certain individuals entertaining doubts whether these two Epistles were written by John the Evangelist. No one regarded them as forged in the name of the Evangelist, for we can by no means perceive for what purpose these Epistles could, in such a case, have been written. They aim at no particular object, but are merely expressive of the tenderest Christian love. Many, however, believed that another John, viz., *John the Presbyter*, before mentioned, with whom Papias was acquainted, was the author of the Epistles. This view appeared confirmed by the fact that, in the salutations of both Epistles, John expressly terms himself *Presbyter;* and as, moreover, the other John likewise lived in Ephesus, it is possible they might have been confounded. But, in modern times, these doubts in regard to the apostolic character of the two small Epistles have been disregarded, because the style and the sentiments of both Epistles are so entirely similar to the style and course of thought in the Gospels, and the first Epistle, that the idea of a different author is totally untenable. Moreover, we are able to show how John, the apostle and Evangelist, might also call himself Presbyter. This expression is nearly equivalent to the Latin *Senior*, or the German *Ælteste*.* In the Jewish synagogues, and also among the primitive Christians, it was applied to the principal persons in the Church (comp. Acts xx. 17), and was at first used in this sense as exactly synonimous with *Episcopus*, *i.e.* bishop. In Asia Minor, as we know from the writings of Papias, there prevailed a peculiar custom of speaking, by which the apostles were called, as it were by way of distinction, *elders*. Whether the intention was thereby to denote the great age of the apostles, or whether all the churches were regarded as forming one general church, and the apostles as their presbyters, is doubtful. It is sufficient that the apostles were thus termed,† by way of eminence, for in this fact is exhibited a sufficient explanation of the inscriptions to the second and third Epistles of John. Thus the case is the same with these two Epistles as with that to the Hebrews. The primitive Church adopted them, but not without opposition, and therefore we must reckon them among the *Antilegomena;* but still the reasons which were addressed against their apostolic origin may be so thoroughly refuted, that not a shadow of uncertainty can reasonably remain in regard to them.

The fourth of the seven Catholic Epistles is the first *Epistle of the Apostle Peter.* As we have now come to the consideration of the Petrine writings in the canon, the question forces itself upon us, how it is to be explained that we have so few productions of Peter, and so many of Paul, who was called latest to be an apostle. When we consider what our Lord said to Peter—" thou art Peter, and upon this rock will I build my Church, and the gates of hell shall not prevail against it," (Matt. xvi. 18), and afterwards—" Feed my lambs," (John xxi. 15 seq.), it must seem strange that the powers of this rock of the Church should have been exerted so little in writings for posterity. It is true, the Gospel of Mark is properly Peter's Gospel, as we have seen; but even this falls into the back-ground by the side of Luke (the Pauline Gospel), and the other Gospels, so that Peter, according to the representation of himself in his writings, constantly appears insignificant compared with Paul.

---

* Or the English *elder*, as it is translated in our version.—Tr.
† Peter calls himself in his first Epistle a *fellow-elder* (1 Pet. v. 1).

This fact finds a satisfactory explanation only in the relation of the two apostles, Peter and Paul, to the propagation of the Gospel in general. In reference to this, they had different destinations. Peter, with the twelve, was called particularly to the dissemination of the Gospel among the Jews. Had the Jewish nation acknowledged Jesus to be the Messiah, Peter would then have exhibited himself in all his dignity and consequence. But that unhappy nation hardened itself against all the operations of the Spirit, and the Gospel was carried to the Gentiles, because Israel rejected the grace to which it was called. Paul was set apart for the express purpose of preaching to the Gentiles (Acts xxvi. 17), and as Christianity first displayed itself in a flourishing condition among them, all the other apostles, with the exception of John alone, fell into the back-ground in comparison with Paul, both in oral discourse, as appears from the Acts, and in these written efforts, as is shewn by the New Testament canon. It is, consequently, not at all strange that Peter should be represented by two Epistles of so small a size, and that the second of these is, moreover, the most disputed book in the whole New Testament canon. His being thrown into the shade by Paul is rather in accordance with the facts respecting the extension of the Church of Christ on earth in the times of the apostles.

As to the *first Epistle of Peter*, we have before seen that it belongs to the Homologoumena, along with the first Epistle of John. In all Christian antiquity there was no one who doubted the genuineness of the Epistle, or had heard of doubts respecting it. And yet the Epistle (1 Pet. i. 1), is addressed to Christian Churches in Asia Minor, where Christianity early gained great success, and where a lively intercourse was maintained between the individual churches. Here, of necessity, must have arisen soon an opposition to this Epistle, if it had not been known that Peter had sent a circular letter to the churches. Now, the oldest fathers of the Church in Asia Minor, Papias and Polycarp, both make use of the Epistle of Peter, as well as that of John, as a genuine apostolic production. This Epistle of Peter does not seem to have made its way to Italy till a late period. At least it is wanting in the very ancient catalogue cited by Muratori, which probably exhibits the canon of the early Roman Church. We can infer nothing, however, from this absence against the genuineness of the first Epistle of Peter, since there is not the slightest trace of its having been disputed in the first three centuries. Yet, in modern times, this decided declaration of Christian antiquity has been thought insufficient. An objection has been founded on the circumstance that Peter writes from Babylon (1 Pet. v. 13), while history does not relate that he ever was in Babylon; as also upon the fact that he directs the attention of his readers to sufferings and persecutions which they should endure, (1 Pet. i. 6; iii. 16; iv. 12 seq.; v. 10), referring, as is supposed, to Nero's persecutions, while he himself, it is said, died at Rome during this persecution, and therefore could not have addressed an Epistle from Babylon to those who suffered under it. Both these remarks, however, are easily obviated. As to the first, respecting the city of Babylon, we know too little of the history of Peter to be able to determine in what places he may have been, and in what not; particularly, as there were several cities of this name in the ancient world, and it is not specified which is meant in the Epistle. It is to be observed, too, that many of the fathers of the Church understood the name Babylon to mean mystically the city of Rome, which shewed itself the enemy of our Lord in the persecution of the faithful. (Comp. Rev. xviii. 2.) If this exposition be adopted, the second remark also is at once obviated; for, in that case, the Epistle was written by Peter in Rome itself, during the persecution, and he gave the believers in Asia Minor Christian exhortations in reference to such a grievous period among them. Yet, as this explanation cannot be *proved* to be correct, we set it aside, and merely observe, that in whatever Babylon Peter may have written his Epistle, his residence there can be easily reconciled with the exhortations which the Epistle contains. For, though these *may* be referred to the persecution of Nero, they may be understood, with equal propriety, as referring to any other persecution, since all individual characteristics, which could suit *only* this first cruel persecution of the Church, are entirely wanting. Such general sufferings as these which Peter mentions must be supposed to have been endured by the Church everywhere and at all times, as it is always comprehended in the very idea of a believer that he should excite opposition in those who are of a worldly inclination, and thus cause a combat. A more important objection than these two remarks, is, that the style and ideas of the first Epistle of Peter exhibit a strong resemblance to the style and ideas of Paul. This cannot be denied, for it is too evident not to be observed; but it does not serve its intended purpose,—viz., to deprive Peter of the authorship of the Epistle. Notwithstanding all its similarity to Paul's manner, it still maintains enough of independence and peculiarity to stamp it as the production of a man who thought for himself. As, moreover, when Peter wrote this Epistle, he was connected (1 Pet. v. 12), with the old friend and companion of Paul, Sylvanus (or, as abbreviated, Silas), nothing is more easy than to suppose that Peter dictated to the latter, and, in all probability, in the Hebrew language, which alone seems to have been perfectly familiar to him. In translating into Greek, Sylvanus, who, from long intimacy with Paul, had become very much habituated to his diction, may have adopted many of its characteristics, and thus have been the occasion of the somewhat Pauline colouring which the Epistle possesses.

CHAPTER VIII.

OF THE SECOND EPISTLE OF PETER.

IN regard to the second Epistle of Peter, its case is very different from that of the first. The former has always been so violently attacked, and suspected on such plausible grounds of not having been written by the apostle Peter, that criticism is encompassed with as much difficulty in relation to it as in relation to any other book of the New Testament. And, moreover, such is the state of the matter, that the critical investigation of this Epistle is of particular importance. For, as we remarked in Chapter I., while, in regard to many writings of the New Testament (*e. g.* the Epistle to the Hebrews, the second and third Epistles of John), the question is, not so much whether they are genuine or spurious, as who was their author, in regard to the second Epistle of Peter, the question is, in truth, whether the apostle Peter composed it, or some other Peter, or somebody of another name, who meant no harm, but still *purposely endeavoured to deceive* his readers into the belief that it was written by Simon Peter, the apostle of our Lord. In the first place, the author of the Epistle not only expressly appropriates Peter's name and title, "Simon Peter, a servant and apostle of Jesus Christ" (2 Pet. i. 1), but he also states particulars respecting his own life, which can have been true only of Peter. He says, for instance, "For we have not followed cunningly devised fables, when we made known unto you the power and coming of our Lord Jesus Christ, but were eye-witnesses of his majesty. For he received from God the Father honour and glory, when there came 'such a voice to him from the excellent glory, This is my beloved Son, in whom I am well pleased. *And this voice, which came from heaven, we heard, when we were with him in the holy mount*," (2 Pet. i. 16—18.) These words, it is clear, refer to the transfiguration on the mount, (Matt. xvii. 1, seq.) But, besides James and John, the two sons of Zebedee, no one was a spectator of this transfiguration except the apostle Peter. If, therefore, the apostle Peter was not the author of this letter, the man who not only presumed to take upon himself the name of an apostle, but designedly endeavoured to make his readers think that he was the apostle Peter, must have been a downright shameless impostor; and his production should by no means retain its place in the canon, but it is necessary that it should be at once thrust out of it.

It is for this very reason, viz., because the necessity of which we have spoken has been sensibly felt, that the friends of the work have so zealously prosecuted the investigation respecting it; though certainly not always with due impartiality and coolness. It has been forgotten that in truth very important objections may be urged against the Petrine origin of this second Epistle, and it has been attempted to establish its genuineness as firmly and incontrovertibly as it is possible to establish that of other writings. The best weapon, however, which can be used in defence of God's word, is always truth; and this compels us to admit that it is impossible to attain so firm and certain proof of the genuineness of the second Epistle of Peter, as of that of other books of the New Testament. But certainly the opponents of the Epistle err greatly when they assert that the spuriousness of the Epistle can be fully established. Such an assertion cannot but be denied with all earnestness, even though, as is often the case, it be connected with the opinion that the Epistle may, notwithstanding, retain its place in the canon as hitherto, and be cited by preachers of the gospel in their pulpit instructions. Such lax notions must be resisted with the utmost moral sternness. For, would it not be participating in the fraud of the author of the Epistle, were we to treat it as the genuine production of the apostle Peter, while we consider it as spurious? If it be really spurious, and can be proved to have gained its place in the canon only through mistake, then let it be removed from the collection of the sacred writings, which, from its nature, excludes every fraudulent production. Christian truth would not at all suffer by the removal of a single work of so slight extent.

We are convinced, however, that no such step is necessary. The most prominent error in the critical investigation of this Epistle has been, that writers have always striven to prove beyond objection either the genuineness or the spuriousness of the production. It has been forgotten that between these two positions there was a medium, viz., an impossibility of satisfactorily *proving* either. It cannot seem at all strange that this impossibility should exist in investigations respecting writings of the New Testament, if it be considered for a moment how difficult it often is to determine respecting the genuineness of a production even shortly after, or at the very time of, its composition, if from any circumstance the decisive points in the investigation have remained concealed. As in regard to the author of the Epistle to the Hebrews it is entirely impossible to come to any decided result, so it seems to me probable, that the deficiency of historical evidence makes it impossible to come to a fixed conclusion in regard to the second Epistle of Peter. It is certain there are several circumstances which give rise to reasonable doubts respecting the apostolic origin of the Epistle; still, so much may be adduced, not only in refutation of them, but in the way of positive argument for the Epistle, that these doubts are neutralized. Only, the favourable points do not amount to a complete objectively valid proof, and therefore, a critical investigation of the Epistle does not result exclusively to its advantage. Now this is certainly a very unpleasant result, and one satisfactory to neither party, for men commonly wish everything to be decided in an absolute manner, and therefore would have the Epistle declared positively either genuine or spurious. But the main object should be the truth, and not an agreeable result; and faithful, impartial examination leads us to the conclusion that in fact no perfect proof is to be obtained in regard to the second Epistle of Peter. This conclusion affords us the advantage, that we may with a good conscience leave the Epistle in its place among the canonical books, since it cannot rightfully be deprived of it until its spuriousness is *decisively proved*. Now, whether it shall or shall not be used in doctrinal argument, must be left to the judgment of each individual; but at any rate no one can prohibit its use so long as its spuriousness remains unproved.

It is time, however, to consider more closely all that can be urged against the genuineness of the Epistle, and to present therewith the counter-considerations which either invalidate the former or argue the apostolic composition of the Epistle. Now, the most important circumstance which presents itself against the genuineness of the book is, that it was to such a degree unknown in Christian antiquity. Not one of the fathers of the first two centuries mentions the second Epistle of Peter; they all speak of but one Epistle from the hand of this apostle. Nor are there any passages in their writings which must of necessity be citations from it. Those passages which seem like parts of it may be explained either on the score of accidental coincidence or of mutual reference to the Old Testament. It was not till after Origen's time, in the third century, that the epistle came into use, and even then doubts were always current in regard to its apostolic origin, and the learned father Jerome expressly remarks that *most* denied it such an origin. It is true, this statement cannot refer to all members of the Church, but only to such as were capable of critical investigations; for the same father of the Church says further, that the reason why most denied it to be Peter's was, the difference in style which was observable on comparison with the first; and clearly, uneducated persons were incapable of judging as to such difference in style. But still, it is extremely remarkable that even in the time of Jerome, *i.e.*, in the fifth century, there should be found in the Church so many opponents of the Epistle.

It is, however, to be considered, in estimating the importance of this fact in relation to the genuineness of the Epistle, that no definite historical arguments are adduced against the Epistle from any quarter. Recourse is had, not to the testimony of individuals, nor to the declaration of entire churches, which denied the Epistle to be Peter's, but merely to internal reasons, deduced by the aid of criticism. This is the more strange, as it would appear that this second Epistle of Peter was addressed to the very same readers for whom the first was designed (comp. 2 Peter iii. 1,) *i.e.*, to the Christians in several churches of Asia Minor. From these, one would think, there must have proceeded a testimony which could not be misunderstood against the Epistle, if Peter had not written to them a second time. Nor do the fathers say that the Epistle contains heresies, or anything else totally unworthy of the apostle; indeed, they do not make the slightest objection of this kind to the character of its contents. If, on the other hand, we look at their objections to other evidently fictitious writings, we find them asserting that they had an impious, detestable character, or that historical evidence was against their pretended apostolic origin. From the manner in which history represents the testimony of the fathers of the Church, we may suppose that their opinion respecting the genuineness of the Epistle was founded in a great measure upon the fact that its diffusion was very much delayed. Since so many writings had been forged in Peter's name, the fathers of the Church probably at once regarded an Epistle which came so late into circulation with some considerable suspicion, and then made use of the difference in language, or something of the kind, to confirm this suspicion. We must therefore say, that no decisive argument against the genuineness of the Epistle is to be drawn from historical considerations. Although it was but little known in the ancient Church, this want of acquaintance with it may have been founded on reasons not at all connected with its spuriousness or genuineness. How many Epistles of Peter and other apostles may never have been much known? And still the circumstance that they have not been diffused abroad does not disprove their apostolic origin.

Thus, as the fathers of the Church themselves had recourse to the internal character of the Epistle, it remains for us likewise to examine this, and as particular historical traditions respecting the Epistle were as inaccessible to these fathers as to us, and the art of criticism has not been carried to a high point of cultivation till recently, we may lay claim to greater probability, as to the result of our investigation, than they could.

Among the striking circumstances to which we are led by a careful investigation concerning the second Epistle of Peter, the first which presents itself is the very ancient observation, that the *style* of this Epistle is quite different from that of the first. According to the most recent examinations, the case is really so. The style of the second Epistle is so different from that of the first, as to make it hardly conceivable that the same author should have written thus variously; particularly as the two Epistles must have been written at no great distance of time from each other, it being necessary to refer them both to the latter part of the apostle's life. But we have seen above that Peter probably employed another person to write for him when he composed his first Epistle; now, how natural to suppose, as Jerome has already suggested, that, in writing the second Epistle, Peter only made use of a different assistant from the one employed in writing the first, which supposition satisfactorily explains the difference in style. If it be insisted, however, that this supposition is a very violent one, we may then admit that the Epistles are in reality not apostolic, but are from Sylvanus, or some other writer. It is certainly true that by this hypothesis we surrender the common opinion that Peter either guided the pen himself, or at least dictated to the amanuensis word for word what he should write. But is it at all essential to admit that the writings of the apostles originated precisely in this way? Is a prince's letter of less value because his secretary wrote it, and the prince himself only signed it? Do we esteem the writings of Mark and Luke any less because they were not apostles? These last writings shew best how the case is to be considered. Say that these two Epistles were written by Sylvanus or Mark; is their importance to us in the least diminished, when Peter has given them the confirmation of his apostolic authority, as presenting his ideas, his mode of thinking?

This hypothesis of Peter's having employed a writer in the composition of the second Epistle, explains, moreover, another remark which it has been usual to urge against its apostolic origin. If the Epistle of Jude be compared with the second chapter of this Epistle, there will appear a very striking similarity between them. This, as in the case of the Gospels, is so great that it is impossible it should have arisen accidentally. An impartial comparison of the two makes it extremely probable that Jude is the original, and was employed in the Epistle of Peter. Now this hardly seems suitable for the apostle Peter, considering him as the author of the Epistle. He, the pillar of the Church, should have been the original writer, though it would not have been strange that Jude, who held a far lower rank, should make use of his production. On the supposition, however, that Peter employed an individual to write for him, the latter might have made use of Jude's Epistle, and what would be totally unsuitable for an apostle, would not be at all strange in his assistant. If it be said that, as Peter must have known the use which was made of Jude, the circumstance still remains very strange, we may suppose that both Peter (with his assistant) and Jude conferred together in regard to combating the heretics, and agreed together in certain fundamental thoughts, and that thus coincidence in details was occasioned by their common written groundwork. Still, it may not be concealed, that, after all attempts to explain these appearances, there nevertheless remains in the mind something like suspicion; and for this reason, although there are certainly not sufficient grounds for rejecting the Epistle, we cannot regard its genuineness as susceptible of proof.

There are other points of less moment which are usually brought forward by the opponents of the Epistle. Among these is the passage, 2 Peter iii. 2, in which the writer, it is said, is distinguished from the apostles, just as in Heb. ii. 2. But, in the first place, the reading in the former passage is not perfectly certain, since several ancient versions give it the same sense as Luther, who translates—" that ye may be mindful of the words which were spoken before by the holy prophets, and of the commandment of *us, the apostles of our Lord and Saviour.*"* But, even though we admit that the correct reading is one by which the author is distinguished from the apostles, we may

---

* So, too, in the English version. The question alluded to in the text is, whether we should translate, *of us the apostles*, or, *of the apostles sent to us* (or *to you*, according to another reading)? See the original Greek.—Tr.

explain the passage by supposing that the writer who was employed, instead of speaking in the name of the apostle, spoke in his own person. This was certainly an oversight, but not a very great one; like that, *e.g.*, which occasioned the Evangelists to differ from each other in respect to the number of the blind men whom our Lord healed, and other points of the kind. The admission of such trifling oversight belongs properly to God's plan in regard to the Scriptures, since literal coincidence would, on the one hand, give rise to strong suspicion in regard to the veracity of the writers, (as it would suggest the inference that there had been a previous concert between them,) and, on the other hand, there would be danger of confounding the letter with the spirit, to the disadvantage of the latter.

Of as little consequence is the reference made to 2 Pet. iii. 15, 16, where Peter says of his beloved brother Paul, whose wisdom he extols—"As also in all his Epistles, speaking in them of these things; in which are some things hard to be understood, which they that are unlearned and unstable wrest, as they do also the other Scriptures, unto their own destruction." These words, it is said, clearly suppose a collection of Pauline Epistles to have been current in the Church; but one cannot have been made earlier than the commencement of the second century, and consequently the Epistle must be regarded as a work of later origin. But this assumption, that the collection of the Pauline Epistles was first made at so late a period, is by no means susceptible of proof. Indeed, in the fourth chapter we attempted to prove it not improbable that even Paul himself made a collection of his Epistles. At all events, no historical fact can be adduced against this hypothesis, and we must therefore consider this much as certain, that the mention of a collection of Pauline Epistles ought not to induce us to conclude against the apostolic origin of the Epistle whose history we are investigating.

Thus is confirmed the position which we laid down above, that not one of the reasons usually adduced against the genuineness of the second Epistle of Peter is a decisive one. Notwithstanding, as has been already mentioned, impartiality enjoins it upon us to allow that, after considering these reasons, there remains a feeling in the mind which does not permit us to place this Epistle in the rank of those universally admitted. We find ourselves constrained to resort first to one expedient, then to another, in order to invalidate the arguments which make against the genuineness of the Epistle. Let us, however, cast a glance at the other side, and consider the arguments which may be adduced *in favour of* the authenticity of the Epistle. The impression made by the genuine apostolic manner in the first and third chapters in particular, is so heart-stirring, the severe moral tone which prevails throughout them is so forcible, that very estimable scholars have found themselves induced to regard these two chapters, or at least the first, as truly Petrine; and the second, or the last two, as, perhaps, merely subsequent additions to the genuine Epistle. This hypothesis, has, indeed, at first view, this recommendation, that we can give proper weight to the reasons for doubt, without being obliged to regard the express statements respecting Peter personally as having been forged. But the close connection of all the chapters with each other, and the uniformity of the language and ideas throughout the Epistle, is too much at variance with the supposition of an interpolation of the Epistle to make it right that it should be admitted.

Still, we cannot but allow the great weight of the reason from which the hypothesis took its rise, viz., that it was an almost inconceivable piece of impudence for an impostor to assume the person of the apostle Peter, so as even to speak of his presence at the transfiguration on Mount Tabor, and venture to invent prophecies of our Lord to him respecting his end. (Comp. 2 Pet. i. 14.) It is true, appeal is made on this point to the practice of the ancients, according to which it was not so strange and censurable, it is said, to write under another's name, as it appears to us at the present day. And it is undoubtedly true, that in the primitive times of the Church, writings were much more frequently forged in the name of others than at the present time. But it is a question whether this is to be referred to the custom of the times, or does not rather arise from the fact, that in the less methodical book transactions of the ancient world it was much easier to get fictitious writings into circulation than it is at present, on account of the great publicity which now attends such transactions. At any rate we must say, that it was a very culpable practice, if it ever was common, to procure currency for one's literary productions by affixing a great name to them; and every honourable man would have avoided it, and written only in his own name. Suppose, however, it was less offensive than now to publish any thing under an assumed name, we must, notwithstanding, protest in the most earnest manner against the idea that a man could permit himself fraudulently to appropriate such points from the life of him whose name he used as could be true only of the latter; which must be the case in regard to this Epistle if it was not written by Peter. Were this to be done in any case, the use of another's name would no longer be a mere form in writing, it would rather be a coarse piece of imposture, such as could not occur without a decidedly wrong intention; and this leads us to a new and important point in the investigation of the origin of the second Epistle of Peter.

The alternative in which we are thus placed is as harsh as it could possibly be. Either the Epistle is genuine and apostolical, or it is not only spurious and forged, but was forged by a bold, shameless impostor, and such a person must have had an evil design in executing a forgery of the kind supposed. Now, in the whole Epistle we do not find the slightest thing which can be regarded as erroneous, or as morally bad. Its contents are entirely biblical, and truly evangelical. An elevated religious spirit animates the Epistle throughout. Is it conceivable, that a man actuated by this spirit can be chargeable with such a deception? Or is it supposed that this spirit is itself feigned? But this idea plainly contradicts itself, for he who is bad enough to forge writings cannot entertain the design of extending a good influence by his forgery. No forgery would be necessary for such a purpose. The design must have been to defend what was unholy in principle or practice under cover of a sacred name. The only probable purpose of the forgery of the Epistle is this—that the unknown author of the production wished to combat the heretics described in the second chapter, and, in order that he might do this with some effect, he wrote in the name of the apostle Peter, and made use of the Epistle of Jude in doing so. But if a man who was honest (in other respects) could have been induced to enter upon such a crooked path, would he not have contented himself with placing the apostle's name in front of his Epistle? Would his conscience have permitted him to appropriate falsely from the life of the apostle such particulars as are narrated in the Epistle? This is really hard to believe, and the efforts made to preserve the genuineness of the first chapter at least, which contains these very particulars, sufficiently prove how universal is the feeling that the statements it contains cannot have been forged.

It is true the case would stand otherwise if it were a wellfounded position, that the Epistle really contains erroneous tenets. But how truly impossible it is to establish this, is very evident from the nature of the points adduced as errors. In the first place, one is supposed to be contained in the passage, 2 Pet. iii. 5, in which it is said, that the earth was formed out of water and in water by the word of God.* It is true, there are parallels to this view of the creation of the earth in several mythical cosmogonies; but is this circumstance a proof that the doctrine of the creation of the world out of water is false? Does the Mosaic account of the creation, or any other passage in the Bible, contain anything which in the slightest degree impugns it? Or does the condition of the physical or geological sciences in our day prove that the earth certainly came into existence in a different manner? It will suffice, in regard to this point, to remind our readers that the formation of the earth out of water was taught by the celebrated De Luc, not to mention many men of less note. At the most, then, it can only be said that, in the passage referred to, there is something openly and definitely stated which is not found thus stated in any other book of the Bible; though it is impossible to deny that the Mosaic account of the creation ("The Spirit of God moved upon the face of the waters") is susceptible of such an interpretation, as to convey the idea which is more plainly declared in 2 Pet. iii. 5. Thus there is no ground for talking about an error in this passage of the Epistle. The same remarks may be made respecting another position, that the doctrine (also presented in the third chapter of the second Epistle of Peter) concerning the destruction of the world by fire, is erroneous. For it can by no means be shown, in regard to this second idea, that it contradicts the common statement of the Bible, or contains anything incorrect.

---

* Our English version gives a somewhat different sense to this passage; but probably the translation above conveys nearly, if not exactly, its true signification.—Tr.

Indeed, there are other passages likewise, that contain an intimation, at least, of the same thing which is here openly stated. (Comp. Isaiah li. 6; Zeph. iii. 8.) And so far are the similar mythical accounts in other religions from arguing anything wrong in this idea, that we should rather consider the coincidence of the mythical accounts with the biblical doctrine as a confirmation of the real verity of the former.

If, therefore, we put together all which has been said of the second Epistle of Peter, this much is certainly clear, that the circumstances which are calculated to excite suspicion respecting the Epistle, are by no means sufficient to constitute a formal proof of their spuriousness. True, the suspicious points cannot be so perfectly obviated, that every doubt will disappear. Some uncertainty will remain in the mind. Still the positive arguments in behalf of its genuineness so far allay these doubts, that it is possible to obtain a satisfactory *subjective* conviction of the genuineness of the Epistle. But a proof of its genuineness, which shall be of perfect validity, and be generally acknowledged, can no more be attained than such a proof of its spuriousness; and, therefore, there will always be something dubious in the position of this Epistle. The ancient fathers of the Church endeavoured to express this uncertainty by the term *Antilegomena*, and later teachers in the evangelical Church by the designation *Deuterocanonical writings*, among which this Epistle is reckoned. Attempts to remove all the obscurity which envelopes the facts in regard to this Epistle will probably always prove vain, from the want of historical accounts respecting the use and diffusion of it in primitive times.

CHAPTER IX.

OF THE EPISTLES OF JAMES AND JUDE.

In investigating the Epistles of James and Jude, the question is, as in the case of the Epistle to the Hebrews, not so much whether they are genuine or spurious, as who was their author. This may seem strange, inasmuch as the authors of both of them mention themselves in the salutations, which is not the case as to the Epistle to the Hebrews. Indeed, Jude, for the purpose of designating himself still more definitely, adds the circumstance that he was the brother of James. But, as both these names were very common among the Jews, and the relations between the persons of this name mentioned in the New Testament are quite involved, it is a very difficult inquiry, what James and what Jude were the authors of the Epistles which we are considering. Now, if it should be probable, on investigation, that the authors of the two Epistles were not apostles, (*i. e.* among the number of the twelve disciples), then will arise a second inquiry, what we are to think of the canonical authority of the Epistles?

The first question is, how many persons of the name of *James* and *Jude* are mentioned in the Scriptures, or by ancient Christian writers? From the catalogues of the twelve apostles (Matt. x. 2 seq.; Mark iii. 13 seq.; Luke vi. 12 seq.; Acts i. 13 seq.) we perceive that two individuals among them were named James. The first was a brother of the evangelist John, a son of Zebedee and Salome; this James is often mentioned in the evangelical history. His brother Peter, and himself, were, of all the apostles, the most intimate with our Lord. He was present at the transfiguration, and at our Lord's agony in the garden of Gethsemane. According to Acts xii. 2, Herod killed him with the sword a few years after our Lord's ascension. As, therefore, this James disappeared from the scene of events very early, he does not cause much difficulty in the investigation. The second James is termed the son of Alphæus, and of this apostle we have so uncertain accounts, that it is difficult to determine much respecting him.

As there were two individuals of the name of James among the twelve, so there were two Judes. One, the betrayer of our Lord, of course is not concerned in this investigation. He cannot be confounded with any one else; especially as he had the surname Iscariot, from his birth-place Carioth. The second Jude, it would seem, bore many names; for while Luke (in the Gospel as well as in the Acts) calls him Jude the son of James, Matthew and Mark call him sometimes Thaddeus, and sometimes Lebbeus. It was not at all uncommon among the Jews for one man to bear several names; and, therefore, we may admit the validity of the prevalent opinion that Lebbeus or Thaddeus, and Jude, the son of James, are the same individuals. In John xiv. 22, a second Jude among the twelve is expressly distinguished from Jude (Judas) the traitor, who is termed Iscariot, and hence the name Jude may have been the one by which the former was most commonly designated.

Now, did we know with perfect certainty that the authors of the Epistles under consideration were of the number of the twelve, it would be easy to fix upon the individuals; James, the son of Alpheus, must have written the Epistle of James, and Jude, the son of James, that of Jude. But as Jude (v. 1.) calls himself the brother of James, he must either mean another man of this name known to his readers, or we must suppose the term *brother* to signify step-brother or cousin, as indeed the word is often used in Hebrew. For the opinion of some, that in the catalogues of the apostles (see Luke's gospel and his Acts of the Apostles), Jude is not called the son but the brother of James, must be totally rejected, because, though it is true that sometimes the word *brother* is to be supplied for the genitive following a proper name, this is only the case when it is clear from the connection what is to be supplied. In the apostolic catalogue, however, *son* is everywhere else to be supplied for the genitive; and hence it is incredible, that, in the case of Jude alone, *brother* must be added.

But that the authors of these two Epistles of James and Jude were among the number of the twelve is very uncertain, (indeed, as we shall show hereafter, improbable), and on that account we have still to determine the difficult question, what persons of these names wrote the Epistles? The following reasons show the uncertainty of the idea that the authors of the Epistles were apostles. In the first place, the fathers of the Church speak of another James, the brother of our Lord, and first bishop of Jerusalem, and another Jude, likewise the brother of our Lord, as the authors of the Epistles; and, moreover, these were disputed by many, and reckoned among the Antilegomena, clearly for this reason alone, that it was supposed perfectly correct to regard them as not apostolical. Thus, in the opinion of the fathers, there were, beside the two James's and Judes among the twelve, two other persons of these names, called *brothers of our Lord*. These are mentioned in the passage, Matt. xiii. 55, with two other brothers of our Lord, Simon and Joses, and with sisters of his whose names are not given. They are also mentioned in the later history of the apostolic age (Acts xv. 13 seq.; Gal. i. 19; ii. 19), particularly James, who is designated with Peter and John as a pillar of the Church. According to the fathers of the Church, he was the first bishop of Jerusalem, and the description which the New Testament gives of his position and operations perfectly accords with this statement. According to the account of the Jewish writer, *Josephus,* and a very ancient Christian historian, named *Hegesippus,* this James, the brother of our Lord, died a martyr's death at Jerusalem shortly before its destruction. He possessed such authority and such reputation for piety among the Jews, that, according to Josephus, the destruction of the city was a punishment from heaven for the execution of this just man. James was succeeded in the bishopric of Jerusalem by another brother of our Lord, viz., Simon (Matt. xiii. 55), who, as well as the third brother, Jude, lived till the reign of the Emperor Trajan, *i. e.,* to the end of the first century after Christ. According to the account of Hegesippus, Simon also died a martyr's death, like his brother; of the manner of Jude's end nothing definite is known. Although, however, we find these brethren of our Lord labouring with ardent Christian zeal after the resurrection of the Saviour, still in the lifetime of our Lord they did not believe on him. This we are told by John expressly (vii. 5), and, therefore, we do not observe these brethren of Jesus among the disciples until *after* his resurrection from the dead. (Acts i. 13.) Probably the vision with which, according to 1 Cor. xv. 7, James was favoured, was the means of convincing them all of the divine dignity of our Lord, which hitherto, perhaps on the very account of their close relationship to him by blood, they had been unable to credit. It is true, the expression, *brothers of our Lord,* is not to be understood as meaning what the words strictly signify: for Mary, the mother of our Lord, appears not to have had any other children. The passages, Matt. i. 25, Luke ii. 7, in which Jesus is called the *first-born* son of Mary, prove nothing to the contrary, since, if no more children follow, the only son is also the first-born. If the statements of Scripture respecting these brethren of our Lord be put together, it cannot be doubted, that the children of the sister of Mary, the mother of Jesus, are intended by the expression. The sister of Mary was likewise named Mary, and was the wife of a certain Cleophas. She stood with the mother of Jesus beneath the cross of our Lord, as did also Mary Magdalene. (John xix. 25.) This same Mary is called in the parallel passage of Mark (xv. 40) the mother of James the Less and of Joses. Here, then, are named two of the persons who, in Matt. xiii. 55, are termed brothers of our Lord. Nothing, therefore, is more natural, as it nowhere appears that Mary had any other children, than to suppose that these so-called brethren of our Lord were his cousins, the sons of his mother's sister. As it is probable that Joseph, the foster-father of Jesus, died at an early period, (for he is not mentioned after the journey to Jerusalem, in the twelfth year of Jesus' age,) Mary perhaps went to live with her sister, and thus Jesus grew up with the sons of the latter, which may have been the reason why it was so difficult for them to give credit to his divine authority. It was very common in the Hebrew idiom to term cousins *brothers*. Hence, in Gen. xiii. 8, Abraham and Lot, who were cousins, are termed brothers. If we were to take the word *brother* in its literal sense, and regard the four brothers of our Lord, mentioned in Matt. xiii. 55, as own children of Mary, the mother of Jesus, we should have to suppose the extraordinary circumstance, that the two mothers of the same name had also children named alike. Now, as we nowhere find mention first of our Lord's brethren, and then of his cousins, but the same relations are always referred to, this supposition cannot be admitted. The same may be said of another supposition, according to which two of these so-called brethren of our Lord, viz., Jude and James, were of the number of the twelve. For it is said that the Hebrew name, which lies at the basis of the Greek one, Cleophas (abbreviated Klopas), viz., Chalpai, may also in Greek become Alpheus. Thus James the son of Alpheus would be equivalent to James the son of Cleophas. Now, it is true, that on the score of philology nothing can be reasonably objected against this supposition; but its validity is overthrown by the fact, that one and the same writer (viz. Luke) presents both forms. Although the name could be differently expressed in Greek, at least the same writer would always have followed the same mode. Moreover, as we have already remarked, it is inadmissible to supply the word *brother*, instead of *son*, after the name Jude. Lastly, it is a decisive circumstance, that in John vii. 5, it is most expressly stated, that the brethren of Jesus did not believe on him. It is, therefore, impossible that they should have been of the number of the twelve. Consequently, the New Testament mentions, besides the James, son of Zebedee, who was early executed, two other persons of this name, first the apostle, who was a son of Alpheus, and next, the brother of our Lord, the first bishop of Jerusalem. Thus, too, the New Testament mentions, besides the apostle Jude, who was the son of a certain James, of whom we know nothing, another Jude, who likewise was a brother of our Lord, and lived to a late period (till the time of Trajan), in Palestine. That these two brothers of our Lord, and not the apostles, were the authors of our Epistles, has been already intimated, and will now be more fully shown.

Of great importance, and indeed almost decisive by itself, is the circumstance, that the fathers of the Church refer the Epistle of James to the brother of our Lord of that name; and, too, the fathers who lived in that very region which was the scene of the labours of this celebrated bishop of Jerusalem, viz., the East. Here they might and must have had the most exact accounts respecting this distinguished man, and information as to his writings must have spread itself very readily from Jerusalem to the neighbouring countries of Syria and Egypt. This historical testimony is confirmed very strongly by the great agreement which exists between the contents of the Epistle and the communications which are made by ancient fathers of the Church, and particularly Hegesippus, in regard to the peculiar habits of James. According to the account of this writer, James distinguished himself by forms of piety which were very like those inculcated in the Old Testament. He fasted and prayed a great deal, so that, as Hegesippus relates, probably with some exaggeration, his knees had become callous. According to the New Testament, too, (comp. Acts xv. with Gal. i. 2), James, the brother of our Lord, appears to have been the head of the Jewish Christians. He, therefore, undoubtedly observed the Mosaic law, even after he became a Christian, and endeavoured to obtain the sanctity enjoined in the Old Testament. That, however, this endeavour* was not a narrow-minded one, as among the Ebionites, but a liberal one, as among the Nazarenes, is plainly shown by the narrative in the Acts, according to which he did not, along with the obstinate Judaizers, desire to impose the observance of the law upon the Gentiles, but only adhered to it himself, as a pious practice of his fathers. Still his whole disposition leaned somewhat to the side of the law, and this is clearly exhibited in the Epistle.

The same is true of Jude likewise. His very designation of himself as *brother* of James can leave no doubt that he desired to represent himself as the brother of that James who was so celebrated, the first bishop of Jerusalem. He does not call himself an apostle, any more than James. Both term themselves merely servants of Jesus Christ, neglecting from modest humility to make any mention of their relationship by blood to our Lord. We have no statements on the part of the early fathers of the Church in regard to the author of the Epistle of Jude. The later fathers, *e.g.* Jerome, call him an apostle, but they did not for that reason mean a different Jude; only, as might very easily happen, considering the confused accounts we have of these men, they sometimes placed Jude, the brother of our Lord, among the number of the twelve, contrary to John vii. 5.

Another as important reason for believing that James the brother of our Lord, and not the apostle James, was regarded as the author of the Epistle, is the circumstance that it was reckoned among the Antilegomena. Doubts did indeed arise, but not till a pretty late day. Clement of Rome, Hermas, and Irenæus make use of the Epistle without scruple. Origen first, then Eusebius, mention doubts. Now, as before the time of Jerome, there is no trace of the Epistle's having been regarded as forged in James' name, the ground of doubt can have been no other than that it was questionable whether an Epistle of any one not an apostle could claim admission into the canon. Jerome observes, that certain individuals believed the Epistle of James to have been forged by some one in his name. This opinion, however, is entirely devoid of probability, because in

---

* The original reads *Schreiben*, which I take to be clearly a mistake for *Streben*, and translate accordingly.—Tr.

such case the author would not have neglected to ascribe the dignity of apostle to the James whom he wished to be regarded as the writer of the Epistle, that it might be more sure of admission into the canon. Those persons, therefore, of whom Jerome speaks, and who undoubtedly resided in the West, probably entertained doctrinal scruples respecting the Epistle. In the West, and particularly in Rome, the centre of the western churches, special regard was felt for Paul and his doctrines. Now, the second chapter of the Epistle of James was supposed to contain erroneous notions in contrariety to Paul, because, as was thought, it inculcated justification by works instead of by faith. This passage even misled Luther into a rejection of the Epistle of James. In his preface to it he says, "This James does nothing but urge his readers to the law and to works, and his manner is so confused, that I imagine he was some pious man who had gathered a few sayings from the disciples of the apostles, and put them down upon paper. . . . Hence the Epistle of James is but a *strawy* Epistle; it has by no means an evangelical tone."

In more recent times, however, it has been proved, by very thorough and impartial investigations, that this harsh judgment of Luther is certainly unfounded, together with the apprehensions of the ancient fathers mentioned by Jerome.

James only opposed misconstructions and perversions of Paul's real doctrine, not the great apostle of the Gentiles himself. The two great teachers of the Church are essentially one in sentiment; only they had reference to different heresies, and thus their language wears a different aspect. In the Epistles to the Romans and Galatians, Paul presents the doctrine of faith, and justification thereby, in opposition to the reliance which the Jews placed on works. James, on the other hand, opposes a dead imaginary faith, which, without any renovating influence over the heart and mind, lulls a man into the sleep of sin, instead of making him active in works of love. If we thus consider the language of the two apostles with reference to the positions which they respectively opposed, we shall perceive the most perfect unity between these two teachers of the Church, notwithstanding all their freedom and peculiarity of manner. Though they taught the same doctrines, their point of view was different. Paul had a predominant leaning towards faith, not meaning by any means, however, to deny that it must bear good works as its fruit; James directed his attention more to the fruit, without, however, disparaging the root of faith from which alone the fruit could spring.*

Thus, leaving wholly out of view the influence of doctrinal ideas, the discrepancy between the ancient fathers of the Church was only whether the Epistle, as proceeding from the brother of our Lord, who was not an apostle, should or should not be admitted into the canon. The East, in general, maintained that it should, because James had exerted so much influence in that region; the Christians of the West were less favourable to it. In reality, then, the question was not in regard to the genuineness of the Epistle, but in regard to the rank of James, whether or not he should be placed on a level with the apostles in respect to the abundance and power of the Spirit poured out upon him, so that a writing of his might be received into the canon as a norm of faith and practice for all future generations of Christians; a question which we will soon consider further.

In regard to this second point, likewise, the case is the same with the Epistle of Jude as with that of James; except that in the accounts concerning this Epistle given by ancient fathers, we do not find the slightest evidence that the Epistle was ever regarded as the production of an impostor who forged it in Jude's name. Such a supposition respecting this Epistle is extremely improbable. In such case, would an impostor have contented himself with designating Jude as the "brother of James?" Would he not at least have expressly called him an apostle of our Lord, in order to gain a place for the Epistle in the canon? When we are told, therefore, of opposition to the Epistle, which caused it to be placed among the Antilegomena, we must refer it all to a refusal to accord to the author of the Epistle, who was not an apostle, sufficient consideration to procure its admission into the canon. Thus, in regard to the Epistle of Jude, likewise, the point in question is, not the genuineness of the Epistle, but

---

* See more complete discussions of the supposed discrepancy between Paul and James on the subject of faith and works, in the Biblical Repository, vol. iii. p. 189, and vol. iv. p. 683.—Tr.

only the personal standing of the author, which by some of the fathers of the Church was considered equal to that of an apostle, and by others inferior. The investigation of this question, then, what we are to think of the admission of two productions of writers who were not apostles into the canon of the New Testament, remains for the conclusion of this chapter.

Now, whether it be said that the Church has forsaken its principle of admitting no writing into the canon which was not either written by an apostle or composed under his supervision and authority, in admitting the Epistles of James and Jude; or that they indeed adhered to their principle, but erred in regarding James and Jude, the brethren of our Lord, to whom they correctly ascribed the Epistles, as apostles, and therefore admitting their Epistles into the canon—either way, it would seem as though we of the present day were entitled to charge antiquity with mistake respecting these Epistles. As to the Epistle of Jude, the case certainly seems to be as we have here stated it. It was written by one who was not an apostle, by a man of whose acts and character we know nothing further; a fact which appears to sustain the scruples of many of the ancients in regard to its being canonical. Moreover, it contains nothing which is not also found in the second Epistle of Peter, so that the Church could dispense with it without suffering the slightest loss. We might therefore be disposed to consider this Epistle as a deutero-canonical production, which was received into the canon only at a late period on the ground that it was more advisable to preserve every writing of the days of the apostles than to reject anything which might be of apostolic origin. It is not to be forgotten, however, that the use of Jude's Epistle in the second Epistle of Peter must be considered as apostolic confirmation of the former, if the latter be acknowledged genuine. Both productions, therefore, stand or fall together. The impossibility, however, of proving beyond doubt the genuineness of the second Epistle of Peter, will not permit the friends of these Epistles to entertain anything more than a subjective conviction in regard to the authority of Jude.

The case is different, however, with the Epistle of James. For this remarkable man appears, both according to the New Testament, and according to the fathers of the Church, to have occupied a very influential position. It is true he was not of the number of the twelve; but the fact that our Lord appeared to him separately, as he did to Peter (1 Cor. xv. 7), indicates his consequence; as does also the circumstance that he was elected bishop of Jerusalem, and especially his relation to the Jewish Christians, of whom James seems to have been the real head. Hence, in Gal. ii. 9, this man, with Peter and John, is called a pillar of the Church, and Josephus represents the consideration in which he was held among the Jews to have been so great, that the destruction of Jerusalem by the Romans was looked upon as a judgment for his death. Although, therefore, James was no apostle, and, moreover, no one of the twelve, so far as we know, afforded his confirmation to the Epistle, still the Church might well have considered itself entitled to insert the production of so influential a man in the canon. It may be said, indeed, that James was in a precisely parallel situation to that of Paul (who, too, was not of the number of the twelve, and still enjoyed apostolic dignity), except that in regard to the appearance of our Lord which was vouchsafed to James, and the commissions which were entrusted to him, we have not such particular information as is furnished us by the Acts respecting his appearance to Paul. Yet, passing by this, we cannot but declare, that an apostolic confirmation of a particular book, such as we suppose in the case of Mark and Luke, according to the testimony of history, is nothing compared with the testimony which we have from Paul's own mouth respecting James. He is designated, along with Peter and John, as a pillar of the whole Church of God upon earth; and thus, though not one of the twelve, still placed entirely on a level with the proper apostles; and hence no objection at all can be made to the reception of the Epistle by the Church. She has not, in receiving it, deviated at all from her principles; indeed, she has thereby rather applied them in their real spirit, not rigorously restricting the idea of *apostolical* estimation to the number of the twelve, but referring it to the fulness and power of the Spirit exhibited in the life. This, however, as appears from the Epistle itself, and from history, was possessed in its utmost potency by James, as well as Paul, on which account the Epistle of the former richly merits a place among the canonical books.

CHAPTER X.

OF THE REVELATION OF JOHN

The sublime book which concludes the New Testament, the Revelation of St. John (ὁ θεολόγος), with its wonderful images and visions, has met with a more extraordinary fate than any other writings of the New Testament. The impressive and absorbing nature of the contents of the book has seldom permitted any one to examine it with cool impartiality; and while some have become the enthusiastic advocates of the book, others have appeared as its most violent opponents, not only rejecting the work as not apostolical, or as forged, but even reviling it as the production of an heretical spirit. Thus it has happened, that, while no production of the New Testament can exhibit more and stronger historical evidence of its genuineness and apostolic authority than the Revelation, none has met with more antagonists; and, indeed, many of its antagonists are men who have merited much gratitude from the Church for their struggles in behalf of the truth. Among these is Luther, who shows himself a determined opponent of John's Revelation. He says, in his preface to it:

"There are various and abundant reasons why I regard this book as neither apostolical nor prophetic. First and foremost: the apostles do not make use of visions, but prophesy in clear and plain language (as do Peter, Paul, and Christ also, in the Gospel); for it is becoming the apostolic office to speak plainly and without figure or vision, respecting Christ and his acts. Moreover, it seems to me far too arrogant for him to enjoin it upon his readers to regard this his own work as of more importance than any other sacred book, and to threaten that if any one shall take aught away from it, God will take away from him his part in the book of life, (Rev. xxii. 19.) Besides, even were it a blessed thing to believe what is contained in it, no man knows what that is. The book is believed in (and is really just the same to us) as though we had it not; and many more valuable books exist for us to believe in. But let every man think of it as his spirit prompts him. My spirit cannot adapt itself to the production, and this is reason enough for me why I should not esteem it very highly."

From this strong language of the great Reformer it is sufficiently evident how repulsive the contents of the Revelation were to him. As he termed the Epistle of James a *strawy* Epistle, because it seemed to him to contradict Paul's doctrine in regard to faith, so he rejected the Revelation, because the imagery of the book was unintelligible to him. This was obscure to him from the fact that he could not thoroughly apprehend the doctrine of God's kingdom upon earth, which is exhibited in the Revelation, and forms the proper centre of everything contained in it.

The same point has at all times in the Church operated very powerfully upon the judgments of learned men in regard to the Revelation; and therefore we must, before any particular examination of this production, make some general observations on the propriety of permitting doctrinal views generally, and the doctrine of God's kingdom upon earth particularly, to have an influence on criticism.

In recent times, critical investigations of the sacred books have pretty generally proceeded on the principle, that doctrinal views ought not to exert any influence upon inquiries respecting the genuineness of the Scriptures. It has been easy to lay down this principle, because generally* the binding authority of Sacred Writ has been denied, and writers have not felt it incumbent on them to admit as an object of faith everything that was stated in genuine apostolic writings. Indeed, to many an investigator it has been very gratifying, that in genuine writings of the apostles things should occur which to him seemed evident errors; since in such case it became more easy to prove that the apostles even had stated many things erroneously, and that therefore what was true in their productions should be separated from what was false. With Luther, however, and all the other old theologians, the case was different. They acknowledged the Scriptures as binding on their faith, and therefore could by no means wholly exclude doctrinal considerations. For, were a book proved to be apostolical by all possible historical and internal arguments, and yet it plainly subverted the Gospel, and preached a different Christ from the true historical son of God and man, no faithful teacher

---

* That is, in Germany.—Tr.

of the Church of Christ should receive and use any such production, notwithstanding all the evidence in its favour, any more than listen to an angel from heaven, who should bring another Gospel, (Gal. i. 8.) Such was Luther's position; and in this view we may respect and honour his opposition to the Epistle of James and the Revelation of John. His only error in this, in itself commendable endeavour boldly to distinguish what was anti-christian was, that he decided too rashly and hastily, and thus did not investigate with sufficient thoroughness, and, on the ground of appearances merely, pronounced that to be not biblical which in reality was so. That this was the case in regard to his judgment concerning the discrepancy between James and Paul, is at the present day universally admitted. In regard to the Revelation, however, many still think that he judged correctly, although, in my opinion, he erred here as much as in relation to the Epistle of James.

We cannot say, therefore, that doctrinal considerations are not of the least consequence in critical investigations; though certainly we must not permit them to have an improper influence, so as to disturb the historical investigation, nor too hastily make an objective rule of our present subjective views, but endeavour to investigate more thoroughly what is at the moment obscure and inexplicable. Such an endeavour will often educe a modification of our views, and we may find that what seemed erroneous contains profound and sublime truth.

In particular, this would undoubtedly be the case with many if they could determine to consider more closely the doctrine respecting God's kingdom upon earth, which has always been the greatest cause of offence in the Revelation. True, it is not to be denied, that the history of the fortune of this doctrine is by no means calculated to favour it; for everything which human ignorance and human malice have been able to devise, appears to have concentrated itself in the misapprehensions of this doctrine. If, however, pains be taken to separate these misapprehensions and perversions from the doctrine itself, and we are impartial enough to consider, that often very profound truths, which take a mighty hold of the human mind, are most exposed to abuse, and may become most dangerous, and that hardly any other religion has been misused to such abominable purposes as the Christian religion itself, and yet that it is not on that account the less true or the less divine, he will easily attain the proper fundamental idea of the doctrine of God's kingdom upon earth; which is so simple, that we cannot understand how its truth could ever be doubted, until we remember the farragos of nonsense which have been propounded under its sanction. This simple radical idea is merely that, as in regard to an individual man, God, by the Saviour, redeems not merely a particular part of him, his spirit alone, his soul alone, or his body alone, but the *whole* man, his body, soul, and spirit, so the redeeming power of Christ has for its object the deliverance of the entire human race, and of the creation in general, from the yoke of sin. As, therefore, the end of salvation for the individual is the glorification of his nature, the end of all things in the universe, on the same principle, is the glorification of the universe. Proceeding from this fundamental idea, the Revelation teaches in sublime imagery, agreeing perfectly with the statements of our Lord and the apostles (which are less formal, and rather take the doctrine for granted, and thus are more incidental), that a period will come in which not only, as had already been the case, the spirit of Jesus Christ should prevail in secret, and guide men's minds, but should also gain the victory externally, and found a kingdom of peace and righteousness upon earth. Now, that, with the arrival of this reign of peace, there will be connected, on the one hand, the appearance of Jesus Christ, and a resurrection of many saints and pious men, and, on the other, a previous mighty struggle on the part of evil—does indeed follow very naturally from the fundamental idea, and the supposed development of good and evil; but these points are only incidental. The principal idea is the perfect return of the supremacy of good, the restoration of the lost paradise to an earth which has been laid waste by sin. Millions desire this most earnestly, hope and pray for it even, without ever imagining that it is the very doctrine which they think themselves bound to oppose, or at least unable to admit, without deviating from correct belief. Even the excellent Reformers had but an imperfect notion of this doctrine, though it is as simple as it is sublime; and, for this reason, in a great measure, that they saw around them senseless fanatics who dishonoured the Gospel, and caused unspeakable injury by the grossest misconstructions and perversions of this doctrine.

It would not have been worth while, with our present purpose, to say even the little we have said on this subject, were there not so many well-meaning men of real piety, who, notwithstanding the most striking historical proof, can never prevail upon themselves to admit the Revelation to be a genuine apostolic production, and therefore entitled to a place in the canon, and thus to become a rule of faith; because they feel that then they must, in consequence, admit the reign of God upon earth into their circle of belief, which they suppose they neither can nor ought to do. May such be led to a thorough investigation of this idea, and of all the passages of Scripture which relate thereto, that the acknowledgment of evangelical truth in this respect may be promoted, and its fulfilment be rendered nearer at hand!

In passing now to the consideration of the historical evidence in favour of the genuineness of the Revelation, we must again call to mind the latter days of the life of John the Evangelist. He lived, as we know with certainty, longer than any one of the other apostles, that is, as late as to the end of the first century. The scene of his successful labours, at the close of his life, was the city of Ephesus, in the vicinity of which were situated all those cities to which were directed the seven Epistles contained in the first chapters of the Revelation. Ephesus, moreover, was one of the great centres of business in the Roman empire, and was much frequented by Christians from all countries.

It must, therefore, be admitted, that it was easy for the Ephesian Church particularly, and indeed for the whole ancient Church, to arrive at the highest degree of certainty in regard to the writings of John. In particular, there could be no uncertainty whether John had composed so peculiar, so very remarkable a production as the Revelation. We must therefore admit, that if among the fathers of the Church in that region, we met with even uncertainty in regard to its author, it would be a very suspicious circumstance; and, on the other hand, unanimity in their conviction of the genuineness of the book must be a very decisive testimony in its favour. Now we meet with this last to a surprising degree. First, we have the testimony of Papias, bishop of Hierapolis in Phrygia, in behalf of the book. This man was personally acquainted with several of the apostles, and, among them, with the Evangelist John. His testimony is, therefore, of the greatest consequence. It is true, an attempt has been made to invalidate it, on the ground that only a late writer named Andreas, attributes to Papias any knowledge of the Revelation; but careful consideration of the principal passage respecting Papias in Eusebius (Hist. Eccl. iii. 39), which certainly ought to be thus examined, will show that Eusebius has given a wrong representation concerning Papias in more than one respect, and everything is in favour of the supposition, that Papias was acquainted with all John's writings. Eusebius is one of those fathers of the Church who were very much prejudiced against the doctrine concerning the Millennium, and it is on this account that he so strongly opposes Papias. Since this ancient bishop was a principal supporter of that doctrine, his testimony may, on that account, appear partial; and yet his close relation to John cannot have permitted him, notwithstanding all his predilection for this doctrine, to attribute to that writer a production which was not his. Justin Martyr, too, along with Papias, testifies in favour of the apostolic origin of the Apocalypse. He was indeed born in Palestine, but he taught in Ephesus, and there had opportunity to learn how things really were. Now, this father expressly declares the Revelation to have been written by the Evangelist John, one of the twelve. So, too, Melito, bishop of Sardis, one of the cities to which the Epistles in the Revelation are addressed. We cannot but presume that such a man would know who was the author of a production which contained an Epistle to the church over which he presided.

The same is true of Polycarp, the celebrated bishop of Smyrna, to which church, likewise, an apocalyptic Epistle is addressed. This man was an immediate disciple of the Evangelist John. Polycarp's pupil, Irenæus, who removed from Asia Minor to the south of France, and, as has been already observed, became bishop of Lyons, gives us an account of Polycarp's relation to John, and makes use of the Revelation throughout his writings, without mentioning even the slightest opposition to it. It is also employed as really apostolical by the western fathers, Tertullian, Cyprian, Hipolytus, &c., without any mention of a doubt as to its canonical authority. Still, it may be said, none of these were either learned or critical; they found in the Revelation their favourite doctrine in regard to the kingdom of God upon earth, and therefore they readily received the book as a production of John's. In decided opposition to such remarks, we adduce the Alexandrian fathers, Clement and Origen. These were not only the most learned men of the day, and the best skilled in criticism, but, in particular, were *opponents of the doctrine of the Millennium;* yet neither had any idea that the Revelation of John was not composed by the Evangelist of that name. They chose to get rid of the odious contents of the book by a forced interpretation, rather than by opposing the tradition of the whole Church. A stronger combination of historical evidence in favour of the apostolic origin of the book is, in fact, hardly conceivable! The weight of this evidence is augmented by what we know respecting those who doubted the genuineness of the book. Of this number was a presbyter of the Roman Church, whose name was Gaius. This man made it a set purpose to oppose the doctrine of the Millennium; and because the defenders of it naturally appealed, first of all, to the Revelation, he declared it spurious, without, however, presenting any historical or critical reasons for doing so. In order to degrade the Revelation, it was even referred by him to a heretic, Cerinthus, who was said to have written it in John's name. But in this, he clearly evinced that he was carried away by his feelings, for no one can by any means attribute the Revelation to an intentional deceiver, for this reason, that it would have been one object with such a man to denote with precision the person of the Evangelist, so as to cause the work to be regarded as his. This, however, has not been done, and thus we are not permitted to take any view in opposition to it, except it be that another John, and not the Evangelist, composed it. This opinion was first stated and defended, in a formal manner, by the learned Dionysius, bishop of Alexandria, a disciple of Origen. But, as this man lived at so late a period that authentic oral tradition was no longer within his reach, no more stress is to be laid upon his doubts, than upon the learned objections of more modern days. We come, therefore, to this result—*All historical tradition is unanimous in behalf of John's composition of the Revelation.*

Now, in order to invalidate this decided testimony of antiquity, very striking arguments ought to be adduced; but observe what are the reasons which prevail upon modern investigators to deny that the Evangelist John was the author of the Revelation, and then judge whether they are strong enough to countervail such testimony. In enumerating these reasons, I follow a distinguished scholar of the present day, whom I very much esteem and love as my former instructor, although I differ entirely from his views. I do indeed believe him to be in general very impartial and unprejudiced; but nevertheless, I think him to be influenced in his judgment of the Revelation by the force of prejudices which were largely imbibed by the Church, and have been widely diffused.*

In the first place, it is urged by this learned man that John never mentions himself in the Gospel and Epistles as the author of these writings; would he act differently, then, in the Apocalypse? It is true, he says only that this circumstance is worthy of attention; but as it stands as one of his arguments, it seems to have been regarded as of considerable importance. Of what consequence, however, is such a difference in practice, since all we can say is, simply, that the author chose in this case to employ a different form from his usual one? What writer is there who does not act as he pleases in regard to such points?

In the second place, the variation from his other writings in point of language is adduced as an argument. The fact is indisputable. The language of the Gospel is pure Greek, smooth and accurate; that of the Revelation, on the contrary, is harsh, rugged, full of inaccuracies of expression, and real grammatical mistakes. But it is not true that all difference in phraseology indicates different writers. Compare, *e. g.*, the earliest writings of Goethe, Schiller, Herder, with the latest productions of the same authors. Especially, take an author who attempts to write in a foreign language; must not his first essays be of a totally different character from his later ones? he has not complete mastery of the language; he struggles not only with the sense, but with the form; and this must necessarily make the phraseology even of the most practised intellect somewhat cumbrous. This is exactly the case with John's Revelation. It was his earliest production in the Greek language, occasioned by the

---

* I mean Professor De Wette, in his "Einleit. ins neue Testament" (Introd. to the New Testament.)

fearful occurrences during Nero's persecution. These cast the sympathizing mind of the beloved disciple of Jesus into deep meditation, during which the spirit of prophecy showed him the future fortunes of the Church, and its final conquest over Judaism and heathenism. It was, therefore, composed some twenty years earlier than the Gospel and Epistles seem to have been written, and in a language which to John, a native of Palestine, must have been a foreign one. Now, the Revelation appears exactly like the production of a man who had not yet acquired the requisite skill in the Greek language, and as its internal characteristics likewise show that it was written in the early part of John's life, before Jerusalem was destroyed, it is in fact impossible to see how one can ascribe importance to this circumstance of the difference of style, in opposition to the tradition that the Evangelist John was the author of the production; the rather as there is undeniably very much in the language which bears close affinity to those writings that are admitted to be John's.

The same may be said of the *third* observation, that the style of the Revelation is in the following respect very unlike that which we find in the Gospel and Epistles, viz., that the former exhibits a lively creative fancy, while, in the latter, quiet, deep feeling predominates. In regard to this remark, which likewise is correct, we are to consider, first, that the same individual in different stages of mental development will make use of different styles of expression. The earlier works of the same writer are accordingly more ardent, more imaginative, than his later. Moreover, the imagery in the Revelation is not by any means to be regarded as the arbitrary production of a rich fancy, but rather as actual appearances to John's mind from the operation of the Divine Spirit within him. I admit that John would not have been selected as the medium of these communications of the Spirit, had there not been in his whole organization a special adaptation for such impressions; but still, susceptibility to them is not the same as positive productive fancy. Finally, it is not to be forgotten in this view, that John's other writings are of a more historical or else purely didactic nature; while, on the other hand, the Revelation is a prophetic production. It would, therefore, be totally unnatural that the same style should be observable in the Apocalypse as in John's other writings.

The only remaining point alleged in confirmation of the difference between the Revelation and other writings of John is, that they exhibit a totally different *doctrinal aspect*. In particular, stress is laid on this circumstance, that in the Gospel nothing at all is found of what forms the main topic of the Apocalypse, viz., the expectation of a visible coming of our Lord, and the establishment of his kingdom upon earth. Moreover, all that is said in the Revelation respecting good and bad angels is of a more Jewish cast, we are told, than we should expect John's views to have been, from examining his other writings. It would appear that, if this be really so, it is a reason of some weight against the genuineness of the book; for we cannot suppose the apostles to have altered their doctrinal views, and, plainly, difference in the character of the writings could not affect the doctrine, as both in historical and prophetical productions there must exist the same fundamental views on the part of the writer. Now, the remark is indisputably correct, but the true reason of the fact has been misapprehended. For, first, the same difference which is exhibited between the Gospel of John and the Apocalypse, also appears, on comparison, between the Gospel of John and the first three Gospels. These latter, like the Revelation, present many doctrines and views agreable to the Jews, particularly the visible coming of our Lord to assume his kingdom upon earth; while nothing of all this is touched upon by the Gospel of John, notwithstanding there was ample occasion for doing so. It does not thence follow, however, that either John or the others err in representing the discourses of Jesus Christ, since the same person *may* have spoken sometimes spiritually, as in John's discourses, and sometimes in a Judaizing manner, as according to the other Evangelists. The correct solution of this difficulty is to be sought solely in the *special purpose* of the Gospel of John, with which the first Epistle stands in such intimate connection that it is not strange it should partake of the same character. The two other Epistles are too short to be here taken into consideration. For above (in the third chapter, in speaking of the Gospel of John), it was observed, that this Evangelist had a particular class of persons in view in his work, viz., men similar to the later Gnostics, and who in certain views coincided with them perfectly. In particular, they, like the Gnostics, speculated on Divine things in a peculiar manner, and sought to idealize the real facts in the history of

Jesus, more than the true apostolic doctrine permitted. These men, among whom were many very sensible and well-meaning persons, were those whom John had particularly in view in the composition of his Gospel. With apostolic wisdom he avoided in this work everything which could offend the prejudices of these persons. Many Jewish ideas, which had a very good and genuine foundation, and, according to the first Gospels, were expressed by the Saviour himself, he kept back, becoming in a manner a Gnostic to the Gnostics, without doing the least injury, however, to the cause of truth. He depicted Christianity, therefore, to their minds, just as they could most easily comprehend it, convinced that when once they had seized this idea, they would gradually learn to understand it thoroughly.

If, now, we adhere steadfastly to this point of view, it will appear perfectly intelligible, how the same John who wrote thus in the Gospel, should appear to express himself so differently in the Revelation, in the composition of which no such reference existed; though still he was always governed by the same doctrinal views at every period of his life. And thus we must declare that no one of these reasons is calculated to disturb us in regard to the correctness and truth of the tradition of the first centuries after Christ. If the repugnance which is felt towards the contents of the Apocalypse be only conquered, men will soon cease to rate so highly the reasons which are adduced against its apostolic origin, and to think so little of the importance of the unanimous tradition of antiquity. And that this may soon happen is the more to be wished, as the progressive development of the Church makes the Revelation more and more important in testing what is now occurring among Christians, and what awaits them in the immediate future!

CONCLUSION.

HAVING thus passed through the entire series of the writings of the New Testament, taking notice of the critical questions in regard to them, we will now, for the sake of convenience, present a compendious view of the *results* at which we have arrived.

We find then most, and the most important, of the writings in the canon of the New Testament, so unanimously acknowledged in ancient times, and so universally made use of as apostolical in later days, that there cannot be the least doubt in regard to them. They are on this account denominated *Homologoumena*, universally acknowledged writings, and form the main sources of the doctrine and history of the Christian Church. Among these Homologoumena, as is stated by Eusebius so early as the commencement of the fourth century, were the four Gospels, the Acts of the Apostles, the thirteen Pauline Epistles, the first Epistle of Peter, and the first of John. If we attend only to the voice of Christian antiquity, as Eusebius correctly observes, the Apocalypse also does in reality belong to the Homologoumena. But the fortune of this book has been so peculiar, that some have not even been willing to class it among the Antilegomena, but have ranked it with the writings which are of a profane character, and are to be utterly rejected. Eusebius was therefore in great perplexity to what class he could properly assign the Revelation. As to the Epistle to the Hebrews, its author is unknown merely; its genuineness is not disputed. It belongs, therefore, to the class of the *Antilegomena* only so far as this, that its position in the canon was disputed; the relation of the author to the apostle Paul not being unanimously acknowledged in the Church.

Properly, the class of the *Antilegomena* among the New Testament writings comprehends the two smaller Epistles of John, the Epistles of James and Jude, and the second Epistle of Peter. These five books were never universally acknowledged and used in the ancient Church. More recent investigations decided in favour of the first three. The two small Epistles of John are certainly apostolical, and from the author of the Gospel of John; that of James was not, indeed, written by one of the twelve, but by a brother of our Lord, who held such a prominent rank in the ancient Church as placed him, like Paul, fully on a level with the apostles. As to the two writings last in the list, however, it appears justly somewhat doubtful whether they are productions of the days of the apostles. The Epistle of Jude is, indeed, certainly genuine, but as certainly not apostolical; and, as history attributes to this brother of our Lord no very prominent station or agency, the Epistle seems not properly to belong to the canon. It can be supported only by the second Epistle of Peter, which is not itself certainly of apostolical origin. For, in regard to the latter, a consideration of the circumstances makes it impossible to establish its genuineness objectively on valid grounds, although it may be made subjectively probable.

These results of the most careful critical investigation of the New Testament are very satisfactory. For, if we could wish that the genuineness and canonical character of the Antilegomena might be established by as valid arguments as we can adduce in behalf of the Homologoumena, still it must be admitted that those books upon which some suspicion rests, are the very books, of all the New Testament writings, with which we can most easily dispense. The chief and best of these writings are the very ones whose genuineness and apostolic authority are certified as strongly as possible.

If, now, we inquire into the relation between the *external* historical genuineness of the books of the New Testament, and their *internal* efficacy and determinate power over the faith and life of the individual, and of the whole community of Christians, it is certainly undeniable, that the former by itself decides nothing in favour of the latter; but still, on account of the circumstances of the Church, demonstration of such genuineness is by no means unimportant or indifferent. It is clear that we may regard the writings of another religious system, the Zend-Avesta of the Parsees, or the Koran of the Mahometans, as genuine, and as having proceeded from the immediate circle of adherents which the founder of that system of religion possessed, without thereby attributing to it any internal efficacy and determining power over the heart and life. But it cannot be said that a conviction of the genuineness of the apostolic origin of the writings of the New Testament, likewise, is a matter of indifference. It is rather of great consequence in its connection with the Church, *i. e.*, the great community founded by our Saviour, and actuated and sustained by his Spirit. You may prove the genuineness of the writings of the New Testament to him who is not within the pale of the Church, or under its spiritual influence, and he may even acknowledge it upon incontestible historical grounds; but, as Christ and his apostles themselves, are of no consequence in relation to his internal life, this proof has no more effect upon his faith or his life, than is produced upon those of the scholar who declares the Zend-Avesta to be a genuine work of Zoroaster. Far otherwise is it with him who lives in the bosom of the Christian Church. Here he cannot completely withdraw himself from the influence of the Spirit of Christ, which operates upon his heart from his earliest youth; he feels himself spiritually affected, and in a manner constrained by it. It is true that sinful man very often strives against the influence of the Holy Spirit, it being troublesome to him, because it does not permit him to continue sinning so freely and peaceably as he could wish. In such case he seeks to obtain plausible grounds on which he may evade the force of the Spirit's influence. One such plausible ground is often presented by the supposition that the writings of the New Testament are spurious, whereby the extraordinary character of our Saviour, with the sublime impression he made on the hearts of men, is encompassed with doubt, and thus its effect is diminished. To members of the Church of Christ, therefore, a firm conviction that the Scriptures are genuine, is of the highest consequence; the opposite opinion, yea, uncertainty merely, in regard to the character of the sacred writings, is ordinarily the natural concomitant of sin. Such a sentiment hinders the efficacy of the Holy Spirit, which manifests itself, in a manner not to be mistaken, to every simple, plain mind, on perusal of the Holy Scriptures, but exhibits its full strength only when the heart feels a quiet faith, undisturbed by any doubt. Hence the conversion of many has taken rise from their acknowledgment of the genuineness of the New Testament writings; and, moreover, the apostacy of many from the truth has arisen out of the circumstance that they denied the authenticity of these books. We may therefore say, that the knowledge of the genuineness of the writings of the New Testament is of essential efficacy where the influence of the Spirit of God, and a susceptibility to its operations, exist in any degree. To him who has already turned aside entirely from the truth, and who resists it with an unfriendly mind, a conviction of the genuineness of these books will be of little use, unless his opposition be first broken by the power of grace. To him who is converted, born again, the sure conviction of their genuineness will always be a pleasing concomitant of grace, and will excite his gratitude; but, as he has experienced in his heart the Divine power which dwells in the

Scriptures, the testimony of the Holy Spirit will always be the proper foundation of his faith, which would support him even though he had no historical proofs in behalf of the sacred books. Persons, however, who have neither experienced a perfect change of heart and mind, nor are actuated by a positively hostile spirit, but ardently desire the former, though they are often assailed by doubts and uncertainties, will find in the firm historical foundation of Scripture, something on which they may lean at first, and from which they may then be gradually led to the full knowledge of salvation. For, if it be only admitted that such a life as that which the Scriptures represent our Saviour's to have been was really spent, that such words as they communicate to us from him were really spoken, the obvious question is, Whence came such a phenomenon? What is its import to the world? to me?

But, it may here be asked, if the case is thus, how happens it that God has permitted many plausible objections to exist against the writings of the New Testament, and that some cannot even be freed wholly from suspicion? Would it not have been more consistent with the purpose of the Scriptures, had all the books been supported by so numerous and so completely incontestible testimonies, that not even a doubt concerning them could ever have entered any one's mind? It may indeed seem so to short-sighted man. But his desires would not stop here, they would reach still further. He would wish to have a Bible without various readings, a biblical history free from the slightest variations; in short, Jehovah himself embodied in the letter of the word. The living God, who is eternal wisdom and love, has not thought anything of this kind suitable for mankind; herwise he would undoubtedly have effected it for their benefit; and the reasons why he has not we may at least conjecture, even with our weak powers. On the one hand, it would have become easier for man to confound the word and the Spirit dwelling in it with the letter; for, even as the case now is, this mistake has not been entirely avoided, from the want of spirituality in many men. On the other hand, the guilt of many persons would have been augmented, since they now have at least plausible reasons for their opposition to the truth, but in the other case would have had no such extenuation, and still would have retained their hostility to God's word. We may, therefore, declare, that the character of Scripture, in this respect likewise, corresponds most perfectly with the necessities of human nature, as well as with the designs of God, notwithstanding all its apparent imperfections and deficiencies.

The observations we have here made in conclusion, are, moreover, such as are best suited to present the correct view concerning the peculiar character of the Old Testament in the light of criticism. For this portion of God's word has so few historical evidences in its favour, excepting those comprehended within its own compass, that it is impossible to frame such an argument for the genuineness of its books as we are able to exhibit in behalf of the New Testament. This want of evidence proceeds in part from the very great antiquity of the writings of the Old Testament, which were almost all composed before there existed any literature among the Greeks, and before the Romans were so much as known by name; and in part, also, from the state of seclusion which the nations of the old world generally, and particularly the Jews, always maintained. The Persians, Syrians, Egyptians, knew scarce anything of the literature of the Hebrews; and had they even been acquainted with it, the circumstance would have been of little advantage to us, as we have but few writings of a date anterior to the time of Christ which originated with these nations. In these few, moreover, we find hardly any mention of the Jews and their productions. Hence, in investigating the earliest writings of the Old Testament, the critic has no other resource than a careful examination of the contents of the books themselves, and a comparison of them with each other. Were this examination and comparison invariably conducted with a believing and humble disposition, not the slightest objection could be made, and we might quietly await the results of such a procedure; but, when the minds of investigators deviate from the proper spirit and disposition, it is very evident how easily such an inquiry, which is in its nature somewhat uncertain and precarious, may lead to pernicious results. Every one will, in such a case, determine the matter according to his subjective ideas and views, without obtaining any objective grounds of judgment from investigation. If we only look at the actual state of the matter, entirely aside from the holy character of the book, we shall be convinced that such a course of investigation could hardly afford any useful result, even with the best intentions. A book is presented to us, which contains the relics of a nation's literature during a period of 1200 years. We derive all that we can know of the history, the manners, the special circumstances of this people, excepting a few points, from this book alone. Thus it is at once the *object* and the *norm* of investigation. Since, moreover, in regard to many of the writings in it, we have no statement as to their author and the time of their composition, the investigation of these writings cannot but have always a character of uncertainty. If we were only familiarly acquainted with the history of a single nation in close vicinity to the Jews, and found in its literature constant reference to the Jewish writings, we might then, by drawing a parallel, communicate more stability to the criticism of the Old Testament, but we have no such advantage, and must content ourselves with individual notices, which have come down to us from the most ancient times, of the nations with which the Jews came in contact. It was not till the time of Alexander the Great, about 300 years B.C., that the Jews, with their literature, became known to the Greeks, through whom we have received much important information in regard to the Old Testament. For, as the Jews, after that period, when they fell under Greek dominion, made themselves acquainted with the Greek literature, and, to some extent, themselves wrote in Greek, as *e. g.*, the celebrated Jewish writers, *Josephus* and *Philo*, so, on the other hand, the Greeks began to take an interest in the Jews and their religious institutions. From this mixture of Hebrew and Greek life proceeded the celebrated *Greek Version of the Seventy*. This, according to the account of the ancients, was executed under the Egyptian monarch, *Ptolemy Philadelphus*, at the instance of the learned *Demetrius Phalereus*, about the year 270 B.C. It is true, the Old Testament was not probably translated all at once, but, at any rate, even according to the most recent opinion, the Old Testament was entirely translated into Greek when Jesus Sirach was composed, *i. e.*, about the year 130 B.C. Consequently, it is placed beyond a doubt that the whole Old Testament, as we have it, existed in Palestine in the Hebrew language long before the time of Christ and his apostles, and in a Greek version in the other countries of the Roman empire, particularly in Egypt, where there resided so large a number of

Jews, and they possessed so great privileges, that they had even built a temple in the city of *Leontopolis* in close imitation of that at Jerusalem. In Egypt, the collection of the Apocryphal books likewise, which were confessedly written in Greek, was inserted in the canon of the Old Testament, which was spread abroad by the version of the seventy interpreters, and from this version they were introduced into the Latin Church-version (the so-called *Vulgate*), thus obtaining the same authority as the writings of the Old Testament, which authority they possess at the present day in the Catholic Church. As, however, they are not *expressly* cited in the New Testament,* and are wholly wanting in the Hebrew canon of the Old Testament, Luther rightly separated them from the rest, but appended them to the books of the Old Testament, as "*Writings not to be equally esteemed with Holy Writ, but still profitable and excellent for perusal.*" The Reformed Church, however, has gone still farther, and dissevered them entirely from the collection of sacred books, in order to prevent them from being confounded with the inspired word. Hence arose this great evil, that the historical connection between the Old and New Testament, which is so well exhibited in the narrative writings of the Apocrypha, was totally sundered; and this connection is by no means a matter of indifference to believers, because it is only through it that God's providence towards his people can be regarded in the light of an united whole. Hence, it would seem best to retain the apocryphal writings along with the Sacred Scriptures, designating, indeed, the distinction between them and the canonical books.

Thus much, then, according to these statements, we know certainly from historical testimony, that the Old Testament, as we now have it, existed more than a century before Christ. It is true, the learned would be gratified to know a great deal more respecting the formation of the canon of the Old Testament, respecting the authors of the individual writings, &c.; but, in view merely of the relation of the Old Testament to the faith of the present day, the knowledge that the Old Testament

---

* Allusions to them are pointed out by *Steir* in his "Andeutungen für Glaubwürdige Schrifterkläung," (or Hints towards the proper interpretation of the Scriptures), p. 486, seq.

was in a complete collected form before the time of Christ, is sufficient to afford us a firm conviction of the genuineness and importance of its books. Now, that the existing Old Testament was generally diffused and in use among the Jews, is attested by the Jewish writers of the apostolic times, who employed the Greek language in their writings. *Philo*, in Egypt, and *Josephus*, in Palestine, make use of the Old Testament throughout their works, thereby confirming the custom of the New Testament, which also everywhere refers to the Old Testament. The *manner* in which the Old Testament is cited by the New, and the definite declarations in regard to the former which are contained in the latter, are decisive as to the faith of Christians of the present day. These afford us more than the mere assurance that the books of the Old Testament are authentic; this might be admitted, without the slightest acknowledgment of the value of the writings, since the most wretched and even hurtful productions may be perfectly genuine. They declare, in the most precise manner, the *Divine character* of these books, which of course presupposes their genuineness, for it is very evident that no writings could be Divine which originated in deceit and imposture.

In the first place, we find in the New Testament citations from almost all the writings of the Old Testament.[*] The principal books, as, *e.g.*, the Pentateuch, the Psalms, the Prophet Isaiah, are cited very often, and even those less important are referred to here and there in the New Testament. A very few are entirely neglected;[†] of this number, in particular, is Solomon's Song, which is nowhere cited in all the New Testament. This circumstance is certainly not accidental. Perhaps it is not too much to conclude, that the books of the Old Testament which are not at all mentioned in the New, should be regarded very much as the so-called deutero-canonical books of the New

---

[*] The Old Testament is expressly cited in the New more than four hundred times, and in a much larger number of places there are allusions to the Old Testament.

[†] The Books of Ezra, Nehemiah, Esther, Ecclesiastes, and Solomon's Song, as also the minor prophets, Obadiah, Nahum, and Zephaniah. It is most proper, however, to consider the twelve prophets as *one work;* and then the fact that these three are not cited loses its force. But in regard to other books of the Old Testament, the circumstance that they are not cited is not unimportant.

Testament; though the circumstance that they are not cited in the New Testament can be nowise objected against their genuineness any more than the position of a New Testament book among the Antilegomena can be considered as a proof of its spuriousness. These non-cited books of the Old Testament, with the exception of the three minor prophets, probably present something like a *transition* to the apocryphal books. At all events, the fact that these books are nowhere mentioned in the New Testament, should inculcate upon us *caution in making use of them.*

Of more importance than the citations are such passages of the New Testament as contain decisive declarations respecting the Old Testament as a whole. These occur particularly in the discourses of our Lord himself. Jesus calls the law (Matth. v. 17 seq.) eternal, imperishable. Heaven and earth, he says, shall pass away, but not one jot or tittle of the law shall pass away till all be fulfilled. In a similar manner, in Luke xxiv. 44, prophecy concerning Christ is represented as something running through the law of Moses, the Prophets, and the Psalms, and as necessary to be fulfilled. In Luke xvi. 17, also, all created things, (heaven and earth,) it is said, will sooner and more easily pass away than the law and the prophets. Thus a lofty Divine character is clearly claimed in behalf of the Old Testament. It may indeed be observed, on the contrary, that, in the passages referred to, allusion is made, not to the whole Old Testament, but only to particular books, the Mosaic law, the Prophets, and the Psalms. But, first, it is to be noticed, that the expression, law, or law and prophets, stands frequently for the whole Old Testament, just as Gospel stands for the whole New Testament. Moreover, the law, the prophets, and the Psalms, was the usual division of the books of the Old Testament among the Jews. The first part of the Hebrew Old Testament comprehends the five books of Moses, the second part falls into two sub-divisions, first the historical writings, the books of Joshua, Judges, Samuel, Kings, and, secondly, the three larger and twelve minor prophets. To the third part (which in Luke xxiv. 44 is termed *Psalms*, from the principal book which it contains) belong, moreover, besides the Psalms, the book of Job, the writings of Solomon, the book of Daniel, and some later historical books, and, lastly, the book of Chronicles. But, entirely aside from this Jewish division of the Old Testament, the connexion of these passages with the citations clearly shews, that they are intended to refer to the whole Old Testament. The citations in the New Testament from the Old are not adduced as mere confirmations, drawn from human productions of great value, but as irrefragable proofs from sacred books. This power of proof could have belonged to them only from the fact that they were not bare compositions of human wisdom, but those of men who were moved by the Holy Ghost. (Compare 2 Pet. i. 20, 21.) Now, as citations from all the principal writings of the Old Testament occur in the New, the general declarations we have mentioned must of course refer to all the writings of the Old Testament, so as to attribute to them *a common character*, viz., that of a Divine origin.

To this it is to be added, that, throughout Scripture, there runs the doctrine of a deep, essential connection between the Old and New Testaments. As the Old Testament is always pointing onward to the New, so the latter is always pointing backward to the Old, as its necessary precedent. Consequently, both alike bear the character of a Divine revelation; only, this revelation manifests itself in a gradual development. In the Old Testament, it appears in its commencement as the seed of the subsequent plant; in the New Testament, the living plant itself is exhibited. On account of this relation, there cannot be anything in the Old Testament specifically different from what is to be found in the New Testament; only, the form of presenting the same thing is at one time more or less plain and direct than at another.

These declarations of the New Testament in regard to the Old are, to Christians, not mere private assertions of wise, good, and pious men, such as many in our day are in the habit of supposing Jesus and his apostles to have been; they exhibit rather authentic information respecting the real character of the Holy Scriptures of the Old Testament. Christ, as the Son of the living God, as absolute truth itself, who alone knew the Father, and as the source of all real revelation from him, can have made such declarations concerning the writings of the Old Testament, only with the strictest sincerity, (as is the case with every thing he did or said,) and must have designed that they should be a rule to his Church, since his whole life on earth had but one single aim, that of developing the heavenly and eternal to the created world. Thus, had Jesus attributed the character of eternity to a production to which it by no means belonged, he would have counteracted his own sole purpose. The same is true of the apostles, who, in that respect to which our attention is now directed, are to be considered as upon a level with Christ himself; they being pure organs of the mind of Christ; though, in themselves considered, they were but sinful men, and desired to be so regarded. Under the influence of the Holy Spirit, they acknowledged the eternal character of the Old Testament, and their declarations on this point are not (any more than those of our Lord himself) mere subjective, private statements, they are rather authentic accounts respecting the character of this part of Holy Writ. In considering the force of the apostolic declarations concerning the authority of the sacred Scriptures of the Old Testament, we are to regard, not merely the citations of individual passages from it, or general statements respecting its authors, such as their being at one time represented as moved by the Holy Ghost (2 Pet. i. 21), and at another Holy Scripture being called instruction unto salvation (2 Tim. iii. 15), which, as the New Testament was not then collected, can refer only to the Old; but we are especially to observe the manner in which the citations are adduced from the Old Testament. This is most remarkable in the Epistle to the Hebrews, although similar passages also occur in the Gospels and other books of the New Testament. In this remarkable Epistle, God or the Holy Ghost is constantly named as the speaker, in the passages which are adduced from the Old Testament; and this not only in regard to those which are accompanied in the Old Testament by the expression, "God said," but also to those in which some man speaks—for instance, David, as author of a Psalm. Herein is clearly exhibited the view of the author in relation to the Old Testament and the writers of it. He considered that God was, by his Holy Spirit, the living agent and speaker in them all, so that, consequently, the Holy Scriptures were to him *purely a work of God*, although brought forward by men. That the genuineness of these writings was equally certain to him, follows of course, because that which is divine, as has been before remarked, can never appear in the form of a forgery.

It is true, however, that such a proof in behalf of the Old Testament is valid only for him who has become convinced, by living experience, of the truth of God in Christ, and the infallibility of the Spirit which actuated his disciples. Where this truth and infallibility are either flatly denied, or even merely doubted, the observations we have made may be of no weight. For such persons we cannot frame an argument in behalf of the Old Testament, which shall be valid against all objections. As to us who live according to Christ, and to whom the power of his Spirit is accessible, everything must radiate from the centre of the New Testament scenes, viz., the Saviour himself. The conviction of his eternal power and Godhead establishes the Old Testament retrospectively, and also establishes the New Testament prospectively, by the promise of his Spirit, which should bring all those things which he had said to his disciples to their remembrance. On this conviction, the assurance of the genuineness and divinity of Scripture for ever rests, and much more securely than upon any external historical proofs; for it wholly takes away the possibility of an attack in any quarter on the part of human sophistry, and leaves assurance safe in the unassailable sanctuary of our interior life.

INTRODUCTION.

§ 1. ON THE ORIGIN OF THE GOSPEL-COLLECTION.*

As the revelations of God to man assume two principal forms,—viz., the Law and the Gospel; so, the Scriptures are divided into two parts,—the first of which relates to God's covenant with man in the *law;* the second, to the covenant in *grace.* Since the living Word of God—the eternal cause of these ever-binding covenants—lives in those writings which refer to the covenants, the writings themselves have been denominated *Old and New Covenants,* (בְּרִית = διαθήκη.† The Vulgate renders it Testamentum. Compare 2 Cor. iii. 14.) It is upon the writings of the New Testament that we have here to fix our attention; these always, however, necessarily presuppose the Old Testament. The New Testament springs from the Old, as the tree from its root; while the Old appears in the New in its completion. (Matth. v. 17.) We do not find the New Testament, as a collected whole, till the end of the fourth century. In the course of this century three smaller collections were united into one,—viz., the Gospels, the Pauline epistles, and the general epistles, together with some more isolated writings, which form the transitions and the conclusion,—viz., the Acts of the Apostles, the Epistle to the Hebrews, and the Apocalypse.

The origin of the first of these smaller collections, the εὐαγγελικόν, chiefly claims our attention. The collecting of our four canonical Gospels is lost in the remotest Christian antiquity. As far back as the historical records of the Church extend,

---

* [*Evangeliensammlung* is the word in the original, which expresses a collection of the Gospels into one volume, forming a subdivision of the whole New Testament.]—*Tr.*

† The word διαθήκη occurs, however, in the New Testament, (Acts iii. 25; Gal. iii. 15; Heb. ix. 16,) also in the sense of "Testament," "leaving an inheritance to children."

we find that collection *everywhere* in use, not only in every quarter of the world, but also in every division of the Church, whether belonging to the orthodox Church or the sects; and even among heathen writers, as Celsus, it was known, used, and respected.* It is true, that many heretics, as Marcion, the Jewish Christians, and others, did not use the Gospel-collection, but only one or other of the Gospels; the collection, however, was known to them, and they did not make use of it on the sole ground that, in accordance with their views, they did not believe themselves justified in regarding the writers as authorities in matters of faith.† This leads necessarily to the supposition of a very early origin of the Gospel-collection, of which, however, we have no definite information. Whether it was the work of an individual, or of a single church, or of a council, remains uncertain. The last supposition is the most unlikely, since we have no account whatever of church assemblies before the middle of the second century. But it is very possible that some eminent man, or an influential church, might have formed the collection. Yet there is no historical trace of such a fact extant; and it seems as if the *universal* dissemination of the collection, appearing, as it does, even in the first half of the second century, pointed to another mode of formation. For, starting with the assumption, that the four Gospels are genuine, and with the further assumption, (which we must do, since there is no credible account whatever of other apostolical Gospels,) that these four *alone* are the work of *apostles*, or enjoy apostolical sanction, we do not then need to suppose a definite time, or a definite place, or any special occasion, in order to explain the origin of the collection of the Gospels; but we may conceive that it was made in different places at the same time. The lively intercourse among the ancient Christian congregations led them to distribute, as quickly as possible, those Gospel histories which had apostolical authority in their favour, as precious gifts bequeathed to the Church of Christ; and, as it was just these four only

---

* For a fuller discussion of this point, see the Author's work: Die Aechtheit der Evangelien, aus der Geschichte der zwei ersten Jahrhunderte erwiesen. Königsberg, 1823, 8vo, S. 267, ff.

† *E. g.* Marcion, the Gnostic, believed St. Matthew, and even St. John, to be Judaizers. (See the Author's work, *ut supra*, S. 359, ff.)

that could shew credible evidence of being genuine apostolical writings, they were consequently united into one collection. Gradually, as they came into circulation in the Church, they were deposited in the Church archives, which must have been early formed by the presbyters and bishops, and were immediately multiplied by copying. If, then, we suppose likewise, (and history supplies no ground of objection to the supposition,) that the evangelists wrote in the order in which the Gospels are arranged in the canon, not only is their general dissemination accounted for, but also the circumstance, that we discover only slight traces of the existence of any arrangement different from the present,*—a circumstance which, apart from the supposition of the Gospels having been composed in that order, might favour the opinion, that some particular individual or church must have arranged the collection just in that order; since, otherwise, the contemporaneous formation of the collection, in different places, would almost inevitably have produced variations in the arrangement, especially such variations as were so founded in the nature of the case, as the placing of St. John and St. Matthew together.

§ 2. ON THE CHARACTER OF THE GOSPEL-COLLECTION.

The ancient Church justly regarded the Gospel-collection as a unity, on which account they call it simply εὐαγγέλιον, or εὐαγγελικόν,† as containing the glad tidings of Him who had appeared as the Saviour of the world, and as relating the life, labours, and passion of Jesus. See *Iren.* adv. haer. i. 17, 29, iii.

---

* Cod. D. and also the Gothic translation, place, for instance, the Gospel of St. John immediately after that of St. Matthew, evidently in order to separate the two apostolical works from those of the helpers of the apostles. See Hug. Introduction to the New Testament, p. 309, (Fosdick's Translation,) and the Postcripts to the Gospels in Schulz' edition.

† The New Testament recognizes the proper signification only of the word εὐαγγέλιον = בְּשׂוֹרָה chiefly in the special reference to the joyful tidings of the Messiah's actual appearance. A secondary signification, in conformity to which the writings that sketch the actions of the Messiah are called εὐαγγέλια, has been incorrectly given to the word in such passages as Rom. ii. 16; x. 16. The titles of our Gospels are of later origin; moreover, in them we should refer the term εὐαγγέλιον simply to the contents, not to the book. In classical use, εὐαγγέλιον signifies likewise a reward for a piece of good news, a present to one who brings good news. (See Liddell and Scott's Lex. s. v.)

11. The uniting into a whole of these four authentic writings concerning the Saviour, they not only further regarded as not merely accidental, but acknowledged a higher necessity in their connexion, as well as in the formation and arrangement of the Scriptures in general. The number of the Gospels could not have been different any more than their arrangement, without disturbing the harmony of the whole. *Irenæus*, (*ut sup.* iii. 11, p. 221, Ed. *Grabe*,) therefore, very appropriately calls the Gospel-collection a εὐαγγέλιον τετράμορφον, *fourfold gospel*, and describes it as a picture, portraying the same sublime object from different aspects. The relation of the Gospels to each other, and to the remaining books of the New Testament, speaks for the correctness of this opinion. The Gospels are supplemental to each other in their accounts of the person of the Redeemer, and in the form of their portraiture. The life of Jesus presented such a fulness of the most varied appearances, and His discourses breathed so rich a stream of life upon the circle of His disciples, that single individuals were incapable of adequately comprehending the exceeding grandeur of His character. In Him there was revealed something that surpassed the power of single human individuals to apprehend; and hence there was need of several minds, which, as mirrors, caught the rays that proceeded from Him, as from the Sun of the world of spirits, and reflected the same image in different directions. The four Gospels contain just such entirely different conceptions of our Lord, in His demeanour, at once divine and human, as must be *blended* together, in order to form a perfect delineation of Christ. But for God's providential arrangement, therefore, by which several persons, and those very different, have narrated the life of Jesus, either His human and natural, or His divine and supernatural, conduct would be presented to us less carefully conceived, according as we were without the one or the other aspect of this grand fourfold picture.

But much as this view of the relation of the Gospels to each other must approve itself to every one who feels that he cannot ascribe the development of the Church, and especially the formation of the Scriptures, to chance, it is yet difficult, in following out that view, to define accurately the character of each individual Gospel—a difficulty which certainly by no means leads to the rejection of the fundamental view, but rather invites to deeper research into the nature of the Gospels. That *St. Matthew* has seized the manifestation of Jesus more in its human and subordinate aspect, and *St. John* more in its higher, is too evident to be overlooked. In St. Matthew, we see the human ascending to the divine exhibited in Him; in St. John, the descent of the divine to the human. It is more difficult to assign a definite position to *St. Mark* and *St. Luke*, since both stand as intermediate between the other two Gospels, as extremes. The comparison of the Gospels with the prevalent tendencies in the ancient Church, is our best guide. That is to say, as St. Matthew unquestionably represents the Judaistic, and St. John the Gnostic element, so far as both are to some extent true, so St. Mark and St. Luke appear to represent the peculiar tendencies of the heathen Christians, the former perhaps more in the Roman, the latter more in the Greek, form. In St. Mark, however, the least of what is peculiar is discernible; yet, that it is not altogether wanting, is evident from the circumstance, that one party in the early Church attached themselves principally to this Gospel. But on the party itself impenetrable obscurity rests. (See the Author's Geschichte der Aechtheit der Evang. S. 96, ff.) As, then, the Gospels, in the manner referred to, represent different tendencies of the early Church, which, under other names and forms, belong to every period; so they correspond to the progressive developments of the inner life, which can never proceed in its growth from the understanding of St. John, downwards to St. Matthew, but, contrariwise, always upwards, from St. Matthew to St. John.

Further, if we consider the Gospel-collection in its relation to the entire New Testament, it appears plainly as the basis of the whole. In the Pauline epistles, the Gospel is unfolded in its separate branches—in its doctrinal and practical bearing; the general epistles continue the exposition of what was included in the Gospels as a germ, and in the Apocalypse appears lastly the prophetic portion of the New Testament vitally connected with the other parts—they being the root and branches, and it the blossom crowning the whole. The whole of the New Testament, therefore, forms a completed unity, and is like a living plant. The beginning and the end are the most difficult to understand, because there the thoughts appear in the most succinct form. Unless inward experience be altogether wanting, it is best to begin the deeper study of the New Testament with the Epistle to the Romans, since that document purposely expounds at length the peculiarities of the Gospel. After the accurate explanations of this important epistle, much that is expressed more concisely and darkly in other portions of the New Testament, may be easily understood. But, as the whole of the New Testament is the subject of our labours, we follow the order of the books as there given, so as not to interfere at all with any one's wishes and views.

§ 3. ON THE AFFINITY OF THE FIRST THREE GOSPELS.

The *investigation* of the difficult problem of the striking affinity of the first three Gospels, which is seen to be interrupted by variations just as striking, cannot, of course, be carried on in this place, any more than we can give a history of the attempts to solve that problem: both belong to the Introduction to the Canonical Books of the New Testament, properly so called, where the subjects of the preceding paragraphs also meet with a more copious discussion. A commentator, however, owes to his readers an account of the way in which he looks upon this remarkable phenomenon, since the view taken of very many passages is determined by his opinion concerning the origin of the Gospels. I shall therefore endeavour here to give briefly the *results* of my inquiries.

The two Gospels of St. Matthew and St. Luke appear to me to have been composed quite independently,—St. Matthew's principally from his own experience and oral tradition; St. Luke's principally from shorter written memoirs (diegeses*) which he edited. That which is found common to both Gospels may, in great part, be accounted for on the supposition of an affinity existing among the sources of information,† both oral and written, which the authors used independently of each other. In another respect, however, the supposition of their having used kindred sources of information, does not appear sufficient to account for the affinity subsisting between St. Matthew and St. Luke. I do not indeed, by any means, discover similarity of form in the general plan of the two works, and especially I do not discover that similarity in the fact, as alleged by some, that the scene of Christ's history, up to His last journey, is confined

---

* [Διήγησις, Luke i. 1.]—*Tr.*

† The copious narrative of the journey, contained in Luke ix. 51—xviii. 14, which is peculiar to him, is probably to be regarded as a *diegesis* of that sort, edited by St. Luke. See on this subject, *Schleiermacher*, über die Schriften des Lucas, S. 158, ff.

to Galilee; for, in respect to the general plan, there is much that is very different; and the above-mentioned limitation of our Saviour's ministry to Galilee, in the Gospels of St. Matthew and St. Luke, is totally destitute of proof, as it depends, not on positive reasons, but merely on the omission of journeys to the feasts, and the want of chronological and topographical notices;—still, there is, in many places, so close a verbal coincidence between St. Matthew and St. Luke, that we can hardly maintain that both, even in such places, wrote altogether independently of each other, or that they only used kindred sources of information. Compare Matth. iii. 7-10, with Luke iii. 7-9; Matth. vii. 3-5, with Luke vi. 41, 42; Matth. vii. 7-11, with Luke xi. 9-13; Matth. viii. 9, with Luke vii. 8; Matth. viii. 19-22, with Luke ix. 57-60; Matth. ix. 5, 6, with Luke v. 23, 24; Matth. ix. 37, 38, with Luke x. 2; Matth. xi. 4-11, with Luke vii. 23-28; Matth. xii. 41-45, with Luke xi. 24-26, 31, 32. Yet the view, that the one made use of the *complete* work of the other, is beset with invincible difficulties, since, in that case, it remains inexplicable for what reason the one should not have either used or noticed the other's narrative of the history of Christ's infancy. To solve this difficulty, I suppose that St. Matthew, who had written his Gospel in Hebrew, himself subsequently prepared* a Greek recension, (no other than our canonical St. Matthew;) and that, for this work, he made use of smaller collections of those memoirs which St. Luke had used, particularly Luke iii.—ix., in which section the closest coincidence is found.

The affinity of St. Mark's Gospel with those of St. Matthew and St. Luke, must be differently explained.† Although he may have taken here and there a circumstance from tradition, or from shorter memoirs, yet, in the main (for there is very little in St. Mark that is peculiar to him; with the exception of additional circumstances in various narratives, two cures, briefly narrated, are all that he alone has) he follows St. Matthew and St. Luke entirely; where he leaves the one, he follows the other, but only to return from the latter to the former. It is impossible for so regular a coincidence to be accidental. Still I do not go so far as to maintain, that St. Mark had *both* the Gospels before him while composing. This is not altogether

---

* This subject is handled more fully in § 4 of this Introduction.
† See *Saunier*, Ueber die Quellen des Marcus. Berlin, 1825. A. *Knobel* de origine evang. Marci. Wratislaviae, 1831.

improbable with respect to St. Matthew's Gospel; but, with respect to St. Luke's, it would suit better to suppose that St. Mark also was acquainted only with the section, chaps. iii.—ix., where the closest agreement is found; so that St. Mark may still have been finished earlier, and, consequently, received into the canon earlier, than the *complete* Gospel of St. Luke. For, had St. Mark had access to the whole Gospel of St. Luke, it would remain inexplicable, why St. Mark should not have incorporated much of the important narrative of the journey in Luke ix.—xviii.* Respecting the early chapters of St. Matthew and St. Luke, which contain the history of the childhood of Jesus, it might be said that St. Mark did not make use of them on this ground,—that it was his purpose to describe only the *official labours* of Jesus.

§ 4. ON THE GOSPEL OF ST. MATTHEW.

St. Matthew, called Levi, the son of Alphæus, (Matth. ix. 9; Mark ii. 14,) is mentioned in the inscription as the author† of the first of our four canonical Gospels; and tradition establishes the fact, that St. Matthew wrote a Gospel; but the question about the genuineness of St. Matthew is so intimately connected with the inquiry into the *language* in which it was composed, that the one cannot, by possibility, be answered apart from the other. All accounts of the Fathers who give any information about the Gospel of St. Matthew, (see the Author's Geschichte der Ev., S. 19, ff.,) agree in this, that St.

---

* See, however, what is said concerning this in the remarks on Luke ix. 51.

† Although we are not, by any means, necessarily *compelled* to explain the inscriptions of the Gospels, as giving the author, yet they *may* be so taken grammatically; it is the comparison of tradition that gives to this possible explanation its probability. The κατά might be taken = *secundum;* so that the meaning of the formula would be—a Gospel of Jesus, after St. Matthew's mode of description, or St. Mark's, which explanation would admit the supposition of other authors of the Gospels. But universally-prevailing tradition, which cannot have arisen out of these superscriptions, because it is too widespread and too ancient, decides in favour of taking κατά as pointing out the author,— a usage found also 2 Macc. ii. 13. This form of expression was chosen to convey the genitive relation, because the simple genitive could hardly stand here, since the Gospel is not that of the author, but of Jesus Christ. As εὐαγγέλιον Ἰησοῦ Χριστοῦ, *Gospel of Christ,* was in use, it was impossible to write εὐαγγέλιον Ματθαίου or Μάρκου, *Gospel of St. Matthew or St. Mark.*

Matthew wrote his Gospel in the Syro-Chaldaic language. But on the relation in which our Greek Gospel by St. Matthew stands to the Aramaic, there rests an obscurity which the investigations that have been pursued have not hitherto succeeded in penetrating. The readiest suggestion is, to pronounce the Greek Gospel a translation of the Aramaic. On closer consideration, however, difficulties arise in the way of this view. *First of all,*—*Papias* (*Euseb.* H. E. iii. 39) might seem to speak against the existence of a translation, as he writes of the Hebrew Gospel of St. Matthew, ἡρμήνευσε δ' αὐτά, ὡς ἦν δυνατὸς ἕκαστος; which words are best taken to mean, that every one had to try to explain the Hebrew book as well as he could, (either from his own knowledge, or from that of some one else,) because there was no translation of it. However, we must not overlook the fact, that Papias says this, not of his own times, but of the much earlier times of the Presbyter John. The passage cannot, accordingly, be adduced to shew, that in the time of Papias, there was no Greek translation of St. Matthew in existence. *Next,* our Greek text of St. Matthew shews traces of originality, which render it extremely unlikely that we have in it a mere translation. In particular, the passages from the Old Testament are quoted in a way so free and independent, that no translator would have so treated them. This character of the Greek text, taken in connexion with the universally current tradition, that St. Matthew wrote an Aramaic Gospel, and with the like universal reception of this very Greek text in the Church, as the genuine Gospel, renders it probable to me, as before observed, that St. Matthew, after the composition of the Aramaic Gospel, himself prepared also a Greek edition of it, or, at least, had it done under his authority. This Greek edition may be regarded as another recension of the Gospel, whereby the difference that subsists between our Gospel according to St. Matthew and that of the Jewish Christians, which was a revision founded more on the Aramaic Gospel, is more easily accounted for. The objection to this view, that scarcely any one would have taken the trouble to read the original Aramaic work if an authorized Greek edition of the Gospel had been extant, (which Papias' account, mentioned above, implies was the case,) is sufficiently refuted by the supposition, that the Greek Gospel was less rapidly circulated in the Church than the Aramaic and the other Gospels; it was regarded only as a translation, and, consequently, not as a new book, and people thought that they possessed it already in the Aramaic copy, which was earlier in circulation. But with the growing circulation of the Greek, the traces of the Aramaic Gospel were gradually lost, because to most it was inaccessible, by reason of the language, and its contents could be read as well in the Greek Gospel.

The view, just detailed, of the relation of the Greek Gospel to the Aramaic, agrees best with the *historical* data. But, very recently, an attempt has been made to disprove the apostolical character of our Greek Gospel, on *internal* grounds.* But, from the nature of the case, such arguments have something most uncertain about them; very much, if not everything, depends on the feeling, and especially on the doctrinal views of the critic. Hence the opinions of the learned differ greatly from each other; where one sees a proof *against* the apostolical authorship of St. Matthew, another sees a testimony in its *favour*. We cannot, therefore, ascribe any importance to the results of internal criticism, as long as they are unsupported by historical proofs. (For further information on this subject, consult the Programmes mentioned in the note.)

Lastly, in reference to the *place* and *time* of the composition of the Gospel by St. Matthew, but little can be said. Doubtless it was written in Palestine, and even in Jerusalem itself, since the tradition of St. Matthew's labours points thither. The circumstance, that the Hebrew recension of the Gospel, under the title of εὐαγγέλιον καθ' Ἑβραίους, was in use principally among the Jewish Christians in Palestine, also implies that it was composed in that country, and for its inhabitants. The Greek recension may certainly have had its origin in a different

---

* Schleiermacher, Schulz, de Wette, Schulthess, were the first to utter these doubts. Heidenreich has endeavoured to refute them in Winer's Theol. Journ., Bd. III., H. 2. They were followed by Sieffert, (Königsberg, 1832.) Klener, (Göttingen, 1832.) Schneckenburger, (Stuttgart, 1834.) Consult also Schleiermacher's Article on the Testimony of Papias, (Stud. und. Kritiken Jahrg. 1832, II. 4;) and Strauss's Review in the Berl. Jahrbücher, 1834, No. 91, ff. Kern, (Tübingen, 1834,) defends the genuineness of St. Matthew against these attacks, still inclining to Sieffert's and Klener's views; he also supposes a re-touching of the original, together with spurious additions, only allowing but few such. I have given my opinion of these works and their arguments more at length in the Erlangen Easter Programme for the year 1835, and the Christmas Programme for 1836. On Sieffert's Work, see the Author's Review in Tholuck's Liter. Anz. Jahrg. 1833, No. 14, ff.

country; yet there are no data to enable us to decide more accurately upon the point, and it still remains just as possible that St. Matthew, in consequence of the very general use of the Greek tongue in Palestine, in the time of the apostles, may have prepared a Greek edition of his Gospel for the benefit of the Greeks who dwelt there. The supposition of the Greek Gospel appearing in any other country would always have this objection against it, that there are no remarks added illustrative of the localities and customs of Palestine, such as we find in St. Mark and St. Luke, but which, in that case, would have been equally necessary in St. Matthew. Respecting the *time* of the composition, we are totally destitute of express authority on the point. The statement of *Irenæus*, (adv. hær. iii. 1,) however, that it was written while St. Peter and St. Paul were preaching at Rome, comes, probably, very near the truth. According to St. Matthew (xxiv.,) the Gospel was certainly written *before* the destruction of Jerusalem, since this event, though near at hand, appears as still future. We can hardly, therefore, be wrong in placing the composition of St. Matthew somewhere between A.D. 60-70.

And now, in conclusion, to say something on the *distinctive character* of St. Matthew, it is clearly seen, as was before observed, to be this, that St. Matthew labours to prove for Jewish readers that Jesus is the Messiah foretold by the prophets. The special regard for Jewish readers shews itself at once at the very commencement, since the genealogy of Jesus is traced up to Abraham only; it appears also in various express statements, (Matth. x. 6; xv. 24;) and lastly, in its being taken for granted that everything relative to the Mosaic law, Jewish customs and localities, is familiar. The distinctive character of St. Matthew is further evident in this, that external circumstances appear to him something by the by and unessential in the description. St. Matthew has conceived the life of Jesus from general points of view. At one time, he pictures Him as a new lawgiver; at another, as a worker of miracles; at another, as a teacher. He presents the character of the Saviour especially in discourses, which are in part made up of elements of addresses that appear to have been spoken at different times.* These discourses, as chap. v.—vii., x.

---

* *Schlichthorst,* Ueber das Verhältniss der drei synoptischen Evangelien, und über den Charakter des Mt. insbesondere, Göttingen, 1835, attempts to sub-

xi., xiii., xviii., xxiii., xxiv., xxv., are connected by historical introductions, which do not seem, however, in themselves, to be of importance to the Evangelist, (almost as in the case of St. John;) for which reason, also, St. Matthew has bestowed less pains on their completion, than on the construction of the discourses. St. Matthew's book, regarded as a whole, undeniably presents him to us as a character thoroughly taken up with the magnificence of Christ's manifestation; still we perceive that he was destitute of that abundant susceptibility and that refinement (*Feinheit*) of spirit, which we admire in St. John, although St. Matthew far exceeds St. Mark in spiritual depth, (*Innerlichkeit*.) The Christ of St. Matthew is by no means a Messiah according to the ordinary popular Jewish conceptions. The delineation which St. Matthew gives of Him, appears rather in opposition to what was false in the Jews' notions of the Messiah; still the Son of God, whom St. Matthew, of course, in common with the other apostles, recognized in Jesus, presents himself, according to St. Matthew's portraiture, in a Jewish garb; while in St. John's, a robe of heavenly light floats around Him; so that the form in which the disciple of love introduces the Son of love, is as much spiritualized as is the holy person himself, who is enveloped in it. As this cannot be said of St. Matthew, the ancients were not wrong in denominating the Gospel of St. Matthew, σωματικόν, that of St. John, πνευματικόν; by which epithet it was not intended to mark that of St. Matthew as unapostolic, but as, in the Saviour, the λόγος was manifested in a σῶμα, so, in a comprehensive delineation of the life of Jesus, the popular and temporal element in His manifestation *must* vividly appear associated with the apprehension of its spiritual aspect.

§ 5. ON THE GOSPEL OF ST. MARK.

John Mark, often called simply Mark, was the son of a certain Mary, (Acts xii. 12,) who had a house at Jerusalem, where the apostles often assembled. He is known from the New Testament

---

stantiate too close a relationship between the separate parts of St. Matthew to each other. Various of his demonstrations are not without foundation; but most of these references are undesigned, simply growing out of the spirit and harmony of the life of Jesus, not out of the reflection of the author.

as the companion of St. Paul. (Acts xii. 25; xiii. 5; xv. 36, ff.) Even during the Apostle's imprisonment at Rome, he is still associated with him, (Col. iv. 10; Philem. 24;) and, if we suppose the Apostle to have been a second time a prisoner at Rome, he appears in connexion with St. Paul till the close of the Apostle's life. (2 Tim. iv. 11.) In this there seems to be some contradiction to the notices of the Fathers, according to which St. Mark appears in company with St. Peter, of which only one trace is met with in the New Testament, and that has some uncertainty attaching to it. (1 Peter v. 13.) But the notices of the Fathers may be reconciled with the statements of the New Testament, by supposing that, after the contention with St. Paul, St. Barnabas, and St. Mark, (Acts xv. 37, ff.,) the last-named joined St. Peter *for a time*. On this point the New Testament is silent, because less is there said about St. Peter than about St. Paul; but afterwards, when the old relation between St. Mark and St. Paul was restored, and St. Peter, moreover, was labouring in conjunction with St. Paul at Rome, St. Mark appears again in connexion with St. Paul. But, together with the account of the connexion of St. Mark and St. Peter, which appears too unvaryingly to have its truth questioned, the Fathers tell us (see *Euseb.* H. E. iii. 39; v. 8; vi. 25. *Tertull.* adv. Marc. iv. 5) that St. Peter authorized the Gospel written by St. Mark, as his interpreter. That the Fathers are not quite unanimous in their relation of secondary circumstances, cannot be any reason for doubting the truth of the main fact; because nothing but such an occurrence can render conceivable the fact, otherwise so astonishing, that the Gospel by St. Mark was acknowledged in the Church without any contradiction. The authority of this companion of the apostles was surely too insignificant, and his previous relation to our Lord too uncertain, for them to have relied on his personal character in receiving his narrative of the life of Jesus into the canon. If it had been the product of a later period, the name of some more renowned man would certainly have been put at the head of the book; so that, even if history did not supply any such account, we must have conjectured something similar from the fact of the reception of St. Mark into the canon. The authority of St. Peter, which this Gospel enjoyed, also alone explains how any persons in the ancient Church could have thought of using this Gospel in preference to any other, as *Irenæus* (iii. 11) tells us was the case. The character of the Gospel itself could not possibly lead them to do so, since it contains too little that is distinctive to gain a party to itself; but it is easily conceivable, that partisans of St. Peter, on account of this very connexion, which, as they knew, subsisted between St. Mark and their leader, used this Gospel on the same principle that the partisans of St. Paul used that of St. Luke. But whether the Gospel by St. Mark suffered corruption in the hands of these Christians of St. Peter's party, as that of St. Luke did among the ultras of St. Paul's party, (the Marcionites,) and that of St. Matthew among the Jewish Christians, is uncertain. We know too little of the εὐαγγέλιον κατ' Αἰγυπτίους, to be able to say anything certain on its relationship to the Gospel of St. Peter.*

On the *time* and *place* of the composition, as little can be said that is exact and certain as respecting that of St. Matthew's Gospel. Here, also, we must rest content with the one circumstance, that it was written *before* the destruction of Jerusalem. (Mark xiii. 14, ff.) From the relation it bears to St. Matthew, we may conclude, with much probability, that it was composed later than the Gospel of that apostle. We come nearest the truth in supposing that St. Mark wrote his Gospel in the period shortly before the overthrow of Jerusalem. Respecting the *place* of its composition, tradition is divided between Alexandria and Rome. The Latin words which St. Mark has admitted into his book, speak in favour of the latter city; and as, in any case, it had its origin in one of the centres of the early ecclesiastical life,† to which circumstance the rapid circulation of the Gospel must be partially ascribed; and as the history of St. Mark is not opposed to the idea that he wrote in Rome, the opinion that he did so seems to deserve the preference.

---

* In my History of the Gospels, (p. 97, ff.) I have too decidedly rejected the possibility of a connexion between the Gospel of the Egyptians and St. Peter, and that of St. Mark. According to the general analogy, it is very probable that the Gospel of St. Mark also suffered corruptions; and it still remains possible that one of the writings belonging to the apocryphal books of St. Peter's partisans was a corrupted Gospel by St. Mark. *Schneckenburger*, Ueber das Evangelium der Aegyptier. Bern, 1834, takes it to be a work related to the εὐαγγέλιον καθ' Ἑβραίους, used by the Ebionites. From the Gospel of St. John, published by Münter, (Copenhagen, 1828,) we see that *it* also, though not till a late period, suffered corruption from the Gnostics. Consult Ullmann in the Studien und Kritiken, Jahrg. I., H. iv., S. 818, ff.

† Consult the Author's Gesch. der Evangelien, S. 440.

No definite *character* is displayed in the Gospel by St. Mark. We see, indeed, at once that St. Mark did *not* write for Jewish readers, because Jewish manners and customs are carefully explained by him, (compare the remarks on Mark vii. 3, 4;) but what particular tendency in the ancient Church he had in view, does not clearly appear. The Latinisms found in St. Mark are not of themselves sufficient to stamp it with a Roman character. The evident pains which St. Mark has bestowed on the vividness of the narrations, which is characteristic of his Gospel, might be regarded as a more conclusive proof. In the popular Roman character, there appears unquestionably a practical tact, which is in some measure reflected in St. Mark. This Evangelist knows how to represent the progress of the actions picturesquely, and to transport his readers to the scene. Compare particularly Mark v. 1-20, 22-43; vi. 17-29; ix. 14, ff., with the parallel passages; also Mark vii. 32-37; viii. 22-26, which are peculiar to him. This vividness manifests itself mainly in the accounts of cures, and among these, most of all in the cures of some demoniacs. (Mark v. 1, ff.; ix. 14, ff.) In his conception of the *inner* aspect of the life of Jesus, and especially of His discourses, he is strikingly inferior. We cannot, therefore, regard the vividness of description as such a superiority in St. Mark as should place him far above St. Matthew. It appears, likewise, that St. Mark intended to place before his readers a vivid picture of only the official labours of Jesus; on which account, he opened his narrative with the baptism of Christ.

§ 6. ON THE GOSPEL OF ST. LUKE.

The person to whom tradition refers the third Gospel, is St. Luke, who is sufficiently known, from sacred history, as the companion of the Apostle Paul. His name is the shortened form of Lucanus,—as Alexas of Alexander, Cleopas of Cleopatros. That he was a physician, is placed beyond doubt, by Col. iv. 14; and there is nothing improbable in the statement of the Fathers, that he was a native of Antioch. He was a heathen by birth, as is satisfactorily proved by Col. iv. 14, compared with verse 11, and still more by the aim of his book. As St. Matthew evidently had the Jewish Christians, so St. Luke had the heathen Christians in view. He might be led to write for them, not only from his national sympathy with them, but also by the example of the Apostle of the Gentiles, who directed the whole of St. Luke's tendencies. According to the tradition of the Fathers, (*Euseb.* H. E. iii. 4, v. 8, vi. 25; *Tertull.* adv. Marc. iv. 5,) St. Paul is also said to have exercised a confirmatory influence on the Gospel of St. Luke, like that of St. Peter on St. Mark's; which information is confirmed in a similar way by the rapid dissemination of the book, and its universal acknowledgment in the ancient Church. But the internal structure of the Gospel shews more than all, that it sprang from the Pauline school, which it represents in the Gospel-collection.

The *universal character* of this Gospel manifests itself at once in its carrying the genealogy of Jesus up to Adam, while St. Matthew stops at Abraham, the ancestor of the Jews; further, in the account of the sending forth of the seventy disciples as the representatives of all nations, while St. Matthew speaks only of the twelve apostles going forth as representatives of the twelve tribes; and equally so in the omission of every circumstance in which anything of Jewish exclusiveness shews itself. It may, therefore, be said, that as St. Matthew represents Jesus as the Messiah of the *Jews,* so St. Luke represents Him as the Messiah of the *heathen,*—i. e., as He in whom all the higher aspirations of the heathen world were realized, and who made the heathen themselves the object of his labours. As respects the form of the delineation, St. Luke has the peculiarity of exhibiting, with great vividness and truth, (especially in the long journey narrated in ix. 51—xviii. 14,) not so much the *discourses,* as the *conversations* of Jesus, with the occasions which gave rise to them, the remarks interposed by the bystanders, and the manner of their conclusion; so that, according to this, each of the Evangelists teaches us, even in the *form of his delineation,* to view the Saviour from a different aspect. Accordingly it was founded in the nature of the relations, that the ultra partisans of St. Paul—and, as such, we must regard the Marcionites—used this Gospel, in which their tendency is most definitely embodied, in preference to the others, and only endeavoured to remove, as Jewish additions, so much as did not agree with their exaggerated or mistaken Pauline views of the law and the Gospel.*

---

* That the Gospel of Marcion is a mutilated Gospel by Luke, has been convincingly shewn by *Hahn* in his well-known work: Das Evangelium Marcions

Regarding the determination of the *place* and *time* of the composition of St. Luke's Gospel, the person of Theophilus, to whom the Gospel is addressed, may, in some measure, guide us. He seems to have been a man of reputation, (see note on Luke i. 3,) and a resident in Italy. For we observe that the Evangelist, in speaking of Eastern subjects, everywhere adds explanations, and particularly, exact descriptions of places, even of the most familiar. These, however, are altogether wanting concerning the most insignificant parts of Italy, because he must have thought himself at liberty to take for granted a perfect familiarity with them in his reader. Rome is, therefore, in all probability, to be regarded as the place of composition for this Gospel also, whither, in particular, we are led, by the close of the Acts of the Apostles, the second part of the Evangelist's work. For, without a formal close, it breaks off with the second year of St. Paul's imprisonment at Rome; and as St. Luke was in company with St. Paul during that imprisonment, we can assign the place of composition with much probability. Further, as nothing is added about the issue of St. Paul's affairs, there remains but little obscurity as to the *time* of the composition of the Gospel. It must have been written shortly before the Acts of the Apostles, during St. Paul's imprisonment at Rome, and about sixty-four years after the birth of Christ. For it is not likely that a great space of time should have elapsed between the composition of the Gospel and that of the Acts, because the two works are so closely connected. In all probability, also, St. Luke's acquaintance with Theophilus could only be the fruit of his stay in Rome. *De Wette* (Einleitung ins. N. T., S. 182,) draws from such passages as Luke xxi. 17, ff., the conclusion, that this Gospel must have been written *after* the destruction of Jerusalem; but our remarks on Matth. xxiv. 15, will shew that this conclusion is untenable.

§ 7. ON THE HARMONY OF THE GOSPEL-HISTORY.

The propensity to look everywhere for connexion and unity, is too deeply seated in human nature not to have sought its

---

in seiner ursprünglichen Gestalt, Königsberg, 1823. Consult the Author's work on the Gospels, p. 106, ff. The counter-assertions of *Schulz* in Ullmann's Studien (B. ii., H. 3) still remain unestablished.

gratification in attempts to form a connected account of the Saviour's life out of the different Gospels. Such an undertaking is very much adapted to meet a practical want, by rendering easier the survey of all the circumstances in our Lord's life; so that it is not surprising to hear, even at a very early period, of attempts to form the different accounts of the Evangelists into a connected whole, such as were made by *Tatian,** Ammonius*, and *Eusebius*. But the narratives of the Evangelists do not admit of being reduced to a unity, with certainty, and in a strictly scientific manner. The difficulties in the construction of a Gospel harmony lie in this, that some of the Evangelists, in the composition of their books, have not thought of any definite arrangement of events in the order of time. They begin their histories, indeed, with the Saviour's birth, and close them with His death, as it could hardly be otherwise in a biography; but the real body of the Gospel-history—the exhibition of the official labours of Jesus—is so treated, that the intention of preserving a definite chronological order in the events narrated is nowhere perceptible. In *St. Matthew*, first of all, no accurately defined statement of time is found from the temptation (ch. iv.) down to the last journey to Jerusalem, (xx. 17,) which might serve for the arrangement of the matter. For the most part, the Evangelist passes from one event to another, without anything to fix the time, (iv. 12, 18, 23; viii. 5, 18, 23, 28; ix. 1, 9, 35;) or he uses an indefinite τότε, to connect them, (iii. 13; iv. 1; ix. 14; xi. 20; xii. 22, 38; xv. 1;) or he arranges the several histories, one after another, with the comprehensive formulas, ἐν ταῖς ἡμέραις ἐκείναις, (iii. 1; xiii. 1,) ἐν ἐκείνῳ τῷ καιρῷ, (xiv. 1,) ἐν ἐκείνῃ τῇ ὥρᾳ, (xviii. 1.) Precise statements as to time (as Matth. xvii. 1, μεθ' ἡμέρας ἕξ) are extremely rare. The great collections of discourses in St. Matthew shew that his prevailing aim was to portray the person of Jesus, apart from time and place, and, by a grouping together of kindred actions and discourses, to bring Him before the reader's mind in the different spheres of his labours. In the

---

* *Tatian's* work I have called, in my History of the Gospels, p. 335, ff., a Harmony of the Gospels; but the zeal with which Theodoret, in the fifth century, caused it to be destroyed, points to grave heretical corruptions which it contained. There is no doubt that Tatian made a compilation from the whole Gospel-collection, such as suited his purposes, and took the liberty of making considerable alterations in the text, which his adherents probably further increased. Concerning other harmonies, consult § 9 of this Introduction.

case of *St. Mark*, this neglect of time and place is still more striking; even these general data are for the most part wanting with him. He usually gives the narrative, without any remarks; he is concerned only to represent the facts themselves vividly, without arranging them according to a certain order of subjects. *St. Luke* appears, at first sight, more exact in the chronology; so that one might expect to discover from him an arrangement of events according to the succession of time. At the very commencement, in ch. i. 3, καθεξῆς, (see comment. on the passage,) seems to point to a chronological arrangement; there follows then (iii. 1) a very important date for the chronology of the life of Jesus; and (iii. 23) he remarks, that the Saviour was thirty years of age at His entrance on His ministry. Yet, in the course of the Gospel, an indefiniteness in the arrangement of the events, similar to that which we find in the others, discovers itself. For the most part, St. Luke, too, joins one history to another, without statement of time, (iv. 16, 31; v. 12, 33; vii. 18, 36; viii. 26; ix. 1, 18;) sometimes the indefinite transitions, μετὰ ταῦτα, (v. 27,) ἐν μιᾷ τῶν ἡμερῶν, (v. 17; viii. 22,) and others are interchanged; so that it does actually become uncertain whether, even in St. Luke, events are always arranged according to the succession of time; but, at all events, even if this be still probable, an arrangement of the events in the life of Jesus throughout cannot be accomplished by means of St. Luke, because no fixed points of connexion with the other Gospels can be laid down in the body of the narrative,—that is, from the baptism of Jesus to His last journey to the feast, (Matth. xx. 17; Mark x. 32; Luke xviii. 31;) for, after this, there is less lack of chronological data. It is true it might be thought, that such a point is to be found in the history of the transfiguration, since all the three Evangelists (Matth. xvii. 1; Mark ix. 2; Luke ix. 28) connect it with what precedes by μεθ᾽ ἡμέρας ἕξ. (The ὀκτὼ ἡμέραι, in St. Luke are the same period, but differently reckoned.) Yet if, commencing at this point, we make the attempt to arrange the events backwards and onwards, the thread is soon lost. But if there appears to be an impossibility of connecting the statements of the Evangelists into an orderly whole in the case of the *events*, it is still more so in that of the *discourses*. What appears in St. Matthew (v.—vii., x., xiii., xxiii., and in several other places) as spoken in connexion, St. Luke gives scattered in the most varied places; so that the very first attempt to restore the different parts of the discourses of Jesus to their chronological connexion, demonstrates the impossibility of so doing, at least if the compilation is not merely to serve a practical purpose, but is to claim scientific certainty.

Thus *St. John* alone remains, whose careful chronological arrangement strikes the eye, and who seems, therefore, to afford very important materials for the chronological arrangement of the chief events, at least in the first three Gospels. For though, now and then, an indefinite μετὰ ταῦτα occurs even in St. John, (as iii. 22; vi. 1; vii. 1, and elsewhere,) he usually states exactly, whether one day, (i. 29, 35, 44; vi. 22; xii. 12,) or two, (iv. 40, 43,) or three, (ii. 1,) or several days, intervened between the events recorded. The discourses, also, are in St. John so connected with the occurrences mentioned, and are so complete in themselves, that they acquire, in their full extent, a fixed chronological place. The chief point, however, is, that St. John gives us great divisions in the life of our Lord, between which we can try to arrange the separate events. Besides the last passover, (xiii. 1,) which is mentioned by the synoptical Evangelists also, he speaks *distinctly* of another passover, at which Jesus was present, (ii. 13;) and between these two fixed points at the beginning and end of the ministry of Jesus, St. John mentions further two feasts which the Saviour celebrated at Jerusalem,—viz., the feast of the dedication of the temple, (x. 22,) and the feast of tabernacles, (vii. 2.) Besides these, mention is made (v. 1) of another feast; but its character is left undetermined. If we possessed only the records of the first three Gospels, we should know nothing certain of these journeys of Jesus to the feasts; we could only arrive at the probable conclusion, that Jesus would certainly not have neglected the Old Testament command (Ex. xxiii. 17) to go up to Jerusalem at the three great feasts, since we find Him so scrupulous in the observance of the law in other points. Yet there is no clear evidence, even from St. John, of the number of journeys to the feasts, which took place during the ministry of Jesus, and hence the relation of the occurrences to the chronology of Christ's active ministry still remains obscure. What St. John narrates, certainly occurred in the order in which he narrates it; but it is uncertain how long a period is included,—whether he details the events of one year, of two years, or of several. First of all, we cannot prove that St. John has left *no* journey of Jesus to the feasts unmentioned. Moreover, the indefiniteness of the passage (v. 1*) makes the whole chronology of St. John uncertain; for although much may be said in favour of the opinion, that the festival there referred to was a passover,† yet this cannot be fully ascertained, particularly as we read so soon as vi. 4 of another nearly approaching passover; for it is, after all, harsh to refer ἐγγύς, to the passover that was gone by, as *Dr. Paulus* does. (See the retrospect quoted in the note.) Whether, therefore, according to St. John's representation, Jesus celebrated three passovers or four at Jerusalem during His ministry, cannot be stated with certainty;‡ but how much more difficult it must be to use the notices of St. John respecting the journeys of Jesus, for the purpose of arranging the historical materials of the other Gospels, appears sufficiently from the one circumstance, that, as St. John gives hardly any information about the life of Jesus but such as the other Evangelists had not given, no point of contact between them and St. John can be assigned. The history of the feeding of the five thousand, (John vi. 1-15,) with the walking on the sea immediately following it, (vi. 16-21,) is the only event which is parallel with St. Matthew, (xiv. 13, ff.,) St. Mark, (vi. 30, ff.,) and St. Luke, (ix. 10, ff.;) and the first two Evangelists, St. Matthew and St. Mark, like St. John, connect Christ's walking on the sea with the feeding of the five thousand. Yet as, on the one hand, the connexion of events cannot be pursued with certainty, and, on the other, the exact time of the miraculous feeding is uncertain, even in St. John, on account of the indefiniteness of v. 1 and vi. 4, so we cannot arrive at anything conclusive for the

---

* *Kaiser*, in his Synopsis, (Nürnberg, 1828,) regards it as a feast of tabernacles. Consult the commentary on the passage.

† Consult the chronological retrospect at the end of the first volume of Dr. *Paulus*' Commentary on the Gospels.

‡ In reference to the chronological difficulties in St. John's Gospel itself, we must further compare the passage (x. 22) in which St. John passes on to the feast of the dedication, in a way that leaves it altogether uncertain how the presence of Jesus at that feast stands related to His presence at the feast of tabernacles, (vii. 2,) since no mention is made either of His going away or remaining. It might even be thought to be the feast of dedication in another year, were it not that the following discourse (x. 27, 28) refers too plainly to the preceding context, (x. 12, 13.)

arrangement of the whole from this single point of contact.*
Whether any particular event belongs to the beginning or the
close of the public ministry of Jesus, is sufficiently shewn, it is
true, partly by its position in the Gospels, partly also by the internal character of the narratives; but the mode of representation
used by the Evangelists, who commonly leave time and place
undetermined, does not admit of our bringing all the separate
incidents recorded of the Saviour, as well as His discourses,
into precise chronological connexion. We, therefore, take the
Gospel-history as it is given to us, following the chronological
order as far as the Evangelists enable us to discover it plainly,
but nowhere bringing it out violently and artificially where it
has not been given. According to the synopsis of *De Wette* and
Lücke, which we take as the foundation of our exposition, we
shall first treat of the history of the childhood of Jesus and His
baptism; and, last, of the narrative of His sufferings, resurrection, and ascension, (combining St. John's description of these
latter circumstances;) but with respect to the intermediate
materials of the Gospel-history, we shall chiefly follow St.
Matthew, incorporating with his narrative—where they appear
to us most probably to belong—those portions which St. Mark
and St. Luke only have, or which one of them only has. The
editors of the synopsis have, indeed, treated this part in such a
manner, as to give the whole matter three times over according
to the order of St. Matthew, St. Mark, and St. Luke. A
threefold exegetical discussion of this part would certainly have
secured no small advantages; these, however, had to be sacrificed, as it would have required too much space.

§ 8. ON THE CREDIBILITY OF THE GOSPEL-HISTORY.

The description given above of the origin of the Gospels from
separate memoirs, whose authors are unknown by name,—
further, the character of the Gospel-history itself, in consequence of which no chronological arrangement of the events

---

* Just so *Lücke* observes in his *Commentar über den Johannes*, Th. i., S. 526:
"How that which St. John has mentioned out of the variety of events may be
chronologically harmonized with what the first three Evangelists narrate in the
above-mentioned (middle) period, is an insolvable problem of historical criticism." See the further remarks, S. 614, 615, of the same work.

can be recovered through a large portion of it,—and lastly, the distinct discrepancies which discover themselves in various events, particularly in the composition of the discourses,—are all circumstances which seem to endanger the credibility of the Gospel-history, especially in such events as lay beyond the field of observation open to any one of the narrators, as, for instance, the childhood of Jesus. The Gospels seem in this way to acquire the appearance of an unarranged aggregate of separate and uncertain reports, which do not precisely agree among each other, and do not even, in each individual Gospel, stand in strict connexion. The older theology was apprehensive, that, by such a view as that which modern criticism has advanced, the sacred character of the Gospel-history would be entirely taken away. Starting from the *literal* inspiration* of the sacred writers, they laboured to force a harmony, and to reconcile all discrepancies in facts and words; but, from the character of the Gospels, this procedure could not but lead to the most arbitrary treatment; —that is to say, wherever there appeared a difference, whether in the events or in the discourses, the event or the discourse was always said to have been twice, and sometimes even thrice repeated. By setting up the principle, therefore, that the Gospel-history must agree in everything external and non-essential, they put weapons into the hands of the enemies of God's Word; the evident non-agreement was used as an argument for denying the divine origin of the Scriptures. It is best, therefore, in this case, also to stand to the truth, plainly to acknowledge the evident fact of discrepancies in the Gospel-history, to seek for a reconciliation of these variations where it

---

* I distinguish *literal* inspiration from *verbal*, and maintain the *latter*, while I deny the *former*. The distinction between them does not lie, as I think, in the *essence* and the *form*, (for the *form*, too, is necessary in one aspect,) but in the *essential* and the *unessential form*. But the question, Where is the *essential* in the form separated from the *unessential?*—what is *word*, what is *letter?*—will never admit of being answered as respects individual cases, so that *all* shall be satisfied, because the mind's subjective attitude exercises too much influence over our views on the point. In general, however, those who are one in the principles, will be able to unite in this canon: *The form of Scripture is to be regarded as essential, as far as it is connected with what is essential in the doctrine, and is, consequently, also to be ascribed to inspiration; it is only where there is no such connexion, that the form is to be regarded as unessential.* Consult, further, Tholuck's excellent dissertation on the contradictions in the Gospels, in his *Glaubwürdigkeit der Evangelischen Geschichte gegen Strauss*, Hamburg, 1837, S. 429, ff., which preserves just the right medium.

presents itself naturally, but not to resort to anything far-fetched or forced. The *external* agreement of the Gospel-history should not be absolutely required as proof of its divinity, any more than it ought to be in the formations of nature; as in them exact regularity is combined with the greatest freedom, so also, in the Gospel-history, complete agreement in what is essential, is found with the freest treatment of what is unessential.* The credibility of the Gospel-history is securely based only on the identity of that vital principle which reigned in all the individual Evangelists, and in which the whole new communion, of which they were but members, shared. That vital principle was the Spirit who guides into all truth. But this Spirit, who inspired the Evangelists and the whole company of the apostles, neither relieved them from the use of the ordinary means of historical inquiry, as, for instance, the use of family memoirs or narratives of single events; nor did He obliterate their peculiarities, and use them as passive organs; He rather spiritualized all the individuals in their capacities and powers, gave them an abiding faculty (*tact*) of testing everything false in matters of faith and in the essentials of the narrative—of recognizing what was genuine and appropriate—and of placing it in connexion, according to a deeper principle of arrangement. Although, therefore, the Evangelists did even combine parts of discourses out of the addresses of our Lord differently from their original connexion, the import of those parts, although modified, is not altered. For, as the living Word, which the Lord himself was, wrought in the Evangelists also, and inspired them, it formed in each of them a new spiritual whole, in which the members of the separated whole appear harmoniously re-united.

This view of Scripture—of its unity in essentials, and its diversity in non-essentials—leads as much away from the superstitious reverence of the *dead letter*, as it does to the search for the *living Spirit;* but it stands aloof from that hollow spirituality which fancies itself able to do without the external *word*, and thereby falls into the danger of taking its empty dreams for the essential ideas of the truth. Although, therefore, Providence intended that the external proofs of the genuineness of the

---

* Literal agreement in the Gospels, would have suggested to the enemies of the truth, the charge of a concert among the authors to deceive; as Scripture now is, it appears at once divine and human.

Gospels should not be wanting, yet it has not permitted that the credibility of the events reported in the Gospels can be incontrovertibly demonstrated. Occasions are left for doubting and suspecting; and by means of these the Gospel-history fulfils a part of its intention, since Christ, when written of, as well as when personally labouring on earth, is set for the *fall* of many. (Luke ii. 34.) In every reader of that history, therefore, a readiness to receive the Spirit of truth is presupposed. Where this exists, the Gospel-history, in its peculiar character, asserts its claims with overwhelming force. For, although the Gospel partakes of the general character of history and biography, yet, as its subject is itself incomparable, it is, in its treatment of the subject, not to be compared with any other work of that kind. The Evangelists write in a manner so childlike and *naïve*, and, at the same time, with a simplicity so noble, as are not elsewhere to be met with thus united. Their individual view (*subjectivity*) disappears entirely,—they narrate without making reflections, without bursting out into expressions of praise, or blame, or admiration, even in portraying the sublimest events. They appear, as it were, absorbed in the contemplation of the mighty picture displayed before them, and, forgetting themselves, reflect the appearance in its pure truth. The Gospel-history, therefore, bears witness to itself and its own credibility, in no other way than our Lord himself; He had no witness to Him but himself and the Father, (John viii. 18;) so the Gospel-history (like the Scriptures in general) bears witness to itself only through the Divine Spirit, who reigns in it. He that is of the truth, hears His voice.

It is only where this Spirit of God has not yet displayed His power, that the conception of the history of Christ being on a par with all other biographies of great men, could arise; and that, therefore, what is miraculous in it, as well as in them, should be regarded as a myth. The want of inward personal experience of the regenerating power of Christ,—the want of the testimony of the Holy Spirit, which alone gives certainty as to the divine origin of the Scriptures, has always caused offence to be taken at the miraculous garb that invests the person of our Lord. In ancient times this offence simply took the form of a hostile attitude towards the Church. It is the experience only of very recent times, to see this offence pretending to be an advance in Christian science. It appeared first in the form of what was called the *natural* explanation, the very *unnaturalness* of which has, however, long since pronounced its condemnation; it needs, accordingly, no further refutation. Then, especially since the time of *Gabler*, it appeared in the form of the *mythical* explanation, which also has been pushed on to self-destruction through its very extreme application by Strauss. The inapplicability of the mythical exposition to the life of Jesus is incontrovertibly manifest: 1. *From the nearness, in point of time, of the sources of information,*—namely, the four canonical Gospels, the antiquity and genuineness of which are satisfactorily demonstrable on internal and external grounds. As long as the eye-witnesses of the miraculous events of the life of Jesus were living, there could be no such thing as myths,—viz., formations of involuntarily inventive rumour,—but only productions of enthusiasm or deceit; 2. *From the acknowledged genuineness of the Acts of the Apostles, and of the Pauline Epistles, as well as of the other principal writings of the New Testament.* Hitherto no one has ventured to pronounce the chief Epistles of St. Paul and St. John to be spurious, and yet they contain precisely the same view of the person of Christ which lies at the basis of the four Gospels. This appears, consequently, to have been the early Christian view. If the mythical explanation is to be defended, nothing is left but to pronounce the Apostle Paul an enthusiast or a deceiver; 3. *The origin of the Christian Church,—the continuity of feeling in it,—the purity of the Spirit that wrought in it, with especial power, just in the first centuries,* do not allow us, in any way, to conceive of merely a beautiful romance as the ultimate foundation of these appearances. That a Church could be formed of Jews and heathen, who worshipped a crucified Son of God, is, according to the mythical view of the life of Jesus, a far greater miracle than all those which are meant to be dispensed with by this means. It is only from the records of the Evangelists, taken as history, that this fact becomes conceivable. Since, moreover, in this Church, while gradually extending itself over the world, there was still a constant connexion of feeling, and a spirit of purity, never previously beheld, inspired it, especially in the very early times, we cannot perceive where we can find room for the pretended formation of myths. It can be found only on the unscientific assumption, that no existing records date from the first Christian century. The mythical scheme appears, accordingly, a partial, indecisive measure. The decided antichristian spirit will pronounce Christianity, together with the whole Scripture, to be the product of enthusiasm and deception.

[The theory which *Strauss*, in his famous "Life of Jesus," attempted to apply to the history of Christ's birth, life, sufferings, and death, needs to be known, as to its general features, before the remarks in the text above, and in many other parts of this work, can be understood. *Strauss* is a philosopher of the school of *Hegel*—an ultra-ideal school—and an avowed Pantheist. Entertaining such philosophical views, a miracle was, to him, impossible, and the history of Jesus could not, of course, be literally true; and, to account for the form of our present Gospel-narratives, he adopted a theory something like the following:—Jesus was a Jew, who, by early training, had become enthusiastically desirous of seeing the fulfilment of the prophecies, and, at length, believed himself to be the Messiah. Filled with the loftiest ideas of purity, and of the high destiny of man, He gathered around Him a band of devoted disciples, who were fired with something of His own enthusiasm. The leading idea enforced in His teaching, was the union attainable between the human mind and the divine. At length He died a violent death, from having incurred the hatred of the Pharisees. A mere skeleton is all that Strauss leaves of His life as historically true. It is not true, he says, that Christ was born of a virgin—that He wrought miracles—that He rose from the dead—and ascended to heaven. Then His disciples must have deceived us, we are ready to exclaim. No, says Strauss. The accounts of Him contained in the Gospels were the product of their fervid imaginations; and, without the slightest intention to deceive, there grew up among His followers a complete history, adorned with all that they thought could render their Master's memory glorious. The Old Testament was the principal source of the additions thus made to the simple narrative of Christ's life. Whatever they found there of endowments from above, was at once ascribed to the Saviour, who, in their view, must possess all that Heaven had ever bestowed on man. And, in particular, they sought to embody the main doctrine of their Master's teaching,—viz., the union of our souls with God, as the aim of life, in His person, by uniting in that person the divine and human natures.

Taken alone, the theory seems too baseless to have been seriously proposed and applied in two considerable volumes; but the history of religious opinion in Germany throws some light on its origin. What Kant and his followers denominated *moral interpretation,*—that is, giving a moral or spiritual meaning to historical facts,—had been exploded some time previously, and had been succeeded by the *natural* interpretation adopted by the Rationalist school, with *Paulus* at their head. This scheme had, in its turn, been exposed as utterly hollow, because it was plain that the Evangelists *meant* to give a miraculous history; and it is dishonest to interpret their language otherwise. Driven from these two refuges, those who would not take the Gospel-history as a miraculous one, were bound to give some explanation of the fact of such a history, so attested, being in existence. And, as it had been the fashion in Germany, to assume a mythical period in the history of Greece, and Rome, and many other nations, Strauss attempted to assign the history of Jesus to such a period. To attain his end, he is compelled to deny the genuineness of every one of the Gospels, and ascribes them all to a period subsequent to the first century of the Christian era. The theory hardly needs refutation. The work is a repository of all the difficulties that beset a harmony of the four Gospels; and, as such, may cause uneasiness to readers who are not properly acquainted with the solutions of those difficulties, both in general and in particular instances; but it could not satisfy any but a thoroughly infidel mind, glad to catch at any hypothesis that gives a semblance of ground for impugning the veracity of the witnesses of Christ's life.]—*Tr.*

§. 9. SURVEY OF THE LITERATURE.

As soon as the activity of the Apostles, who laboured chiefly in the living Word, ceased in the Church, the people betook themselves to those written legacies which they had bequeathed to the Church,—partly to gain a deeper acquaintance with the acknowledged truth through the contemplation of the written Word, and partly to separate, according to it, truth and falsehood. Since the second century, many distinguished men have devoted their powers to the exposition of the Holy Scriptures, and of the New Testament in particular. Nevertheless, its contents are yet unexhausted. The depth of the Word of God is so great, that it affords full satisfaction for all times and all relations, for every degree of cultivation and development. It is founded, however, in the nature of the Church's progress, that the ability of penetrating still more deeply and thoroughly into the understanding of the Scriptures, should be acquired by gradual advances. In particular, our times have made an immense advance in this point, that, in recognizing more and more the comprehensive sense of Scripture, we have learnt to regard the greatest part of the different expositions as not so much absolutely false, as rather taking in but one phase of the thought, whereby the labours of centuries to understand the Scriptures appear as connected and supplemental to one another; while, according to the view formerly prevalent, it was necessary to pronounce all the various expositions, except the *single* true one, a mass of errors. According to this, the Church of former ages could not, for the most part, have at all understood the Scriptures, which would be to say, in other words, that the Spirit had not been in the Church. We must rather say, that the Church has always understood the Bible aright in essentials; but that we have penetrated, step by step, more deeply into its correct comprehension.

In the first place, as respects the *general works* which comprise the whole New Testament, we do not possess a complete exposition of the whole New Testament by any of the teachers in the early Church; they used to apply themselves at first to single books. It is not till the ninth century, that the *Glossa Ordinaria*, by Walafrid Strabo, appears as a continuous commentary on the New Testament, if, indeed, it deserves the name of a commentary at all. Subsequently to him, Nicolaus de Lyra and Alphonsus Tostatus, Bishop of Avila, in Spain, wrote complete commentaries on the entire Scriptures—the latter in twenty-three folios. At the time of the Reformation, Calvin commented on the whole New Testament except the Revelation of St. John; as well as Johann Brenz, among the Lutherans, seven folios of whose works are filled with expositions of almost all the books in the Bible. In the seventeenth century, several works appeared, embracing the whole New Testament. Besides Hugo Grotius, (in his *Adnotationes in N. T.*, 2 vols. 4to,) we may notice particularly the collection of expositions under the name *Critici Sacri*, (London, 1660, 9 vols. fol.,) of which Polus [Pool] prepared an abridgment; and further, *Calovii Biblia*

Illustrata, (Francof. 1672, 4 vols. fol.,) a work which was directed against Grotius, and includes the exegetical works of the author. These were followed by Pfaff's edition of the Bible, Tübingen, 1729; Wolfii Curæ Philologicæ et Criticæ, Hamburg, 1738, 4 vols. 4to; Heumann's Erklärung des N. T., Hanover, 1750, 12 vols. 8vo; Moldenhauer's Erklärung der Schriften des N. T., Leipzig, 1763, 4 vols. 4to; J. D. Michaelis' Uebersetzung des N. T. mit Anmerkungen, Göttingen, 1789, 3 vols. 4to; Bengelii Gnomon N. T., Tubingæ, 1773, 4to; J. G. Rosenmülleri Scholia in N. T., Norimbergæ, 1777, 5 vols. 8vo. (The last edition [the sixth] appeared in 1825.] Henneberg planned a complete commentary on the New Testament; but only the first volume, containing St. Matthew, appeared, Gotha and Erfurt, 1829. The author died in 1831. H. A. W. Meyer has begun to prepare a commentary on the New Testament, of which four volumes have appeared up to the present time, containing the Gospels, the Acts of the Apostles, and the Epistle to the Romans.* Of De Wette's Exposition of the New Testament, the Epistle to the Romans and the synoptic Gospels have come out.† Among the general works on the New Testament, we must also reckon the well-known Observationen-Sammlungen, by Raphelius, (out of Xenophon, Hamb. 1720; out of Polybius and Arrian, Hamb. 1715; out of Herodotus, Lüneb. 1731,) Alberti, (Leiden, 1725,) Kypke, (Breslau, 1725,) Elsner, (Utrecht, 1728,) Palairet, (Leiden, 1752.)

As regards the *Gospel-collection*,‡ the expositions of Theophylact and Euthymius Zigabenus have come down to us. The ancient exposition which Theophilus of Antioch is said to have composed on the four Gospels, is lost. Of the time of the Reformation, Mart. Chemnitzii Harmonia Quatuor Evangeliorum, continued by Polycarpus Lyser and Johann Gerhard, (Hamb. 1704, 3 vols. fol.,) is particularly distinguished. Clericus also composed a similar harmony. (Amsterd. 1669, fol.) Of more recent times, the following include all the four Gospels: Köcheri Analecta, (Altenb. 1766, 4to,) which are supplementary to Wolf's Curæ; J. F. G. Schulz, Anmerkungen über die vier

---

* [This commentary is now nearly completed.]—*Tr.*
† [This commentary has since been completed.]—*Tr.*
‡ For the complete literature of the Gospel harmonies, see Hase's Leben Jesu, S. 18, ff.

Evangelien, Halle, 1794, 4to; Ch. Th. Kuinoel Commentarius in Libros N. T. Historicos, Lips. 1807, 4 vols. 8vo, (including the Acts of the Apostles;) Paulus, philologisch-kritischer Commentar über das N. T., Lübeck, 1800-1808, 5 vols.; also his Exegetisches Handbuch über die drei ersten Evangelien, Heidelberg, 1830, 1831, 2 vols.; Fritzsche, evangelia quatuor cum Notis, Lips. 1825, 1830, 8vo. The first volume comprises St. Matthew, the second St. Mark.

Lastly, as regards the *single* Gospels. Among the Fathers we possess fragments of a commentary on St. Matthew by Origen. Chrysostom wrote ninety-one homilies on the Gospel by St. Matthew. Possin published a *catena* on this Evangelist, Tolosæ, 1646. In later times Salomo van Till, Frankf. 1708, and Jac. Elsner, Zwoll. 1769, 4to, wrote upon St. Matthew. Also, Götz, Erklärung des Matthäus aus dem Griechisch-Hebräischen und dem Hebräischen, Stuttgardt, 1785, 8vo; Heddäus, Erklärung des Matthäus, Stuttgardt and Tübingen, 1792, 2 vols; Der Bericht des Matthäus von Jesus dem Messias, by Bolten, Altona, 1792, 8vo; Kleuker's Biblische Sympathicen, Schleswig, 1820; Das Evangelium Matthäi, erklärt von Gratz (of Bonn,) Tübingen, 1821, 2 vols. 8vo; Pires, Commentarius in Evangelium Matthæi, Mogunt., 1825.

On the Gospel by St. Mark we have, likewise, a *catena* edited by Possin, Rome, 1673. Jac. Elsner wrote a commentary upon St. Mark, Utrecht, 1773; and Bolten also, Altona, 1795, 8vo; Matthäi published an Exposition of St. Mark, by Victor, a presbyter of Antioch, and other Greek fathers, Moscow, 1775, 2 vols. 8vo.

Lastly, in reference to St. Luke, we have *catena* on it by Corderius, Antwerpen, 1628. This Gospel was separately commented on by Pape, Bremen, 1777, 1781, 2 vols. 8vo; by Bolten, Altona, 1796, 8vo. We have also Morus, Prælectiones in Lucæ Evangelium, published by C. A. Donat. Leipz. 1795, 8vo. The latest works on Luke, are Scholia in Lucam scripsit Bornemann, Lips. 1830; and Stein's Commentar über den Lucas. Halle, 1831.

SYNOPTICAL EXPOSITION

OF THE

FIRST THREE GOSPELS.

FIRST PART.

OF THE
BIRTH AND CHILDHOOD OF JESUS CHRIST.

FIRST SECTION.—ST. MATTHEW'S ACCOUNT.
CHAPTERS I. AND II.

§ 1. GENEALOGY OF JESUS.

(Matth. i. 1-17; Luke iii. 23-38.)

WHILE St. Mark at once, in the title of his Gospel, (Mark i. 1,) describes Christ as the Son of God, St. Matthew represents Him as the Son of Man, since he first characterizes Him as the descendant of the two great heads of the Old Testament economy,—Abraham and David,—and then introduces His entire genealogy. The character of St. Matthew's Gospel, as σωματικόν, in the nobler sense of the word, and its special adaptation for Jewish Christians, shew themselves, in this form of beginning, too plainly to be mistaken. Since Jesus is introduced as υἱὸς Ἀβραάμ, He appears as the descendant of him whose family is blessed among the families of mankind; but, as Son of David, He was more definitely assigned to a branch of the Abrahamites,—viz., the family of him who, even in the Old Testament, is described as the representative of the future head of the kingdom of God. Both expressions, therefore, point out Jesus as the promised Messiah. Yet this is more expressly conveyed in the name Ἰησοῦς Χριστός. Ἰησοῦς* denotes primarily only the

---

* The LXX. use Ἰησοῦς for יְהוֹשֻׁעַ or יֵשׁוּעַ, which latter form is first found in writings after the time of the captivity. The name marks out our Lord's spiritual character, and was given to Him by divine command, (Matth.

human individual—the historical person of the Saviour; Χριστός, on the other hand, is the official name for the desired deliverer of Israel. It corresponds to the Hebrew מָשִׁיחַ, which word is used in the Old Testament, sometimes of kings, (1 Sam. xxiv. 7, 11; xxvi. 16, and frequently;) sometimes of high-priests, (Lev. iv. 3, 5, 16, and frequently;) sometimes of prophets, (Psalm cv. 15;) because all these persons were consecrated to their office by the symbolical rite of anointing, (on the anointing of prophets see 1 Kings xix. 16,) to intimate, that for the due discharge of their office, they must be endowed with spiritual powers. It is only rarely that the expression is used in the Old Testament of the royal prophet and high-priest of the kingdom of God. (Psalm ii. 2; Daniel ix. 25.) Out of these passages, with which others were connected, in which the anointing was viewed spiritually, arose the name Χριστός, which, even at the time of Christ, was the prevailing official designation of the great desired one. (See Isaiah lxi. 1, compared with Luke iv. 18.) In this view, the name "Christ" expresses the union of the divine and human natures in the person of the Saviour, since the humanity is the anointed—the endowed; the divine power is the anointing—the endowing. Originally the Saviour was called either ὁ Ἰησοῦς, with reference to His historical *individuality*, or ὁ Χριστός, with reference to His *dignity*; also, Ἰησοῦς ὁ λεγόμενος Χριστός, (Matth. i. 16, on which consult the commentary.) It was not till afterwards that the two terms were compounded into the united appellation Ἰησοῦς Χριστός, which, however, is always, properly speaking, to be resolved in the manner above-mentioned.

The first verse in St. Matthew does not, in all probability, form merely a superscription for the subsequent genealogy. Βίβλος γενέσεως (= סֵפֶר תּוֹלְדֹת Gen. v. 1) means primarily, "book of the descent," "genealogy." The expression cannot possibly have reference to the *whole* life of Jesus, because γένεσις nowhere means "life." The meaning, "family memoirs," however, which תּוֹלְדוֹת undoubtedly has, (see Gen. xxxvii. 2, αὗται αἱ γενέσεις Ἰακώβ, where no genealogical tables whatever are mentioned,) is quite applicable in this place, and warrants our refer-

---

i. 21,) to intimate His exalted calling. Just so the Old Testament names, Abraham, Israel, and others, denote the spiritual character which those persons were called to exhibit amongst mankind.

ring the expression to the history of the childhood of Jesus contained in the first two chapters. This supposition would agree very well with the view, according to which the early chapters of St. Matthew (and St. Luke) are regarded as separate memoirs, which, having had their origin in the bosom of Mary's family, afterwards came into the hands of the Evangelists. But the genealogy in St. Matthew, compared with that of St. Luke, shews plainly the different character of the two Gospels. While St. Matthew begins with Abraham, the ancestor of the Jewish people, St. Luke ascends to Adam, the first father of the whole human race,—of the heathen also,—and thus connects the Saviour with human nature as such, apart from all national individuality. But in the particulars we find the two genealogies at variance from David downwards, since St. Matthew continues the line of generations through Solomon, St. Luke through another son of David—Nathan. Two names only—Salathiel and Zorobabel, (see Luke iii. 27, compared with Matth. i. 12)—are the same in both, the rest being quite different; but these persons must be regarded as living at different times, because in St. Matthew nine persons are enumerated between them and Jesus, and in St. Luke seventeen.* The difficulty, that St. Matthew and St. Luke give quite different genealogies of Jesus, was the subject of learned investigations, even in the earliest times of the Church; *Julius Africanus*, in particular, gave his attention to it, (*Euseb.* H. E. i. 7.) Three hypotheses† for the solution of this difficulty have been framed with uncommon acuteness : 1. The supposition of a levirate marriage, (Deut. xxv. 6 ;) in which case, however, to explain all, we must further suppose, that the two brothers, who had the same wife, one after the other, were not properly brothers, but step-brothers, sons of the same mother by different fathers; because, if they had been by one father, the genealogy would have been the same. This hypothesis was first propounded by *Julius Africanus* (*ut supra.*) Agreeably to it, the descent would be as follows:—

---

* [There are ten in St. Matthew, and nineteen in St. Luke, including Joseph in both cases.]—*Tr.*

† Other attempts at explaining this difficulty are to be found in *Wolf's* Curæ, and *Köcher's* Analecta, but they are futile. Consult also *Surenhusius'* βίβλος καταλλαγῆς, page 322, *seqq.*

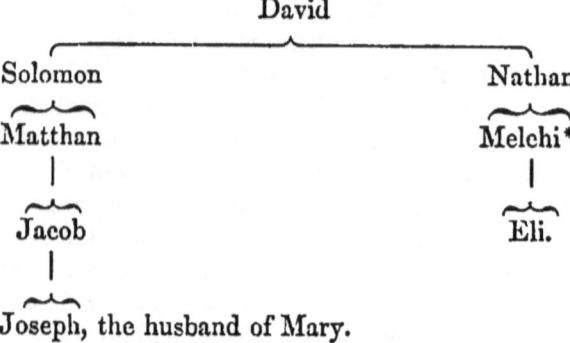

Joseph, the husband of Mary.

This hypothesis explains the difference; yet, in the first place, the supposition that Jacob and Eli had the same wife, one after the other, and were, moreover, step-brothers, is rather harsh; further, it cannot be demonstrated with certainty that it was the practice to take the *name* of the real father in the case of obligatory marriages; and lastly, both genealogies would be those of Joseph, which appears unsuitable on this account, that Jesus, according to the flesh, was descended from David and Abraham, not through Joseph, but through Mary. That step-brothers, and still more distant relations, were also bound to fulfil the levirate marriage, is shewn by *J. D. Michaelis*, in his Commentaries on the Laws of Moses, (Smith's translation.) 2. The assumption that Mary was an heiress, (ἐπίκληρος,) in which case she would be obliged to marry within her own tribe. (Numb. xxxvi. 5-8.) The husband of an heiress was at the same time obliged to enter himself in the family of his wife, and so came to have as it were two fathers. In this way one of the genealogies would indeed be that of Mary; but the latter circumstance, —viz., the being received into the wife's family, and the taking the name of the father-in-law on the part of those who married heiresses, which in this case is all-important, is exactly what is uncertain; at least Nehemiah vii. 63 is not sufficient to establish it.† This hypothesis, however, though it does not suffice for solving the difficulty, is very suitable for explaining Mary's journey to Bethlehem. (Luke ii. 4.) In general it seems

---

* *Julius Africanus* omits Matthan and Levi, and appears, therefore, to have had another reading before him, or to have transposed the names. The name, however, make no difference to the hypothesis.

† See *J. D. Michaelis'* Commentaries on the Laws of Moses, (Smith's translation.)

appropriate for the development of David's family, that that line of it out of which the Messiah was to proceed, should close with an heiress, who ended it in giving birth to the promised everlasting heir of the throne of David. We may, therefore, combine the opinion, that Mary was an heiress, with (3) the third hypothesis, according to which the genealogy of Mary is given by St. Luke, that of Joseph by St. Matthew. Thus Jesus is shewn, as well on the father's as the mother's side, to be of the house of David. On the mother's side the descent had a real importance, on the father's an ostensible one. For, as Jesus passed in the eyes of the world for the son of Joseph, (see note on Matth. xiii. 55,) the Jews acknowledged Him in this respect also to be of the house of David; and on this account not a doubt of His descent from David is ever uttered by His enemies. Agreeably to this hypothesis, Eli (Luke iii. 23) would be the father of Mary, (with which the Jewish tradition coincides, see *Lightfoot, ad loc.;*) and when Joseph is called his son, "*son*" (υἱός) is here to be taken in the sense of "son-in-law," as Ruth i. 11, 12, and frequently. Genealogical tables are, indeed, unusual in the case of women, but for heiresses they *must* necessarily exist; besides which, the case of Mary was altogether of an extraordinary kind. The real descent of Jesus from David through Mary, is, moreover, by no means to be regarded as a merely external fact, intended to fulfil the prophecies. The prophecy that the Messiah should descend from Abraham and David, is rather itself to be viewed as more deeply rooted. The appearance of the Messiah among mankind, presupposes conditions and preparations, of a kind not merely *negative*, inasmuch as the need of salvation had to be brought home to the minds of men, but also *positive*, inasmuch as the coming of the Messiah, as the flower of mankind, could not be anything separate from the root. We must look upon the incarnation of Christ as a fact, for which preparation was made, by a vein of nobler life flowing through the whole line of our Lord's ancestors. The virgin chosen to be the mother of the Messiah could not be born on a sudden in the midst of a sinful family. Although not without sin, she was the purest of that generation. And that she was such, was in consequence of her election by grace—her being born of the holiest family of mankind. As in the development of the human race we observe certain families growing in sin and wickedness, so we find families, also, in which the noblest germs of life are possessed and cherished from generation to generation. Of course, this is not to be interpreted as if those families which have been, through grace, more defended from the corruption of sin, had no need of salvation,—that need is rather to be viewed as absolute and equally necessary for all men,—but their readiness to receive salvation is greater, since, as being of the truth, they more certainly hear God's call.

In the following enumeration of the links of the genealogy, St. Matthew omits several, e. g. ver. 8, between Joram and Josias. (See 1 Chron. iii. 11; 2 Chron. xxi. 17.) St. Luke, on the contrary, inserts Cainan in iii. 36, whom the Hebrew text does not mention. Doubtless, this name is derived from the LXX., which St. Luke, as a Hellenist, used for the most part. The LXX. translators may have received it from tradition. (Respecting such variations of the LXX. from the original Hebrew, which have been admitted into the New Testament, see the remarks on Luke iv. 18.)

Ver. 2.—Throughout the whole genealogical table, St. Luke appears in the character of a relater merely, while St. Matthew adds reflections; he divides the list into certain classes, and adds particular observations. Of Judas he remarks that he had brothers; probably because the patriarchs of Israel—the twelve sons of Jacob—appeared to call for special notice. The same remark is made of Jechonias (ver. 11;) in which passage, however, the term ἀδελφοί must be taken in a wider sense, like אח (Gen. xiii. 8.) of father's brothers, as Jechonias had no actual brothers. (1 Chron. iii. 15, 16.)

Ver. 3.—It is also peculiar to the genealogy in St. Matthew, that it several times mentions women,—a circumstance which did occur in Jewish genealogies, if anything remarkable gave them special interest. (See *Surenhusii*, βιβλ. καταλλ. p. 110.) Tamar, (Gen. xxxviii.) Rahab, (Josh. ii.) Ruth, Bathsheba, are named by St. Matthew. Tamar, Rahab,* and Bathsheba, appear scandalous in their lives; Ruth as a heathen (Moabitess.) That they were nevertheless counted worthy to be among the

---

* Whether it is Rahab ἡ πόρνη, that is meant, might seem uncertain, because of the chronology; she comes too near to Obed and Jesse, David's ancestors; yet the expression ἡ 'Ραχάβ (with the article) plainly points to the well-known Rahab mentioned in Josh. ii. Perhaps St. Matthew has omitted some links.

ancestors of our Lord, could not therefore but give them a peculiar importance. St. Matthew makes this circumstance still more prominent by the designation ἐκ τῆς τοῦ Οὐρίου, in order to point to the wondrous leadings of God in the arrangement of the Messiah's lineage. As examples of the election of grace, of renovation by faith and repentance, and of being received out of heathen families among the people of God, the persons named are noticed even by the Rabbins. (See *Wetstein's New Test.*, on ver. 3 compared with Heb. xi. 31.) If it had not been St. Matthew's intention to point out these leadings of God, he would have preferred the mention of the renowned names of Sarah, Rebecca, Leah, in the genealogy of the Messiah.

Ver. 6.—David, as a principal person, as it were a knot in the genealogical tree of the Messiah, is called emphatically ὁ βασιλεύς, as a type of the Messianic king. (Ezek. xxxvii. 24, and other places.) A similar break is made afterwards, (ver. 11,) by the μετοικεσία Βαβυλῶνος = αἰχμαλωσία. The LXX. use μετοικεσία for גָּלוּת (Ezek. xxxiii. 21.)

Ver. 16.—The term ἀνήρ in this verse, answers to *sponsus*, (v. 19;) according to Jewish law, the bridegroom was already regarded as the possessor of the bride. (Gen. xxix. 21; Deut. xxii. 23, 24.) St. Matthew expresses himself very carefully: ἐξ ἧς ἐγεννήθη Ἰησοῦς, in order to mark the supernatural character of the generation of Christ; γεννᾶν is used as equivalent to τίκτειν. (Luke i. 13.) In the phrase, Ἰησοῦς ὁ λεγόμενος Χριστός—Χριστός appears evidently as the official name. With the exception of this phrase, St. Matthew almost always uses ὁ Ἰησοῦς, or ὁ Χριστός. It was only gradually that, in the usage of the Church, the name expressive of the human individuality of the Saviour grew up into so close a connexion with His official name, that the two have formed a whole, as is particularly the case in the Apostle Paul's writings. (See *Gersdorf's* Beiträge zur Sprachcharacteristik, S. 38, ff., 272, ff.) The λέγεσθαι, in the phrase under remark, like καλεῖσθαι = נִקְרָא (on which see comment. on Luke i. 32,) has, in this place, the pregnant meaning, "to be called, and really to be." In the opposite sense, "to be called, without being," the expression occurs in Ephes. ii. 11, and Matth. xxvii. 17. The phrase has frequently no emphasis, either the one way or the other, as in Matth. xxvi. 14, Mark xv. 7.

Ver. 17.—St. Matthew closes his genealogical account with a

review of the different divisions which may be made in the generations from Abraham to Christ. He notices three such, of fourteen generations each,* which may, however, be reckoned in more than one way. That reckoning appears the most convenient, according to which David and Josias are reckoned twice,† (at the close of one and the beginning of another division,) and Jesus omitted. If the person of Jesus is to be reckoned as forming the close of the third division, David only ought to be reckoned twice. The former plan appears to me, however, preferable. It is fitting not to include Jesus himself in the generations, just as we do not ordinarily in reckoning a person's ancestry. Besides, since St. Matthew, as was remarked, has omitted some links, it cannot be his intention to lay stress on the number fourteen, and as little ought this arrangement to be regarded as a mere help for the memory. Rather it is the Evangelist's purpose, by means of the equal number, to point out the inward symmetry and regularity of the historical development.‡ As the whole history of the world moves forward in its development by measured periods, and as, in general, every greater or lesser whole, in the wide creation of God, has its inward gradations of progress, through which it advances to its completion, so there is a regularity in the development of that family also, as it were the inmost life-pulse of mankind, of which the Messiah was to come. *Bengel* recognized correctly this fundamental view, (in his Gnomon on the passage ;) but

---

* Whether the number fourteen has a reference to the name David, the Hebrew letters of which, reckoned according to the Jewish custom, make up the number fourteen, it might be difficult to decide. Such a supposition might, however, agree well enough with the complexion of St. Matthew's whole description. The number fourteen is moreover to be regarded as twice seven,—a number which the Scriptures treat as a sacred one. The three times fourteen thus become six times seven, and the seventh seven opens with the person of Christ.

† Similar modes of reckoning are met with in other cases. A simple Nazarite vow lasted thirty days, a double one not sixty, but only fifty-nine days, because the day in the middle was reckoned twice. The Germans call a week eight days, "acht Tage," but two weeks, fourteen days, "vierzehn Tage;" while the French call two weeks, "quinze jours."

‡ The omission of some links may be ascribed to the authors of the genealogy in Joseph's family. St. Matthew took it as he found it, without making any alteration in it, and, of course, the remarks made upon it could only apply to it in its present form. The want of some of the links can have no influence on the truth of the remarks themselves, inasmuch as the fundamental thought, that all things unfold themselves in God's world according to measure and number, applies no less to the complete genealogy than to the shortened one.

the particulars which he adds, as well as his whole chronological system, which he brings into connexion with it, appear to me untenable. (Compare further remarks on this subject in the Commentary on the Revelation of St. John.)

Something unique and unexampled presents itself, too, in a family table of three times fourteen, and seventy-five ancestors respectively, extending through 2000 or 4000 years, with which the Evangelists open the life of Christ. The possibility of exhibiting such a genealogical table, always proceeding in the directest line of descent from father to son, and that, too, of a family long living in the deepest obscurity, would be inexplicable, (since even the distinguished families, on whose genealogies millions gaze, cannot trace their pedigree a thousand years, and none of them, too, ascends in a direct line,) if there had not been constantly given to the members of this line of ancestors, a clue by which they were enabled to trace themselves out in the midst of the number of families, into which each trunk and branch was subdivided, in order to hold fast *that* member which was destined to continue the succession. This clue was the hope, that the Messiah would be born in the family of Abraham and David. The desire of beholding Him, and of participating in His grace and glory, suffered not the attention to weary through thousands of years.* Agreeably to divine arrangement also, from time to time, as the member that continued the succession might become doubtful, it was again plainly marked out; so that the hope of the final fulfilment was anew excited and maintained in activity up to its realization. An excellent view of the wonderful circumstances discoverable in the construction of these genealogies, is given by *Köppen* in his book: Die Bibel ein Werk der göttlichen Weisheit, (Leipzig, 1798, 2 vols. 8vo, compare B. ii., S. 199, ff. ;)—a new edition of this work is being prepared by Scheibel.

§ 2. THE BIRTH OF JESUS.
(Matth. i. 18-23.)

St. Matthew's account of the birth of Jesus is characterized

---

* That the Jews of later time also bestowed great care upon their family registers, is shewn by *Julius Africanus*, as quoted by *Euseb.* i. 7. *Herod* had them all sought out and burnt, so that no one should be able to prove that his family was more ancient than the king's.

by the greatest simplicity and brevity. There
chronological or topographical reference in the
persons are supposed to be, in general, alread
readers. The great fact of the supernatural l
simply narrated as sober history, without any
the fulfilment of Old Testament prediction in i
last of all, the providential guidance of Joseph,
event, is recorded. We readily pass by the
stantial vividness, which this part of St. Matthe
common with his whole Gospel, discovers, for
sober earnestness of really historical narrative
minent throughout; the more so, as the poetica
Luke's narrative render that feature less perv
scholars, therefore, are in error, who, while
application of the mythical interpretation of the
throughout, have yet thought it necessary
mythical influences in the history of His birt
For it is just at this part that the inadmissi
supposition most strikingly appears, since, if tl
take place just as the Evangelists record the
ceptions about the origin of Jesus obtrude ther
For as Christ is undeniably a historical person,
fore have been begotten and born, to affir
character of the Gospel-history, can only favou
destructive of the notion of a Saviour,—viz.,
into existence in an impure manner, since Mai
at the time she conceived Him. The suggesti
an escape, that Jesus might have sprung from
Mary and Joseph, is self-refuted by its unhist
for if the circumstance, that Mary was with
marriage, is to be reckoned among the myths, t
that she gave birth to Jesus, and even that Jo
may equally well be reckoned among them.

Besides, it appears, on closer consideration
parently most recommends the mythical inter
history of the childhood of Jesus, is rather
it. This holds good particularly of the appe
to the traditions of the birth of great men fr
($\pi\alpha\rho\theta\epsilon\nu o\gamma\epsilon\nu\epsilon\tilde{\iota}\varsigma$,) as of Buddha, Zoroaster, Plato, ar
traditions are in no way opposed to the Bible h
than are analogous longings for a Saviour wl

expected. They rather witness to the thoroughly correct feeling of the noblest men among different nations, that, in the way of *natural* generation, nothing can proceed answering to the ideal exhibited in the human spirit. They witness to the general longing and desire for such a fact—to the truth of it in some one historical manifestation. Now, as we have so sober a historical account of the supernatural generation of Jesus in a pure virgin, as that of St. Matthew, which appears to be made studiously dry, in order to keep everything fanciful at a distance; further, as the whole manifestation of Jesus during His life confirms the opinion that He was born in a supernatural manner, since the ideal of all ideals is realized in Him, which could never proceed from sinful humanity and the power inherent in it; there is perfect historical foundation for the conviction, that this general longing is fulfilled in the person of Jesus. *In addition to this*, the narrative of the generation of Christ by the Holy Ghost, stands in necessary connexion with His whole destination to be the physician and the Saviour of diseased mankind, since it is impossible that any one who is himself descended from lost mankind could have any power to heal the hurt from which they suffer. It was necessary, indeed, that He should be most closely united with men, flesh of their flesh, bone of their bone, (Ephes. v. 36,) yet, at the same time, without sin; wherefore, He was not begotten by any man of sinful seed, but Mary was touched with pure divine fire from heaven. If, then, we see in the person of Christ not a merely human appearance, however exalted in power, but believe in an incarnation of the Word of God in Him, (John i. 1, 14,) not only can the narrative of the supernatural generation of Jesus present nothing astonishing, but it becomes even natural to the Saviour. A Saviour conceived in sin—sprung from the sinful race of man, is a self-contradictory notion; the very idea of a σωτήρ requires, that in Him there should be manifested something higher, something heavenly, that cannot be derived from what exists in human nature itself.* But, *lastly*, the mythical view of the

---

* The opinion that we might conceive, that, as the transfer of anything sinful from Mary to Jesus was prevented, *it could just as well have been prevented if Joseph had been His father in the ordinary way*, only shifts the miracle to a different quarter, without getting rid of it. If we actually suppose such an influence of the Holy Ghost to stay the transfer of what was sinful to Jesus, that is no less a miracle than His generation by the Holy Spirit. But wherefore should we make the miracles other than it has pleased the Spirit of God to present them to us?

history of Christ's childhood must be seen to be untenable for this reason, that Mary, the mother of Jesus, lived until a considerable time after the ascension. Her statements were accessible to each of the Apostles,—any error could immediately have been set aside by her testimony.

With respect to *the appearances of angels*, the mention of which in St. Matthew's narrative might be regarded as the most important point in proof of its mythical character, we must, in interpreting, chiefly keep in view, that the historian *reports as facts* the appearances of angels in this, as well as in other places of his Gospel. Quite after the manner of the Old Testament, St. Matthew places the visions of angels, as real occurrences in the present economy, along with the other facts to be recorded, without the slightest hint being given that the author himself intended them to be regarded either as a mythical expression for internal pyschological occurrences, (tricks of thought called up by surrounding circumstances,) or as in any other respect different. The business of the expositor extends beyond the ascertaining of the author's view only in so far as he not merely expounds, but also vindicates the result of the exposition; a duty which, in the position that science now takes up, cannot be neglected. The following observations may suffice to meet the requirements of the present case. On the testimony of the Scriptures, we are not to conceive of the angels as separated from men by an impassable gulf; according to it, they are, on the contrary, actively employed around and in men,—especially in the faithful. (Heb. i. 14.) Usually, however, their service is an invisible one. The possibility of their becoming visible lies in the nature of spirit itself, whose indwelling energy involves a capacity of making itself visible. This possibility exists, however, actually, by God's direction only, in those cases where it subserves men's good,—that is, for the purpose of instruction and guidance. For the appearances of angels, like other σημεῖα, are intended to give to man the assurance of his being led by God, to save him from his tendencies to error. In this consists their importance in the divine economy; but, compared with other forms of divine communication, they are manifestly of a subordinate nature. The agency of angels has reference principally to the physical part of existence. They are the living supports and springs of motion to the world, for which the modern mechanical view of the world has substituted what are called powers of nature. The religio-ethical world is the scene of the divine Spirit's agency. On this principle we can explain why to one, an angel appears, (sometimes in a dream, sometimes waking,) and to another, the Lord. Caprice is inconceivable in the case; on the contrary, the different forms of the revelations are calculated for the condition of those to whom they are granted. Communication by dream is plainly seen to be the lowest grade of divine revelation; it is, as it were, one that takes place in an unconscious state; it is the kind made to Joseph, as, from the Gospel narrative, there is no decidedly spiritual character apparent in him. From the appearances of angels seen in a waking state, the form of communication rises to a revelation received through the word within, which was the usual form of receiving the higher influences in the cases of Moses and all the prophets. The revelation of Jehovah himself, or of *the* Angel κατ᾽ἐξοχήν, appears to be the highest grade, which was granted only to the princes among the saints,—an Abraham, a Jacob, a Moses, and a Paul. The Church of Christ needs no longer any appearances of angels, as it possesses the very source of all truth in the Holy Ghost given to it. The *form* in which angels appeared (with wings, garments, and the like) should be regarded as quite accidental, determined solely by the conditions under which the appearance happened to take place. On the part of him who sees the angels, the unclosing of the inward eye is an invariable prerequisite. Appearances of the heavenly world cannot, like the objects of the outward world, be beheld by every one with the bodily eye. Even if other persons are present, he only for whom the appearance is appointed, sees the angel. Thus the angels were ascending and descending upon Jesus at the very moment that He was speaking the words in John i. 51 to the Apostles; but their inward eye was still closed to the transactions of the world of spirits. Every appearance of angels, accordingly, should be conceived not merely as an outward act, but also as an inward effect in the subject who sees it. (See Numb. xxii. 31.) Lastly, Christ, the Lord, *had* no revelation,* but *was*, not merely *a*, but *the*

---

* It is in appearance only that such passages as Luke xxii. 43, which speaks of an angel appearing to Christ in Gethsemane, are opposed to this thought. For that angel revealed nothing to Him, but was concerned only with His physical exhaustion;—he appeared to Him merely for the purpose of strengthening Him in body.

revelation of God in human nature itself; on Him the angels of God ascended and descended,—*i. e.*, He is the centre and the medium of connexion between the visible and the invisible world; so that the entire reciprocal action of these two portions of existence is conducted and ordered by Him. (See note on John i. 51.)

Ver. 18.—The first narrative after the genealogy is introduced with a special title, in which Ἰησοῦ is, in all probability, a spurious addition. (See *Gersdorf, ut sup.* p. 39.) Γένεσις, as the more Hebraizing reading, (= תּוֹלְדוֹת,) is preferable to γέννησις. Μαρία, also Μαριάμ, corresponds to the Hebrew מִרְיָם. (Exod. xv. 20; Num. xii. 1.) The anxiety of the Evangelist to represent Mary as pure and innocent, cannot fail to be noticed. In addition to μνηστευθείσης γὰρ τῆς μητρὸς αὐτοῦ, he says expressly, πρὶν ἢ συνελθεῖν αὐτούς. Συνελθεῖν (parallel with παραλαβεῖν, ver. 20, 25) denotes living and dwelling together as husband and wife. Εὑρίσκεσθαι is not used absolutely for εἶναι, any more than נִמְצָא is so used; it rather expresses "being," with the additional idea of "being recognized as such." (On ἐκ πνεύματος ἁγίου, see note on Luke i. 35.)

Ver. 19.—St. Matthew's account leaves the impression, that Mary did not make known her condition to Joseph. (On this point, see further the remarks on Luke ii. 39.) When he noticed it himself, he sought to put her away without a stir, (λάθρα,—*i. e.*, without mentioning the cause in the writing of divorcement.) Ἀπολύειν denotes the formal dismissal by a written declaration. (Deut. xxiv. 1.) According to Jewish custom, Joseph treated his betrothed just as his wife;[*] but shewed himself to be δίκαιος. This term cannot here, as in Luke i. 6, signify one who diligently fulfils the precepts of the law; for, according to them, he ought to have preferred an accusation against his betrothed. (Deut. xxii. 23, ff.) But he is called kind, mild. *Chrysostom:* χρηστός, ἐπιεικής. (Concerning the significations of δίκαιος and its derivatives, compare the remarks on Rom. iii. 21.) Παραδειγματίζειν, to make a παράδειγμα, contains the idea of φανερῶσαι, but with the accessory idea of disgrace. (Heb. vi. 6.) Thus, therefore, the Father left His only-begotten Son

---

[*] *Maimonides* apud Buxt. de divort. pag. 76. Femina ex quo desponsata est, licet nondum a viro cognita, est uxor viri et, si sponsus eam velit repudiare, oportet ut id faciat libello repudii.

and His mother, just as He does His people in the Church, to pass through evil and through good report! That God permitted even the appearance of having committed sin to rest upon Mary, (for her pregnancy must, in any case, have appeared premature,) must be regarded, in reference to Mary, as a trial intended to perfect her faith; but in reference to Christ, as an additional trait in the character of His humiliation: He had to appear as sent in the likeness of sinful flesh. (Rom. viii. 3.)

Ver. 20.—That this intention, to which he thought himself compelled, should have caused a great commotion in Joseph's soul, may be supposed probable. But, apart from what naturally passed in his mind, or from any dreams or sports of fancy possibly arising thence, a higher influence is distinguished, which was imparted to Joseph in a dream, and which determined him in his conduct towards Mary, as narrated ver. 24, 25. There is nothing in the text to call for the supposition of anything externally visible in the appearance of this angel; as Joseph saw him in a dream, it is best to view the vision as an inward one. That same God, who most expressly warns against false dreams, (Jer. xxiii. 32, xxix. 8,) not unfrequently directs His people by true ones, (Numb. xii. 6;) since, for the sincere, who were really concerned for the truth, and for what was well-pleasing to God, He discovers infallible criteria of genuine appearances by dreams, in order to distinguish them from false ones. Yet these are modified by individual disposition, and cannot, therefore, be reduced to any objective rules; all divine directions, whether by dreams or any other communications, are dependent upon the inward earnestness and sincerity of the heart; the insincere man always hears and sees falsely, when he is determined hastily to seize divine hints for himself.— ('Ενθυμεῖσθαι is, to revolve in the θυμός, with the exercise of the affections. [See Matth. ix. 4; Acts x. 19.] Κατ' ὄναρ occurs only in Matth. ii. 12, 13, 19, 22; xxvii. 19. The phrase καθ' ὕπαρ is its opposite, but does not occur in the New Testament. Ἐν αὐτῇ = ἐν τῇ κοιλίᾳ αὐτῆς, the child unborn, yet reposing in the womb of its mother, but still already existing. The preposition ἐκ, denotes the Holy Spirit to be the creative cause of the child's existence.)

Ver. 21.—The indefinite neuter (γεννηθέν) is more precisely characterized as Son; the name to be given to Him is mentioned, and the meaning of His name, in relation to His appointed work, is set forth. A significance in names is found throughout the Scriptures. A name, according to its proper intention, should not be arbitrary, but should express the nature of him who bears it. By sin, this original meaning of names is destroyed, since it extinguished the capacity of ascertaining the inward essence; in the principal characters, however, who stand as the bearers of what is noble among our race, the Spirit from above supplied this deficiency. The last words of the verse declare the great and exalted appointment of this divinely-begotten one; He is described as the σωτήρ (יְהוֹשׁוּעַ) of His people. The expression λαός = עַם stands for the Jewish people, in opposition to the ἔθνη = גּוֹיִם, although ἔθνος also sometimes denotes the Jewish people. (John xi. 51.) That the angel, on this occasion, regards the appointment of the Messiah only in relation to the Jewish people, is in the same sense as Jesus himself describes it. (See note on Matth. x. 5, 6.) The Jews had, in fact, according to the whole divine economy and plan of salvation, the first call and appointment to the σωτηρία. The relation to the heathen is by no means excluded thereby; the Saviour's people (λαός) is, in a wider sense, the whole spiritual Israel,—all minds desirous of righteousness and truth, among all people, tribes, and tongues. (John x. 16.) The addition of ἀπὸ τῶν ἁμαρτιῶν, is significant of the character of the promised salvation. The moral import of the redemption to be looked for through the Messiah, which, at the time of Christ, was lost among the common mass of the Jews, but not among the noble-minded of the people, is very prominent in this phrase, and cannot be denied, except by such as are blinded by partiality; for it corresponds to the expression in the parallel passage, (Luke i. 77,) the ἄφεσις τῶν ἁμαρτιῶν. Σώσει ἀπὸ τῶν ἁμαρτιῶν denotes, as it were, their removal,—*i. e.*, their extinction. To refer ἁμαρτία to the punishment of sin, (and, indeed, to the most external, the oppression of the Romans,) is incorrect, for this reason, that ἁμαρτία never does, and never can, signify the punishment of sin *without* the sin, but only *together with* it.

Ver. 22, 23.—The following words are evidently not the words of the angel, but of the Evangelist, who is referring his Jewish readers to the Old Testament, in order to prove to them, that what was new in the Gospel, already existed in the sacred foundation on which their faith rested. The Lord himself appears as the effective cause, (ὑπό like ἐκ above, is used of the source, the origin;) the prophet appears only as the intermediate organ. (Διά, as distinguished from ὑπό, denotes the instrument, by means of which something is accomplished.) But, with respect to the formula: ἵνα or ὅπως πληρωθῇ, which appears to be a standing one, particularly with St. Matthew, it is evident, in the first place, that the New Testament writers themselves understood it, according to the natural meaning of the words;—that is to say, πληροῦσθαι, in the sense of something that was promised in time past, being realized at the present time; so that πληροῦσθαι always supposes a previous promise. The conjunction ἵνα cannot be translated *so that*, denoting a *result*, (ἐκβατικῶς,) but must always be taken as expressing an *intention*, (τελικῶς,) *to the end that, in order that*. In the whole formula it is evident, that the event being *intended*, is just what is meant to be brought into notice; and πληροῦσθαι itself necessarily leads us to this idea. We may, therefore, supply ὑπὸ τοῦ κυρίου after τοῦτο γέγονεν, since that which took place must not be regarded as accidental. The formula does receive its simple grammatical explanation in those cases where it seems to the expositors that real prophecies from the Old Testament are implied; but when they are not thought to be such, a wider sense is wont to be given to the phrase in this way: the result is such, that the words of the Old Testament may be suitably applied to this case. This explanation is defended on the ground, that ἵνα is used in the New Testament to express the event, (ἐκβατικῶς;)*

---

* The question of the use of ἵνα is of great importance doctrinally. It comes under special notice in the subject of predestination, as well as in that of the prophecies from the Old Testament. (See observations on Matth. xiii. 14, 15; John xii. 39, 40.) But it is worth noticing, that to assert that ἵνα is *very frequently* used ἐκβατικῶς, tends to take away the force of many passages, no less than is done by asserting that it is *never* so used. This is the case, for instance, with John xvii. 3, where the words αὕτη ἐστὶν ἡ αἰώνιος ζωή, ἵνα γινώσκωσι θεόν, are translated by some: "vita aeterna in hoc cernitur studio, ut te cognoscant." Instead of the knowledge of God itself, nothing is left for us but a mere striving after it. It appears to me that, in this case also, the truth lies midway between the two, and that St. John, in particular, certainly does use ἵνα of the event. This Evangelist has used ὥστε once only (John iii. 16) in all his writings; and in that instance it is after a preceding οὕτως; ὅπως, too, occurs only in John i. 57. But it is inconceivable that St. John should not sometimes have wished to express the notion of mere consequence without intention. Such passages as John

but from the fact that ἵνα *may* be so used, it does not follow that it *must* be so taken in *some* of the passages which contain this phrase. This expression, which appears so constantly in the New Testament, can have but one and the same sense in *all* the places where it is used. To appeal to the custom universally prevalent among the Jews, of applying passages of the Old Testament in relations quite different from those in which they stand according to their connexion, cannot in this case be allowed; because, in the first place, it is inconceivable that the sacred writers should have accommodated themselves to a custom so unmeaning, and so much exposed to abuse; and then, further, even if such were the state of the case, the meaning of the phrase, ἵνα πληρωθῇ, would not be altered, since, if the New Testament writers did follow this habit, they must have held, in connexion with it, the principle out of which it arose,—viz., that the Scriptures contain endless references, and can, therefore, be applied to all possible circumstances. The Rabbi imagines it really to be so with his quotations of Scripture, (nonsensical as they may be;) and agreeably to this view of the multifarious applicability of the contents of the sacred Scriptures, he believes that he finds a real fulfilment of the Bible language where he applies it. In my opinion, therefore, it is nothing but doctrinal prejudice which gave occasion to an interpretation varying from the simple grammatical explanation. Certain passages from the Old Testament were quoted as prophecies in the New, which it was thought impossible to regard as such, according to their original connexion; then, in order that it might not seem as if the New Testament writers quoted passages from the Old which did not contain any prophecies, as if they did, ἵνα πληρωθῇ, with such quotations, was translated in the manner above named. If this difficulty be removed, there remains no occasion for a departure from the literal sense of the words.

But the difficulty can be removed by our acknowledging in the Old Testament prophecies a twofold reference to a present lower subject, and to a future higher one. With this supposi-

---

iv. 34; ix. 2; xv. 13; xvi. 7; xvii. 3, show that he employed ἵνα for this purpose. It appears to me, therefore, that *Winer* (Gr. of the N. T. Idioms, § 57) goes somewhat too far when he admits the less forcible meaning of ἵνα only after verbs expressing command, desire, request; but denies altogether that ἵνα and ὥστε are interchanged.

tion, we can everywhere adhere to the immediate, simple, grammatical sense of the words, and still recognize the quotations of the New Testament as prophecies in the full sense. And it belongs to the peculiar adjustment and arrangement of the Scripture, that the life and substance of the Old Testament were intended as a mirror of the New Testament life, and that in the person of Christ particularly, as the representative of the New Testament, all the rays of Old Testament ideas and institutions are concentrated as in their focus.* (Consult the Author's dissertation: *Ein Wort über tieferen Schriftsinn*, Königsberg, 1824. On the opposite side: *Steudel* in Bengel's Archiv, B. iii., St. 2. Lastly, *Kleinert's* observations in Tholuck's Literarischer Anzeiger, Year 1831, No. 28.) This general character of the Old Testament shews itself in the passage here quoted from Isa. vii. 14. The immediate, grammatical sense of the words of the passage, necessarily requires a reference to something present, since the παρθένος, who was to bring forth Immanuel, is represented by the prophet as a sign to King Ahaz;—a reference to the Messiah, born of a virgin centuries after, appears to answer no end whatever for the immediate circumstances. It is most natural to suppose, that by παρθένος is meant the betrothed of the prophet, called in Isa. viii. 3, נְבִיאָה, as being his wife. (Παρθένος, equivalent to עַלְמָה, *unmarried woman*, is indeed in itself different from בְּתוּלָה, which necessarily denotes pure virginity; but the word עַלְמָה, too, *may*, and *must*, in this case, be taken for a pure virgin.) The passage, then, affords the natural sense, that Isaiah gives Ahaz the sign, that she who is now his betrothed, and will soon be his wife, shall bear a son, named Immanuel; and before this son shall have come to knowledge, (that is, in two or three

---

* See *Hamann*, in the history of his conversion (Werke Th. i., S. 211, ff.): "I found the unity of the divine will in the redemption by Jesus Christ, inasmuch as all history, all miracles, all God's commands and works, tended to this centre." In Hamann's works, a spiritual exposition, like that which the writers of the New Testament employ, may be seen in a modern author. *Bengel* also says very truly, (Gnomon ad. h. 1,) "Saepe in N. T. allegantur vaticinia, quorum contextum prophetarum tempore non dubium est, quin auditores eorum *ex intentione divina* interpretari debuerint de rebus jam tum praesentibus. Eadem vero *intentio divina*, longius prospiciens, sic *formavit* orationem, *ut magis proprie deinceps ea conveniret in tempora Messiae*, et hanc, intentionem divinam apostoli nos docent, *nosque dociles habere debent*."

years,) his prophecies shall be fulfilled. Thus the King Ahaz had given to him a sign (אוֹת) close at hand, and intelligible; but, at the same time, the birth of Immanuel had its higher reference to the Messiah, by whom the prophecy was fulfilled in a far higher sense, since He was born of a virgin, and as a sign (אוֹת) for the unbelieving world, which Ahaz represents. This agrees well with the symbolizing manner in which Isaiah named his sons throughout. He represented a whole chain of ideas and facts, which were especially important to him, from the circumstances of the times, in the names of his children, one of whom was called Shear-jashub, (Isa. vii. 3;) the second, Maher-shalal-hash-baz, (viii. 3;) and the third, Immanuel. Thus he formed with his family, as it were, an embodied and personified circle of ideas, in which his spirit moved. Such a form of teaching is quite in agreement with the prophetic agency; and, at the same time, St. Matthew was perfectly justified in referring the event of the birth of Immanuel to the birth of Christ, because that parallel was intended by the Spirit of prophecy himself.* The words of St. Matthew, more-

---

* I have not been convinced of the untenableness of the interpretation just given to the passage Isa. vii. 14, even by the able defence of the opposite view —viz., that no inferior subject is intended by the prophet's words—set up by Hengstenberg in his Christology, vol. i., p. 307, ff. It seems to me that he has not succeeded in solving the difficulty, how the reference to the Messiah could be a sign for Ahaz. Looking at it free from prejudice, one is necessarily led to expect that Ahaz must have had something given him, which *he* would live to witness. It is very forced to refer the period of two or three years spoken of to the coming of the Messiah, born centuries after. At any rate, the prophecy could not then have any meaning for Ahaz. The reasons brought forward against my view, seem to me unimportant; for when Hengstenberg reminds us, that there is no likeness between the birth of Immanuel in a natural manner, and that of the Messiah in a supernatural manner, it is certainly true that St. Matthew lays stress on the term παρθένος, which in the prophet has not the emphasis; but such a free use of prophecies is not uncommon in the New Testament, particularly in the Epistle to the Hebrews, and is quite safe when the passage so used is a real prophecy or a type, as in this instance. In this passage the unity of the reference lies in the *name Immanuel;* Isaiah's son had the *name,* but Christ the *essence.* He *was* God manifested, whom the former merely represented. Besides, discordant features are necessarily found in every type or symbol, for otherwise it would not be a type, but the thing itself. All prophecies of Scripture have, therefore, points of similarity enough to be *understood* by him who needs them, and who, because of his need, seeks for them; but likewise dissimilarities enough to be *misunderstood* by him who will not perceive. In the main, I agree in my view of Isaiah vii. 14, with *Umbreit's* Observations in the Studien und Kritiken, Year 1830, II. iii., S. 538, ff. The late Professor *Kleinert's* hypothesis in *Tholuck's* Anzeiger, Year 1832, No. 25, ff., that we should

over, do not follow the LXX. precisely, and differ from the original, also, in translating קָרָאת, (*thou shalt call*, 2d pers. sing. fem.) by καλέσουσι, *they shall call*.

Ver. 24, 25.—Joseph was in everything obedient to the divine command, believed in the purity of his wife, took her to himself, and gave the child, after His birth, the appointed name. But the Evangelist adds a remark worthy of notice, in the words, οὐκ ἐγίνωσκεν αὐτὴν, ἕως οὗ ἔτεκε τὸν υἱὸν αὐτῆς τὸν πρωτότοκον. It is unnecessary to prove, that in these words γινώσκειν = יָדַע is used of connubial connexion; the only question is, whether the meaning of the words is, that it did not take place in Joseph's marriage at all, or merely that it did not *previous* to the birth of Jesus? The words suggest, *at first sight*, the latter, particularly ἕως οὗ and πρωτότοκος. The former appears to suppose connubial intercourse *after* the birth of Jesus; the latter seems to say that Mary had several children. As, however, it is not probable, from the Gospel-history, that Mary had other children, (see note on Matth. xiii. 55, for a more particular account,) no conclusion can be drawn from the word πρωτότοκος to compel us to suppose, that afterwards connubial intercourse between Joseph and Mary took place. The term is merely equivalent to בְּכוֹר or פֶּטֶר רֶחֶם in Hebrew, which may signify either the *first* among others, or the *only* child. (It should be particularly noticed also, that the expression is πρωτότοκος αὐτῆς, HER *first-born*. The term has, of course, quite a different meaning in the phrases, πρωτότοκος ἐν τοῖς ἀδελφοῖς, (Rom. viii. 29,) ἐκ τῶν νεκρῶν, (Rev. i. 5,) πάσης κτίσεως, (Col. i. 15.) So also in Heb. i. 6, where the term stands alone. (Concerning these passages, compare the remarks in the Commentary.) The formula ἕως οὗ = עַד כִּי does not necessarily assert, that what is said not to have taken place *before* a certain time, did happen *after* it. In the Old Testament, this is proved by such passages as Gen. viii. 7, 2 Sam. vi. 23. In the New Testament, indeed, there is not one of the passages quoted as proof that it is quite conclusive,—*e. g.*, Matth. xxii. 44, (compared with 1 Cor. xv. 28,) Matth. v. 26,

---

conceive the facts respecting the virgin and Immanuel as a vision which God shewed to Ahaz by the prophet, would in fact explain several circumstances, if there were but one word in the text intimating, that this was the account of a vision. Without such an intimation, however, the supposition of a vision remains purely gratuitous.

xviii. 30. But it is in the very nature of the particle, that it does not necessarily affirm that what had not taken place up to a certain point of time, has taken place since. All depends on the circumstances and relations. (If we were to say, we waited till midnight, but no one came, that does not imply, that after midnight some one came; it means, no one came at all.) We must say, therefore, that from this passage no conclusion can be drawn either for the one view or the other; St. Matthew merely states as fact,—"Till the birth of Jesus he knew not Mary." It is evident, however, that after what he had passed through, Joseph might justly think that *his marriage* with Mary had another purpose than that of begetting children. Perhaps the words of the Evangelist are framed purposely thus, in order to prevent any inference that might be drawn from these events against the sanctity of the marriage; but, nevertheless, it seems, in the order of nature, that the last female descendant of David, in the family of which the Messiah was born, closed her family with this last and eternal scion. (The opposite view is defended by *Stier*, Andeutungen für gläubiges Schriftverständniss, Th. i. S. 404, ff.)

§ 3. ARRIVAL OF THE MAGI—FLIGHT INTO EGYPT—MURDER OF THE CHILDREN—RETURN TO GALILEE.

(Matth. ii. 1-23.)

Ver. 1.—It is only in passing, and as a supplementary remark, that St. Matthew notices that Jesus was born at Bethlehem, in the time of Herod,[*] (that is, the Great, the son of Antipater,) while he gives no exact account of the dwelling-place of Joseph and Mary; it is hence clearly seen, that the Evangelist, in his description of Christ's life, intentionally disregards the circumstances both of place and time,—a fact which is not unimportant in the apparent contradictions between St. Matthew

---

[*] As St. Matthew gives no more definite statement as to the person of Herod, several princes of which name reigned in Palestine, (see the first chronological table before the Exposition of the Acts of the Apostles,) it is clear that he supposes his readers to possess some knowledge of the circumstances, which accounts for several peculiarities in his narrative.

and St. Luke, which will presently come under notice. (Βηθλεέμ = בֵּית־לֶחֶם lay two hours* distant from, or six Roman miles south-west of, Jerusalem. The town was originally named Ephrath. [Gen. xxxv. 19, xlviii. 7.] The addition, τῆς Ἰουδαίας, is to distinguish it from another Bethlehem in Galilee, in the tribe of Zebulun, mentioned in Joshua xix. 15. As being David's birthplace, it is called simply, "City of David." See Luke ii. 4, 11.)

The most important circumstance in St. Matthew's eyes is, that the new-born Messiah received at once the homage of the Magi. (Μάγοι is well known to have been originally the name of the learned class among the Parsees. In Jer. xxxix. 3, the term רַב־מָג is used of the head of the College of the Magi. The Greek explanation of the word, as given in Suidas, φιλόσοφοι, φιλόθεοι, is not so correct as that which gives the meaning, *great, excellent*, from a Persian root. In later times, the name μάγος, like mathematicus, Chaldaeus, was used of all who were attached to occult science—especially of astrologers. See Acts xiii. 6.) This narrative is most simply explained, if we regard the Magi as adherents of the Zoroastrian worship of light, which, even before the time of Christ, was widely spread in the western part of Asia. Pompey found the worship of Mithras, a branch of the Zend religion, among the Cilician pirates. Cf. *Plut.* vit. Pomp. cap. 37. The expression, ἀπὸ ἀνατολῶν,† will be best left in the indefinite generality proper to it; it applies, like מִקֶּדֶם, to all that is situated east of Palestine—to adjacent Arabia, as well as to more distant Persia. Now, the hypothesis that these Magi were Parsees, is highly probable; in the first place, because there are remarkable germs of truth in the Zend system itself,—*e. g.*, the idea of a Sosiosh—an expected Saviour; and further, because an intermixture of Jewish ideas is more easily conceivable in their case than in that of any other nation. But such an intermixture must on this occasion be supposed, since the Persians expected their Saviour from the family of Zoroaster; but these Magi come to seek for the King of the

---

* [*Stunde, hour*, is used in Germany as a measure of distance. It is something less than three English miles.]—*Tr.*

† Ἀνατολή, used of a quarter of the world, appears, like δυσμός, chiefly in the plural, (see Matth. viii. 11, ἀπὸ ἀνατολῶν καὶ δυσμῶν,) perhaps because of the daily return of the rising and setting sun.

Jews, (ver. 2.*) The circumstance, too, that a star guided the Magi, points to the pursuit of astronomy, which was not uncommon among the Parsees. With respect to the recorded fact, that, although about the time of the birth of Christ, the prophecy of the appearance of a great universal monarch in the East, was spread far and wide, even among the heathen, (*Suet.* Vesp. c. 4. *Tacit.* Hist. V. 13. *Joseph.* B. J. i. 5, 5; vii. 31,) which is a proof how great events, concerning the whole of mankind, are ushered in by a sort of previous surmise; yet this feeble expectation can scarcely be used in explanation of the visit of the Magi. Their faith rested clearly on firmer props than so indefinite a rumour could supply. They recognized in the newborn one, whom they were seeking, not merely a ruler, but the Saviour himself—their Sosiosh. But, correct as their knowledge in the main certainly was, we must still beware of ascribing sharply defined doctrinal ideas to these believing strangers. The early Church, moreover, looked upon these Magi as the representatives of the heathen world, which, in them, offered its homage to the Lord;—an ingenious thought, full of deep truth! Agreeably to Old Testament hints of this fact, (Ps. lxviii. 30, 32; lxxii. 10; Isa. xlix. 7; lx. 3, 6,) the Magi were early taken to be kings, and, in the legend, bore the names of Caspar, Melchior, and Balthazar.

It was an easy step for the advocates of myths in the New Testament, to view this occurrence of the appearance of the Magi, before the new-born Redeemer, as a philosophical myth, without any historical foundation whatever, by which tradition intended to express the idea called forth by the passages of the Old Testament just referred to, that the Messiah would exercise a universal influence, extending beyond the limits of the Jewish people.† But this view is altogether at variance with the circumstance, that it is precisely in St. Matthew that this universal character of Christ's mission is least prominent. As related

---

* These Magi might also be thought to be Jews, perhaps of the dispersed ten tribes; but the words, Βασιλεὺς τῶν Ἰουδαίων, evidently lead us to think them not to be Jews.

† The advocates of the mythical view are quite arbitrary in using sometimes this and sometimes that circumstance, to defend their view, without regarding internal consistency. At one time, they make the Apostles imagine that the mission of the Messiah was to be confined to the people of Israel; and yet, on the other hand, they make them invent myths, for the purpose of shewing His universal mission.

by contemporaries, this narrative could be nothing but gross deception, if destitute of historical truth.

Ver. 2.—The words which the family memoirs here employed by St. Matthew report as being used by the Magi, indicate a knowledge of the special relation in which the new-born one stood to the Jewish people. The "King of the Jews" is not a king who rules over the Jews *alone*,—the Magi represent their own subjection under His (spiritual) power by a symbolical action,—but a King, who springs from the Jews, and from them, as His centre, extends His kingdom. Thus it expresses properly the true idea, "salvation is of the Jews." (John iv. 22.) As the sure sign of His birth, they mention the sight of *His* star, εἴδομεν αὐτοῦ τὸν ἀστέρα. They knew, therefore, that a heavenly sign would stand connected with the earthly appearance of this (spiritual) king. That great events on earth had their corresponding appearances in the heavens, which shewed themselves principally in stars, was a very general opinion of antiquity, (see, for instance, *Justin.* Hist. xxxvii. 2. *Sueton.* vit. Caes. c. 88,) and is not without truth, though it commonly served the purposes of superstition.* In the life of the Saviour, the surmise expressed in this opinion attained to reality and truth. In what this ἀστὴρ Βασιλέως consisted, is hardly to be ascertained with certainty. The idea that an appearance in the air is meant, is the most improbable; it could not find any support but in ver. 9, where it is said, "the star *stood* over where the young child was." *Chalcidius*, the Platonist, (Opp. Hippolyti edid. J. A. Fabricius, pag. 325,) understood a comet to be meant by the star. The learned Bishop Münter of Copenhagen takes it to be a constellation, and refers to the conjunction of planets which took place in the year 1825. (See the Dissertations of the Academy of Sciences at Copenhagen, for the year 1820.) It is most probable to me that a particular star is intended,† because of the parallel between this passage

---

* In the tract, Yalkut Rubeni, it is said: "Qua hora natus est Abrahamus, stetit sidus quoddam in oriente, et deglutivit quatuor astra, quae erant in quatuor coeli plagis." (See *Bertholdti* Christol. Jud. pag. 55.) The words evidently describe a conjunction of planets, according to the sensible impression. Four stars united and formed a whole, so that one great star seemed to have swallowed the four little ones.

† *Ideler*, who follows the Abbot Sanclemente, so celebrated as a chronologer, has made me doubt whether the star ought not still to be regarded as a

and Matth. xxiv. 30, where, in like manner, a sign of the Son of Man in heaven is foretold, with reference to Christ's second coming; just as in Numb. xxiv. 17, it is held up as a prophecy of the first coming of our Lord. (In order to apply this passage to himself, the well-known false Messiah, took the name of Barkochba,—*i. e.*, son of the star.)

Ver. 3, 4.—This intelligence was a message of terror to the king and the city of Jerusalem, (in its representatives—the ecclesiastical rulers of the Jews;) partly, because in general what is great and mighty, when it comes into our immediate neighbourhood, seizes us with a feeling analogous to terror, (for we cannot suppose that all the chief priests and scribes would be terrified at the appearance of the Messiah, on account of their sins;) partly, because conscience announced to Herod, now grown grey in sin, as well as to the priestly caste, from selfishness (at least in the majority) alive only to their own interest, that with the appearance of the King of Righteousness, their kingdom of iniquity was drawing near its end. From the external character which the expectations of a Messiah had acquired among the Jews, it is more than probable that, with most of those who heard of the appearance of a King of the Jews, political fears or hopes would be excited. Only we must not forget to notice, that the correct view of the spiritual character of the Messiah had maintained itself in the little circles of true believers, (see note on Luke i. 76,) and that the change in outward circumstances was regarded by them only as the consequence of His inward influence.

---

conjunction of planets. The above-mentioned scholars employ their view of it to fix the chronology of the year of Christ's birth, and shew that, six years before the Christian era, a most remarkable conjunction of all the chief planets in our system did take place. Now, as the planets, according to the latest and most exact calculations, were sometimes close together, at others, farther off from each other; so that sometimes the star seemed to be there, and then, at others, to disappear,—all which agrees well with St. Matthew's narrative,—I am inclined to think this hypothesis very probable. In addition to this, according to Jewish tradition,—*e. g.*, of Abarbanel, (in his Commentary on Daniel,) such conjunctions are said to have happened at the birth of Moses also, and of other men of note in the kingdom of God. See *Ideler's* Handbuch der Chronologie, Th. ii., S. 410, ff., and in the *Lehrbuch*, S. 428, where there is a new calculation by *Encke*. *Keppler* already held the same opinion, only, from his calculation not being quite correct, he fixed the date of conjunction somewhat too late. *Ignatius* (epist. ad Ephes. c. 19) describes the star as a remarkable one, surpassing all others in the splendour of its light.

(By the ἀρχιερεῖς in this place, are meant, not only the high priests [כֹּהֵן הַגָּדוֹל] properly so called,—that is, the one in office, and those who had before passed through it, but also the heads of the twenty-four classes (courses) of priests. [See note on Luke i. 5.] Since these heads, as such, were members of the Sanhedrim, every member of the Sanhedrim was also called ἀρχιερεύς, [John xii. 10.] The γραμματεῖς, = סֹפְרִים, include all who were skilled in the law, like νομικός, νομοδιδάσκαλος; so that every ἀρχιερεύς was a γραμματεύς, but not *vice versâ*.)

Like the Magi, (ver. 2,) the king (ver. 4) inquires only for the birth-*place* (ποῦ γεννᾶται) of the new king. The birth itself appears to all indubitably certain, which indicates a general expectation of the Messiah. The present γεννᾶται does not require to be taken as a future; this tense is rather used in relation to the prophecies of Scripture, by which the scribes were to decide; so that the meaning is,—Where is the King (of whom the prophets speak) to be born, which leaves it undecided whether He be already born, as the Magi declared, (ποῦ ἐστιν ὁ τεχθεὶς βασιλεύς, ver. 2,) or should yet be born.

Ver. 5, 6.—The learned Jews quite correctly assign Bethlehem as the birthplace of the Messiah, according to Micah v. 1, in which remarkable prophecy, acknowledged as such by most expositors, so minute, and so literally fulfilled, the insignificant town (hence called κώμη, in John vii. 42) is described as the birthplace of the Messiah, and its spiritual glory is contrasted with its worldly lowliness. In the quotation, the Evangelist follows neither the Hebrew text nor the LXX.; he quotes freely from memory.* The *meiosis*, which appears in the words οὐδαμῶς ἐλαχίστη εἶ, is not contained either in the original or the translation of the LXX. Still the variation is purely formal. St. Matthew gives merely the thought of the prophet, which is just this, that Bethlehem, notwithstanding its mean exterior, is highly honoured.

(The words γῆ Ἰούδα added by St. Matthew himself, refer probably to the tribe of Judah, of which, according to Gen. xlix. 10, the Messiah was to be born. The γῆ is put by *synecdoche* for πόλις,

---

* *Jerome* observes strangely on the passage: " Arbitror Matthaeum volentem arguere scribarum et sacerdotum negligentiam sic etiam posuisse, (sc. verba prophetæ) uti ab eis dictum est." But in that case St. Matthew must, in other places, have laid himself open to the charge of the same "negligentia."

as, *e. g.*, in Jerem. xxix. 7, עִיר is translated γῆ by the LXX. [See Matth. x. 15; xi. 24; xiv. 34.]—Instead of ἐν τοῖς ἡγεμόσιν, as in St. Matthew, the LXX. have ἐν χιλιάσιν, after the Hebrew בְּאַלְפֵי. The Jewish people were divided into families, [אֲלָפִים, Judges vi. 15,] over which heads [שָׂרֵי אֲלָפִים, ἡγεμόνες, Ex. xviii. 21; Numb. i. 16] presided. The heads of families are, therefore, in St. Matthew put for the families themselves, and these again for the chief towns in which they were settled.)

As the characteristic mark of Him who was to be looked for from Bethlehem, (יָצָא, ἐξέρχεσθαι in the sense of "being born,") the Evangelist makes His dominion over the people of Israel prominent by the manner in which he applies the Old Testament quotation. The terms in which that dominion is described, appear chosen purposely to signify its mild and gracious character. (Ἡγούμενος = מוֹשֵׁל expresses the idea of guiding to an object, rather than that of laying down law and restraining by force; the additional clause ποιμανεῖ τὸν λαόν μου, which is wanting in the Hebrew text, is perhaps inserted from 2 Sam. v. 2, another prophetic passage. The ideas of governing and tending are closely related, and are often interchanged; yet ποιμαίνειν gives greater prominence to the ideal character of the true ruler, who has the good of his subjects at heart, than βασιλεύειν.) The special relation of this shepherd to Israel (λαός = עַם, the opposite of גּוֹיִם) is to be regarded partly as again expressive of the view most readily suggested of the influence of the Messiah, (see notes on Matth. i. 21; x. 6; xv. 24,) and partly as inclusive of its further extension to the whole spiritual Israel, scattered among all nations. (See note on Matth. viii. 11; Rom. ii. 28, 29.)

Ver. 7.—In order to smother all political excitement, the suspicious tyrant kept the arrival of the Magi, and the purpose of their journey, a secret,—using them, as he imagined, for his own ends. After having ascertained from his doctors the *place* of the birth, he tried to discover the *time* likewise. This he connected with the appearance of the star, (ἠκρίβωσε τὸν χρόνον τοῦ φαινομένου ἀστέρος,) but whether from the hints of the Magi or not, is uncertain. From ver. 16, therefore, we might conclude that the star had already been seen some time,—perhaps, since the time of the conception of Jesus. (Ἀκριβόω, see ver. 16, = ἀκριβῶς ἐξετάζω, ver. 8.)

Ver. 8, 9.—By his outward smoothness Herod hoped the more surely to deceive the simple men, and induce them to return to him; but God preserved them and the young child from his malice. (Πορεύεσθαι is used certainly according to the analogy of the Hebrew הָלַךְ, but is not redundant, as the inquiry in this case involved a journey.) The position of the wise men, while travelling, in reference to the star, as stated in ver. 9, is not clear. First of all, with respect to προῆγεν αὐτούς, it is not necessary to conclude thence that the star had disappeared, and then re-appeared. The matter may be easily imagined thus,—the star, which they had seen rise in the east, (ἐν τῇ ἀνατολῇ, ver. 2,) they discovered, from its change of position in the progress of its course, in the direction in which the road from Jerusalem to Bethlehem led them. It continued, therefore, to precede them as a guiding star. (Προάγειν is taken in its proper signification.*) But what follows is more difficult still,—ἐλθὼν ἔστη ἐπάνω οὗ (sc. τόπου) ἦν τὸ παιδίον, where mention is made of the star moving and arriving at a destined point. Now, it is not easy to see how a star in the heavens, whether a comet or a constellation, could even apparently rest over a house. A fiery appearance in the air would more easily account for this, if there were any probability at all that anything of that sort could be designated by the term ἀστήρ. The whole of St. Matthew's description evidently indicates a star that shone for some considerable time. It is simplest to take the expression, ἐλθὼν ἔστη, as the natural conception of their childlike feeling; so that the usual mode of inquiry after the child Jesus was not meant to be excluded, while the result, as well as the beginning, of the journey is still ascribed to the heavenly guide.

Ver. 10, 11.—The remark again made, that the Magi beheld the star, (ἰδόντες τὸν ἀστέρα,) is not by any means to be referred to what precedes, so that ἰδόντες would be taken for a pluperfect. It is better to refer the expression to the ἔστη before mentioned, so that the view of the star, so to speak, terminating its office, filled them with a peculiarly joyful surprise. (Ἐχάρησαν χαρὰν is a familiar Hebraism, [see 1 Sam. iv. 5;] something analogous to

---

* *Ideler* (*ut sup.*) explains this of the approach, or dispersion of the planets, which seemed, while in conjunction, to form one large star.

which is found in all languages. The periphrasis of the superlative with σφόδρα [מְאֹד], is also well known as a Hebraism.) In the description of the visit of the Magi, *Mary* only, the mother of the child, is mentioned. Joseph recedes quite into the back-ground throughout the whole Gospel-history, and presents no perceptible spiritual character. (The reading εἶδον, is every way preferable to the εὗρον of the Textus Receptus.) Two things are distinctly noticed in the actions of the Magi; first, the προσκυνεῖν, then the presenting of their gifts. We may imagine both included in one in this way, that they desired to testify their dependence in the presentation itself. The action was to be προσφορά, a solemn recognition of the superior character of the new-born one, as also the prophecy in Isaiah lx. 6, intimates. Προσκυνῆσαι, therefore, answering to the Hebrew הִשְׁתַּחֲוָה, is no proof, so far as the words go, of the view entertained by the Magi of the young child's dignity. The word often denotes nothing more than the well-known oriental form of political homage. Still the connexion of the narrative makes it certain, that the Magi ascribed a spiritual character to the child; and their προσκύνησις, combined with the ceremony of the προσφορά, acquires a more spiritual meaning. Only we must not, as before observed, by any means ascribe to the Magi any doctrinal ideas of the divinity of Jesus; but merely a surmise of the divine power *accompanying* and resting *on* Him. We may say, they worshipped God, who had made this child for salvation to them also, but not the child.

Further, as regards the gifts presented to the child, (and His mother,) we are not at liberty to conclude from the fact of their being Arabian produce, that the Magi came exactly from Arabia; the articles were common throughout the East, as being necessary to their worship, for gold also was among the gifts usually presented to the gods. The idea of many expositors, that these valuable presents must needs be brought to Mary in her poverty, on occasion of her journey into Egypt (ver. 13,) may not be altogether inadmissible; the Gospel-history shews that, in after life also, the Saviour committed himself, in reference to His bodily life, to the love of His friends. (See note on Luke viii. 3.) (The term θησαυρός signifies, like אוֹצָר, Deut. xxviii. 12, "vessel," "place of keeping;" the idea of "what is kept,"—"costly" is the derived one. Λίβανος = לְבוֹנָה, signifies "incense," the produce of a balsamic plant of Arabia. In the

Old Testament the term is found very frequently, because incense is so often mentioned in connexion with the sacrifices; in the New it occurs only once more,—viz., in Rev. xviii. 13. Σμύρνα = מֹר, *myrrh*, is a similar product, obtained from a tree like the acacia. [Ex. xxx. 23; Psalm xlv. 9.] Incense and myrrh were also used medicinally by the ancients; but such a use of the presents is here totally inadmissible. On the history of the Magi in general, see *Kleuker's* Bibl. Sympathieen, S. 36, ff.; and *Hamann's* Kreuzzüge des Philologen, Werke, Th. ii., S. 135, ff.)

Ver. 12.—As above, so here also, we should observe that the thoughts of the Magi, which arose within them on the natural consideration of the circumstances, must not be confounded with the higher impulse, which induced their determination not to return to Herod. (Χρηματίζειν signifies, in profane authors, "to manage public affairs"—"to give answers and commands;" χρηματίζεσθαι, "to receive commands." In the Hellenistic Greek, the term appears in the same signification, but with reference to divine transactions; χρηματίζειν, "to give divine commands," Heb. xii. 25; χρηματίζεσθαι, "to receive divine commands." Thus it is found in the New Testament, ver. 22 of this chapter, and frequently; and in the Old, in Jer. xxvi. 2; xxix. 18. Lastly, it means, also, merely "to call," [Acts xi. 26; Rom. vii. 3,] a meaning which is quite common in profane writers.)

Ver. 13, 14.—As the Saviour, after He had attained to a full consciousness of His divinity, and of His unity with God, (*Gottesbewusstseyn*,) did and said nothing of himself, but always at the instance of the Father, (John viii. 28,) so the divine agency prevailed among the circle surrounding Jesus during His infancy, and before He was conscious of this unity. The history of Jesus, even the child Jesus, is a divine history. By divine impulse, therefore, Joseph brings the holy child with His mother to Egypt.* (On the appearance of the angel "in a dream," [κατ' ὄναρ.] see i. 20. Ver. 13, ἴσθι is imperative from εἰμί, and not to be confounded with a similar form from οἶδα. Εἶναι is to be taken here, as הָיָה is also used in the sense of "being continuously,"—*i. e.*, "remaining." Ἕως ἂν εἴπω σοι

---

* On the Flight into Egypt, see *Schleiermacher's* excellent sermon in the Magazine edited by him, *Röhr* and *Schuderoff*, vol. vi., Madgeburg, 1829, S. 301, ff.

intimates another appearance to be looked for. The whole narrative of the flight indicates haste and secrecy [νυκτός, ver. 14] in their removal. The expression, τὸ παιδίον καὶ τὴν μητέρα αὐτοῦ, delicately intimates that Joseph was only in the place of a father.) Tradition names Matarea as the place where Jesus is said to have remained with Mary in Egypt. The temple of Onias (at Leontopolis) stood in the neighbourhood,—a circumstance which made many Jews resort thither.

Ver. 15.—The observation, that Jesus remained with His mother in Egypt till the death of Herod, is not without importance for the chronology, since the death of Herod, and the beginning of Archelaus's reign, (ver. 22,) can be accurately determined. True, the date is not void of uncertainty from the circumstance, that the Evangelist does not remark, either how old the child Jesus was at the time His mother fled with Him into Egypt, or how long He was there; nor do the passages, Luke iii. 1, 23, remove the uncertainty. Yet thus much is certain from this passage, that Jesus must have been born *before* the death of Herod; and agreeably to this fact, the vulgar Christian era is at least three years too late. (See *Paulus* in his Commentary on the passage.) The investigations of *Sanclemente* and *Ideler*, as was observed, place the birth of Christ as long as six years before our era.—But with respect to the flight into Egypt, the Evangelist refers to an Old Testament prophecy,—viz., Hosea xi. 1. The Greek words in St. Matthew differ from the text of the LXX. in a remarkable manner; the latter reads, ἐξ Αἰγύπτου μετεκάλεσα τὰ τέκνα αὐτοῦ sc. τοῦ Ἰσραήλ. In this form, the passage was wholly useless for the purpose of the quotation; St. Matthew, therefore, follows the Hebrew text, which has the singular, (קָרָאתִי לִבְנִי.) We see, hence, that in the Greek text of this Gospel, St. Matthew treats the quotation independently, which we should not look for in an ordinary translator. (See Introd. § 4.) In its connexion in the prophecy, the passage evidently refers to the recall of the people out of Egypt by Moses; the people being regarded as one man, are called God's son—God's first-born. (Ex. iv. 22; Jer. xxxi. 9.) This passage, however, the Evangelist regards as so far a prophecy, since Israel after the flesh is spiritually represented in the person of Christ. The fortunes of the earthly Israel are a type of the fortunes of the Messiah, in whom Israel is first found in his true essence. (See 1 Cor. x. 1, ff.; Gal. iii.

28.) If, on the principle that every author is to be explained by himself, we view this idea as one that was familiar to the New Testament writers, quite apart from its intrinsic and eternal truth, we obtain at least the advantage of being able to proceed more simply and naturally in the exposition.

Ver. 16.—The lengthened absence of the Magi now rouses the wrath of the tyrant Herod. He perceives that he is deceived, and hopes, by means of a revolting barbarity, to destroy the dangerous child. To be certain of not missing his aim, he causes all the children in Bethlehem under two years of age to be killed.

(Ἐμπαίζειν means, first, "to deride," "to jeer at;" then, "to deceive," "to beguile," since deceiving often involves derision. Θυμοῦσθαι = הָרָה, *to burn with rage*, does not occur elsewhere. The immediate neighbourhood of the town, the "coasts" [ὅρια = גְּבוּלִים, *suburbs, precincts,*] were included in Herod's cruel order.)

The relation in which this note of time stands to the account of the Magi, (ver. 7,) makes it probable that the star appeared before the birth of Jesus, and that the Magi did not arrive immediately after His birth, (see note on Luke ii. 40;) in which case Herod might think it necessary, in order to be sure, to extend the limit to within a little of two years. (Διετής, *bimus, two-year old;* ἀπὸ διετοῦς stands for διετῶν, from the two-year old children downwards.) The fact of the murder of the children at Bethlehem has been doubted, because neither Josephus nor any other historian makes any mention of it;* and further, because it would have been a cruelty scarcely conceivable even for a Herod, while the whole event seems without sufficient motive, as simpler means for accomplishing the removal of the child would have suggested themselves to Herod. But, in the *first place*, as respects the silence of the historians on an event so unimportant in a political point of view, (the only view taken by all ancient historians,) as the death of some children in a small Jewish town must have seemed to them; this is the less surprising, because, according to ver. 7, the whole matter was kept secret as to its real connexion. *Then,* too, the murder of

---

* *Macrobius* (Saturn. ii. 4) mentions the occurrence, but mixes it up with the murder of Herod's own son,—a confusion which might easily occur, as no other royal offspring could be thought of, who could have been the object of Herod's persecutions.

a few children was lost among the atrocities of a Herod, as a drop is lost in the sea. The number of those slaughtered on this occasion has been erroneously thought to be great, and the deed itself a horrible massacre; whereas, in the nature of things, there could be but a few children under two years in a little town like Bethlehem, and these might be put out of the way without any stir. *Lastly,* the remark that the affair is without adequate motive, since Herod could easily have sent secret messengers to accompany the Magi, appears to be not altogether unfounded. Yet we must consider, that we are not to transfer modern arrangements of police to antiquity; and, again, that, according to the king's intention, the birth of the King of the Jews was to be kept a secret, and he thought he might repose full confidence in the Magi; and, lastly, that in the history of all times there occur unaccountable oversights, which shew that a higher hand overrules history.

Ver. 17, 18.—The Evangelist finds in this event also the fulfilment of a prophecy, Jer. xxxi. 15. The prophet's language refers, in its connexion, to the carrying away of the Israelites by way of Rama, to Babylon, by Nebuzaradan, (Jer. xl. 1;) and Rachel, Jacob's beloved wife, the progenitrix of Israel, is represented as weeping over this misfortune. This circumstance of the mother bewailing her unhappy children, was regarded by the Evangelist as repeated in the murder of the children at Bethlehem, and, indeed, with increased force, because it was the Messiah, near to whom, and on whose account, this affliction happened. While, in general, the forefather of the people is mentioned, the mother is here brought forward as bewailing those who fell a sacrifice in order to save the life of the Messiah, because sympathizing sorrow for the pains of her tender charge, shews itself more naturally in the mother. The words of the quotation deviate again from the translation of the LXX., yet not so as to discover an independent construction of the original; the passage is quoted from memory.

(Φωνή = קוֹל is here *lamentation, cry of sorrow.* The town Rama, in the tribe of Benjamin, lay scarcely a-half day's journey from Bethlehem, [Jud. xix. 2, 9, 13.] It might, therefore, be put for Bethlehem itself, as, in specifying this place, it was only intended to designate the land of Palestine in general. Besides which, Rachel was buried in the neighbourhood, [Gen.

xxxv. 19; xlviii. 7;] so that it seemed as if the progenitrix of the nation was disturbed in her peaceful grave by the cruelty of Herod.)

Ver. 19, 20.—The return from Egypt is again instigated by special divine admonition; and the death of the tyrant is assigned as the determining circumstance. The words Ιεθνήκασι γὰρ κ. τ. λ. contain a reference to Exod. iv. 19, where nothing but the formula ἵνα πληρωθῇ is wanting to make it completely parallel with the previous references to Old Testament passages. What was there said of Moses and his flight from Pharaoh, St. Matthew interprets in reference to Jesus; so that Moses appears here as a type of Him. The plural οἱ ζητοῦντες, applies to Herod as the representative of all God's enemies in general. (The expression γῆ 'Ισραήλ—not γῆ 'Ιούδα—readily suggests Galilee, which, according to ver. 22, the parents of Jesus chose for their dwelling. Ζητεῖν τὴν ψυχήν corresponds to אֶת־נֶפֶשׁ בִּקֵּשׁ.)

Ver. 21.—The time of the return of Jesus from Egypt is not indeed stated; but, as it was an event consequent on Herod's death,* his residence there cannot have been of long continuance. This circumstance of itself, therefore, is sufficient to overthrow the hypothesis that Jesus obtained His knowledge from Egyptian philosophers, which stands, too, in absolute contradiction to the idea of a Saviour. It must have been in very early childhood that Jesus returned to Palestine, at which period the depths of Egyptian wisdom cannot have been accessible to Him.

Ver. 22.—On their return, report represented Archelaus to the holy family as not less cruel than his father Herod. They chose Galilee, therefore, for their residence, where Antipas reigned. Augustus, who confirmed the testament of Herod, appointed Archelaus Ethnarch of Judea, Idumea, and Samaria; Philip obtained Batanea and Auranitis; Antipas, Galilee and Perea.† Archelaus held his dominion only nine years. At the expiration of that period, Augustus deposed him, banished him to Vienna, and made Judea a Roman province. (*Josephus,* Ant. xvii. 10, 12; xviii. 1.)

---

* On the death of Herod, see *Euseb.* H. E. i. 6, 8; and, in respect of the chronology, the detailed discussion in *Dr. Paulus'* Exegetisches Handbuch, Th. i., H. i., S. 227, ff.

† On this point, see the first chronological table to the Acts of the Apostles.

(Γαλιλαία = גָּלִיל, גְּלִילָה signifies, like כִּכָּר, *circuit, district.* The name in full is גְּלִיל הַגּוֹיִם, γαλιλαία ἀλλοφύλων, or γ. τῶν ἐθνῶν. [1 Macc. v. 15; Matth. iv. 15; Isa. ix 1.] As in this district heathenism was much mixed with Judaism, the strict exclusive character of the Jewish people appeared in a milder form; but for this very reason the inhabitants of Galilee were despised among the rest of the Jews. [Matth. xxvi. 69; John i. 46; vii. 52.] According to *Josephus,* [de Bell. Jud. iii. 2,] the district was divided into Upper and Lower Galilee; the former bordered on Tyre and Sidon, the latter on the Jordan and the Lake of Gennesaret. Tiberias first, and afterwards Sephoris, was the capital of Galilee. Ἐκεῖ is put for ἐκεῖσε, like שָׁם for שָׁמָּה. It is often so in the New Testament.)

Ver. 23.—In Galilee, the parents of Jesus made the town of Nazareth their dwelling-place. (The preposition εἰς is to be connected with ἐλθών, and not, therefore, to be confounded with ἐν. When ἐν is joined with words of motion, or εἰς with words denoting rest, we are not to suppose an interchange of particles, but rather that the idea of previous or subsequent rest or motion is to be supplied, according as the case requires. See *Winer's Grammar of the New Testament,* translated by *Agnew* and *Ebbeke,* § 51.) This little town of Galilee, of which neither the Old Testament nor Josephus makes mention, was situated in the tribe of Zebulun, not far from Capernaum, on a hill (Luke iv. 29) some miles distant from Tabor. The derivation of the name from נֵצֶר, *bush, shrub,* is proved by Hengstenberg (Christol. vol. ii., i. 1, ff.) to be the only correct one. Bengel derives it incorrectly from נֵזֶר, *a crown.* In this choice of the town of Nazareth as the residence for the mother and the child, the Evangelist sees also the fulfilment of the Old Testament predictions; he connects this fact with the name Ναζωραῖος, which was given to the Saviour from His residence at Nazareth. But as there is no passage in the Old Testament where the Messiah is so called, the meaning of this reference is obscure. Some have supposed the Nazarite vow to be intended, and have imagined in this place a *paronomasia* between the name of the town and the word נָזִיר, (Numb. vi. 1.) But, in the *first place,* it does not agree with the Saviour's character to compare Him with a Jewish Nazarite, because He did not, like John the Baptist, appear with outward legal rigour; and *then* the Nazarite is called in Greek Ναζιραῖος, less frequently Ναζαραῖος, or

Ναζηραῖος, while the inhabitant of Nazareth is called Ναζαρηνός, or Ναζωραῖος. (See *Schleusner* in his Lexicon to the LXX.) It is quite as untenable to refer to the term נֵצֶר, *shoot, branch,* by which the Messiah, as a descendant of David, is frequently denominated,*—*e. g.*, Isa. xi. 1. Had the Evangelist intended it so, he would have quoted a distinct passage from the prophets, where this term occurs, as he did in the former quotations from the Old Testament. But he could not, in that case, have employed the formula ὅπως πληρωθῇ, for there is no connexion between the name נֵצֶר, *shoot,* and the dwelling in Nazareth. In our view of this passage we must, therefore, be guided by the expression ἐχθὲν διὰ τῶν προφητῶν. (The reading διὰ τοῦ προφήτου is obviously a mere correction without critical authority.) The *plural* indicates that the Evangelist had not any single quotation in view, but meant only to adduce a collective citation; and the article compels us to think of all the prophets, or of some in particular, whom St. Matthew supposed to be known. Accordingly, the view becomes most probable, that the Evangelist had regard to the common usage of the language, in which Nazarene signifies a mean, despised one. In that case he would have had those passages in view in which the Messiah is portrayed in His humiliation,—as, *e. g.*, Ps. xxii.; Isa. liii. An etymological allusion to נָזוּר, *the despised one,* (from זוּר,) may be combined with this view, and is not improbable, particularly on the supposition of a Hebrew original of the Gospel. The endeavour of St. Matthew to represent Jesus as the Messiah, according to the Old Testament predictions, is most plainly evidenced even in these first chapters.† As he wrote for Jews, it was his chief aim to prove the connexion of the various events at the birth of Jesus with the important testimonies of the Old Testament. (On καλεῖσθαι, see note on Luke i. 32.)

If now, at the close of the first two chapters of St. Matthew, we glance at the objections which have been raised against their genuineness, we may take it for granted that, in our day, they

---

* It was in this way that the learned Nazarene Jewish Christians explained the quotation to Jerome. See *Hieronymi* comm. ad loc. Jes. xi. 1.

† *De Wette* is wrong in assuming, contrary to his other declarations, a double sense;—the reference, according to him, is first to the town of Nazareth, and the residence there; and then, further, to the word נֵצֶר.

may be regarded as set aside. No external reasons can be adduced for the opinion, that these chapters did not form part of the original Gospel, since it is proved that the "Gospel καϑ' 'Εβραίους" contained the history of the childhood of Jesus. (See the Author's History of the Gospels, p. 73, 76.) The Ebionites, indeed, had not the first chapters in their edition of that apocryphal Gospel; but the fact of their having omitted them confirms their genuineness. (See *Epiph.* haer. xxx. 13.) And with respect to the internal reasons, *Gersdorf* (Sprachcharacteristik, S. 38, ff.) has shewn convincingly the affinity of the style which prevails in the first chapters with that of the following parts; although it must be admitted that *Fritzsche* (Excursus iii. in Matth.) has here and there refuted *Gersdorf's* remarks. There is nothing left, then, to give any colour to these doubts, except the doctrinal objections taken against the contents; but this reason, of all others, will never be urged by judicious critics against the genuineness of the first two chapters, as, at most, it could only be brought against the authenticity of the history narrated, not against the genuineness of this part of the work, since the Evangelist, in the subsequent parts, exhibits the same fundamental views from which the form of description prevailing in the first chapters resulted. Moreover, as reference is made, in what follows, (see iii. 1; iv. 23,) to the preceding part, the first chapters are very manifestly seen to be an integral part of the Gospel.* Precisely the same observations apply to the arguments brought forward against the genuineness of the first chapters of Luke. (For the Literature on the subject, see *Kuinoelii* comm. in Luc., vol. ii., p. 232.) In this case, likewise, there is no external evidence whatever, since the character of the Marcionite Gospel is a testimony, not against, but for, the genuineness, because Marcion omitted the early chapters, which he found in St. Luke's Gospel as generally used. (*Tertull.* adv. Marc. iv. 7.) No internal reason can be adduced, except the miraculous character of the history narrated in them—a character which agrees perfectly with that of the whole. We shall presently treat particularly of the contradictions which appear to exist between the accounts of St. Matthew and St. Luke, in the history of the childhood

---

* Compare the Dissertation of *J. G. Müller*, (Trier. 1830,) which defends the genuineness of these chapters.

of Jesus; but on the ground occupied by our opponents, even in case they were irreconcileable, no argument could be derived thence against the *genuineness* of the early chapters, because those contradictions could be urged as evidence only against the *credibility* of the history.

SECOND SECTION.—ST. LUKE'S ACCOUNT.
CHAPTERS I. AND II.

---

§ 1. PRÖEMIUM.

(Luke i. 1-4.)

THE four verses with which St. Luke opens his work, consisting of two parts, (see Acts i. 1,) are worthy of notice in more than one respect. As regards the style, we perceive that the Evangelist's own style, which is pure Greek, as the first period shews, differs from the Hebraising style apparent in the subsequent part, where St. Luke communicates documents, whether unaltered or worked up, with which tradition had supplied him. His words next inform us, that, previous to the composition of his work, other accounts of the Gospel-history were in existence, the accuracy (ἀσφάλεια, ver. 4) of which was, however, questionable; lastly, St. Luke indicates the sources of information which he had employed, the principles which he had followed in the composition of his work, and the special object which he had directly in view. The construction of the Pröemium is subject to a certain indefiniteness, which is the more calculated to give room for diverse explanations, as the views entertained of the origin of the Gospels naturally influenced them in various ways. The sense of the whole passage depends on where the *apodosis* is made to begin; it may begin either with καθὼς παρέδοσαν, or with ἔδοξε κἀμοί. According to the latter division, the words καθὼς παρέδοσαν κ. τ. λ., which are connected with ἐπειδήπερ πολλοί κ. τ. λ., contain an observation on the *quality* of the earlier Gospel records; for to refer them to the mere *existence* of those records, as if St. Luke had not personally known these older works, but had only heard of them by παράδοσις, is evidently forbidden by the expression ἀπ' ἀρχῆς αὐτόπται, which necessarily implies a tradition respecting the history of Jesus.* St. Luke's opinion of the character of those older writings would, in that case, be a favourable one, since he claims the same sources of information for himself, (καθὼς παρέδοσαν ἡμῖν;) a supposition which would very well agree with an hypothesis, according to which these many Gospels were shorter, and our Gospels more lengthened, editions of the same original Gospel. But as (ver. 4) blame is plainly imputed to the πολλοί, since St. Luke leads Theophilus to expect historical certainty nowhere but in his Gospel, which could not therefore possibly be found in the accounts of the earlier narrators,† it might be thought necessary to prefer that division of the sentence which places the beginning of the *apodosis* at καθὼς παρέδοσαν ἡμῖν κ. τ. λ. In that way, the tradition of the eye-witnesses would refer only to St. Luke's narrative; and his narrative would stand distinguished from the earlier ones. But here, again, we are met, first, by the circumstance that, grammatically, the *apodosis* is more definitely pointed out in ἔδοξε κἀμοί, than at καθώς, since κἀμοί appears evidently in contrast with the πολλοί; besides, too, the change from ἡμεῖς to ἐγώ is remarkable. It is, therefore, undoubtedly most correct to begin the *apodosis* with ἔδοξε; but to join the clause, καθὼς παρέδοσαν κ. τ. λ., not to ἀνατάξασθαι—so that it would contain the description of the quality of the sources used by the πολλοί—but to πράγματα ἐν ἡμῖν πεπληροφορημένα. In accordance with this construction, the ἡμῖν after παρέδοσαν would be quite parallel with ἐν ἡμῖν πεπληροφορημένα, and the meaning would be, "since many have undertaken to put forth a narrative of the events which are regarded among us (members of the Christian Church) as historically established, just as the eye-witnesses have reported them to us, (to myself and all members of that communion;) so I also have determined," &c. Thus, therefore, the *events* only appear perfectly ascertained by the tradition of the Church. The quality of the narratives is left at first undetermined; but is afterwards represented as suspicious by the

---

* *Hug* (Introd. p. 387, ff., Fosdick's Translation) interprets καθὼς παρέδοσαν "as the eye-witnesses put them,—*i. e.*, the writings of the πολλοί, into our hands;" an interpretation which stands or falls with the opinion of this learned author, that the writings of the πολλοί are works of the Apostles.

† Thus *Origen* explains it correctly in Luc. hom. 1. Quod ait "*conati sunt*" latentem habet accusationem eorum, qui absque gratia spiritus sancti ad scribenda evangelia prosilierunt.

contrast exhibited between St. Luke and the πολλοί, and particularly by ver. 4. This view agrees best with the opinion which we endeavoured to establish in the Introduction,—viz., that the apostolical tradition concerning the person of Jesus and His history was concentrated in our four canonical Gospels alone, and that all older writings of that sort bore more or less of an apocryphal character.

Ver. 1.—The words πολλοί ἐπεχείρησαν διήγησιν ἀνατάξασθαι, can hardly be understood of single documents relating to single portions of the Gospel-history, (which from this passage are usually, though not very appropriately, called *diegeses*,) since the use of the singular suggests only connected narratives (whether more or less full) of the whole of the Gospel-history. Indeed ἀνατάξασθαι leads to the supposition, that the πολλοί themselves composed their memoirs from shorter records. But to what writings St. Luke refers cannot be determined; for, as St. Luke most probably was not acquainted with our canonical Gospels, (see Introd. § 3,) we are left to imagine the works of the πολλοί to have been apocryphal attempts to delineate the life of Jesus, which, however, for want of historical information, cannot be more accurately characterized. The πράγματα ἐν ἡμῖν πεπληροφορημένα are mentioned as the subject of the writings of the πολλοί. As this Pröemium must be viewed as introductory to St. Luke's whole work, (the Acts of the Apostles being regarded as a second part of the Gospel,) the expression applies to more than the period of our Lord's earthly sojourn,—it embraces also the growth of the Church up to the time when St. Luke wrote. But when the Evangelist immediately adds, in the words πεπληροφορημένα ἐν ἡμῖν, a remark on the *credibility* of the events, (those in the life of Jesus, as well as those which happened afterwards in the early Church,) it is probably because their character is such, that their miraculous form appears at first sight to contradict their credibility.

(The signification "happen," "take place," cannot be assigned either to πληροφορεῖσθαι, or to מָלֵא, which some have thought to resemble it. Πληροφορέω has, in the first instance, the same meaning as πληρόω; then, as transferred to what is spiritual, "to afford conviction, certainty."* So it is found, particularly

---

* *De Wette's* assertion, that πληροφορέω, in this sense, can be used of persons only, is indefensible.

in the writings of St. Paul, who uses πληροφορία as parallel with πίστις, πεποίθησις. The participle πεπληροφορημένα is therefore equivalent to βέβαια, and should be connected with ἐν ἡμῖν. Immediately after the notice of the firm conviction of the members of the Church of the important events, [which the πολλοί had made the subject of their writings,] there follows appropriately the mention of the vouchers for them.)

Ver. 2.—As vouchers, St. Luke mentions the οἱ ἀπ' ἀρχῆς αὐτόπται and the ὑπηρέται λόγου. As the Evangelist begins with the birth of John the Baptist and Jesus, we ought not to limit the ἀπ' ἀρχῆς to the time of Christ's active ministry; St. Luke meant to delineate the whole new phenomenon from its first commencement.* The αὐτόπται in this place are doubtless Mary the mother of Jesus, and other members of the families of whose private history the first chapters treat; but, for the subsequent history of Jesus and of the Church, the Apostles also are eye-witnesses. Παρέδοσαν is, accordingly, to be understood of oral as well as written tradition, since most probably the family information, as conveyed to us in the early chapters, is founded on written records. It is incorrect to take the αὐτόπται to mean the Apostles, and the ὑπηρέται λόγου their assistants; for though ὑπηρέτης is used, it is true, of apostolical assistants, (see Acts xiii. 5, although the reading there is not quite certain,) yet ὑπηρέτης λόγου, sc. Θεοῦ, is never so used. This name designates the Apostles and all teachers in the Church in common; the expression does not therefore indicate a new class of witnesses, but only describes the same witnesses more fully. In reference to one portion of the events which St. Luke is about to describe, they were merely eye-witnesses; but in reference to the other (later) portion, they were themselves the acting parties, so that there they bore witness of themselves. This whole clause relates accordingly only to πράγματα ἐν ἡμῖν πεπληροφορημένα. On the manner in which the πολλοί used these sources, St. Luke, in order to spare them, says nothing definite; only, the subsequent statement of the principles on which he proceeded in the composition of his own work, quietly intimates the insufficiency of their productions.

---

* *De Wette* asserts boldly, that the narrative of the Gospel-history usually began with Christ's entrance on His official work. Why? Because St. Mark (i. 1) begins so!

Ver. 3.—St. Luke specifies three points, in which he expounds, as it were, his historical method; the terms ἄνωθεν, ἀκριβῶς, and καθεξῆς, here come under notice. The first two words apply to the use made of the sources of information, the last to the description itself. (In παρακολουθεῖν, the mind's action in following—living over again, as it were,—the whole train of events [which implies inquiry and search] is intimated.) In the works of the πολλοί, the opposites of all the three points are tacitly implied. In the first place, as respects ἄνωθεν, it refers to ἀπ' ἀρχῆς, ver. 2; St. Luke meant to bring out to view the earliest germs of this new phenomenon, and fully to detail them; of course, the πάντα are only to be understood as implying all that appeared to St. Luke to claim a place in the description of the whole; in the choice of facts, the subjective views of each Evangelist appeared. But by no means ought πᾶσι to be referred to αὐτόπται; it belongs to the πράγματα, on account of which alone the persons are mentioned. Ἀκριβῶς, characterizes the historical investigation as a clear and careful process—opposed to the uncritical method of the apocryphal writings. Lastly, καθεξῆς can apply only to the chronology, as in Acts xi. 4. (In Acts xviii. 23, it is used of contiguity in space.) The plan of the book shews that St. Luke *intended* to observe that order in the main; but this intention, it must be confessed, does not extend to the very minute chronological details, since in them St. Luke seems to have deviated from the order of time. (See Introd. § 7, and the commentary on Luke ix. 51.)

Ver. 4.—The laying down of these historical principles was intended to give historical certainty and warrant (ἀσφάλεια) to Theophilus, who, as being acquainted with classical literature, probably made stricter demands than the uncritical apocryphal writings could satisfy. In the first place, St. Luke wrote from the reports of eye-witnesses, and, next, with a discriminating use of those reports. Doubtless, he laid much stress on the character of the persons with whom those reports originated; and the credibility of the whole Gospel-history rests, therefore, upon the Spirit, who animates a whole circle of individuals linked together by His living communication.* Facts such as

---

* Justly does *Osiander* exclaim, in his *Apologie des Lebens Jesu*, Tübingen, 1837, S. 63: "What shall be said when *Strauss*, instead of refuting the strong anti-mythical argument afforded by St. Luke's preface, imagines it invalidated

the agency of the Holy Ghost in the birth of Jesus, could be attested only by Mary herself; but he who was moved by the same Spirit that enabled her to give such testimony, received her witness, and needed no other; he who was a stranger to that Spirit, found no other testimonies, and accordingly left the matter uncredited. The acknowledgment of the ἀσφάλεια of the Gospel-history always presupposes, therefore, faith in the Spirit of truth; and as in human life truth and falsehood appear side by side indeed, but yet are at the same time opposed, being distinguished as the kingdom of God and the World,—*to him who is conversant with the world and its spirit, which everywhere suspects falsehood and deceit, because it carries them about in itself—to him, as such, the Gospel-history cannot and will not be accredited.* But St. Luke's narrative afforded complete assurance to Theophilus, because he was not out of this sphere of the Spirit of truth, but lived within it. He was a member of the Church, (and the early Church possessed the Spirit of truth fully,) as indicated by the words περὶ ὧν κατηχήθης λόγων, and the Spirit of the αὐτόπται was therefore in him also. (Κατηχεῖσθαι, is the usual term for attending on instruction in religion. See Acts xviii. 25; 1 Cor. xiv. 19; Gal. vi. 6.) Only we must not conceive of the κατήχησις in the earliest times of the Church to have consisted of a communication of doctrines; it was founded on history only, (λόγοι,—*histories, narrations.*) Reflection was not yet developed in the Church, and doctrines had not yet been deduced from God's mighty acts by logical process. The Apostles were content with bearing witness to the great facts of the life of Jesus; on this real foundation the Church was reared. Mere opinions, doctrines, dogmas, could never have given rise to such an appearance as the Christian Church presents. But after its formation, there could not fail to arise within it systematizing doctrinal activity, because the Spirit of Christ is destined to pervade all the powers of human nature. But though the instruction of the ancient Church was historical, yet it was not on that account merely of a narrative nature; rather, the testimony of the first ministers of the word was accompanied by a power which attracted those hearts which received it into the new sphere of life opened by the Saviour;

---

by the empty assertion, 'that St. Luke certainly might speak so, if he had no idea that he was narrating myths,' and degrades a historian, who begins so discreetly, to a thoughtless collector of unconsciously framed myths?"

and, by the agency of that Spirit, those who had received the testimony of the truth, became themselves, in turn, witnesses of those same great facts, which were not merely outwardly known to them as things past and over, but exerted a living power within, through the agency of the living Spirit. The Church was thus built up purely from within itself; nothing foreign could intrude into its circle: first, the testimony to the truth had to be received and embraced with the accompanying power of the Spirit; then followed incorporation into this new sphere of life, and belief in its decisions. Even so the Church is built up at this day, and will be till the end of time; it needs, therefore, no further warrant for the truth of the Gospel-history than the reports of eye-witnesses, which are open to us, and which are still accompanied by the same power of the Spirit of truth, as their oral narrations formerly were, causing in those hearts which give it admission, the same assurance as was produced by the words of the witnesses of Jesus in the apostolic age.

Who and what Theophilus was, (compare Acts i. 1,) cannot be determined further, than that the character of St. Luke's work leads us to conjecture it to have been addressed to one who was familiar with Rome and Italy, and, consequently, in all probability resident there.* The opinion that the Theophilus to whom St. Luke wrote, is the high-priest Theophilus spoken of by Josephus, (Antiq. xviii. 6, 3; xix. 6, 4,) is therefore to be rejected, since we cannot imagine him to have been so well acquainted with Italy. Besides, the title κράτιστος, like the Latin *splendidus*, intimates considerable dignity, with which this Theophilus was invested. It was granted to proconsuls in the provinces, (Acts xxiii. 26; xxiv. 3; xxvi. 25;) at a later period, however, inferior officials also enjoyed it. (See *Hug's* Introd., p. 395, Fosdick's Translation.) Although, therefore, the Gospel of St. Luke, as well as the Acts of the Apostles, were, in the first instance, addressed to a distinguished private person, yet the Church has justly received them into the canon, like the Epistles to Timothy, Titus, and Philemon; because the individuals for whom they were immediately intended, shared, as members of the Church, its general wants; and, therefore, what was adapted to them might be given to all.

---

* The opinion that Theophilus should be taken as an appellative,=Friend of God, and as including all believing readers, may be regarded as antiquated.

§ 2. ANNUNCIATION OF THE BIRTH OF JOHN THE BAPTIST.

(Luke i. 5-25.)

St. Luke places ἄνωθεν, in ver. 3, so far back, that he begins the history of Christ, and of the formation of the Church, as early as the birth of John the Baptist. This view results from the nature of the phenomenon which he was to describe historically. For after the spirit of prophecy became silent, from the time of the building of the second temple, and seemed entirely to have vanished from among the people, a prophet, in the person of John the Baptist, appeared again, for the first time, in the Old Testament form. His history, therefore, could not but be included within the limits of the description, since it formed an integral part of the Gospel-history. There is something striking, too, in the change of style in the body of the work, as compared with the preface; while in the former, pure Greek prevails, in the latter, the strongest Hebraisms appear. This sudden change is most naturally accounted for on the supposition, that St. Luke, in the narration of the history, made use of written sources of information, and that he incorporated them into his work, often quite unchanged, or only slightly amended. The character of the narratives, moreover, particularly in the first two chapters, renders this conjecture extremely probable; for events are recorded in them, which took place in the bosom of two families, and which must have been preserved in them as a sacred treasure, till the hopes expressed of the two scions of the families had been made good by the result. But afterwards, when the Saviour's great work was accomplished, and Mary, the mother of our Lord, was numbered among the multitude of the first disciples, (Acts i. 14,) nothing was more natural than that she should impart to the community the wonders that clustered round the birth of Him whom she herself now adored as her Saviour. The holy family had, as it were, expanded; and, in connexion with it, the sacred histories also, of which it had been the scene, could be more widely diffused.

Ver. 5.—St. Luke begins with defining the time in the general, (see note on Matth. ii. 1,) by setting out from the reign of Herod the Great, and then portrays the family which is to be the immediate subject of his narrative. In conformity with his object, he could not, like St. Matthew, assume much as already known. He rather describes all the characters fully. Zacharias and Elisabeth were both of a priestly family, (as Joseph and Mary were both of the lineage of David,) which gave lustre to their offspring.* Of Zacharias we are further told, that, as priest, he belonged to the course or class of Abia. This was the eighth of the twenty-four classes of priests appointed by David. (See 1 Chron. xxiv. 10.) Each of these classes took the service in the temple for a week. (In *Josephus* [Antiq. vii. 15, 7,] they are called πατριαί, with reference to the relationship which existed among them. The name ἐφημερία, which does not occur elsewhere in the New Testament, is chosen with reference to their daily duty in the temple.) The use which *Scaliger* (opus de emendatione temporum) and *Bengel* (ordo temporum) have attempted to make of the definite succession of the twenty-four classes of priests in the temple service, as a chronological datum, cannot afford any results to be at all depended upon, because the *terminus a quo* of the rotation cannot be definitely fixed.

Ver. 6.—The mention of their personal standing succeeds the description of their family relations. Both were δίκαιοι, and that not merely outwardly before men, but ἐνώπιον τοῦ Θεοῦ. The idea of δικαιοσύνη used of persons under the law, (as it is in Luke ii. 25, of Simeon, and 2 Peter ii. 7, of Lot,) can of course be understood of legal righteousness only, as is shewn by the explanatory clause, πορευόμενοι ἐν πάσαις ταῖς ἐντολαῖς καὶ δικαιώμασι τοῦ Κυρίου ἄμεμπτοι. The ἐντολαί and the δικαιώματα, are the individual declarations and statutes of the law, which they had striven to follow with upright mind, and without pharisaical hypocrisy. But when, in this and other passages, (Matth. x. 41; Luke xv. 7,) δικαιοσύνη is ascribed to certain persons, there is no opposition or contradiction to Rom. iii. 20, according to which passage the law causes knowledge of sin. The δικαιοσύνη τοῦ νόμου never is an absolute righteousness, (Gal. iii. 20;) but, relatively, it always implies, in those who strive for its attain-

---

* Josephus (vit. c. 1) remarks, Παρ' ἡμῖν ἡ τῆς ἱερωσύνης μετουσία τεκμήριον ἐστι γένους λαμπρότητος.

ment, repentance and faith; and hence a longing for the finisher of that which is wanting to them. Thus, on account of their δικαιοσύνη, the desire for a σωτήρ was lively in Zacharias and Elisabeth. (On δικαιοσύνη, and all cognate words, see the complete exposition in the note on Rom. iii. 21.)

Ver. 7.—But the want of a blessing in respect of offspring formed a contrast with their δικαιοσύνη, as in the case of Sarah. Elisabeth was barren, (στεῖρα, see Luke xxiii. 29; Gal. iv. 27,) and both were no longer young.* The age of Zacharias must be considered relatively only,—viz., with respect to his office. According to Numb. viii. 25, no one was permitted to perform the functions of a priest beyond the fiftieth year of his age. If we take into account also the oriental custom of marrying early, Zacharias and Elisabeth might well have given up the hope of offspring on account of their long childless marriage, notwithstanding that the age of Zacharias, considered in itself, was not so great.

(Καθότι is found only in the writings of St. Luke, sometimes with the meaning *siquidem*, as in this passage and xix. 9; Acts ii. 24; sometimes meaning "according as," "as far as," Acts ii. 45; iv. 35. The phrase προβεβηκὼς ἐν ταῖς ἡμέραις = בָּא בַּיָּמִים, Gen. xviii. 11, and frequently elsewhere.)

Ver. 8, 9, 10.—After these prefatory observations, which inform the reader of the circumstances of the family whose history is about to be told, there follows, introduced by an ἐγένετο δέ = וַיְהִי, the special narration of the events connected with the birth of John. According to the arrangement of the Jewish service, incense was offered twice daily,—at the morning and evening sacrifice. (Ex. xxx. 7, 8.) The ministering priest carried the censer with incense (θυμίαμα) into the holy place, (ναός = הֵיכָל, the temple properly speaking, while ἱερόν includes the courts also; see Matth. xii. 5; John ii. 14,) in front of which the courts extended, where the multitude assembled for prayer stood, awaiting the return of the priest. The twenty-four classes of the priests alternated according to a determinate

---

* It was the same with the mothers of Isaac and Samuel. The *Evangelium de nativitate Mariæ* (Thilo. vol. i., p. 322,) remarks appropriately on this point:— Deus cum alicujus uterum claudit, ad hoc facit, ut mirabilius denuo aperiat, et non libidinis esse quod nascitur, sed divini muneris cognoscatur.

cycle; but the priest who was to minister for the day was chosen by lot (ἔλαχε τοῦ θυμιάσαι) from among the priests who constituted each class. This had become the established custom of the priest's office. (Ἱεράτεια differs from ἱεράτευμα, *priesthood*, 1 Peter ii. 5, and ἱερωσύνη, *priestly service*, Heb. vii. 11, 12, 14.) Once upon a time, then, as the turn (τάξις) came to his class, it fell to Zacharias, by lot, to fill this office. (In ver. 8 ἔναντι is preferable to the more common form ἐναντίον. It is found in the New Testament only in this passage, and corresponds with ἔναντα used by Homer. In the Old Testament the LXX has ἔναντι in the passage Job xvi. 21.)

Ver. 11.—It is possible that the lot brought Zacharias into the temple for the first time, and the quiet sanctuary around powerfully affected him. These possibilities cannot make a sober expositor doubt that the narrator intends the appearance of the angel to be regarded as a fact; nor can they lead a believing critic of this narrative to require the commonness of everyday life even in the most glorious moments of the life of our race. At the time when the eternal Word descended to become flesh, (John i. 1, 14,) manifestations of the spiritual world appeared in the world of mankind, such as were not needed in less powerfully excited seasons. (See note on Matth. i. 18 ; ii. 8.) As the result of a vivid conception, minute features are given, which confirm the historical fact, and are unfavourable to the mythical view. The angel appeared by the altar, on the right side of it. (The θυσιαστήριον τοῦ θυμιάματος is described Ex. xxx. 1, ff.; it stood in the holy place, and must be carefully distinguished from the great altar of burnt-offerings in the court, Heb. vii. 13.)

Ver. 12-14.—Although the vision was to be a blessing to Zacharias, yet fear seized him when he saw it, as was frequently the case in similar circumstances. (Compare Luke i. 29; Rev. i. 17; Dan. x. 7, 12.) *In one aspect*, this fear, at the immediate view of appearances from the unseen world, is an expression of the feeling of sinfulness. But for sin, man would see in what is divine something akin to himself; and instead of fear, he would experience ravishing delight. *In another aspect*, however, this fear is expressive of a susceptibility to perceive this contrast between what is pure and what is unholy; and in this consists its nobler character. On this account, such fear of God is never considered as blameworthy, but as the beginning

(Psalm cxi. 10) and the end (Isaiah xi. 2) of all wisdom. This fear of God, which is consistent with love, (see Rev. i. 17, where the disciple of love falls to the earth with fear at the sight of Him whom he loves,) must not, therefore, be confounded with the φόβος, which the πνεῦμα δουλείας engenders. The latter implies being afraid of God, (*vor* Gott,) which is absolutely culpable; the latter might be called fear at ourselves, or fear *for* God, (*für* Gott.) (See note on Rom. viii. 15.) The heavenly messenger quiets this holy fear, and then communicates his message of joy. (The δέησις indicates that Zacharias had not altogether given up the hope of offspring. Γεννᾷν is equivalent to τίκτειν, as Gal. iv. 24.) At the same time a name is given, as Matth. i. 21, to the promised son, and in the name his spiritual importance is expressed. (Ἰωάννης = יְהוֹחָנָן.) Thereby he will bring joy not only to the parents by his physical existence, but also to all the pious by his spiritual manifestation and agency, which are here, by anticipation, connected with his birth. (Ἀγαλλίασις is a stronger term than χαρά. In this passage, as in Matth. i. 18, the reading γενέσει is preferable to the common one γεννήσει.)

Ver. 15.—In the following verses the words of the angel describe, first, the *character* of this promised one; next, his *labours;* and lastly, his *relation* to the Messiah, in whom all the hopes and expectations of believing Israelites centred. In reference to his character, it is first observed in general, that a spiritual importance would attach to him. (Μέγας = גָּדוֹל, in respect of influence, as Hosea i. 11. The additional clause ἐνώπιον Κυρίου, sets aside the idea of worldly importance; he bears a purely spiritual character.) Then the form of his piety is more precisely described by the circumstance, that he will live the life of a Nazarite. (See more particularly the note on Matth. ix. 14. Σίκερα = שֵׁכָר is used of all intoxicating drinks; the passage has reference to Numb. vi. 3, ff.) In the life of a Nazarite there appears concentrated the strict legal character which John, who was, as it were, the top-stone of the Old Testament, was called to exhibit. This form of piety is not, therefore, the highest, because a heavenly appearance ascribes it to John as an excellence; it is assigned to him rather because it agrees with his whole calling and destination. The wisdom of God takes up every character in its individuality and in its surrounding circumstances, and neither requires everything from, nor gives everything to, each. The negative characteristic (οὐ μὴ) is followed by the positive one, (πλησθῆναι πνεύματος ἁγίου.) That this does not imply furnishing with natural capacities, is sufficiently plain from πνεῦμα ἅγιον, which always denotes a superior, heavenly life-power, that does not belong to fallen man as such. To suppose this power at work in John, (as in all Old Testament prophets,) would not be attended with any further difficulty; but the phrase ἔτι ἐκ κοιλίας μητρός is obscure. (Ἐκ κοιλίας μητρός = בְּמֵעֵי אִמִּי, Psalm lxxi. 6. Ἔτι is not precisely equivalent to ἤδη; it is rather to be taken in its proper sense, as the writer conceives the agency of the Holy Spirit continuing from the mother's womb down to a later period.) Considered in itself, the expression ἐκ κοιλίας μητρός might indeed mean merely "from early youth onward;" but, in connexion with ver. 44, we must allow, that, without doubt, the writer intends us to conceive of an active influence in the Baptist *before* his birth. But this thought becomes perfectly intelligible if we consider, *first*, that the πνεῦμα ἅγιον in this passage, is not to be taken as identical with the Holy Spirit, whose outpouring is connected with the completion of the work of Jesus. (See note on John vii. 39.) The expression denotes here the divine power, in so far as it is a holy power, as Psalm li. 13; Isaiah lxiii. 10. And *further*, too, as the Divine Spirit influences even the κτίσις, (Rom. viii. 19,) we can have no hesitation in admitting the fact of His influence in the elect *before* birth. In like manner we must conceive of the influence of baptism on unconscious children; but not as if it should be thought identical with regeneration.

Ver. 16.—The active influence of this prophet promised anew, after so long a silence of the prophetic spirit, is now described as being limited to the people of Israel, warning of destruction, and awakening to repentance. (Ἐπιστρέψει = הֵשִׁיב refers to μετάνοια, which forms the centre of John's labours, Matth. iii. 2.) A new and higher principle of life John could not impart, and that was not his destination; but the Spirit in him was intended to awaken the sense of the higher end of life,—to point men back to God. His ministry was confined to Israel, like that of the Saviour, (Matth. xv. 24,) not as if the other nations were to be excluded from the favours of God, but because what took place in the central nation of mankind was for the benefit of all. There a hearth had first to be prepared for the holy fire, and for that reason the influence of God's messengers was concentrated on that spot. That it was not, however, the whole nation, but only certain members of it, that would be gained, is expressed plainly in the words: πολλοὺς τῶν υἱῶν τοῦ Ἰσραὴλ ἐπιστρέψει. Just so when God is called Θεὸς αὐτῶν, as in the Old Testament, "The God of Abraham, Isaac, and Jacob,"—that does not imply at all the exclusion of other nations (Luke ii. 31) from the blessing of the true God, nor a limitation of it to Israel, but the thought that the relation of God to different nations is no more alike than His relation to different individuals. The Bible knows of no national God of the Hebrews; it teaches only, that it hath pleased the one true God, the maker of heaven and earth, to bring Israel into special relation with himself, (Lev. xx. 26; Sirach xxiv. 13,) and in Israel again, certain individuals. The angel speaks here, certainly, in a *human* and Jewish manner,— *i. e.*, so as men and Jews could understand; but, at the same time, in a *divine* manner, since it is purely divine determinations to which his words refer, and with which they connect new divine ordinances.

Ver. 17.—*Lastly*, The appearance of the new prophet is shewn to be connected with the Messiah, as prophesied by Malachi, (iii. 23;) according to which passage, Elijah was to precede the appearance of the Messiah, exercising a preparatory influence, (Matth. iii. 7, ff.—Προέρχεσθαι, involves preparation.) But the expression · ἐν πνεύματι καὶ δυνάμει Ἠλίου, gives this passage an explanatory character. John was not to be Elijah raised from the dead, but his antitype; being of a like spiritual nature, he was to exercise a kindred influence. While πνεῦμα denotes what is more general,—his peculiar tendency, regulated by the higher principle of life that animated him,—δύναμις refers more to what is special. In Elijah, the idea of divine *power*, as punitive, is, as it were, personified; this same spiritual character is that of John. (Comp. more particularly in note on Matth. xi. 14.) The angel's referring to the language of Scripture, is parallel with the quotation from Scripture in Christ's temptation, on the part of the devil. (Matth. iv. 6.) It is wrong to make use of these passages to impugn the historical view of the appearances of angels. Such circumstances are, evidently, not to be viewed as if angels were quoting *from* the Scriptures; but it is in the Scriptures, because it is so determined in the heavenly world, to which the spiritual persons speaking belong. The attaching of the thought to the words of Scripture, is to be viewed as merely clothing them in the form familiar and intelligible among men. Angels do not, therefore, quote the words of Scripture, because they wish to derive from the Bible a proof or an illustration of what they say; but the thoughts expressed by them are in the Bible, because they contain a truth, which stands good, as well in heaven as in earth. This verse is, further, of the highest importance on account of the expression, ἐνώπιον αὐτοῦ, which refers grammatically to Κύριον τὸν Θεὸν αὐτῶν, ver. 16, so that God himself is conceived as appearing in the Messiah. Were this thought foreign or contradictory to the doctrine of Scripture, a less natural explanation might be attempted, (as, *e. g.*, that αὐτός = הוּא denoted the Messiah, that well-known, that desired one;) but as even the Old Testament (Isa. xl. 3, 5; Jer. xxiii. 6; xxxiii. 16; Joel iii. 26; Mal. iii. 1) intimates the same truth, and the New Testament (John i. 14) expresses it clearly in doctrinal form, the expositor must abide by the simple construction of the words. It was the exalted destination of the Baptist to lead the hearts of men, alienated by sin from what is divine, to the Lord of all lords, who revealed himself in Christ visibly and near. The concluding words of ver. 17 are a free quotation from Mal. iii. 23. The LXX., which substantially follows the Hebrew text, translates ὃς ἀποκαταστήσει καρδίαν πατρὸς πρὸς υἱὸν, καὶ καρδίαν ἀνθρώπου πρὸς τὸν πλησίον αὐτοῦ. In this way the words affirm only that he will remove the alienation of men's spirit, and restore love and peace. But, according to the words in St. Luke, the second half of the sentence, ἐπιστρέψαι ἀπειθεῖς ἐν φρονήσει δικαίων, acquires, apparently, a different meaning. But if we look on ἀπειθεῖς as corresponding to "the children," and the δίκαιοι as corresponding to the "fathers," the thought remains essentially the same; he will produce a great moral effect on the people, restraining the fierce outbreakings of sin; he will awaken a salutary endeavour after righteousness, and thus call forth a λαὸς κατεσκευασμένος, whose character consists in the sense of a need of salvation. (Φρόνησις is here nearly related to σοφία, [הָכְמָה,] although not identical with it; it is בִּינָה in the noblest sense; so that ungodliness appears as the true folly, godliness as the true wisdom. [Matth. x. 16.] 'Εν φρονήσει in construction with ἐπιστρέψαι must be viewed as another case, where a verb of motion is joined immediately with a preposition of rest.)

Ver. 18.—The promise on the part of the angel of a son, was not to exclude natural generation; Christ's birth happened differently from John's. This is a parallel with Isaac's birth in the Old Testament; but the unbelief of Zacharias forms a striking contrast to Abraham's faith. Of Abraham it is said, οὐ κατενόησε τὸ ἑαυτοῦ σῶμα ἤδη νενεκρωμένον, Rom. iv. 19. Zacharias looked at his age and his long unfruitful marriage in a doubting spirit. It is not, therefore, the forethought exercised by the father that is blamed, but his unbelief;* he was certainly convinced that the vision in the temple beside the altar, which filled his heart with holy fear, was a heavenly one, but, nevertheless, he allowed unbelief a place in his heart. The wrong lay not in the words of the question, but in the disposition from which it proceeded. (Mary's question [Luke i. 34] *sounds* like one that proceeded from doubt, and yet she was really believing as a child.) The asking for a sign (אוֹת, σημεῖον) in confirmation of the promise, is never misinterpreted, (see Gen. xv. 8, where Abraham asks בַּמָּה אֵדַע = κατὰ τί γνώσομαι τοῦτο;) on the contrary, under certain circumstances, not to ask for one is rebuked. (Isa. vii. 13.) Zacharias' request for a sign is therefore granted; but, on account of his unbelief, he receives a sign that is a punishment.

Ver. 19.—To accredit himself, as it were, (and to correct the unbelieving Zacharias,) the heavenly messenger makes himself known in his high dignity; he calls himself Gabriel, (גַּבְרִיאֵל, Dan. viii. 16; ix. 21,—*i. e., man of God*, representing the creative power of God.) That the angel applies a Hebrew name to himself, loses all that might be surprising in it, if we view rightly the meaning of names. A name is nothing else than the term which corresponds to the inmost essence of the object named. Inasmuch, therefore, as the beings of the spiritual world possess definite characters, they have their names; whether those names assume a Hebrew form or any other form of human speech, depends on circumstances. Here we have, at the same time, an explanation of the fact, that the names of the angels are not met with till the later periods of the Jewish

---

* Such an expression of unbelief at such an instant, is not so much to be conceived as proceeding from reflection and intention, but should be viewed rather as an involuntary utterance of the inward condition of the soul. In such moments, the inmost being of the soul becomes manifest; it is seen whether faith or unbelief occupies the heart's core. The event had, therefore, for Zacharias himself, a perfecting effect on his spiritual life.

state; for the general idea of a world of spiritual beings could be much more easily formed, than that of a clear conception of distinct individuals in this higher world, and not till then could names be framed to denote such individualities. By the adjunct: παρεστηκὼς ἐνώπιον τοῦ Θεοῦ, the individual that appeared is further associated with a certain class of angels. (See more fully in note on Matth. xviii. 10.) The gradation of existences everywhere prevailing throughout creation, is quite consistently conceived by men to exist in the world of spirits also. In the doctrine of the Zendavesta, likewise, there appear degrees among the angels; the seven Amshaspands are imagined to be nearest to the throne of God.* That there is truth in this mode of conceiving the matter, is proved by the Scriptures, which, long before the Jews had any connexion with the Persians, represent angels in the more immediate presence of God. (Isa. vi. 1, ff.) The descriptions in Dan. vii. 9, ff. and Rev. iv. 1, ff., also evidently convey the idea of the existences of the spiritual world standing at various degrees of distance from God, and of a corresponding modification of their dignity.

Ver. 20.—Zacharias, for his unbelieving language, has inflicted upon him the punishment of dumbness; but, at the same time, the period of healing is foretold as an alleviation, and for a sign of the promise given.

(Μὴ δυνάμενος λαλῆσαι is merely an explanatory clause of σιωπῶν for κωφός, which term is used, ver. 22. Ἀνθ᾽ ὧν [Luke xii. 3; xix. 44] answers both to אֲשֶׁר תַּחַת, Deut. xxviii. 47, and to אֲשֶׁר עַל, Jer. xxii. 9. Εἰς τὸν καιρὸν αὐτῶν is to be taken " according to the succession of the several incidents;" first the birth of the child must take place, and then he would shew himself to be the promised one.)

Ver. 21, 22.—According to the later tradition, the priests are said not to have remained long at prayer in the temple, in order not to excite the fear of some misfortune having happened

---

* Agreeably with this, we find in the Persian constitution, which was intended as a copy of the heavenly order, *seven* princes of the kingdom, (or chamberlains,) who stood first round the king's throne. (Esther i. 10, 14.) The supposition that the Jews derived their doctrines about angels from the Parsees, is discountenanced by the fact, that the Hebrews had only *four* throne-angels, as well as by general reasons. (See note on Matth. viii. 28. Compare also *Buxt. lex. talm.*, p. 46.) It must be confessed, however, that they had the number seven as well as four. (See more fully in note on Rev. iv. 5, 6.)

to them in the temple, which, as the officiating priest was regarded as the representative of the nation, would have been viewed in the light of a national calamity. Hence the continued stay of Zacharias in the temple, though not in itself long, was already beginning to excite surprise. The observation that they perceived he had seen a vision (ὀπτασία = מַרְאָה), does not refer to his silence, but probably to his whole appearance, in which violent excitement may have been expressed, which, from his coming out of the temple, was immediately referred to a spiritual cause. Zacharias confirmed the opinion thus expressed, by signs, (αὐτὸς ἦν διανεύων αὐτοῖς.)

Ver. 23, 24.—After the completion of the week, during which the class of the priests to which Zacharias belonged had fulfilled their service, he returned to his house, and his wife became with child. During the first period of her pregnancy, however, she kept herself retired, in order that all uncertainty might be removed.

(In the New Testament λειτουργία, from λεῖτος = δημόσιος, never means political service; yet it is used of external service, as Phil. ii. 30; 2 Cor. ix. 12. The term commonly denotes holy service, as Heb. ix. 21, and is applied also to purely spiritual relations, as Phil. ii. 17, λειτουργία τῆς πίστεως.)

Ver. 25.—The happy mother acknowledges, with gratitude, the divine blessing in her pregnancy. According to the Old Testament notion, to be without children was a reproach, (Isa. iv. 1; Hos. ix. 11, 12;) and in this the prevailing tendency to what is external is plainly expressed. In the New Testament, the idea of spiritual activity prevails, in comparison with which the external is placed in the shade.

(Ὅτι, introducing the direct sentence, often appears in the New Testament according to the analogy of the Hebrew כִּי. [See Exod. iv. 25; xviii. 15.] רָאָה and פָּקַד are often used, like ἐπεῖδω, in the sense of "to direct the countenance to anything as a token of favour." In the opposite signification—which פָּקַד also often has—ἐπεῖδω occurs in Acts iv. 29.)

§ 3. ANNUNCIATION OF THE BIRTH OF JESUS—MARY'S VISIT TO ELISABETH.

(Luke i. 26-56.)

St. Luke's record is here more specific as to time and place than St. Matthew's. We can, therefore, by his help, render St. Matthew's account more full and circumstantial. The words ἐν τῷ μηνὶ τῷ ἕκτῳ, which refer to ver. 24, furnish a datum of some importance for the age of Jesus in relation to John; and the observation, that the annunciation took place at Nazareth, explains to us Matth. ii. 23. Doubtless Mary (or Joseph) had property in Nazareth as well as in Bethlehem; on which account Nazareth is called, in Luke ii. 39, πόλις αὐτῶν. (On Nazareth and Galilee, see note on Matth. ii. 22, 23. Μνηστεύεσθαι = אָרַשׂ, see Deut. xxii. 23.)

Ver. 28, 29.—The description which follows, of a secret transaction of the most delicate character, is conceived with such simplicity and tenderness, and, at the same time, with such freedom from any uncalled for intermixture of subjective reflection, that it confirms the fact to every mind open to truth; and it is only by force that it can be perverted to any impure associations. With a heavenly salutation the messenger of the higher world introduces himself to the humble, child-like Mary,—Χαῖρε κεχαριτωμένη. (Χαριτόω, to MAKE pleasant, agreeable, is found only in Ephes. i. 6, besides in this place. It is in use also among the later authors,—e. g., Libanius.) The expression does not mean and self-produced holiness and excellence in Mary, but only her election by grace. The Lord had chosen her, even in the line of her ancestors, to be the mother of the Saviour. With child-like innocence she was not aware of her high destination, and thought herself not worthy of this happiness,—the highest that a daughter of Abraham could imagine. While, therefore, κεχαριτωμένη applies to her whole spiritual state, the subsequent expression, εὐλογημένη ἐν γυναιξίν, refers to the announcement of her destination; so that γενήσῃ may be supplied.* Mary fell

---

* Εὐλογεῖν, like בֵּרֵךְ, has a double sense, according as it is used of the relation of superior to inferior, or of inferior to superior. In the former relation it means "to bless;" in the latter, "to praise," "to thank," which presupposes our having been blessed.

into meditation on the meaning of this salutation, (ποταπός denotes as much the quantity as the quality, Matth. viii. 27; 1 John iii. 1;) and on the appearance of the heavenly messenger (on διεταράχθη, see note on i. 12,) she did not know how to apply it to herself. (On διαλογισμός, διαλογίζεσθαι from λόγος = νοῦς, see note on ii. 35.)

Ver. 30, 31.—The further execution of the commission begins with a quieting μὴ φοβοῦ, (see i. 13,) and an assurance of the favour of God. The idea of "favour" (χάρις = חֵן, εὑρίσκειν χάριν = מָצָא חֵן) involves here the free exercise of divine love, which does not appear determined by anything existing out of or in her. It is consequently an expression of the pure choice of grace, which leaves the creature no possibility of personal merit. The announcement, that Mary was to become a mother, is accompanied, as in Matth. i. 21, with the mention of the name which the child was to receive.

Ver. 32, 33.—The character of this expected child of God is now described by infinitely more exalted traits than was that of John above, ch. i. 16, 17.* He comes as υἱὸς ὑψίστου, (John as δοῦλος,) and as the ruler over the house of Jacob, to which John himself belonged.

(On μέγας, see note on ver. 15; and on υἱὸς ὑψίστου, further remarks in note on i. 35. The term ὕψιστος corresponds to the Hebrew עֶלְיוֹן, Gen. xiv. 18. Καλεῖσθαι is sometimes used of false, empty speaking; and then the essence, as being something superior, is opposed to it; but, sometimes, of being named, in as far as it is a correct denomination of the essence; and in this latter meaning it is (like נִקְרָא) synonymous with εἶναι, but with the accessory idea of being recognized to be such. This meaning, which is connected with the use of ὄνομα, (שֵׁם,) is often found; e. g., immediately after in ver. 35, 76; Matth. v. 9, 19; and frequently. The former meaning appears ver. 36, and frequently.)

Then, with respect to the dominion assured to the promised offspring, it is, in the first place, connected with the person of David. The principal passage which establishes this connexion is 2 Sam. vii. 13, ff. In its immediate literal sense, it applies

---

* See *Theremin's* incomparable Sermon on the words, "He shall be great," in his *Kreuz Christi*, Th. i., Serm. 2.

to Solomon, who, however, is, at the same time, viewed as a type of the true Prince of Peace. The passage is so treated even by the prophets, (Psalm lxxxix. 5; Isaiah ix. 7; Jer. xxxiii. 15, ff.) Next, the dominion of the expected King is described as an everlasting one. The indefinite phrase εἰς τοὺς αἰῶνας (LXX. have εἰς τὸν αἰῶνα in 2 Sam. vii. 13, 16) is defined more accurately by οὐκ ἔσται τέλος; so that the dominion of Jesus is here described as an everlasting, endless one, in its proper sense. This thought conducts to the right view of the limitation we here perceive of the Messiah's kingdom to the house of Jacob. A dominion that extends beyond all time, cannot, at the same time, be conceived as limited by political boundaries. The particular reference to the house of Jacob is to be viewed here in the same manner as in Luke i. 16; and, at the same time, the people of Israel is regarded (as in Matth. ii. 6) as a type of the sanctified race of mankind brought together in the kingdom of the Messiah. (John xi. 52.)

Ver. 34.—With child-like innocence Mary expresses her doubts at this wonderful language; she does not live in marriage connexion with any one, (γινώσκω = יָדַע,) and cannot, therefore, be a mother. According to the entire form of the answer, it *might* have proceeded from unbelief; at least the words are not expressive of faith. The connexion, however, favours the idea, that Mary believed, but wished to know *how* this promise could be accomplished. Believing inquiry, directed in a child-like spirit, is therefore not blamed.

Ver. 35.—In answer to this question, the angel discloses to her, that the Son of God, whom she was to bear, would be conceived in a pure and chaste manner in her virgin womb. In words of deep import the heavenly messenger declares this sublime mystery to her. In the first thought, πνεῦμα ἅγιον ἐπελεύσεται ἐπί σε, the πνεῦμα ἅγιον is, as in i. 15, the divine essence in general, which, in its nature, is holy. As the generation of Jesus, according to His *physical* existence, is here spoken of, we cannot refer the creative agency to the Holy Spirit in the narrow sense, as it would not be in conformity with the fundamental view of the Trinity, agreeably to which the world of conscious moral agents is the sphere of His agency.*

---

* If we were to hold this to refer literally to the third person of the Godhead, it would, moreover, follow that the Holy Ghost was the father of Jesus Christ;

The absence of the article is in favour of this view; πνεῦμα ἅγιον has indeed acquired the nature of a proper name, but δύναμις ὑψίστου could not have been without the article, if the third person of the Godhead had been intended. In ἐπελεύσεται ἐπί σε there is also, most probably, an allusion to the description of the creation of the world, (Gen. i. 2, where the LXX. translate, מְרַחֶפֶת, ἐπεφέρετο ἐπάνω τοῦ ὕδατος,) of which the creation of the first man is a copy, which has its antitype in the regeneration. (John iii. 5, 8.) The latter half of the verse explains the former more particularly. Δύναμις ὑψίστου here corresponds to πνεῦμα ἅγιον, and indicates the correct notion of it as the creative power of God. (אֱלֹהִים, Gen. i. 2.) Ἐπισκιάσει σοι stands as explanatory of ἐπελεύσεται ἐπί σε. Ἐπισκιάζειν does not at all involve the idea of "protecting, screening," (according to the analogy of the Hebrew סָמַךְ;) the connexion leads evidently to the idea of generation. It is best, therefore, to compare it with the Hebrew פָּרַשׂ כְּנָפַיִם (Ruth iii. 9; Ezek. xvi. 8) in the signification of spreading out the wings, (= skirts of a garment,) consequently "to surround," "to overshadow,"* which is an euphonistic expression for connubial intercourse. Perhaps the term contains also a remote allusion to מְרַחֶפֶת in Gen. i. 2. The word רָחַף is well known to have the meaning "to hover over;" and in Deut. xxxii. 11, it is placed in parallelism with פָּרַשׂ כְּנָפַיִם. The whole thought of the remarkable verse is, therefore, no other than this, that Mary, without the intervention of a man, would become a mother;—the pure and chaste power of the creative divine Spirit would be the generator. Consequently, the appearance of the Saviour among mankind is represented as a new, immediate, and divine act of creation, and thus the transmission of sinfulness from the sinful race to Him is excluded. But inasmuch as this act of creation did not altogether exclude the substance of human nature, in consequence of Mary's relation to Jesus, the Saviour, though free from sinfulness in the

---

a mode of speaking very rightly never sanctioned by the Church, since the Holy Ghost does indeed proceed from the Son, but the Son has not His origin from the Spirit. God the Father is the Father of Jesus in His divine and human nature.

* The cherubim also spreading their wings over the ark of the covenant, denote the active presence of God. Exod. xl. 32; Numb. ix. 18, 22. See also *Suiceri Thes.*, vol. i., p. 1175.

principle of life, yet partook in common with men of the ἀσθένεια τῆς σαρκός, (2 Cor. xiii. 4.) On this depended his capacity of suffering, which again was a necessary condition of the whole work of the Saviour.* In *His* human nature He glorified human nature *in general*. The fact of the promised offspring being referred to the πνεῦμα ἅγιον as His origin, necessarily shews Him to be a ἅγιον himself, and as such He is called υἱὸς Θεοῦ. (The words ἐκ σοῦ were probably subjoined to γεννώμενον by the transcribers, to whom the thought appeared imperfect; no tenable reason can be given for their having been intentionally omitted.)

The name υἱὸς Θεοῦ, like υἱὸς ὑψίστου in ver. 32, has here undeniably a reference to the *human* nature of Christ. He is called υἱὸς Θεοῦ, because He was born, *corporeally*, of Mary, from the overshadowing of the Holy Spirit. That the same *physical* meaning of the word υἱὸς is to be assumed in ver. 32, is shewn partly by the connexion with ver. 31, and partly by David's being denominated πατήρ. Passages like Mark xiii. 32; Heb. v. 8, (in which, however, υἱὸς stands alone,) appear likewise to come under this head. Jesus is therefore here called υἱὸς Θεοῦ in the same sense as Adam in Luke iii. 38, inasmuch as He received His being immediately from God's hand;—the first and second Adam are parallel in this respect also. Both form a contrast to the υἱοὶ τῶν ἀνθρώπων, who, as descendants of fallen Adam, bear in themselves the image of the fallen one, (Gen. v. 3.) On the contrary, when Jesus is called ὁ υἱὸς τοῦ ἀνθρώπου, (with the article, which is very rarely omitted, as it is in John v. 27,) this name is very nearly allied to the physical meaning of the name υἱὸς Θεοῦ, mentioned above. It refers also to the human nature of our Lord, but in such a manner that this nature is conceived in its *ideal* existence. The term has its origin in the Old Testament, which, in several remarkable passages, (forming the basis of the rabbinical dogma of *Adam Kadmon*,) transports the

---

* If Jesus had come into the world by ordinary generation, He would have shared in the *necessitas* moriendi, together with general depravity; if He had not been born of a human mother, the *impossibilitas* moriendi would have belonged to Him; accordingly, only the narrative presented in the Gospels fulfils all that is required in the idea of a Saviour. Being born as man, the Saviour passed a really human life; but, like that of Adam *before* the fall, with a *possibilitas* tentationis et mortis, which then, by His victory, become an *impossibilitas*. (See further note on Matth. iv. 1, ff.)

human nature in its *ideal* into the divine essence itself. (Compare 2 Sam. vii. 19; 1 Chron. xviii. 17; Ezek. i. 26; Dan. vii. 13, 10, 16, with 1 Cor. xv. 45, ff.) Hence an intimate oneness with the Father and the heavenly world is ascribed to the Son of man, (John iii. 13,) and all power and glory, without reference to the humiliation, is ascribed to Him, (John v. 27; Matth. xxvi. 64; Acts vii. 55.) Yet, as the apostles *never* use this name of Him, (out of the Gospels it occurs *only* in Acts vii. 55, and that with a special reference to the *bodily* appearance of our Lord,) and Jesus, on the contrary, chiefly uses it when speaking of himself; it is probable that He desired in that way to bring himself near to man, and intended, at the same time, to set before their eyes the *ideal* of human perfection. In recent times, some would allow the name ὁ υἱὸς τοῦ ἀνθρώπου to be nothing more than a customary name of the Messiah; but this view is very improbable,—for this reason, that then the people would sometimes have given Jesus that name,* or a false Messiah would have assumed it. It is probable, that only a very few of the enlightened among the people understood the name בַּר אֱנָשׁ in the true sense of those prophetic passages, agreeably to which the idea of an original man—an *ideal* of mankind is embodied in it. The name for the Messiah most usual among the people at the time of Jesus, was ὁ υἱὸς Δαβίδ. By this name our Lord was commonly addressed by those who implored His help, and who thus acknowledged His power to help; and the Saviour himself presupposes this name, as so well known and familiar, that He argues upon it, and proves thence the superior dignity of the Messiah. (See Matth. ix. 27; xii. 23; xv. 22; xx. 30, 31; xxi. 9, 15; xxii. 42, 45.) That this name became so familiar as a designation of the Messiah, is partly because the prophecies of the Old Testament declared very fully and distinctly, that the Messiah was to come of David's descendants; on which account the prophets often use the name of David for that of the Messiah, (Isa. xi. 1, 10; Jer. xxiii. 5; xxxiii. 15, 21; Ezek. xxxiv. 23, 24; xxxvii. 24, 25; Psalm lxxxix. 4, 21;) and partly, because David

---

* In the Apocryphal book of Enoch, the name does indeed occur; but undoubtedly it is only through Christian influence that the name has been put there. John xii. 34 shews that the name was quite strange to the Jews.

was to the Jews the splendid *ideal* of a ruler over His people, under whom their dominion was most widely extended. The use of this name, therefore, was connected with the circle of the worldly ideas of the Messiah which were current among the Jews. In order not to countenance these, our Lord therefore, in speaking of himself, avoided the use of that name altogether, and endeavoured rather, by the use of the more obscure expression, υἱὸς τοῦ ἀνθρώπου, to give another direction to the inquiries about the Messiah's import; for although the name was not a familiar one, yet Jesus might assume it as understood among the better portion, from those prophetic passages in which it occurs. But the phrase υἱὸς Θεοῦ, is commonly used in the New Testament in a sense very different from the *physical* one, in which it occurs in Luke i. 32, 35; and then the article is awanting. The phrase usually denotes, in a *metaphysical* sense, the eternal existence of Christ, which He has with the Father,—His relation as God to God, as the manifestation of the unseen God. In the Old Testament, the name ὁ υἱὸς τοῦ Θεοῦ does not occur to express this idea; for in passages like Psalm ii. 7;[*] 2 Sam. vii. 14, the prevailing reference is to an earthly manifestation. But although the *name* is wanting, (as is the case with the idea of the βασιλεία τοῦ Θεοῦ,) yet the idea itself is widely diffused in the Old Testament. It appears as early as Genesis, (see *Steinwender* diss. Christus Deus, in V. T. Regiom. 1829, where the passages from the historical books are collected,) and often subsequently in the prophetic writings, Isa. ix. 6, 7; xi. 1, 2; Micah v. 1; Jer. xxiii. 6; xxxiii. 16, and often. In the Apocrypha, see Wisdom vii. 25, ff.; viii. 3; Sirach xxiv. 4, ff. In the formation of the name υἱὸς τοῦ Θεοῦ, passages like Psalm ii. 7, probably exercised important influence at a later period, since the different relations in which the phrase might be employed, were not sufficiently discriminated. Moreover, we find it in many passages in the New Testament; and, indeed, while Jesus himself prefers to call himself υἱὸς τ. ἀ., the Apostles, for the most part, use the name υἱὸς τ. Θ. The Saviour, as υἱὸς τ. ἀ., brings himself near to men. Men elevate Him, as υἱὸς τ. Θ., above themselves. Yet our Lord (in John's Gospel) often

---

[*] The words בְּנִי אַתָּה (Psalm ii. 7) do not, as ver. 6 shews, refer to the eternal generation of the Son by the Father, but to the appointment of the Son to universal dominion in the world.

calls himself υἱὸς τ. Θ. too, or υἱὸς with pregnant meaning. But of this—that the name υἱὸς τ. Θ. was merely a name for the Messiah common among the Jews, and without a deeper meaning—they will hardly be convinced, who consider, *first*, that the ordinary and vulgar popular opinion among the Jews regarded the Messiah as merely a distinguished man, who, on account of His excellencies, was chosen by God κατ' ἐκλογήν for the office. (*Justin Martyr* dial. c. Tryph., p. 266, sq.) According to this view, names, such as Χριστός, βασιλεὺς τῶν Ἰουδαίων, υἱὸς τοῦ Δαβίδ, and others, would be more readily suggested. *Further*, if the name had been so familiar, there would not have been such astonishment at Jesus so calling himself. (John v. 18, ff.; x. 33, ff.) *Lastly*, too, we never find any false Messiah calling himself "Son of God." The passages John x. 33, ff.; xix. 7, ff., rather shew that the people regarded it as presumption, even in the Messiah. The only plausible support to this low view of the phrase is, that υἱὸς τοῦ Θεοῦ is found, in some few places in the Gospels, joined to Χριστός; but, on closer inspection, it is plain that no one of them warrants the conclusion; that, at the time of Christ, this name was in common use, as synonymous with that of the Messiah; and that, therefore, the same ideas were attached to it which were usually associated with the names of the Messiah. With respect to the passages in which υἱὸς τοῦ Θεοῦ is joined with Χριστός, we should *first* distinguish carefully between those in which Χριστός precedes, and those in which it follows. In the former, (*e. g.*, Matth. xvi. 16; John vi. 69; [according to the Textus Receptus, *Griesbach* reads, ὁ ἅγιος τοῦ θεοῦ;] xi. 27; xx. 31,) the phrase υἱὸς τοῦ Θεοῦ contains only the more precise determination of the idea of the Christ The disciples thought Jesus to be the Christ immediately after they united themselves to Him, (John i. 41;) but it was not till after prolonged intercourse that the idea of the *Son of God*, who had appeared in Christ, was unfolded to them, through the revelation of the Father. (Matth. xvi. 16.) *Again*, when the High Priest asks (Matth. xxvi. 63; Mark xiv. 61) whether He is the Christ, the *Son of God*, this question had reference, not to the conceptions prevalent among the people, but to what Christ affirmed of himself; and because of these declarations the people cried out, "If thou be the Son of God, come down from the cross," Matth. xxvii. 40. The words of the centurion (Matth. xxvii. 54, and the parallel passages) refer to the heathen mythology. But it does certainly appear to be different with those passages, in which υἱὸς τοῦ Θεοῦ stands first, which, however, are very few, as John i. 50; ix. 35, compared with ix. 17. But that, even from these passages, it cannot be concluded that υἱὸς τοῦ Θεοῦ was only a common name for the Messiah, is shewn in the particular exposition of them in their connexion. (See Commentary on those places.) Thus there remain only the passages, Matth. iv. 3, 6; viii. 29, and the parallel passages, in which Jesus is addressed as υἱὸς τοῦ Θεοῦ, as in other cases He is called υἱὸς Δαβίδ. But these passages occur only in the history of the temptation, or in reference to demoniacs; and it is therefore more than probable that they are to be so understood,—that only the superhuman demoniacal power recognized Jesus in His divine nature and dignity. We must, therefore, say, that υἱὸς τοῦ Θεοῦ does, indeed, designate the Messiah;* but *so far only* as He was born of the essence of the Father; that, therefore, whoever so called Him, either acknowledged Him as such, or blamed Him for declaring himself to be such. *Lastly,* with respect to the relation of the name υἱὸς τοῦ Θεοῦ, in as far as it is applied to Christ, and the same name so far as it is applicable to man, we have to observe, that υἱοὶ Θεοῦ, or τέκνα Θεοῦ,† are used in a twofold reference, corresponding to the two meanings, which belong to the phrase, as applied to the Saviour. On the one hand, it has reference to the physical existence of men. They are called υἱοὶ τοῦ Θεοῦ, inasmuch as God (indirectly) is their Creator. This meaning, however, is very rare; but

---

* On this construction *Schleiermacher's* opinion, too, is set aside, who says in the *Glaubenslehre*, Th. ii., S. 707: "Son of God" denotes probably not the divine nature *alone*, but the *whole* Christ, in His divine and human nature. Passages, such as 1 John i. 7, certainly shew that the physical and metaphysical meanings were conjoined, as, indeed, the Scriptures in general are far from any Nestorian separation of the natures. Still, *Son of God* denotes the whole Christ, inasmuch as He was born from eternity of the essence of the Father. *Son of Man,* on the other hand, denotes the whole Christ, inasmuch as He represents the *ideal* of humanity.

† Τέκνον is not used of the person of Christ, though παῖς is. (Matth. xii. 18; Acts iii. 13, 26; iv. 27, 30.) This term does not, however, so much correspond to υἱός, as to the Hebrew עֶבֶד יְהוָה, which is so often applied to the Messiah, especially in the second part of the book of Isaiah. (See note on Acts iii. 13.) Τέκνον could not be used of Christ, for this reason, that the notion of something undeveloped predominates in the word, while υἱός denotes what has manly force and energy.

Ephes. iii. 15, John xi. 52, and Mal. ii. 10, come under this head. Otherwise, even in passages of the Old Testament, as Isa. lxiii. 16, Deut. xiv. 1, the reference to salvation predominates. In the latter sense it appears also in very many passages of the New Testament, (1 John iii. 1, 2; v. 2; Rom. viii. 14, 16, 17; ix. 8; Gal. iii. 26, &c.,) and denotes the regeneration which, as a new act of creation, restores to the condition of children those who were estranged from God by sin. This reference corresponds to the deeper signification of the name υἱὸς τοῦ Θεοῦ, as applied to the Saviour. In regeneration there is the likeness of His eternal generation from the essence of the Father; and in reference to the spiritual children of the one Father, our Lord calls himself also the first-born among many brethren. (Rom. viii. 29; Heb. ii. 11.) He who from eternity was Son of God, lived as Son of Man on earth in time, in order to raise the children of men from earth to heaven, that, as children of God, they might be like Him, and become partakers of the divine nature. (2 Peter i. 4; 1 John iii. 2.)

Ver. 36-38.—Mary, too, receives a sign, (σημεῖον, אוֹת,) like Zacharias, (i. 20;) but it is a favourable one. As what had happened to Elisabeth is here made known to Mary from above, so also what had happened to Mary was made known to Elisabeth, (ver. 41.) Such dispensations were necessary under such extraordinary circumstances; and, just for that reason, we may assume similar facts for the solution of difficulties in those instances where they are not expressly noticed. (See note on Luke ii. 39.) The address concludes with the general truth, that the Divine Omnipotence accomplishes its plans notwithstanding all apparent impossibilities. The words are from Gen. xviii. 14, where they are used of Sarah in similar circumstances. The truth thus expressed, in its widest generality, should also be conceived as so far limited, that everything true ($ῥῆμα$ = דָּבָר) is also capable of expression; for what is contradictory is, as such, not a $ῥῆμα$, and, consequently, impossible with God, precisely *because* He is God. Mary, believing with childlike humility, submits herself to God; she acquiesces in her destination for the fulfilment of the divine purposes. The birth of the Saviour became thus an act of her faith also. Mary's faith repaired Eve's unbelief. (In ver. 36, for the common reading γήρᾳ, which form stands for γήραϊ, and that again for γήρατι, from nominative γῆρας, *Griesbach* reads γηρει for γήρει, from γῆρος. [See Winer's Grammar of the New Testament, translated by Agnew and Ebbeke, p. 59.]—Ver. 37. The expression οὐκ—πᾶν ῥῆμα is a pure Hebraism; it corresponds with לֹא כָל־דָּבָר.)

Ver. 39.—In consequence of the suggestion of the angel, (ver. 36,) Mary visits Elisabeth, to whom, as a relative, she was, probably, already known. Zacharias' place of abode, which was left undetermined in ver. 23, is now stated more precisely. He lived in the hill country of Judah, (ὀρεινή scil. χώρα,) in a Levitical city called Juda, more correctly spelt 'Ιούδα or 'Ιούττα. In the Old Testament it is called יוּטָה, (Josh. xv. 55; xxi. 16,) for which the LXX. write 'Ιτάν in the first passage. The reading 'Ιουδαίας is at all events a correction; if we retain the form 'Ιούδα, the name of the city must be supplied. In that case, Josh. xxi. 11 affords an appropriate parallel, where it is said of Hebron, Χεβρὼν ἐν τῷ ὄρει 'Ιούδα. (Μετὰ σπουδῆς corresponds with the more common expression σπουδαίως. It is found in the LXX. also, Exod. xii. 11; Ezra iv. 23; Dan. vi. 19.)

Ver. 40, 41.—The narrative evidently implies that there was no previous communication between the two women about what had happened. As Mary knew nothing of the circumstances of Elisabeth before she was informed by the angel, (ver. 36,) so Elisabeth also was ignorant of Mary's fortunes. Both were led and taught by the Spirit. Neither was there time for such communications, according to the dates given us. As Mary received the visit of the angel in the sixth month of Elisabeth's being with child, (ver. 26, 36,) and stayed three months with her, (ver. 56,) she must have repaired to Elisabeth immediately after the annunciation. Joseph was then, undoubtedly, altogether ignorant of the circumstances, and did not become acquainted with them till Mary was advanced in pregnancy. (See more fully on this point in note on Luke ii. 39.) Being espoused, she might, therefore, without exciting attention, spend some months with a distant relative, by permission of her intended husband. The sacred emotions of soul experienced by the mother, are shared by the child yet unborn, and the Spirit from above filled the happy mother, who saw the most ardent hopes of her soul realized. Like Hannah, the mother of Samuel, she, doubtless, often devoted her earnestly-desired child to God. (1 Sam. i. 11.) Respecting the πνεῦμα ἅγιον, see note on i. 15.

($Σκιρτάω = κινεῖσθαι$ is used particularly of the leaping motion, to which joy incites. The LXX. translate Mal. iv. 2: $σκιρτήσετε ὡς μοσχάρια$. In Gen. xxv. 22, it is used also of the motions of children in the womb.)

Ver. 42, 43.—Elisabeth, as the elder, here blesses Mary and her child, ($καρπὸς κοιλίας$ = פְּרִי בֶטֶן,) as afterwards John the Baptist, though the inferior, had to baptize our Lord. Elisabeth, though she blesses, still makes herself inferior to Mary, when she says, $καὶ πόθεν μοι τοῦτο κ. τ. λ.$* ($Καί$ in questions, is emphatic; see Mark x. 26.) Elisabeth's words, $ἡ μήτηρ τοῦ κυρίου μου$, are very remarkable. Turn them as we may, it cannot appear appropriate to call an unborn child $κύριος$,† except upon the supposition, that Elisabeth, by the illumination of the Holy Spirit, like the ancient prophets, recognized the divine nature of the Messiah, as the mother of whom she greeted Mary. The passage is therefore parallel with ver. 17, where, in the address of the angel, the same idea of the incarnation of God in the Messiah was hinted at, and $κύριος$ is emphatic—equivalent to the Hebrew אֲדֹנָי or יְהוָה.

Ver. 44, 45.—Elisabeth's language passes, towards the close, into the third person. She speaks *of Mary* in prayer, and extols her *faith*. By the Holy Spirit, she probably recognized this as the fundamental disposition of Mary's heart, and as the condition of her happiness. The $τελείωσις$ has reference to the fulfilment of all that had been promised of her son in ver. 32, 33. But with respect to the nature of the $πίστις$, it is clear, that this word does not here mean faith in any doctrinal proposition, but describes only the spirit of submission to the divine will, in which Mary was found at the announcement of the heavenly message.

---

* The words $ἵνα ἔλθῃ$, involve the idea of some previous instigation or command, and might be paraphrased, "Who arranged that the mother of my Lord must come to me?" She regards it as a fresh proof of the favour of her God.

† Dr. *Paulus* is of opinion, that $κύριος$ stands simply for $βασιλεύς$; and that Elisabeth merely expresses her faith that Mary will give birth to the Messiah. But as not even Augustus and Tiberius ventured to use the name $κύριος$ of themselves, it is plain that this mode of designating kings was then very uncommon. Least of all, then, can it be believed, that pious Jews, who called God alone "the Lord," should have so applied the term. Certainly, if we do not regard these accounts of the history of the childhood of Jesus as family documents, the hypothesis is feasible, that, from a later and more matured conviction of the dignity of Jesus, such an expression was put into Elisabeth's mouth. But her divine illumination is sufficient evidence of her knowledge.

Faith is susceptibility to the operations of divine grace and their reception into the heart.* (See further remarks in note on Matth. viii. 2.)

Ver. 46, 47.—If we imagine Mary as living in close familiarity with the Sacred Scriptures, whose promises had doubtless often affected her soul, and drawn forth the wish, that God would at last help His people, and send the Saviour, and even that she might become the blessed mother of the Messiah, there is then nothing surprising in such an expression of enthusiastic joy as now follows. Under the consciousness of having become partaker of the highest happiness, she gave thanks for the mercy she had experienced, and for the fulfilment of God's promises, which she viewed as already performed; expressing her thanks with prophetic intuition, and in words of Scripture familiar to her, particularly after the pattern of Hannah's song of praise, uttered under similar circumstances. (1 Sam. ii. 1-10.) Thus viewed, these poetical effusions lose all that strangeness which at first sight appears to attach to them. Even *Schleiermacher* made use of them to support the opinion, that the history of the childhood of Jesus had been cast into a mythical form. If the poetical effusions were independent poems, they would be calculated to awaken some suspicion; but as they are merely reminiscences from the Old Testament, which we must suppose to have been quite familiar to the parties concerned, their introduction here is no way inconceivable or even inappropriate. The following song of praise (ver. 46-55) is usually called the *Magnificat*, from the first word in the Vulgate; we have an excellent practical exposition of it by Luther. (Μεγαλύνω = הִגְדִּיל, Acts x. 46; xix. 17; Phil. i. 20.) The combination of πνεῦμα and ψυχή, the distinction between which will be found at length in note on 1 Thess. v. 23, denotes the whole internal being; the powers of the soul, both high and low, were moved with joy. (See Psalm ciii. 1, נַפְשִׁי and כָּל־קְרָבַי.) In ἐπὶ θεῷ τῷ σωτῆρί μου, the reference to an external σωτηρία, should not be altogether excluded, (see ver. 52;) doubtless Mary looked forward to the exaltation of David's family. But the deep religious

---

* [It is scarcely necessary to point out the defective view of faith expressed in the text. It does not agree with the definition in Heb. xi. 1, nor with the Calvinistic view of the nature of faith. Faith necessarily implies truth or facts as its object, and whatever else is included, this reference cannot be excluded.]—*Tr.*

feeling (*Innigkeit*) expressed in the song, does not leave us at liberty to assign a prominence to this reference, or even to conceive of it in a coarse and sensual manner, particularly as we must certainly suppose Mary to have been illuminated by the Holy Spirit, agreeably to ver. 41. The entire fulness of blessings, consummated by the appearance of the Messiah, lay spread out before her, and she applied the general salvation (spiritual as well as external) to herself also. God was in Christ her Saviour also; and as she was now about to give birth to the Son of Man, so she was afterwards to receive the Son of God also into her heart. (See note on Luke ii. 35.)

Ver. 48-50.—Taken in a religious point of view, the mention of the ταπείνωσις does not refer directly to Mary's outward political lowliness, since she was of David's family; it is rather the expression of the humble consciousness of inward poverty, which could discover no pre-eminence in herself, because of which such happiness should have fallen to *her* lot. (Ταπεινός = עָנִי, אֶבְיוֹן, [see note on Matth. xi. 29,] is closely related to πτωχός, Matth. v. 3.) We ought not, however, entirely to exclude a reference to what is external; as a *result* of the mercy of God bestowed upon her, Mary probably pictured external splendour, too, for herself. This fact, also, has been used to indicate the Saviour's training, and to intimate that we may here see what sort of hopes of a Messiah were imbibed by Christ with His mother's milk; but it is clear that in this way His glory is only increased, since He spiritualized the doctrine of the Messiah in the highest degree.* Besides, the notion that the Messiah was to exercise a mighty influence on the outward affairs of this world, is not a false one. The error in the popular conception consisted in their desire for the external *without* the internal. If the people of Israel had been brought to a thorough change of heart, they would have acquired a powerful influence ex-

---

* [The views referred to above may not be familiar to some English readers. It has been the great aim of the schools of theology opposed to the Gospel truth, to account for the extraordinary character of Jesus on merely human grounds. One of these explanations is alluded to above. Jesus Christ is supposed to have been trained by a mother full of ardent hopes and aspiring ambition to conceive of himself as the Messiah. But, as our author observes, the explanation, so far from accounting for the most extraordinary parts of the Saviour's character—the spiritual views of His kingdom—renders these more inexplicable.]—*Tr.*

ternally also. Though Mary, therefore, as she was not sinless, may, for single moments, have been tempted by vanity, yet her views of the Messiah were entirely those of the Bible. The Old Testament, as well as the New, ascribes to the active influence of the Messiah in the spiritual world, the entire transformation of the external also. Christ is the King of all kings; the highest earthly power is made His footstool. In the first instance, Mary brings into notice only the idea of the after-glory which would be her portion as the mother of the Messiah, —a prediction which has been fulfilled in a more extensive sense than she could have wished. (Γενεά = דּוֹר, *generation*, those who are living contemporaneously; πᾶσαι γενεαί, the whole succession of future generations.) In the light of the Spirit she duly estimated the importance of the Messiah's birth for all times and circumstances. (Μεγαλεῖα = גְּדֻלּוֹת, as in Psalm lxxi. 19; ὁ δυνατός = גִּבּוֹר.) From a definite reference to herself, Mary's language, in the last words from ver. 49, καὶ ἅγιον τὸ ὄνομα αὐτοῦ, becomes more general; but the succeeding thoughts are always to be conceived as having their special bearing on the present case. (Φοβούμενοι τὸν Θεόν, believers, in opposition to the unbelieving world, are the constant objects of His care, notwithstanding all appearance to the contrary. *Ὄνομα*, as the designation of the essential character in general, is more accurately defined by the special term ἔλεος.)

Ver. 51, 52.—God's rigour in the punishment of the ὑπερήφανοι, is put in contrast with His grace in blessing the ταπεινοί, who are equivalent to φοβούμενοι, and on that account ἔλεος is chosen. Mary, in the Spirit, views both—the blessing for the humble as well as the curse for the proud—as connected with the birth of the Messiah. The words καθαιρεῖν δυναστὰς ἀπὸ θρόνων, compared with ver. 32, 33, render it not improbable that Mary contemplated external dominion also for her son. Like the prophets, she connected, in perspective, the future manifestation of the kingdom of Christ with its first appearance. But though she did conceive of a dominion of Christ in externals, an idea which has a true foundation in the Bible, (see note on Matth. xxiv.,) still her conception of it was doubtless different from the coarse material views of the great mass of the Jewish people. (With respect to the phrase ὑπερήφανοι διανοίᾳ καρδίας,—καρδία, in the biblical anthropology, is the seat of life, and of the most general and immediate manifestations of life, and therefore of sensation, and of thoughts and wishes influenced by sensation; while σπλάγχνα denotes pure sympathetic emotion. Hence we can explain the frequent combination of διάνοια and its synonyms λογισμός, διαλογισμός, νόημα, διανόημα, ἐπίνοια, with καρδία. This does not imply that the διάνοιαι are actions of the καρδία,—they are rather actions of the νοῦς or λόγος,—but that the incitement to these actions of the νοῦς proceeds from the καρδία. See the fuller remarks in note on Luke ii. 35; Matth. ix. 3.)

Ver. 53-55.—A kindred thought is expressed in several similar figures; poverty and hunger, wealth and fulness, are kindred ideas. The satisfying of longing desire—the repelling of the sated curiosity after divine things, are both included in the notion of the Messiah. Nowhere does Mary betray anything false in her views of the Messiah; for the relation which, at the close, she represents His manifestation to bear to Israel and the predictions of its prophets, is to be explained agreeably to i. 16. (Ἀντιλαμβάνεσθαι = βοηθεῖν; see Acts xx. 35; Sirach ii. 6. Israel is viewed as παῖς Θεοῦ, agreeably to Exod. iv. 22, if παῖς does not here stand equivalent to עֶבֶד. Ἕως αἰῶνος* is not to be connected with μνησθῆναι, but with σπέρμα, to intimate that the blessing of the Messiah would have a future influence on the whole human race in its nobler members, which the seed of Abraham represents. The datives are to be viewed as *dativi commodi*. The construction μνησθῆναι τινὸς τινί is classical.)

Ver. 56.—After three months Mary returned; as she was probably unmarried at the time of her journey, (see note on Luke ii. 39,) the expression οἶκος αὐτῆς, leads us to suppose that she resided at Nazareth.

§ 4. JOHN'S BIRTH AND CIRCUMCISION—PROPHECIES OF ZACHARIAS CONCERNING HIM AND CHRIST.

(Luke i. 57-80.)

Ver. 57-59.—Shortly after Mary's departure to Nazareth, Elisabeth gave birth to the promised son,† who, according to

---

* Some editions read εἰς τὸν αἰῶνα.—Tr.

† The ancient Alexandrian Church celebrated John the Baptist's birthday on the 23d April (28th Pharmouti.) Subsequently, the Greek Church, as well as

very ancient usage, was named at the time of circumcision. (Gen. xxi. 3, 4.) This took place, agreeably to the Mosaic law, on the eighth day. (Lev. xii. 3.) The happy mother's joy over this son of her old age was shared by the circle of her acquaintance. (Μεγαλύνειν ἔλεος = הִגְדִּיל חֶסֶד, Gen. xix. 19.)

Ver. 60-62.—According to the wish of those present at the circumcision, a family name was to be given to the child; but the mother (from the command, ver. 13) insisted on his being named *John*. In this dilemma they apply to the father to decide. The word ἐννεύειν does not warrant us in supposing him deaf; in the first place, the expression does not actually exclude accompanying words, and then again we easily get into the habit of treating dumb people as if they were deaf. (Ἀποκρίνεσθαι = עָנָה, means not merely giving a reply to a previous question, but beginning to speak in general,—a use of the word well-known, and of frequent occurrence in the Gospels. In ver. 61, instead of ἐν τῇ συγγενείᾳ, Codd. A.B.C.L. read ἐκ τῆς συγγενείας, which Lachmann has rightly preferred. In the question τὸ τί ἂν θέλοι κ. τ. λ., the τό stands as connecting with the verb the whole sentence which contains the question. It is used similarly in Mark ix. 23.)

Ver. 63-65.—The father decides for the mother, (ver. 60,) and writes down the name John. (Λέγειν, in connexion with γράφειν, has only the general meaning, "to declare," "to make known one's mind," as in Luke iii. 4, and in the oft-recurring phrase, λέγει ἡ γραφή. Πινακίδιον = γραμματίδιον, *a little writing tablet.*

Agreeably to the prediction, (ver. 20,) the punishment of unbelief inflicted on Zacharias was removed after the birth of the child. He speaks, and immediately makes use of his tongue to proclaim the praises of God, who had so glorified himself in the fulfilment of His promises. As ἀνεῴχθη did not seem to agree well with γλῶσσα, some Codd. of inferior value have added ἐλύθη, διηρθρώθη, which may properly enough be supplied. As the sense of a higher superintendence in these events forced itself upon those present, they were seized with the holy awe, seen in those who fear God, when divine influence

---

the Latin, devoted the 24th June to that purpose, evidently from the datum supplied by the Bible, that Elisabeth was with child six months earlier than Mary. They reckoned six months backward from the 25th December.

comes perceptibly near them. (See note on Luke i. 12.) What had happened in the family was spread by report through the whole neighbourhood. It was confined, however, to the hill country, (ὀρεινή i. 39,) without reaching Jerusalem, the theocratic centre. Without the Pharisees and scribes having any idea of it, the mightiest events of the kingdom of God were preparing among the simple-minded. (Διαλαλεῖσθαι, *to be talked or spoken of up and down*, Luke vi. 11. 'Ρῆμα = πρᾶγμα, after the analogy of the Hebrew דָּבָר, see Luke i. 37.) He who does not agree with *Schleiermacher*, in regarding this narrative as "a nice little invention by a Christian of the refined Judaizing school," will have no hesitation in taking the fact of the healing of Zacharias, as well as his dumbness, and the appearances of angels, as historically true. In the light of Scripture we see that all physical appearances subserve the advancement of the spiritual world; and, if this event be thus viewed as discipline for Zacharias, no objection can be brought against its historical character, which does not arise from a false view of the fundamental relation in which God stands to the world. If we do not conceive of God as an extra-mundane being, who leaves the phenomena of nature to roll on according to laws left to themselves, but as sustaining the world by His breath, and as the inherent cause of all physical phenomena, then the miracle lies not in the single external fact, (which always has its connexion in laws higher or lower, known or unknown ; for the Spirit of God itself is the law,) but in the harmonious agreement of the individual phenomenon with the highest interests of the whole. Without this agreement the miracle would be on a par with a magical trick. (See more fully on this subject the note on Matth. viii. 1.) The supposition, that we have here not a fact, but a myth, (apart from the general reasons already mentioned, which forbid the supposition of myths in the sacred Scriptures at all,) is further discountenanced by the circumstance, that such a fabrication as the infliction of dumbness for a punishment, is most improbable, since it is altogether destitute of analogy.* The peculiarity of the event testifies to its truth. Such things are not easy to invent.

---

* *Strauss* does not hesitate, notwithstanding this decisive point, to hold to his opinion, even in the second edition of his work, (B. i., S. 141,) though the production of analogies is the only means which he has in order to give the semblance of support to his arbitrary views.

Ver. 66.—A passing reference is made to the impression produced in the neighbourhood by these events in the family of Zacharias. In this way, expectations of the importance of the infant were excited, which his progress fully justified.

(Χεὶρ κυρίου = יַד־יְהוָה. The hand, as the most general organ of action, is here viewed in the light of protecting and blessing. That this hand of the Lord was with the child in his growth, is mentioned by anticipation, in order to intimate that men's expectations were realized. The phrase τιθέναι ἐν τῇ καρδίᾳ = שׂוּם, with the prepositions עַל, אֶל, בְּ, with לֵב, includes, not merely retaining in the memory, but also turning over and considering the matter with interest.)

Ver. 67.—There is not, properly speaking, any break here, as ver. 66 only anticipates certain thoughts. The following prophetic words of Zacharias are rather in immediate connexion with ver. 64. (On πνεῦμα ἅγιον, see note on ver. 15, 41.) It is only to such an elevated moment, in which heavenly power strengthened Zacharias, bodily and spiritually, and raised him above himself, that the following words are suited, in which he speaks prophetically of his son's relation to the Messiah, and of the fulfilment of all the hopes which the seers of the Old Testament had excited. Zacharias begins with the main subject, (ver. 68-75,) and then places John (ver. 76-79) as exercising a preparatory influence, in his proper relation to our Lord, in whom all the promises of the prophets are fulfilled. Although here, too, the work of the Messiah is chiefly referred to the people of Israel, and the whole representation bears a national colouring, *yet nothing false appears anywhere;* for which reason those special references, as they are based on a truly moral conception of the Messiah's kingdom, (ver. 74, 75,) admit the same transference to the general, which we have already vindicated above, (ver. 16, 54.) The language is, moreover, so strongly tinctured with Hebraisms, that it may be re-translated, word for word, into Hebrew—a circumstance which, as already hinted, makes it extremely probable that we have here presented to us family memoirs, which Luke adopted as he found them. As such, these precious narratives have a double value, because they throw light on the circle of ideas in which John grew up; and there is no difficulty whatsoever in supposing, that he would be made familiar with these by conversation and actual instruction, as it is only in the case of the Saviour that we are compelled to suppose an absolutely free development from within.

Ver. 68, 69.—In true prophetic ecstacy Zacharias contemplates, as completed, the work of salvation, which appeared now in its germ, in the birth of the forerunner of the Messiah, (for which reason the Aorists are not to be confounded with Futures.)* His unbelief (ver. 20) appears, therefore, here transmuted into the most assured faith, which enabled him to behold unseen things as visibly present. (On ὁ Θεὸς τοῦ 'Ισραήλ, see note on ver. 16. It expresses nothing more than the true exclusiveness displayed in the Scriptures, to which the Saviour and the Apostles adhered. The relation of the Israelites to the Lord was different from that of all other nations.) In the birth of his son—whom Zacharias, however, views only in connexion with the appearance of Christ—he sees a rich visitation of God's favour, after long waiting on the part of the pious. ('Επισκέπτεσθαι is used quite like פָּקַד in the Old Testament; only that there the idea of visiting for the purpose of punishing is the more prominent; while in the New Testament that of visiting in order to benefit prevails, agreeably to the pervading character of the two economies. Λύτρωσις = פְּדוּת, see more fully on the idea in note on Matth. xx. 28.—Ver. 75 plainly forbids our thinking of political deliverance merely; but that Zacharias connected external blessings with the appearance of the Messiah, is more than probable, and, regarding the work of the Messiah as completed, not incorrect.) In sending the Messiah, divine grace was revealed as both saving and defending. (Κέρας σωτηρίας = קֶרֶן יְשׁוּעָה, Psalm xviii. 3, is used here with reference to passages like Psalm cxxxii. 17, where we read of "the horn of David." The point of comparison in the figure is the power, which is here conceived as protecting the godly, and punishing enemies.)

Ver. 70.—The whole subject is at once connected with the hallowed company of ancient seers, who had prophesied the general feature, (the λύτρωσις τοῦ λαοῦ,) as well as the special, that a descendant of David should accomplish it. (Καθὼς

---

* This description ill accords with the supposition, that the Gospels were fabricated in the second century, and falsely ascribed to the Apostles; for at that time the Church had acquired so little external splendour, that no one could have been prompted to such descriptions by its condition.

ἰλάλησα sc. ὁ Θεός is to be referred to the whole previous sentence.) The prophets are conceived, as stretching in a continuous succession through the history of the people of Israel, and through the human race. The result of their prophecies appeared at last realized in the present. ('Απ' αἰῶνος, ἐκ τοῦ αἰῶνος, and similar forms of expression, are used with indefinite generality, so that they must be more precisely determined by the context. There is, however, always this included in the idea, that what is spoken of should be carried back to the beginning of the period [αἰών] to which it naturally belongs. [See Luke i. 2, ἀπ' ἀρχῆς.] In this place ἀπ' αἰῶνος, agreeably to the context, may be referred to the beginning of the Jewish nation,—that is, to Abraham, [ver. 73,] if it is not preferable to go back to the beginning of the human race itself, since the earliest advocates of righteousness and of the fear of God are regarded as prophets. [2 Peter ii. 5; Jude, ver. 14.] See more fully on αἰών in note on Matth. xii. 31.)

Ver. 71.—After the intermediate thought, the idea of the σωτηρία is again taken up from ver. 69, and is viewed, first of all, as deliverance from enemies. (ἐχθροί, μισούμενοι.) In these words the political view of the Messiah's influence appears to come out most distinctly, and it is certainly not to be altogether omitted in this case. Just as in ver. 47, there was combined with Zacharias' view of the appearance of the Messiah; the contemplation of His completed work, in which what is without agrees with what is within, as will be the case in the kingdom of God. But that very glance at the distant future, shews that the idea of enemies is to be taken in a deeper sense, and includes all whose life was under the influence of hostile principles. Then, too, this salvation is only one aspect of the Messiah's work; it is completed by the λατρεύειν ἐν ὁσιότητι καὶ δικαιοσύνῃ, (ver. 74,) and thus the σωτηρία ἐξ ἐχθρῶν acquires a deeper meaning, since the mere freeing from the dominion of the Romans would fail to confer any true holiness and righteousness.

Ver. 72, 73.—The construction proceeds entirely after the Hebrew mode; (the infinitives ποιῆσαι, μνησθῆναι, are put for the common form εἰς τὸ ποιῆσαι = לַעֲשׂוֹת חֶסֶד, see Winer's Grammar of New Testament Idioms, p. 256;) ποιῆσαι ἔλεος, &c., is evidently not to rank as something different from the σωτηρία, (ver. 71;) but this thought stands in the relation of an adjunct to the main thought. In the words: ποιῆσαι ἔλεος κ. τ. λ., it is not the present that is spoken of, but the past. By the salvation at the present time, mercy was to be shewn also to the fathers in the past. (Ποιεῖν ἔλεος μετά corresponds with the Hebrew עָשָׂה חֶסֶד עִם "to be gracious to any one,"—"to shew favour." Gen. xxiv. 14.) With respect to the thought, it is peculiarly calculated to bring out the spirituality and depth of view expressed in the conceptions of the Messiah, which the words of Zacharias unfold. The work of the Messiah is viewed as a saving one to the whole body of forefathers, since in Him first they all *really received* salvation and forgiveness, which they had *believed in* up to the time of His manifestation. The σωτηρία ἐκ ἐχθρῶν appears here to be such as confers benefits on the dead also; and this shews clearly enough, that the enmity*—salvation from which is celebrated—is meant to be viewed as essentially deeper in its character. (The reference to the covenant and oath sworn to Abraham is put, as a *part* only, for the whole of the revelations and promises of God to the forefathers. The idea of the divine oath [ὅρκος] implies something inviolable, and, consequently, now fulfilled by the faithful God. It is best to construe ὅρκον also with μνησθῆναι, [see Is. lxiii. 7; Wisd. of Sol. xviii. 22,] so that it stands parallel with διαθήκης.)

Ver. 74, 75.—Zacharias, taking up the idea of the σωτηρία in the words: ἐκ χειρὸς τῶν ἐχθρῶν ἡμῶν ῥυσθέντας, now adds a second thought, expressive of a new effect of the appearance of the Messiah, which exhibits itself at the present time,—(*i. e.*, according to the prophetic view of Zacharias, who beheld the kingdom of God already complete,)—viz., ἀφόβως λατρεύειν θεῷ ἐν ὁσιότητι καὶ δικαιοσύνῃ. As this clause is dependent on τοῦ δοῦναι ἡμῖν, the true worship of God, described in it, is marked out as an effect and a gift resulting from the Messiah's appearance. It is not merely a *result* of the removal of enemies, so that the emphasis should be laid on ἀφόβως, but something newly bestowed—never before realized. The words are parallel with all those passages of the prophets in which

---

* To apply it *merely* to political enemies, as the Romans, is inadmissible. They are not, indeed, to be excluded altogether; and Zacharias was not in error, if he thought of an altered political condition of his nation; it was nothing but the sin of the Jews that had made them then subject to the Romans, as they had before been to the Chaldeans,—true repentance would have made them free again.

the establishment of righteousness is connected with the appearance of the Messiah. This view alone is in agreement with what follows in ver. 77, where Zacharias first speaks of the gift of the knowledge of σωτηρία and of its connexion with the forgiveness of sins; while John was to awaken the feeling of need, the Saviour was appointed to provide the ὁσιότης and δικαιοσύνη themselves, and the λατρεία which springs from them. Λατρεύειν ἐν ὁσιότητι καὶ δικαιοσύνῃ may be appropriately compared with προσκυνεῖν ἐν πνεύματι καὶ ἀληθείᾳ, (John iv. 23,) which also stands connected with the appearing of the Messiah. In Ephes. iv. 24, both terms (ὁσιότης and δικαιοσύνη) are used, just as in this place, to mark the new man created after God. (See also 1 Thess. ii. 10; Tit. i. 8.) The two terms here include the whole extent of true piety. Only, ὅσιος = חָסִיד applies more to the pious man's relation to God; δίκαιος = צַדִּיק more to his relation to those around.* Δικαιοσύνη is here conceived more after the manner of the Old Testament, for δικαιοσύνη, as St. Paul describes it in the Epistles to the Romans and Galatians, includes ὁσιότης. (See more fully on this point in note on Rom. iii. 21.) In the concluding words of ver. 75, πάσας τὰς ἡμέρας ἡμῶν, a more earthly conception of Messiah's kingdom seems again to show itself, since its glory is limited to the duration of life. The words may, however, be viewed as a simple expression of the indefinitely protracted enjoyment of the blessings of the Messiah, whose kingdom is most plainly designated (in ver. 33) as a lasting one. Still I am disposed to reckon this passage among those in which, without compromise, there may be seen a leaning towards prevailing popular ideas, which, in this case, appear also to be founded on some passages of the Old Testament. (See Isa. lxv. 20.) For we are not to imagine all as being of the same standing in the Messiah's kingdom; and hence the variety in the mode of expression which we meet with in Scripture on this subject. (The words τῆς ζωῆς are spurious; they were added as explanatory of ἡμῶν.)

Ver. 76.—Zacharias now, for the first time, speaks of his son, and of the place which he occupies in reference to the Saviour. He views him as His prophet and forerunner. (Προφήτης

---

* See *Polybius*, (xxiii. 10, 8,) who thus characterizes these relations: τὰ μὲν πρὸς τοὺς ἀνθρώπους δίκαια, τὰ δὲ πρὸς τοὺς θεοὺς ὅσια.

ὑψίστου stands in contrast with υἱὸς ὑψίστου, ver. 32. On καλεῖσθαι, see note on Luke i. 35.) Προπορεύεσθαι and ἑτοιμάσαι ὁδούς describe John's work according to the terms of the Old Testament. (See Isa. xl. 3, and note on Matth. iii. 3.) That work was to awaken a sense of need, the satisfying of which was afterwards to be accomplished by the Saviour himself. The words: πρὸ προσώπου κυρίου, contain, again, as in ver. 43, an intimation of the divine nature of the Messiah, to which we are also led by the actions ascribed, and the epithets applied to Him in the following words. The degree of consciousness and of clearness on the mystery of the manifestation of God to mankind, which Zacharias possessed, cannot be any further defined. Probably the stream of divine light which poured through his soul at this sacred moment, bore him beyond the bounds of his everyday knowledge.

Ver. 77.—Zacharias proceeds to describe the labours of John, using the same construction as above, ver. 74, ff. The γνῶσις σωτηρίας is specified as the object of his preparatory labours. The Lord himself gives the σωτηρία, (ver. 71,) John awakens to an insight into its necessity. (The special connexion of this γνῶσις with the λαὸς Θεοῦ, appears here as in ver. 68.) There can be no doubt how the following clause: ἐν ἀφέσει ἁμαρτιῶν, should be connected. The σωτηρία itself consists in this, and, as a divine act, (Psalm xlix. 8, 9,) it can proceed only from God. (It is best, therefore, to complete the phrase: σωτηρίας ἐν ἀφέσει ἁμαρτιῶν οὔσης.) The forgiveness of sin appears here, consequently, as the great prerogative of the times of the Messiah, which was lacking to the Old Testament economy. The sacrifices of the Old Covenant could not effect an inward, essential ἄφεσις, but merely a καθαρότης τῆς σαρκός, (Heb. ix. 13,) inasmuch as they restored the interrupted relation to the Old Testament theocracy. Sin itself remained through the forbearance of God. (See note on Rom. iii. 25.) But in the New Testament essential forgiveness was bestowed, on the one hand, by the actual removal of the consequences of sin; on the other, by the implanting in man of a new, higher life,—that of ὁσιότης and δικαιοσύνη. The purity of Zacharias' views of the Messiah is here strikingly evident; and hence we must, from this passage, gather a more precise meaning for the previous indefinite expressions, if we wish to interpret the speaker by himself.

Ver. 78.—The sending of the Sin-destroyer is now set forth as the effluence of God's mercy, (just as in John iii. 16,) and thus Zacharias is led back again to the person of the Saviour; so that the view of his son merges, as it were, in the wider, grander view of the work of Christ, just as John himself modestly withdraws behind the person of Jesus, (John iii. 30,) like the morning star that fades before the rising sun. (Σπλάγχνα = רַחֲמִים frequently in the LXX., thence σπλαγχνίζεσθαι. The term is derived from the lower organs below the heart being regarded as the seat of the purely sympathetic emotions; but especially the womb, [רֶחֶם, *uterus*,] which, as the organ of maternity, was put for mother's love. In some respects, therefore, the term appears to denote the lowest grade of love, as if it were purely physical love. But, because this shews itself to be, at the same time, the most immediate and the strongest, it is used also to denote the love of God, in order to express its essential and immediate nature, of which maternal love itself is but a faint image. The addition of ἐλέους defines the divine love more precisely to be such as is directed towards the miserable —the unfortunate.) As the effect of the divine compassion, Zacharias now brings forward the appearance (see note on ἐπισκέπτεσθαι, ver. 68) of the ἀνατολὴ ἐξ ὕψους. The terms ἐπιφᾶναι and κατευθῦναι, used in the following verse, shew that the Messiah is called a ἀνατολὴ, inasmuch as He is the light of men, φῶς τῶν ἀνθρώπων. In itself, the term may be appropriately compared with the Hebrew צֶמַח, *shoot*, according to passages such as Isa. iv. 2; Jer. xxiii. 5; Zech. iii. 8; vi. 12, (where the LXX. translate it by ἀνατολή,) but that the word ἐπιφᾶναι following it, seems to make the former view preferable. The rising, namely, is put for the rising sun itself, (Mal. iii. 20,) which gives light to the wanderers, and shews them the right way. The addition of ἐξ ὕψους marks the appearance as a heavenly one, descending hither from a higher system. (Ὕψος = מָרוֹם.)

Ver. 79.—In these concluding words there is reference to passages in the Old Testament, (particularly Isa. ix. 1; lx. 1,) in which the Saviour is described as the light of a world shut up in the night of ignorance and alienation from God. (See Matth. iv. 16.) The expression: ἐν σκιᾷ θανάτου καθήμενοι, corresponds exactly to the Hebrew יֹשְׁבֵי בְּאֶרֶץ צַלְמָוֶת, Isa. ix. 1. (On צַלְמָוֶת, see note on Matth. iv. 16.) Lastly, restoration to the way of peace is described as the result of the enlightening of those who sit in darkness. (Ὁδὸς εἰρήνης denotes that walk, that course of life, which is carried on with inward peace, and leads thither as its final aim. This presupposes the absence of peace in those that sit in darkness.)

Ver. 80.—A concluding formula, which depicts, in grand traits, the physical and spiritual growth of the Baptist, and which speaks of his life up to the time of his public appearance, concludes the family history of Zacharias. A similar formula closes likewise the family history of Mary, (ii. 40, 52,) which may indicate, perhaps, that both memoirs are by the same author. The words: ἦν ἐν ταῖς ἐρήμοις, refer to i. 15, and denote the Nazarite form of the Baptist's life. (Ἔρημος = מִדְבָּר, does not mean strictly *a desert*, but still a comparatively uninhabited tract of country. The solitude of his early life is intended to be contrasted with the ἀνάδειξις, as the formal opening of his official labours as a prophet. On ἀναδείκνυμι, see note on Luke x. 1.)

§ 5. BIRTH, CIRCUMCISION, AND PRESENTATION OF JESUS IN THE TEMPLE.

(Luke ii. 1-40.)

A few months after the birth of John, Jesus also was born. The Evangelist here first narrates how, by the leading of Providence, an external political circumstance was made the occasion of Mary's journeying from Nazareth, her usual dwelling-place, (Luke i. 56,) to Bethlehem, the original residence of her family, where, agreeably to the prophecies, the Messiah was then born. (See note on Matth. ii. 6.) A decree of the heathen emperor Augustus brought the mother of our Lord to the city of David, to show that "the king's heart is in the hand of the Lord as the rivers of water: He turneth it whithersoever He will." (Prov. xxi. 1.)

Ver. 1.—The previous verse gave by anticipation, and only briefly, some notices about the Baptist. The words ἐν ἐκείναις ἡμέραις refer, therefore, to the history of John's birth detailed in the former chapter. The passage contains some not unimportant historical difficulties, which have been employed by the advocates of the mythical interpretation, to demonstrate the unhistorical character of St. Luke's Gospel. However, *Savigny's* investigations into the Roman taxation, contained in the *Zeitschrift für geschichtliche Rechtswissenschaft*, B. vi., have shewn that Augustus did, in fact, contemplate the introduction of a uniform system of taxation throughout the whole Roman empire,—a fact which had long been doubted. (*Liv.* epit. lib. 134; *Dio. Cass.*, liii. 22; *Isidor.* orig., v. 36; *Cassidor,* iii. 52; *Suidas,* s. v., ἀπογραφή.) That this undertaking was extended to Palestine, too, though not at that time a Roman province, is divested of all that appears strange, if we take the ἀπογραφή to mean the mere registering of the landed estates, and not an assessment of property,—the proper term for which is ἀποτίμησις. The emperor might well take the liberty of making such a register, in consideration of the Jewish kings being so dependent on him, that the Jews had, along with the oath of allegiance to Herod, to take one to the emperor. (See *Tholuck's* Glaubwürdigkeit der evangelischen Geschichte, S. 191.)

Ver. 2.—The words of ver. 2, which seem to fix the enrolment with greater historical precision, are still more difficult, since the most obvious meaning does not agree with the accounts of historians; for the Κυρήνιος* (*Quirinus*) here spoken of was proconsul of Syria at a much later period, since, about the close of Herod's life, *Sentius Saturninus*, after him, *Quinctilius Varus,* and not till after both of them, *Publius Sulpicius Quirinus,* were respectively invested with this dignity. (*Joseph.* Ant. xvi. 13; *Tacit.* annal., iii. 68.) If, therefore, the census were meant, which, according to *Joseph.* xviii. i. 1, was made by Quirinus in Syria and Palestine, the birth of Jesus would have to be placed ten years later,—whereby the whole chronology would be thrown into confusion.† According to both St. Matthew

---

* Josephus (Ant. xviii. 1, 1) says of him: Κυρήνιος δὲ, τῶν εἰς τὴν βουλὴν συναγομένων ἀνὴρ, τάς τε ἄλλας ἀρχὰς ἐπιτετελεκὼς, καὶ διὰ πασῶν ὁδεύσας ὡς καὶ ὕπατος γενέσθαι, τά τε ἄλλα ἀξιώματι μέγας, σὺν ὀλίγοις ἐπὶ Συρίας παρῆν, ὑπὸ Καίσαρος δικαιοδότης τοῦ ἔθνους ἀπεσταλμένος, καὶ τιμητὴς τῶν οὐσιῶν γενησόμενος.

† With respect to the time of Christ's birth, this passage, on account of its internal uncertainty, cannot well be used to determine the *year*. Besides the star, (see note on Matth. ii. 2,) *the death of Herod*, before the end of whose reign Christ was born, contributes to the determining of this date. He died, according to *Josephus*, (Ant. xvii. 9, 3,) shortly after the insurrection of a certain Matthias. Herod had him and forty companions burnt on a night, in which there occurred a total eclipse of the moon, which was soon followed by the Passover. This eclipse took place in the night of the 12th and 13th March, A.U.C. 750; and as there were no eclipses visible in Palestine for some years either before or after, Christ must have been born before A.U.C. 750. His birth, then, falls in

(ii. 1, 19) and St. Luke, (i. 5, compared with iii. 1, 23,) the Saviour was born during the reign of Herod; a census, consequently, under this monarch could have been carried into effect only by the proconsul Sentius Saturninus, to whom, indeed, Tertullian (adv. Marc. iv. 19) assigns it, without any historical confirmation, but probably by conjecture only. From this passage we cannot so much as conclude that there was a different reading in the MSS. used by Tertullian. But even if there were, it would have no value, since it must be regarded as a correction of the original text. As the common text has been so perfectly established by the critical authorities, none of the conjectures that have been hazarded can obtain any sanction. Some have wished to insert πρὸ τῆς between πρώτη and ἡγεμονεύοντος κ. τ. λ., so that the sense would be: "this taxing took place before that (well-known one) under the proconsul Quirinus." It would be better to read αὑτή instead of αὕτη, so that the words would convey this thought: "the taxing itself (which was then attempted only) did not take place till under the proconsulate of Quirinus;" for the change of an accent cannot be regarded as a change in the text; for this reason, that the oldest MSS. are written without accents. It would perhaps be most suitable to take πρώτη for προτέρα (as John i. 30; xv. 18) in the sense, "this taxing took place before the proconsulate of Quirinus." Yet I do not deny, that the observations, by which *Tholuck*, in his Glaubwürdigkeit der evang. Gesch., S. 182, endeavours to defend this explanation, are not quite satisfactory to me; (see *Winer's* Grammar of the New Testament Idioms, p. 193;) in particular, it seems to me harsh to take πρώτη ἡγεμονεύοντος for πρὸ τοῦ ἡγεμονεύειν, although the LXX. have a kindred construction

---

a time of universal peace, on which the Fathers lay so much stress. In A.U.C. 746, the temple of Janus was shut on the return of Tiberius from Germany, and it was not opened again till A.U.C. 752, on occasion of the war with the Parthians. See *Jo. Kepleri*, liber de J. Chr. vera anno natalitio. Francf. 1606, 4; *Wurm's* astron. Beiträge zur Bestimmung des Geburtsjahres Jesu in *Bengel's* Archiv., B. ii., St. 1; and further, the dissertation on the year of the birth of Jesus in *Kleiber's* Stud., B. i., H. i., S. 50, ff., (Jesus cannot have been born later than the beginning of March 4710 of the Julian period,—*i. e.*, the year of Herod's death, A.U.C. 750,) and the supplement, *ib.*, H. ii., S. 208, ff. With respect to the *day* of our Lord's birth, the ancient Alexandrine Church, according to Clemens Alexandrinus, assigned it to the 20th May, (25th Pachon;) while, in the Western Church, the 25th December was fixed for it.

in Jer. xxix. 2. Be that as it may, Tholuck, in his masterly treatment of this passage, has manifestly proved, in answer to Strauss, that, even supposing all the difficulties in it should not be solved, we cannot draw any conclusion thence against the credibility of St. Luke, who everywhere shews himself to be intimately acquainted with Jewish and Roman history, and, in particular, with this first complete census under Quirinus. (Compare Acts v. 37 with *Joseph.* Ant. xviii. 1, 1.) If, on the most accurate historical inquiry, St. Luke's main assertion, so long doubted, that a taxing of the whole Roman empire took place under Augustus, is confirmed, we may be sure that the minor circumstance he mentions will also prove correct. But even though there were an error in it, or ver. 2 must be regarded as a gloss, it need excite no apprehension whatsoever in those to whom the divine origin of the Scriptures is made certain by the testimony of the Holy Spirit.*

Ver. 3.—That the families had to go to their *own cities*, either was the result of the state policy of the Romans, who accommodated themselves to the Jewish custom, or else the Jewish authorities made use of the Roman arrangement of the taxation for their own ends. In particular, according to Roman custom, it was indispensable for Mary to accompany her husband. (See *Dion. Halic.* Antiq. Rom. iv. 15.)

Ver. 4, 5.—The fact that Mary too went to Bethlehem, is explained only on the supposition of her being an heiress, and possessing landed property in Bethlehem. (See note on Matth. i. 1.) As in journeying to Jerusalem, so in the journey to Bethlehem, the term ἀναβαίνειν = עָלָה has the secondary signification, implying to go up to what is elevated in a moral and religious point of view. (See *Gesenius* in the Lexicon, s. v.) Mary's being called μεμνηστευμένη, ver. 5, is explained by Matth. i. 25.

---

* ["The testimony of the Holy Spirit" was universally held among the older Lutheran divines to be the most convincing proof of the truth of the Scriptures to the individual Christian. The modern Rationalists discard or sneer at the doctrine. But the operation of that conviction is not, as indicated in Olshausen's remark in the text, to lead us to admit the possibility of the existence of errors in the Word of God, as if they were compatible with its inspiration; but rather to make us feel, that whatever difficulties there may be, they are difficulties only, not *errors*, and are capable of a satisfactory explanation, whether we may have succeeded in discovering that explanation or not.]—*Tr.*

Ver. 6, 7.—In Bethlehem, whither the taxing had brought them, Mary gave birth to the Saviour of the world, without show—in the deepest seclusion. (Ἐπλήσθησαν αἱ ἡμέραι τοῦ τεκεῖν αὐτήν, corresponds to the Hebrew וַיִּמְלְאוּ יָמֶיהָ לָלֶדֶת. See Gen. xxv. 24; Luke ii. 21.) As there was no room in the inn, (κατάλυμα = ξενοδοχεῖον,) she laid the infant down in the φάτνη. (See ver. 12, 16.) This indicates that it was a stable which the mother of our Lord was obliged to choose for her resting-place, as the house was occupied. Ancient tradition speaks of a σπηλαῖον as the place where Jesus was born. They were frequently used, in mountainous districts, as folds for flocks. As it is mentioned as early as *Justin Martyr*, (dial. c. Tryph. Jud., p. 304,) and *Origen*, (contra Cels. I., xi. 3,) and as it is not in any way improbable in itself, it may, perhaps, be looked upon as established. (On πρωτότοκος, see note on Matth. i. 25. Σπαργανόω, *to wrap in swaddling clothes*, does not occur elsewhere, except in ver. 12.)

Ver. 8, 9.—The communication of the news of what took place in the holy night is again limited to the humble unknown circle of a few shepherd-families,—to whom this very cave, which our Lord chose for His first dwelling, might belong. The unostentatious character which adorns the whole history of Jesus, is manifest in this feature also. The shepherds were, doubtless, like Simeon, ver. 25, waiting for the consolation of Israel; the angel announced to their desire the fulfilment of all God's promises in Christ. Although notions about the Messiah were dispersed among the whole nation, yet the sacred Scriptures make a distinction between the coarse, carnal expectations of the mass, and the hopes of the few nobler spirits, which were founded on a deep-felt religious and moral need. (Ἀγραυλέω, *to remain in the open field*, particularly by night. In the words ἄγγελος ἐπέστη, the idea of something sudden and unexpected in the appearance is conveyed. Δόξα κυρίου = כְּבוֹד יְהוָה, the radiant light, which is imagined as floating round all heavenly appearances.)

Ver. 10, 11.—We must explain the contents of the angel's announcement by the previous more definite passages. (See i. 17, 32, 33, 74, 75, 78.) As the idea of the ἄφεσις τῶν ἁμαρτιῶν is associated with the σωτήρ, (ver. 78,) so in κύριος the divine dignity of the Sin-destroyer is implied. (On λαός, see note on Luke i. 68.)

Ver. 12.—The angel, of his own accord, gives to the believing shepherds a sign, (σημεῖον, אוֹת,) which is not in itself necessarily a miraculous one. Still we may lay the stress on εὑρήσετε, to which ἀνεῦρον answers in ver. 16. In that case, we do not need to seek any external circumstances by which the shepherds were guided to look for the child just where he was; a secret spiritual influence guided them to the right place through the darkness of the night.

Ver. 13.—This representative of the heavenly world, who communicated the joyful intelligence, was suddenly joined (ἐξαίφνης ἐγένετο = ἐπέστη, ver. 9) by a heavenly host, (στρατιὰ οὐράνιος = צְבָא הַשָּׁמַיִם,) transferring the employments of their superior existence to this poor earth, which so rarely echoes with the pure praise of God. In this appearance there is a prefiguration of the realization of the kingdom of God, the idea of which implies the union of things heavenly and earthly.

Ver. 14.—It is from this import of the angel's appearance, and its relation to the birth of the Messiah, that the words of the angelic song of praise are to be explained. Since all that was desired was restored by the Messiah, and His work is contemplated as complete, it is more suitable to supply ἐστί than ἔστω, which latter gives to the words the form of a wish. On this the division of the words depends. If we put a period after δόξα ἐν ὑψίστοις Θεῷ, it would not be suitable to supply ἐστί, and ἔστω would be preferable, which would make the words more evidently an expression of thankful joy; but then, ἔστω must be supplied for the latter part also; and thus the thought would assume the form of a kind wish to be fulfilled in the future, while it is infinitely more significant to take it as an enthusiastic announcement of what is present in the Messiah. Accordingly that division is undoubtedly preferable which places a period after γῆς; so that the thought is this: "God is now glorified, as in heaven, (ἐν ὑψίστοις = בַּמָּרוֹם in contrast with ἐπὶ τῆς γῆς,) so on earth." The words then prominently point out the characteristic feature of Christ's work; He makes earth heaven, and transplants hither a heavenly spirit, (*Wesen*,) thus fulfilling His own prayer: "Thy will be done, as in heaven, so on earth." In the language of enthusiasm, the plant of God's kingdom is represented in its maturity. According to this division, εἰρήνη is connected with what follows, and we must

necessarily read εὐδοκίας, so that the whole forms but two parts.*
The thought of the second half thus connects itself very naturally with the subject of the first. As the true glory of God (which results from the recovery of the lost) is restored by the Messiah, so also is peace restored on this earth accustomed to war, both externally and internally, and the ἄνθρωποι ὀργῆς are transformed into ἄνθρωποί εὐδοκίας. The critical authorities are certainly much more in favour of the reading εὐδοκία, (only Codd. A.D., some translations, and several Fathers, defend the reading εὐδοκίας;) still an erroneous punctuation of the first half might so easily make an alteration appear necessary in the second, that the origin of the reading εὐδοκία is, in that way, very easy to be accounted for. If there existed a further misunderstanding of the import of the words as a lively announcement of the present, and ἔστω was supplied, then the tripartite division appeared the easier, inasmuch as it seemed incongruous for men to be called ἄνθρωποι εὐδοκίας before the Saviour had finished His work and exercised His influence. The song of praise is more spirited and profound, if we take it as consisting of two parts, and not as a wish, but as an announcement of grace bestowed. Besides, with the threefold division, it is difficult to avoid the tautology in ἐπὶ γῆς εἰρήνη, and ἐν ἀνθρώποις εὐδοκία; in that case we must interpret εἰρήνη, very superficially, of external peace merely in the relations of men among one another; εὐδοκία = רָצוֹן, of men's relation to God.

Ver. 15-17.—The heavenly ones returned to the heavenly place—the men went to Bethlehem, found what was foretold, and made known what they witnessed to the circle of like-minded friends, (ver. 18;) for, that the angels' words did not appertain to the multitude, was well understood by those to whom they were addressed. (On ῥῆμα, see note on Luke i. 37. Διαγνωρίζω = divulgo scil. τὰ περὶ τοῦ ῥήματος.)

Ver. 18-20.—Those who heard the glorious intelligence were amazed; the shepherds praised God, like the angels, (ver. 13,) and with child-like faith viewed what they had seen as the fulfilment of that which was foretold, trusting to the accounts of the mother; but Mary thankfully received this homage as

---

* The preponderance of reasons still seems to me to be in favour of those who divide the angelic song into two parts. Men such as *Beza, Mill, Bengel, Nösselt, Morus,* likewise viewed the passage in this light.

a confirmation of her faith. (Συντηρεῖν implies rather the active exercise of memory; συμβάλλειν ἐν τῇ καρδίᾳ intimates meditation with pleasurable emotion and interest. In ver. 51, ἐν τῇ καρδίᾳ is connected immediately with διετήρει; and thus both the actions of the memory and of the heart are combined in one expression.)

Ver. 21.—Agreeably to the Mosaic law (Lev. xii. 3) the circumcision of the child was performed on the eighth day, and, at the same time, the name of Jesus was given to Him, as the angel had commanded, (i. 31.) The Son of God—the pure and the purifier—was in all things made under the law, (Gal. iv. 4;) and as He appeared even ἐν ὁμοιώματι σαρκὸς ἁμαρτίας, (Rom. viii. 3,) the Father called Him to undergo circumcision also, as the symbol of purification from the σὰρξ ἁμαρτίας. In all respects (κατὰ πάντα, Heb. ii. 17) He was made like His brethren, yet without sin. (Heb. iv. 15.) This divine arrangement had, in the first place, a relation to the *work* of the Saviour. In order to save those that were under the law, (Gal. iv. 5,) He himself descended into all the depths of human misery, and with toil ascended the steps which the Father himself had appointed. It had a relation to His *person* also. Participation in the cleansing rites of the Old Testament on the part of the Saviour was not an unmeaning action for appearance sake, but one of essential import. Holy, pure, and perfect in His divine nature, He shared the common infirmity of human nature in reference to His body. He was θνητὸς σαρκί, (1 Peter iii. 18,) and the temple of His body was only gradually spiritualized to ἀφθαρσία by the indwelling of the heavenly Spirit. (See note on Matth. xvii. 1, ff.) The circumcision, therefore, the participation in the purification, (ver. 22,) in the baptism of John, and in all the sacrifices at the temple, were proofs that the Saviour declared them to be divine institutions, and that, by taking part in them, He placed himself on an equality with His brethren, according to one part of His being. It is true, there was no absolute *necessity* for exacting this method of bodily perfecting for the Saviour, (see note on Matth. iii. 15, πρέπον ἐστὶν ἡμῖν,) as there was for the other members of the Jewish nation; in whose case the omission of circumcision would have occasioned their being cut off from among the people. But the harmony of God's scheme of salvation required just this form of development in His human life; agreeably to which, by means of the same sacred act, which in all Israelites united and strengthened the bond of the covenant with God, He was received as a member of the theocracy of the Old Testament, in order that, after He had attained to a full consciousness of His divine nature, He might raise the whole community, to which He was bound by so many different ties, to share in the superiority of His own life.

Ver. 22.—The participation in the καθαρισμός is explained on a similar principle. The woman was obliged, according to the Jewish law, (Lev. xii. 1,) to remain at home as unclean for forty days after the birth of a boy, and for eighty after the birth of a girl, and then to purify herself by an offering. The period was much too long for sanatory purposes—the ordinance had a religious and moral import. It kept alive a consciousness of sin, which, from the first, displayed itself so prominently in the sexual relations, (Gen. iii. 10, 16,) and directed her view, through the offering that followed, to the coming deliverance from all impurity.

(The reading αὐτοῦ is remarkable; for although it is certain that αὐτῆς is an alteration, which arose from doctrinal narrow-mindedness, since the καθαρισμός did not seem to be required for the σωτήρ; yet we cannot imagine that any one would have altered the text to αὐτοῦ. With the exception of Cod. D., it has only some Codd. of inferior authority in its favour; still it is a question, whether the reading αὐτοῦ is not preferable to the common one αὐτῶν.)

Ver. 23.—According to the law of the Old Testament, (Exod. xiii. 2,) every first-born, (בְּכוֹר = פֶּטֶר רֶחֶם = διανοῖγον μήτραν,) if a male, was holy to the Lord, (קָדוֹשׁ, ἅγιος, *sacer*, signifies primarily only what is separated from that which is profane, and destined for sacred use.) But as, according to Numb. iii. 12, 13, the Lord had taken the tribe of Levi for himself, instead of all the first-born, the first-born sons had indeed to be presented before the Lord, (παραστῆσαι, = הִקְרִיב,) as a symbolical act of consecration, surrendering for His service; but they could be redeemed for five shekels. (Numb. xviii. 15, 16.) Jesus was thus redeemed, according to the forms of the law, from service in the earthly tabernacle, that He might build a greater, a more perfect tabernacle. (Heb. ix. 11.)

Ver. 24.—The offering had immediate reference to the woman, (Lev. xii. 8,) with whom, however, the child was regarded as one. The circumstance that Mary offered doves, is a proof that she was poor,—the rich presented a lamb. Nevertheless, she may have possessed some small plots of ground at Bethlehem and Nazareth; for the regulation of bringing a lamb of the first year, as an offering, for purification, applied only to the rich, strictly so called. (Lev. xii. 6.)

Ver. 25.—The sojourn at Jerusalem gave occasion for a fresh confirmation of Mary's faith, from the circumstance, that a certain man, Simeon by name, uttered words prophetic of the child's importance. Simeon's personal history is not known; for the conjecture that he was father to Gamaliel, (Acts v. 34,) and son of Hillel, is extremely improbable. The indefinite expression ἄνθρωπός τις, indicates rather that he belonged to the lower ranks, where the deeper religious life appears to have concentrated itself at the time of Christ. Simeon, like Zacharias and Elisabeth, (i. 6,) is called δίκαιος, which denotes the external legal aspect of his life; while εὐλαβής, akin to ὅσιος, (i. 75,) denotes rather the internal aspect, the disposition towards God; but, of course, in relation to the Old Testament form of piety, since εὐλάβεια is equivalent to φόβος τοῦ Θεοῦ. His religious life is characterized most definitely by the words: προσδεχόμενος παράκλησιν τοῦ Ἰσραήλ,* which are akin to the following phrase: προσδεχόμενος λύτρωσιν, (ver. 38.) The former expression regards the *deliverance* from sin and misery in the appearance of the Messiah; while the latter specifies the *consolation* afforded by it. Both are included in the phrase, προσδέχεσθαι τὴν βασιλείαν τοῦ Θεοῦ.

(With respect to παράκλησις, it is only in this passage that it is used for the concrete παράκλητος. Παράκλητος = מְנַחֵם, in Rabbinical writers, though פְּרַקְלִיט or פְּרַקְלִיטָא is also found in them, occurs frequently, but in the New Testament principally of the Holy Ghost; [John xiv. 16, 26; xv. 26; xvi. 7;] yet of Christ also in 1 John ii. 1, although in a modified sense. The term as here used of the Messiah, has a reference to the suffering state of the people, which is conceived to be removed by the appearance of the Messiah.) This pious man also, at the richly blessed season, when the greatest that earth ever saw was being prepared in secret, had received the Holy Spirit, (see note on Luke i. 15,) and, in His power, prophesied of the Saviour.

---

* The expression ἐλπὶς τοῦ Ἰσραήλ, in Acts xxviii. 20, is very similar.

(The phrase ἦν ἐπ' αὐτόν [see ver. 40] is to be explained by supplying ἔρχεσθαι, which is involved in ἦν. "The Spirit came upon him, and consequently wrought in him.")

Ver. 26, 27.—Simeon, waiting for the consolation of Israel, had been assured by the Spirit, that he should not die before being honoured with a view of the Messiah. (On χρηματίζεσθαι, see note on Matth. ii. 12. As to the form of this χρηματισμός, whether it came to him when awake, or in a dream, the narrative is silent.—Instead of ἰδεῖν θάνατον, γεύσασθαι θανάτου [Matth. xvi. 28] is also used elsewhere, since perception by the senses is put for actual experience of every kind.) The same Spirit who had given the promise, conducts him also at the proper moment to its fulfilment. Such a guidance by the Spirit, which stands in contrast with choice from reflection, is seen in the life of all Scripture saints, from Abraham to St. Paul. It is the prerogative of the true children of God, who possess innocence in the noblest sense of the word, that they know the voice of truth, (John x. 4,) and are enabled to follow it without falling into error, though they do not on that account neglect the use of natural means, such as reflection and attention to circumstances. (See *e. g.* Acts xvi. 6.)

Ver. 28, 29.—By the power of the same Spirit, Simeon, with indubitable certainty, recognized the promised Saviour in the child, without needing any information from Mary of what she had experienced. With fervour the old man immediately pours out his grateful heart to God, who had fulfilled His promise to him. (The words κατὰ τὸ ῥῆμά σου scil. πρὸς ἐμὲ ἐρχόμενον, refer to ver. 26.) This sight of the desired One he regards likewise as the end of his earthly existence, and, with a swan-like song concerning His glory, he takes leave of life below. (In ἀπολύειν ἐν εἰρήνῃ, there is an allusion to the service and the spiritual office of Simeon; he was a prophet in his day, and doubtless maintained a lively and vigorous hope in the circle of those who looked for redemption. [Ver. 38.] In εἰρήνῃ there is not merely a reference to the fulfilment of the hope of still beholding the Saviour, which inspired Simeon; the term denotes, further, the peaceful consciousness in general, that the people of Israel, and himself with them, had attained the long promised end in the Messiah who was now manifested. Δεσπότης is used several times of God, [Acts iv. 24; Jude, ver. 4; Rev. vi. 10;] once only of Christ. [2 Pet. ii. 1.] The term differs from κύριος in this, that it denotes more precisely the relation of a ruler with unlimited power; while κύριος suggests the milder idea of possession or property.)

Ver. 30, 31, 32.—Simeon, in prophetic rapture, follows up this thanksgiving with a description of the influence of the Messiah, whom he had seen bodily. (The expression οἱ ὀφθαλμοί μου, refers to bodily sight, for with the eye of the Spirit he had long beheld the coming of the Saviour; he longed for His appearance in the flesh, John i. 14.) Although, therefore, Simeon's hopes of the Messiah were conceived (ver. 25) with only a national reference, as the Saviour was called the consolation of Israel, yet here there appears most distinctly a consciousness that this desired One would, by God's appointment, exercise an influence over *the whole human race*. In the light of this plain assertion, therefore, we may judge of the former passages in which such expectations were set forth. Their seeming limitation to Israel, and their reference to earthly relations, form but the one aspect of the idea of the Messiah, which we must complete by the other, even where it is not expressly mentioned. The Messiah's closest connexion is certainly with Israel, but thence the vivifying influence of His Spirit extends to all nations; and though His agency commences in the depth of the soul, yet it thence influences the external relations also; so that, in the most proper sense, the human race, as such, in all its members, and in all its external and internal relations, is the subject on which the Messiah exercises His saving and sanctifying power. As this connexion of the Messiah's work with the entire human race, even with the most distant nations, is just the doctrine of the Old Testament also, (see Gen. xii. 3; xviii. 18; xxviii. 14; xlix. 10; Psalm lxxxvii.; Isa. xi., xix., xlii., and other passages,) we are the more obliged to presuppose this correct view in the pious at the time of Christ, for they appear as living in the spirit of the Old Testament. That the connexion with their own nation, however, and the improvement in its external condition, should occupy the foreground with them, is completely accounted for by their circumstances. The same form of representing the subject is sanctioned by the Old Testament, which never permits the connexion with the nation to degenerate into bigoted exclusiveness, whilst its hopes of external good are never destitute of a moral and religious foundation. But the contrary was the case as to the conceptions of the grossly sensual multitude, who rejoiced in excluding all heathen, as such, from the blessings of the Messiah, and who, with their carnal dispositions, and without true change of heart, hoped to be allowed at once to follow the Messianic King, as their general, to the war of extermination against the heathen. That such gross conceptions are not to be confounded with the noble views which were preserved in the circles of the pious at that time, is shewn by ver. 38, where those who waited for redemption are spoken of as a special class. But the expectations of a Messiah were as already intimated, a common property of the nation at the time of Christ; if, therefore, those which were current among the multitude were acknowledged as the true ones, then the waiting for redemption could not have been used as characteristic of a certain class of men. (In ver. 30, as in i. 71, the abstract is put for the concrete person, σωτήριον = σωτηρία for σωτήρ. It is called "God's salvation," both because it springs from God, and because it is agreeable to His nature; and these two coincide, since only what is godlike comes from God.—Ἐτοιμάζειν = προορίζειν [Rom. viii. 29, 30] marks the relation towards the heathen, as founded on God's gracious purpose, which Simeon correctly perceived in the prophecies of the Old Testament.— In κατὰ πρόσωπον = ἐνώπιον = לִפְנֵי, there is implied not only being known externally, but having also an inward efficacy, since everything beheld externally produces kindred internal effects. The expression reminds us of Isa. xi. 10, where the Messiah is called עֹמֵד לְנֵס עַמִּים, since He stands before the people as a sign of gathering—as forming a spiritual centre. In like manner, in ver. 32, φῶς εἰς ἀποκάλυψιν ἐθνῶν refers to passages, such as Isa. xlii. 6; [John i. 4;] Isa. xxv. 7.—The being covered [פְּנֵי הַלּוֹט, Isa. xxv. 7] is opposed to ἀποκάλυψις. But the blessing of the heathen is, on the other hand, a δόξα of Israel.—Λαός and ἔθνος are here interchanged, as Israel is also called ἔθνος, John xi. 48, ff. It is only when used in the plural that ἔθνη = גּוֹיִם has the meaning "heathen.")

Ver. 33, 34.—The parents of Jesus did not wonder, probably, so much at the thoughts uttered concerning their Son's influence, as that the Spirit uniformly asserted the spiritual importance of the child from the most different quarters. (The reading Ἰωσήφ for πατήρ is evidently the offspring of doctrinal scrupulosity. Copyists feared that the term might be misunderstood. Simeon's being here represented to us as *blessing* the Saviour, must be explained on the principle expounded in the notes on Luke ii. 21 and Matth. iii. 15. On the principle, "the less is blessed of the greater," (Heb. vii. 7,) Simeon here appears exalted above the Saviour, just as do John who baptizes Him, (Luke ii. 46,) and the Rabbins whom Jesus questions. In His human development, the Saviour takes His place among men just according to the stages of the ordinary development of life; and, consequently, as a child He is *really* a child, and therefore in subordination (ver. 51) to those more advanced in life. The *ideal* that was dormant in Him, was unfolded only by degrees, and yet, at every stage, He expressed its appropriate character purely and truly.—In the succeeding context, Simeon specifies more particularly Christ's work, which is viewed as separating and discriminating according to the conditions of men, and appears as causing ruin as well as blessing. A slight intimation of the path of sorrow by which the end must be attained, is then appended. (Luke xxiv. 26.) The figure employed, to which the expression refers, is that of a stone, (Isa. xxviii. 16; Dan ii. 34; Zech. iii. 9; Matth. xxi. 42,) which becomes a πρόσκομμα (1 Pet. ii. 7, 8) to the proud, who stumble at it, but, to the humble, a means of elevation from their low condition. (Ἀνάστασις is here simply the opposite of πτῶσις.) In these opposite departments of His work, the Saviour manifests himself according to divine intention and arrangement. (Κεῖσθαι is by no means absolutely synonymous with εἶναι; the term, combined with εἰς, involves a reference to an intention—a purpose, Phil. i. 17.) And it is not merely at His first appearance, but also as His work extends through the whole of the world's history, that the Saviour manifests himself at all times and places, quite as much in the way of punitive justice, as in that of redeeming efficacy; the two are the supplementary parts of our Lord's work. (The remark, that not *all*, but *many* individuals among the people, were affected by it, may be thus explained, that, so far as Christ's intention is concerned, all should be saved; but unbelief prevents this result; to many He is salvation, to many ruin.) In the concluding words, καὶ εἰς σημεῖον ἀντιλεγόμενον, there is an intimation of Christ's passion. Those who stumble at Him are the ἀντιλέγοντες. (Ἀντιλέγειν is taken as a general expression of hostile disposition, which involves the act also.) But even in this ἀντιλογία the Saviour appears as a σημεῖον, set before the world by the Father, and, indeed, as much before the unbelieving as the believing world, though certainly in different relations. The expression is to be taken in the same way as Isa. viii. 18. God speaks to the world by the Saviour and His whole appearance—by the Man with the cross and the crown of thorns, and the eternal Son of God, the Judge of the quick and dead—in the mighty language of fact, and sets Him up, in truth, as a miraculous sign for mankind, as Isaiah and his sons, with their symbolical names, were in their time. (See note on Matth. i. 23.)

Ver. 35.—At the mention of the opposition of the world to the Anointed, the far-seeing prophet gives a glance at the development of the blessed mother's life. She who gave birth to the Son of God was not as yet born of God. She was, as all mankind are by nature, γεννητὴ γυναικός, (see note on Matth. xi. 11,) and therefore, like them, needed regeneration, which cannot be effected without tribulation, Rev. vii. 14. But the words: τὴν ψυχὴν διελεύσεται ῥομφαία, cannot contain the idea of unmixed trouble, without including that of consolation; this would cast a shade over the joyful tone of the whole prophecy. The idea of the deepest, most exquisite agony of soul, rather includes here the idea of salvation and perfecting through it, just as the ἀντιλέγεσθαι (ver. 34) comprises the victory over every ἀντιλογία. Mary's distress, which was one with her Son's, appears at once killing and quickening. At the sight of Him she must endure not only the struggle of a mother's love, but that of faith also, which appeared to die in her along with Him, who was bestowed from above.—The revealing of the secret depths of the hearts—of the good as well as the bad—is declared to be the end of this discriminating, judicial work. Christ appears here as Judge of worlds, even during the progress of the human race; wherever He appears, His pervading agency compels to a decision for or against. (The διαλογισμοί are here again, as was observed in note on Luke i. 51, connected with the καρδία. So also the less usual terms, ἐπίνοια, [Acts viii. 22,] ὑπόνοια, [1 Tim. vi. 4,] νόημα, [Baruch ii. 8.] All these expressions, as indeed the etymology intimates, denote actions of the νοῦς or λόγος, and correspond to the word "thoughts." Καρδία cannot therefore denote that power to which they belong. But the Sacred Scriptures, according to a view which is psychologically quite correct, never conceive of the active exercise of the thinking faculty apart from the inclination and the bent of a man's whole life; they refer every rising thought to the latent inclination of the heart.* As the centre of personal life, the Bible regards the καρδία = לֵב, [see Prov. iv. 23; כִּי מִמֶּנּוּ תוֹצָאוֹת חַיִּים.] Hence 'Εκ καρδιῶν points out quite correctly the impulse given to the διαλογισμοί from the heart, though they themselves belong to the νοῦς.)

Ver. 36, 37.—One other individual is mentioned to us by name† out of the pious circle at Jerusalem—probably a very narrow one,—Anna, who also had received the Spirit, (Προφῆτις = πνεῦμα ἅγιον ἔχουσα, ver. 27.) It is remarked, as the distinction of this woman, who is otherwise unknown to us, that, although eighty-four years of age, she had been united to her husband only seven years. It is the tender fidelity with which she treasured up the memory of her husband, that is here meant to be brought into notice. The description of her piety is agreeable to her Old Testament spiritual standing. Her religious life assumed an ascetic and Nazarite form. (See i. 15.)

Ver. 38.—She repaired to the temple at the same time, perhaps at the hour of prayer, (ἐφιστάναι, *to appear suddenly*, see Luke ii. 9,) and joined in the praise of God, when she received the intelligence that all her hopes were fulfilled in the appearance of the Messiah. (The term ἀνθομολογεῖσθαι means, in profane Greek, "to strike a bargain," "to agree," "to make mutual concessions." In the Hellenistic language it is used for הוֹדָה, *to praise*, Psalm lxxix. 13. 'Εξομολογεῖσθαι is used in the same sense in Gen. xxix. 35, and the simple verb, in Job xl. 9. The term is not found anywhere else in the New Testament.) With zealous haste the aged woman imparts the joy of her heart to the like-spirited members of the circle of the Messiah's friends in Jerusalem. On προσδέχεσθαι λύτρωσιν, see Luke i. 68; ii. 25.—Λύτρωσις is here put for λυτρωτής.—Περὶ αὐτοῦ refers to the

---

* Old *Michael Montaigne* has a very beautiful remark in the *Stimme der Wahrheit*, Th. i., S. 4: "In man," he says, "we may overlook the *head*, though it is always good not to do so, if it be in the right place, and gives birth to nothing wrong; but the *heart* is still the main thing. We need the head for *life* only, but the heart for *death* also."

† Even *Schleiermacher* has observed, that this mention of a second individual, who reiterates Simeon's testimony, is against the mythical character of the narrative. One event of that sort would have satisfied the tendency in the Church to the formation of myths.

object of praise, though not mentioned, it is true,—viz., the Messiah who was come.

Ver. 39, 40.—After the completion of the ceremony of purification, (ver. 22,) the mother and child returned to Nazareth. The mention of the end of the journey, from its being Mary's actual place of constant abode, does not directly exclude other journeys. (See the subsequent narrative of the history of the childhood of Jesus.) At this point the memoirs evidently become more general, and ὑπέστρεψαν εἰς τὴν Γαλιλαίαν is not so much a new fact intended to be recorded by the narrator, as a form of conclusion. The more particular and accurate accounts were wanting here, and therefore he brings back the mother and the child to the place where he knew they constantly resided (Πόλις αὐτῶν, see Luke i. 56.)—The last verse, just as it was said of John, (i. 80,) notices our Lord's progress in body as well as in spirit, according to the laws of human development, to which the life of Christ, according to the human aspect of His existence, was subject. The only peculiar feature is that which is added in the words πληρούμενον σοφίας. But that the idea of σοφία is to be used relatively only, is shewn partly by ii. 52, which describes the wisdom of Jesus himself as still unfolding itself; and partly by the idea of childhood, to which the character of wisdom always belongs only relatively. But this is precisely the idea of the Messiah in His human development, that He presents each stage of life pure and unsullied by sin; but in such a way, that He never obliterates the character of the stage itself; which would be the case on the supposition that the child Jesus possessed perfect σοφία.* Χάρις ἦν ἐπ' αὐτό, (see ii. 25,) not merely expresses God's being well pleased in Jesus, but it also intimates the effective cause of the pure unspotted development of the Saviour's life. Grace is nothing else than love revealing itself—shewing itself actively; and in every moment of the life of Jesus the love of God shone forth in active exercise in Him. He was completely a child—completely a youth—completely a man; and thus hallowed all the

---

* *Schleiermacher* observes very justly in the *Glaubenslehre*, Th. ii., S. 178,—"If we choose to deny the gradual development of the Saviour, we must either suppose, that His whole childhood was a mere semblance, and that in His first year, for instance, He had entire command of language; or we must return to the solution of Cerinthus, and separate that in which Christ was similar to all men from that which was archetypal in Him."

stages of human development; but nothing incongruous ever appeared in Him, which would have been the case if utterances of a riper age had escaped Him in childhood.

Here, at the close of the history of Jesus' infancy, we must cast a glance at the relation of the narratives of St. Matthew and St. Luke, of which it is maintained, that they do not supplement, but contradict each other; that they are the offspring of totally different traditions, and are, as it were, lines running parallel with each other. According to St. Luke, the parents of Jesus live at Nazareth, and His being born at Bethlehem appears as the result of accidental circumstances; in St. Matthew, on the contrary, it seems as if the parents of Jesus lived at Bethlehem. Further, St. Luke's narrative of the annunciation appears irreconcileable with Joseph's being ignorant at first of the nature of Mary's pregnancy, and his being informed by the angel, as St. Matthew says; and again, the adoration of the Magi, Herod's slaughter of the children, and the flight into Egypt, as recorded by St. Matthew, appear irreconcileable with St. Luke's account of the journey to Jerusalem for the purification. On closer consideration, however, the first objection, that St. Matthew appears to follow a different tradition as to the residence of Jesus' parents, resolves itself into something purely negative. For St. Matthew evidently does not follow any tradition whatever concerning the residence of Jesus' parents, and gives no remarks at all as to time and place; he merely recounts the facts. The circumstance of his naming Bethlehem (ii. 1) as the birthplace of Jesus, happens, as the following verses shew, only in consequence of that place being so assigned in a prophecy of the Old Testament. If that had not been the case, St. Matthew would hardly have named the place of birth at all. Just so he would have been content with the general statement, εἰς τὰ μέρη τῆς Γαλιλαίας, (ii. 22,) had not a reference to the prophecies induced him (ii. 23) further to mention Nazareth. Besides, the passage Matth. ii. 22, 23, does not oblige us, as *Sieffert* asserts, to understand it as if St. Matthew had been ignorant of Mary's having been at Nazareth before the birth of Jesus; we have only to suppose that, during the stay in Egypt, it had appeared desirable to Joseph to establish himself at Bethlehem, but from fear of Archelaus, he gave up the plan, and returned to Nazareth. Accordingly, we can only say of St. Matthew, that he passes over the particulars of place, and notices incidentally one or two points, which must be more precisely fixed by a reference to St. Luke, the more exact narrator.*

Next, as regards the supposed contradictions in the details of the two narratives, no such thing as an impossibility of reconciling them can be talked of, if only in St. Luke ii. 39 the words ὑπέστρεψαν εἰς τὴν Γαλιλαίαν be understood with proper latitude. To regard this expression in its immediate connexion with ver. 40, as a form of conclusion, and, consequently, as intended only to point out the habitual abode of Jesus, where the development described in ver. 40 proceeded, must be called at least an available escape, which no one, who feels himself called upon to avoid the quicksands of myths, will hesitate to adopt. In point of fact, therefore, there remains nothing in the two narratives that necessarily appears contradictory; for no one will seriously urge the objection, which Schleiermacher brings against the supposition of a return from Jerusalem to Bethlehem, after the purification was accomplished,—viz., that the return is improbable, because the mother would have been placed in inconvenient circumstances there; for these circumstances were evidently produced only by the enrolment, which, in the nature of the case, increased the numbers in the town but for a few days. But should any one think it too bold to take Luke ii. 39 as the form of conclusion, still, in this view of the case, the historical interpretation might be defended by supposing a journey back to Nazareth. For Matth. ii. 14 is not expressed in such a manner as would altogether exclude the supposition of an intervening journey to Nazareth. The relation of the accounts in the two Gospels is therefore such, that both may be very well reduced to a connected whole by supplementing the little circumstances that are passed over in silence. And what historical narration, composed by different historians, who give their accounts independently of each other, and who follow different

---

* *De Wette* (in his Commentary, B. ii., S. 25) accuses me of an almost unpardonable perversion, because I regard St. Matthew's specifications of localities as merely incidental. I have supported this opinion at length in my two *programmes* on the genuineness of St. Matthew's Gospel; no unprejudiced person can fail to see from them the correctness of that opinion. It is only where unbelief has blinded sound sense, and men seek for the semblance of support, in order to give countenance to the most false assumptions, that the opposite opinion can still be boldly maintained.

points of view in them, does not stand in need of such supplementing?

It must be confessed, that the reconciliation of the two Gospels in reference to Joseph is more difficult. Yet the difficulty lies not so much in the reconciliation of their accounts, as in the obscurity of the recorded event, which can be cleared away only by a comparison of both. For it is left uncertain from Matth. i. 18, 19, how and when Joseph became aware of Mary's being with child. Εὑρέθη, however, appears to indicate, that Mary did not tell Joseph anything of it; and what we read in Luke i. 36, 39, 56, increases this probability to almost a certainty; for, according to these passages, Mary went to Elisabeth when the latter was six months advanced in pregnancy, stayed there the next three months, and returned shortly before Elisabeth was delivered. Such a visit of three months, supposes that Mary was not yet married; but if Mary had discovered her situation to Joseph before her journey, and if what is told us in Matth. i. 20, ff., followed immediately, Joseph would certainly have taken her to himself as his wife, in order to prevent any ill appearance, which must be the more likely to arise if he postponed the marriage. But then the history presents the startling fact, that Mary told her intended husband nothing about the appearance of the angel and her expectations, but, immediately after the annunciation, took her journey to Elisabeth, and remained there three months. This fact is certainly startling to one who regards these events in the light of ordinary social relations; but, in the case of events so extraordinary as those which are narrated in the first chapters of St. Matthew and St. Luke, the human scale of natural probability is not applicable. The events that had happened to Mary were of so unusual a kind, that she could not communicate them without having any other voucher than her word. The same childlike faith with which she said: "Behold the handmaid of the Lord; be it unto me according to thy word," could not but inspire her with the confidence, that divine compassion would find ways and means to satisfy her intended husband that she was the pure bride of heaven.* It is just in this, therefore, that she waited patiently

---

* There is an absurd attempt to explain this difficulty in the *Protev. Jac.*, c. xii., xiii., in which it is supposed that Mary had forgotten that the angel had announced her being with child of the Holy Ghost, which she then confessed to

for God's guidance until the secret of her pregnancy should be known to Joseph from above; that we have an unquestionable proof that we have to do, not with human history, but divine, the peculiar beauty of which is tarnished if we suffer ourselves to be seduced to interpret its uncommon occurrences by the events of every-day life.

§ 6. JESUS CONVERSES WITH THE PRIESTS IN THE TEMPLE.

(Luke ii. 41-52.)

The import of this *apparently* insignificant occurrence—the only one told us of the life of Jesus up to the time of His public appearance—demands a few passing remarks.* Viewed in its connexion with the whole manifestation, it presents to us unquestionably the sacred season, when the higher divine consciousness arose within Him. As was partially noticed before, the Saviour, in His human manifestation, followed the general course of human development; and though the child's consciousness in Him was a pure, holy, and glorified one, yet it was a *child's,* and, consequently, not a divine one. This latter appeared as a gradual result in the progress of the general development, (Luke i. 80; ii. 40, 52,) and on occasion of His being present for the first time in the holy city, to which the child's desire had probably long aspired, the thought then first presented itself distinctly to Him, as glowing embers burst into a flame, that *He* was God's Son, and God *His* Father. The divine nature of Jesus appears, therefore, a distinct thing from the knowledge of that nature. To the latter He attained gradually, as the result of the progress of His human development. The springing up of that consciousness bore Him at

---

Joseph with tears; but this attempt only shews, that there was an actual fact, which needed clearing up; and this is no other than that reported by our Evangelists,—viz., that Mary had concealed from her intended husband what had happened to her.

* That Strauss reckons even this occurrence among the mythical portions, proves undeniably the exaggerated, wanton rage for doubt that possesses him. A history, which might cast an imputation of disobedience on Jesus, or of a want of care on His mother, certainly would not have been fabricated in later times.

that instant to His real home, of which the temple appeared to Him the type, and, in spiritual rapture, He might forget the earthly representatives of His heavenly Father. But this forgetting was not in Him an act of disobedience, but, in fact, of superior obedience. He followed faithfully the stronger attraction from above, and therefore He reunited himself to His parents with childlike submission, when they reminded Him of the *rights* of parents, while they had forgotten the *duty* of parents. The mother had done wrong in having neglected her highest duty to God—the care of the divine child—to follow the distractions which Jerusalem offered to the senses,—a deep symbol of the relation of the human and the divine agencies in the work of regeneration, in which, after a similar manner, the new man, after his birth, is entrusted to his soul, which has to fulfil the duties of a mother towards him! This occurrence thus affords us a glance at the exalted moment of the first kindling of this light of the Divine Spirit, and its piercing through the human covering, but only again to let fall the vail. But it is just in this historical purity that the divine character of our Gospels shews itself, particularly when compared with the apocryphal ones, which fill up this vailed period with absurd fables. During this period the divine plant of righteousness was invisibly unfolding within itself; and the reason that nothing is narrated of this period doubtless is, that there was nothing special to narrate. Jesus presented probably the *ideal* of a quiet, truly childlike child and youth; and it was only in the depth of His soul that His nature was unfolding, which, at most, may have been betrayed by His look and bearing. The influences from the spiritual world, which He was intended to manifest, gradually descended into Him; and all surrounding circumstances, conversations, sights, and reading the Scriptures, must have become the occasions of one spring after another opening in Him. For, to imagine that, according to the ordinary process of training, any formative power was exercised over Him, or direction given to His mind, through Egyptian, Essenaic, or Rabbinical wisdom, is altogether at variance with the functions of the Messiah, whom we are to regard as of supreme authority. His development is, therefore, purely independent, and altogether internal—a continual outpouring from the heavenly world into the earthly tabernacle, of which outward circumstances must be considered as merely the exciting cause.* It is in this light that the position which Jesus occupied towards the priests in the temple is to be viewed. The questions He put to the priests, and their answers, were exciting, awakening incidents for His inner life. But the idea that Jesus *taught* in the temple, must be rejected as monstrous. A child teaching, demonstrating, would be a contradiction which it is impossible the God of order could have designed. Ἀκούων and ἐπερωτῶν, *hearing* and *asking*, (ver. 46,) point plainly enough to His capacity for receiving impressions. The Scriptures, and the lofty hopes which they excite, formed probably the basis of His questions. He inquired respecting himself; and we may say, the whole endeavour and desire of the child Jesus was nothing but a longing for a revelation of himself. The miraculous union of opposites in the God-man, the conjoining of temporal and eternal, of individual and universal, is here presented before the reader's mind in its growth; and ruling and serving, unfettered dominion and child-like submission, are here united to form an ineffable whole, which the parents of Jesus, like the unregenerate man in general, might indeed wonder at, (ver. 48,) but were not able to understand.

Ver. 41-43.—According to the law of Moses, (Ex. xxiii. 14, ff.; xxxiv. 23,) the males had to go up to Jerusalem three times yearly at the principal feasts;† children used to accompany them in these journeys from their twelfth year. They were called in that year בְּנֵי הַתּוֹרָה, *sons of the law*, and were then under an obligation to keep the law. This time of legal maturity coincides, therefore, very appropriately with the first awakening of His spirit to a higher consciousness.—The feast of the passover lasted seven days, (to which τελειωσάντων τὰς

---

* It is not meant in this to advocate anything like the views of the Docetae, but only to bring forward to view the specific character of the Saviour's advancing development. If His human nature, as sinless, was specifically different from fallen human nature, then the progress of His training must also have been so; and it must be conceived, too, in the way indicated; because if put in any other form, Christ is rendered subject to the sinful influences around Him. In point of form only, we can conceive of Christ as receiving,—that is, as purely passive, *e. g.*, in learning language and letters. The substance of His knowledge is, however, to be conceived as active at every stage of development, because in that way alone it can be pure. *Tholuck's* remarks to the contrary in his *Glaubwürdigkeit der evangelischen Geschichte*, S. 219, ff., do not appear to me decisive.

† The words οἱ γονεῖς αὐτοῦ, contain an intimation, that Joseph the father was yet living; but from this time he does not re-appear in the Gospel-history. He died, probably, before the public appearance of Jesus. See Matth. xiii. 55.

ἡμέρας, ver. 43, refers,) the first and last of which were observed as Sabbaths, Exod. xii. 14; Deut. xvi. 4.

Ver. 44-46.—The parents, accustomed to the prudence and obedience of the child, commence their journey without Him, supposing, doubtless, that He was among their kindred or acquaintances. Συνοδία from συνοδεύω, signifies one of the festal caravans, which were common among the pilgrims journeying to the feasts, to afford each other more protection and convenience on the journey. (See the charming description of such a journey of pilgrimage in *Strauss'* beautiful romance, "*Helon's Pilgrimage*.") It was not till after three days, full of anxiety and trouble, that they found the holy child in the holy place. The ἱερόν, to be distinguished from ναός, (see note on Luke i. 9,) was an extensive structure, and had many halls and separate rooms, in which judges pronounced their decisions, or Rabbins taught their schools. In such a school (מִדְרָשׁ) we have to imagine Jesus.

Ver. 47, 48.—In that company the child was an object of universal astonishment; and this again was a matter of wonder to His parents. Though informed of the high destiny of their child, they could not comprehend this sight. (Σύνεσις generally stands in the same relation to φρόνησις, that νοῦς does to σοφία and γνῶσις; σύνεσις denotes "the understanding," = בִּינָה. Yet this term [Isa. xi. 2] is often applied to divine things and the comprehension of them,—*e. g.*, Col. i. 9; Eph. iii. 4; 2 Tim. ii. 7.) The mother's exclamation (τί = διατί = לָמָּה) contains a gentle reproof; but its force is invalidated by the following words. The fault was the mother's, who had forgotten the spiritual destiny of her son.

Ver. 49, 50.—Without its being intended, the words of Jesus convey the blame which attached to Mary, because they exactly declare the truth. If she had had her son's spiritual character completely present to her soul, she would herself have led Him to those scenes, whither the higher Spirit now attracted Him. (Ζητεῖν, in connexion with the following δεῖ εἶναί με, conveys the notion of uncertainty, indecision; this was what was wrong in Mary's state of mind; she might have known where alone Jesus would naturally be found.) Τὰ τοῦ πατρός refers certainly immediately to the temple, as the visible dwelling-place of the invisible God. But in the child's higher consciousness, which tended upwards, the meaning of the words goes further. This deeper sense of the words, which respects the oneness of the Son with the Father, was not understood by the parents, standing, as they did, on Old Testament ground; for they could hardly fail to perceive, that He spoke with immediate reference to the temple. Still the mother felt a strong impression from the deep saying, (ver. 51,) and laid it up in her heart, (ver. 19,) where it revived at its time, so that she could tell of it.

Ver. 51.—The words: καὶ ἦν ὑποτασσόμενος αὐτοῖς, are evidently intended here to guard against the possible misunderstanding, that Jesus had manifested a will not subject to His parents; not so much in the sense of ordinary disobedience, which is inconceivable in an offspring of the Spirit, as in a higher relation. It might be supposed, that the spirit of Jesus would now have assumed the appearance of *ruling* over the parents; this the Evangelist contradicts by the express observation, that the Son of God always submitted himself to the human will of His parents. The general idea of our Lord's voluntary humiliation (Phil. ii. 7, ff.) appears, therefore, here again, as already pointed out in the note on Luke ii. 21, 22.

Ver. 52.—The history of the childhood closes with a new mention (see Luke ii. 49) of the bodily and spiritual advancement of the child. (Προκόπτειν, in the sense of "to advance," "to grow." [See Gal. i. 14; 2 Tim. ii. 16; iii. 9.] Ἡλικία is not to be taken in the sense of "greatness," "stature," as in Luke xix. 3; it is better to take it as "age," in which the whole physical part of life is included. Χάρις is to be taken in a different sense from that which it has in ii. 40. It is here represented as being in a state of development, which is not applicable to the divine love; for, towards the Son of God, that was always alike and the same. The reference to God *and man* shews that the idea of being pleased is prominent in χάρις, so that it may be taken = εὐδοκία. This might increase, in so far as more and more of that glory was unfolded in the life of Jesus, which must have been the object of God's satisfaction, and that of all the good.

SECOND PART.

OF

JOHN THE BAPTIST—CHRIST'S BAPTISM AND TEMPTATION.

Matth. iii. 1—iv. 12; Mark i. 2-13; Luke iii. 1—iv. 13.

§ 1. JOHN'S DOCTRINE AND BAPTISM.

(Matth. iii. 1-12; Mark i. 2-9; Luke iii. 1-20.)

In the second part of the Gospel-history, the reader is brought nearer to its great cardinal events. The Evangelists tell us, in the following paragraphs, how the public appearance of Jesus was prepared for. First, the Baptist visibly and outwardly prepared the way for our Lord; then, inwardly and in the narrow circle of those who feared God, the outpouring of the Spirit, and the temptation of Jesus, completed the preparations.

John appears here quite in conformity with the angel's prediction in Luke i. 17, repeated by Zacharias in ver. 76, as a prophet in the spirit and power of Elias. In the whole of his labours he represents the law, which *demands* holiness and righteousness, but *supplies* no power. The outward form of his appearance answers to the inward character of his person; he presents himself austere and stern, separated from the world, and revealing to it the strictness of the Divine Judge. His preaching of repentance is a commentary on Rom. iii. 20: "By the law is the knowledge of sin." John was appointed to awaken the slumbering minds, to rouse to a sense of the need of salvation, that the Saviour might find hearts prepared to receive the fulness of blessings, which He came to bring; whence, too, Jesus begins at once to invite to himself the poor and the hungry. Though John, therefore, stands so near the New Testament as to be in contact with it, yet, in his character and work, there is no approach to the spirit of the Gospel; he represents the law purely, and forms only the point of contact between the Old and New Testaments, as the top-stone of the former. (Here compare Matth. xi. 9, ff.) This close *proximity*, and yet undeniably wide *separation*, of Jesus and the Baptist, expresses very vividly the difference of the two economies; the law and the Gospel are two separate spheres of life, which ought not to be mixed; faith alone, and the mysterious act of regeneration thence resulting, conduct us from the one to the other. John, therefore, inasmuch as he is the top-stone of the Old Testament economy, and perfectly expresses its character, stands exalted among those who are born of women; but the least in the kingdom of God (as being born of God) is greater than he.* But with respect to the Baptist's work, it was not confined to the "preaching of repentance," but shewed itself also in an external rite—namely, baptism.† As regards this rite, we are here less concerned with its relation to proselyte-baptism, than with its relation to the Christian sacrament of baptism. With reference to the baptism of proselytes, it seems probable to me, that an actual baptism,—*i. e.*, a lustration performed on the proselyte by another, did not take place *before* the baptism of John; subsequently, it may have arisen out of the lustrations so long customary, which every one performed on himself.‡ But had such a baptism existed, the choice of just this rite would have been less appropriate; for it was by no

---

* See Hengstenberg's Christol., B. iii., S. 460, ff., where this view is opposed, and a higher character claimed for John. But if the New Testament is not to relinquish all that is specific, regeneration and the real experience of the forgiveness of sins ought not to be anticipated. Under the Old Testament there was only the faith in the forgiveness *to come;* sin itself remained, under divine forbearance, till the sacrifice was offered on Calvary. (Rom. iii. 25.) All that the Old Testament possessed and could give, the Baptist did possess; but the *essence* of the New Testament was not his, since he died before the completion of Christ's work. (See 1 Pet. i. 10, ff.; Heb. xi. 39, 40.)

† See a fuller discussion on John's baptism in note on Acts xix. 4, from which passage it is probable that John baptized with the formula: Βαπτίζω σε εἰς τὸν ἐρχόμενον.

‡ The preponderance of arguments seems to me to be on the side of *Schneckenburger:* Ueber das Alter der Proselyten-Taufe, Berlin, 1828; the opposite opinion, that John adapted the custom already existing to his purpose, is defended by *Bengel*, in a book with the same title, Tübingen, 1814. As the Old Testament furnishes no *data* for the decision of the question, and all Rabbinical writings can be but uncertain testimonies on matters before the Christian era, it would be difficult to arrive at any well established conclusion as to the earliest customs at the receiving of proselytes. See also *Matthies* de Baptismate, Berol. 1831. 8vo.

means John's intention to set up a new communion, into which he intended to initiate by his baptism; it was only that those who were living under the Old Testament economy should be thereby represented as provisionally cleansed, and consequently not unworthy to receive the Messiah. Just as little does it seem possible to prove the view of the more modern Jews respecting the Messiah's baptism to have existed before the time of Christ; the very circumstance, that John baptized, seems opposed to the supposition of its existence; for, if it had been generally regarded as the prerogative of the Messiah to baptize, John would not have assumed it to himself. (See this point more fully treated in note on John i. 25.) No special historical incident is necessary to account for the origin of John's baptism. Since lustrations were common in the Jewish worship, it would readily occur to him to represent, by a symbolical rite, the μετάνοια which he preached. Certainly this was not done by his own arbitrary will—the Divine Spirit who quickened him was his guide in this institution, as in all that he did;—he was *sent* to baptize with water, John i. 33. The question, how John's baptism should be viewed in relation to Christian baptism, is of more importance. It is evident, that the baptism of John cannot be identical with the sacrament of baptism, which was not ordained till after the resurrection, (Matth. xxviii. 19; Mark xvi. 16;) the former was wanting in the essential power of the Spirit, (John i. 26;) it was a λουτρὸν μετανοίας, but not a λουτρὸν παλυγγενεσίας, (Luke iii. 3; Tit. iii. 5.) The baptism of John for repentance was quite parallel with the baptism of the disciples *before* the perfecting of our Lord and the appointment of the sacrament, to which St. John refers particularly, John iv. 1, 2. Since the regenerating Spirit was yet wanting, (John vii. 39,) that baptism could only exercise a negative effect, just as the preaching of the disciples before the Saviour's glorification, had more of the character of John's. (Matth. x. 7, compared with iii. 1.) Notwithstanding the similarity in the form of the action,* the essence was very different. In Christian baptism, according to its ideal conception,

---

* John's baptism was most probably like the Christian, not only in this, that, in it, the baptizing party performed the immersion on the baptized, (which was the specific difference between baptism ahd all other lustrations,) but that a *formula* was used at the immersion, as remarked above.

(Rom. vi. 1,) the birth of the new higher being, which the Holy Spirit alone can impart, should coincide with the extinction of the old life. In the baptism of children, however, which the Church, for wise reasons, introduced subsequently, the sacred action returned, as it were, again to the lower standing of John's baptism; for which reason a fresh act must be joined to it after the baptized attains to actual consciousness, in order to complete that which can take place only in a conscious individual. If, therefore, John's baptism was on a much inferior level to the Christian ordinance, yet it was not an empty custom; only, it could not impart more than he who administered it possessed. It completed the blessing of the law in those who received it, since it brought μετάνοια to perfection; but then, indeed, it pointed to another baptism, which bestowed the Spirit,—a sense of whose need that first baptism had only excited.

Luke iii. 1, affords us an important datum for the chronology. John the Baptist began his ministry in the fifteenth year of Tiberius; as John was six months older than Jesus, (Luke i. 36,) the mention of this circumstance (compared with Luke iii. 23) is a hint as to the Saviour's age. True, it is not more than a hint. For, in the *first place*, the age of Jesus is not given exactly, (Luke iii, 23,) ἦν ὡσεὶ τριάκοντα ἐτῶν; then, too, the interval which lay between the public appearance of John and that of Jesus, is not mentioned. In any case, the year of Christ's birth, as is evident from the previous remarks on that point, is placed too late in the chronology of Dionysius, as the fifteenth year of Tiberius begins with the 19th August of the year 27 after Christ.* The mention of the different princes ruling in Palestine at that time, is another useful circumstance for determining the date of John's public appearance.

(The term ἡγεμονεύω, like διέπω, is used for different gradations in the Roman provincial administration. Pilate was only procurator of Judea, which office he sustained ten years, and laid it down about the time of Tiberius' death, being deposed by

---

* In this way the years of his associated rule with Augustus are not included. It is according to this date that the calculation of the Abbot *Dionysius Exiguus* is made, with whom our era had its origin. *Huse*, in his Leben Jesu, S. 39, ff., whom *Meyer* follows in his commentary on this passage, is inclined, erroneously, to hold to this interpretation as the correct one, as he regards the rest of the information in the history of the childhood as mythical.

Vitellius, at that time pro-consul of Syria. (Τετραρχέω meant originally to govern the fourth part of a great territory, then in a wider sense to rule in general, but still in an inferior capacity. Thus Cicero calls Deiotarus a tetrarch, [Cic. ad. div. i. 15.] Ethnarch was a higher title; it was borne by Archelaus, Herod the Great's eldest son. St. Luke comprises the two provinces of Batanea and Auranitis, under the name 'Ιτουραία.)

The only remarkable circumstance in St. Luke's enumeration is, that the governor of Abilene, the territory of the town Abela near Antilibanus, which lay beyond the boundaries of Palestine, is mentioned in the words, Λυσανίου τῆς 'Αβιληνῆς τετραρχοῦντος. Besides, no Lysanias is spoken of as governor of this region in the time of Tiberius; but thirty years earlier, a man of that name was governor, who was slain by Antony. If we consider, however, that the town, and the territory belonging to it, was so insignificant, that it could not possibly be expected that all its rulers must necessarily have been mentioned by the historians, the silence of the authors about this prince is not at all surprising. To remove all the uncertainty, we need only to suppose that Augustus restored a son or a descendant of that elder Lysanias. As Abilene was on the borders of Galilee, the scene of Christ's ministry, this might induce the Evangelist to mention the prince of this limited territory.* What St. Luke has narrated so precisely, St. Matthew gives (iii. 1) in the indefinite formula ἐν ταῖς ἐκείναις ἡμέραις. It is not impossible that the memoirs, which St. Matthew undoubtedly used in the first chapters, extended further, and that in them this formula would be in connexion with some nearer event. It has, however, like the Hebrew בַּיָּמִים הָהֵם, often a more extensive reference, (see Exod. ii. 11.) After the chronological reference to the political rulers of that period, St. Luke subjoins a notice of the heads of the ecclesiastical government at that time. Two high priests are mentioned, Luke iii. 2—Annas and Caiaphas. The reading ἀρχιερέως is doubtless preferable to the plural. From the circumstance of two names following, the singular was changed, which, however, in the meaning of the Evangelist, referred to the proper high priest—the one actually in office. The latter was the

---

* See *Tholuck*, Glaubwürdigkeit der ev. Gesch., S. 198, and *Schneckenburger's* article in the Studien und Kritiken, 1833, H. 4.

officiating high priest; but his father-in-law Annas, who had held the office before, and was deposed, still possessed great influence. (See this point more fully discussed in the history of the passion in the note on Matth. xxvi. 57, ff.) At this time, then, John came forward publicly (παραγίνεται in Matth. iii. 1, = ἦλθεν in Luke iii. 3) and preached repentance. The wilderness (ἔρημος) is spoken of as the place where he preached, which is not to be understood, of course, as literally void of men, but rather as pasture ground, (מִדְבָּר.) But in the fact, that John preached in the ἔρημος, and not in towns, the peculiar character of this witness to the truth may be seen. It belongs to John's essential character to *flee* from man, (Luke i. 80,) and to preach to those who seek him; while the Redeemer himself *seeks* men. (The wilderness of Judea [Matth. iii. 1] bordered on the Jordan and the Dead Sea. See *Joseph* de. bell. Judg. i. 3, 10. St. Luke [iii. 3] calls it therefore περίχωρος τοῦ Ἰορδάνου = כִּכַּר הַיַּרְדֵּן, Gen. xiii. 10.) The subjoined clause, ἐγένετο ῥῆμα Θεοῦ ἐπὶ Ἰωάννην, is peculiar to Luke iii. 2. It corresponds to the phrase so common in the prophets הָיָה דְבַר יְהוָֹה עַל. This remark, in the first place, represents the public appearance of John, not as something originating from himself, but as an action dependent on influence from above. Then, too, according to it, the manner in which the upper world influenced the mind of John, was not different from the influence on the prophets of the Old Testament. While in the New Testament we find a more quiet, continually active influence of the Divine Spirit in the minds of believers, as peculiar to them, (expressed by μένειν, in St. John's language,) in the Old Testament the influence of the Holy Spirit appears more as a sudden, momentary one, which was then succeeded by other dry, and, as it were, spiritless periods, such as appeared afterwards in the life of the Baptist. (See note on Matth. xiv. 1, ff.) For this reason the formula יַד יְהוָֹה עַל is frequently applied to the inspired moments of the prophets, to denote the violent and sudden character of the influence. Such formulas are, of course, not used of Jesus, because divine things were not manifested to Him at single moments of His life; but He himself was the one eternal manifestation of the Divine— the Word. (On the relation of ῥῆμα and λόγος, which imply the same fundamental idea of the relation of λέγεσθαι and εἶναι, see note on John i. 1.)

The object of the Baptist's preaching, which is not specified in Matth. iii. 1, St. Luke describes more definitely, by designating it, in iii. 3, βάπτισμα μετανοίας. (See Matth. iii. 11, where John says, βαπτίζω εἰς μετάνοιαν.) Μετάνοια denotes here the result of the law in its effect on the mind. By its form of inflexible requirement, it rouses to a sense of weakness, and to a longing for a power sufficient to satisfy it. It is therefore, in fact, a change of mind (νοῦς) in its deepest vital principle. Considered in itself, indeed, it is something merely negative, which stands in need of something positive to complete it; and that something is the Spirit, whom Christ obtained, and whom men receive by faith. This is conveyed in the additional clause in Luke iii. 3, and Mark i. 4, εἰς ἄφεσιν ἁμαρτιῶν. John's preaching was not itself to effect the remission, but to prepare for that remission, which was to be accomplished by Christ. It is not inappropriate therefore to supply ἐρχομένην. (On this point see note on Acts xix. 4, where St. Paul instructs the disciples of the Baptist in the import of their baptism.)

Matth. iii. 2.—The presence of the kingdom of God is put forward as a motive for μετανοεῖν, since it excluded persons in their natural unchanged state of heart. (The perfect ἤγγικε, is to be taken in a present sense; so that the meaning is, the kingdom of God is already present,—that is, in the person of the Messiah, who represents it, and of whom John says: μέσος ὑμῶν ἕστηκεν, ὃν ὑμεῖς οὐκ οἴδατε. John i. 26.)

The phrase βασιλεία τῶν οὐρανῶν does not occur except in St. Matthew. In 2 Tim. iv. 18, we find βασιλεία ἐπουράνιος. The more common phrase is βασιλεία τοῦ Θεοῦ, τοῦ Χριστοῦ,[*] or simply βασιλεία, Θεοῦ being left to be supplied, (Luke xii. 32, and frequently.) In the Old Testament, the expression מַלְכוּת הַשָּׁמַיִם, or מַלְכוּת אֱלֹהִים, does not occur, nor does it appear, except in the later Jewish writings. In the Apocrypha we meet with βασιλεία Θεοῦ as early as Wisdom x. 10. On the other hand, the *idea* of the kingdom of God pervades the whole of the books of the Old Testament, but appears in its most mature form in the prophets. See Isa. ii. 1-4; Micah iv. 3, ff.; Isa. xi. 1, ff.; Psalm lxxxv. 11, 12; Jer. xxiii. 5, ff.; xxxi.

---

[*] It is very seldom that the phrase βασιλεία τοῦ υἱοῦ τοῦ ἀνθρώπου is put for βασιλεία τοῦ Χριστοῦ, as in Matth. xiii. 41. In the passage Mark xi. 10, βασιλεία τοῦ Δαβίδ occurs, inasmuch as David is viewed as a type of Messiah the King.

31, ff.; xxxii. 37, ff.; xxxiii. 14, ff.; Ezek. xxxiv. 23, ff.; xxxvii. 24, ff.) Daniel describes the expected holy state of things, which all the prophets regarded as future, expressly as a kingdom of everlasting duration. (Dan. ii. 44; vii. 14, 27.) Just as the Messiah also is often described as a king, (in which respect David is especially regarded as His type, Dan. ix. 25; Psalm ii. 6; Zech. xiv. 9; Ezek. xxxvii. 24.) The fundamental idea of the anticipated kingdom of God, as presented in the Old Testament, is not different from what it is according to the description in the New. The idea of a kingdom necessarily implies the distinction of the governor and the governed. But in the kingdom of God the divine will appears as ruling absolutely. Inasmuch, however, as in a sinful world the will of God is conceived of as being contemned, the period of His absolute rule must yet be future. The βασιλεία τοῦ Θεοῦ, therefore, forms a contrast to the βασιλεία τῆς ἁμαρτίας, or of its representative, the ἄρχων τοῦ κόσμου τούτου. The coming of the former kingdom involves the destruction of the latter: the prevalence of the latter limits the influence of the former. But as the Old Testament, in its prophecies, does not usually develope the ideas, which are the subjects of its contemplation, and especially does not present them in their gradual unfolding in successive ages, but, as it were, concentrated in a single picture; so it is likewise in its declarations respecting the kingdom of God. The prophetic communications contain lively delineations of it, agreeably to which the dominion of sin, both internal and external, is depicted as overthrown, and the dominion of God, and His will, established; but as the external and internal are not kept sufficiently distinct by them, but are mixed up with one another, so, in particular, succession in time is not distinguished, or rather, the grand picture of the purely vital development of the creation is drawn at once in perspective; whence it happens, that things separated by wide intervals appear to stand together. What is included in the Old Testament as a germ, appears in the New in its free expansion, and thus first reveals in its fulness the fundamental idea which it includes. The kingdom of God appears, accordingly, as a kingdom always existing —established among fallen men contemporaneously with the first announcement of the Gospel—typically represented in the Mosaic theocracy—bestowed in Christ essentially complete in its conception—since then secretly advancing among the souls of men—destined to a final conquest over everything, and to penetrate harmoniously all the forms both of outward and inward life throughout creation. With respect to the manner in which the New Testament writings unfold this idea of the kingdom of God, there is in them, first, a marked separation between the external and internal aspect. In reference to the *latter*, the kingdom of God appears according to the New Testament conception as one really present, not merely in the person of the Saviour himself, but also in His believing followers, who were translated into the spirit of His life. In the spirit's inner life and consciousness,—*i. e.*, in faith, the absolute dominion of the divine is realized. We find it thus viewed as the kingdom of God in the soul, in Luke xvii. 21: ἡ βασιλεία τοῦ Θεοῦ ἐντὸς ὑμῶν ἐστιν. (See Rom. xiv. 17.) But in its *external* relation, the kingdom of God appears in the New Testament also as yet future, and the object of desire. The Spirit of Christ, as the principle which begins by securing to itself dominion in the depths of the inward life, strives for an unconditional supremacy over all its concerns. But the extension of the divine dominion in Christ, so as to include external circumstances, is gradual, and therefore to be looked for, even by believers, as to be realized only step by step. In its relation to external things, we find, however, a *twofold* modification of the idea in the New Testament. *First*, the sphere of life in which the Christian element prevails—that is, the Church—is conceived in its visible form as an external communion. In this respect the kingdom of God itself is progressive—expanding gradually in this sinful world—still mixed, to a certain extent, with sinful elements. (See note on Matth. xiii. 47, ff.) For it was only in the person of the Saviour that the βασιλεία was exhibited as complete at once, externally and internally. But *further*, its external condition also is conceived as having been made homogeneous with the internal, and as having been likewise thoroughly subjected to the sole authority of the will of God; and in this view the βασιλεία appears absolutely complete, but future. That which had first to exercise its influence in the souls of men, presents itself in the end as ruling in the κτίσις likewise. (Rom. viii 19, ff.) In this respect the βασιλεία might be called ἐπίγειος, (in contrast with ἐπουράνιος, 2 Tim. iv. 18;) but for wise reasons this epithet is not applied to it; the idea itself, however, is everywhere to be met with in the New Testament, in the promise, that at the coming of Christ the kingdom of God will become externally dominant; (see note on Matth. xx. 21; xxvi. 29; Luke xxi. 31; John xviii. 36.) In very many passages, however, the internal and external aspects are not strictly separated, but are blended with greater generality and indefiniteness, as in the Old Testament. The βασιλεία is then the *ideal* future world, (see Luke xxiii. 42, the words of the thief,) which, as being present in the souls of believers, but absent in its completeness, may be spoken of as at once near and distant. —There is another division in the idea of the kingdom of God in the New Testament, which is equally unknown to the Old, —viz., that idea being taken sometimes in relation to the *individual*, at others to the *human race collectively*. According to these different relations, again, the kingdom is represented sometimes as already come, at others, as to come. For in so far as the spiritual element, which in Christ diffuses itself through mankind, and establishes among them the kingdom of God, has taken possession of an individual, so far the kingdom of God is present *to him*, and *he* is in the kingdom of God; but it is also still *to come* with respect to the individual, not merely in so far as the higher principle of life will gradually take possession of all his faculties, but also in so far as the principle which lives in him will be that of the entire race, and will meet his view as manifested among them. The relation of the whole human race —viewed as an individual—is similar; for though the kingdom of God (*i. e.*, the Church) exists in the race, and the race (*i. e.*, viewing believers as representatives of it) in the kingdom of God, yet, on the other hand, the kingdom is still to come with respect to the race also.

Thus the one idea of the kingdom of God appears in the New Testament alone, applied to different relations; and from the various aspects in which it is regarded, sometimes one of these relations is more prominent, sometimes another. Among the great mass of the Jews held captive by the Pharisaical spirit, the idea of an external manifestation of the Messiah's kingdom prevailed. In opposition to this material view, the Saviour put forward the *ideal* aspect of the βασιλεία τοῦ Θεοῦ. As early as the apostolic times, the germs of Gnostic idealism sprung up, by which a real outward manifestation of the divine dominion, at any future period, was denied in the doctrine of the βασ. τ. Θ.; this point had therefore to be defended in opposition to that heresy. On the other hand, the Alexandrine school had, at a later period, to oppose the *ideal* aspect of the kingdom of God to the gross millennarian views of the ancient Church; and through their influence the view was again gradually forced into the back-ground—that it is in the nature of the divine to pursue its subduing and ruling course from within to without— from the individual to the universal. The pure *realism* of the Bible points out the medium between the two false paths of materialism and spiritualism in the doctrine of the βασιλεία. It is not ἀπὸ τοῦ κόσμου τούτου, but yet ἐν κόσμῳ, (John xviii. 36;) and as, in the individual, its process of formation is from the inmost fountain of life, on which it first seizes, up to the sanctification and glorification of the body also; so it proceeds gradually from the individuals, who at first represent the kingdom of God, to the whole, and not merely raises the earth to paradisaic purity, but at last consummates the universe, so as to be new heavens and a new earth. (2 Pet. iii. 13; Rev. xxi. 1.)

If now, in conclusion, we cast a glance on the passage under consideration, (Matth. iii. 2,) and ask, in what sense John the Baptist may have understood the βασιλεία, it is most probable, that, agreeably to his position towards the law, he conceived of it with the generality and indeterminateness of the Old Testament, perhaps even with some predominance of the external aspect, but without incorporating anything false with the idea. It may always be conceded, that there was some affinity between John's notions of the Messiah's kingdom, and those that were prevalent among the people. That they believed that the kingdom was to appear as an external one, was not in itself false; for that is rather its consummation. What was false, was only that they desired the external without the true internal part. Therefore, as the carnal man makes his God for himself, so he makes his kingdom of God for himself. The spiritual man has a spiritual God, and a spiritual kingdom of God; but as the true God became man, so the kingdom of God, or of heaven, comes down to earth, that heaven and earth may celebrate a perfect reconciliation.

Ver. 3.—The Evangelists establish the divine appointment of the Baptist's appearance by passages from the Old Testament. All four Evangelists (see John i. 23) quote the passage Isa. xl. 3-5. St. Luke gives it most fully. In common with the other two, he follows the LXX. with but slight variations. St. Mark introduces Mal. iii. 1 before it.* This passage, however, appears to have first occurred to him as parallel, while in the act of writing; for, on the one hand, he quotes it (from memory) with great variations, from the LXX., and, on the other, he has applied the formula, ἐν Ἡσαΐᾳ τῷ προφήτῃ to the passage out of Malachi also. The transcribers have indeed given ἐν τοῖς προφήταις as a correction; but that this reading is without value needs no proof. This passage of St. Mark is an unequivocal sign that he had documents before him, and made use of them. He took the formula of quotation from St. Matthew and St. Luke, but inserted from memory the words out of Malachi, without altering the formula.† The whole prophetic passage is founded on the figure of the triumphal entry of a king, for whom the road is made straight. In so far as the king, as well as his kingdom, are spiritual, the heights and depths are also to be taken spiritually, and are to be understood of those mental states of unbelief and despair, of pride and self-sufficiency, which stand in the way of the Saviour's work. Φωνή forms an interesting contrast with λόγος, (John i. 1.) In the notion of "word," the idea is likewise included, which is conveyed by the articulate word. The "voice," as such, denotes simply that which awakens, excites. John did not introduce any new idea among mankind. He did not claim supremacy over any peculiar department of life, to which he could have introduced men. He was a mere organ for a powerful spiritual effect in the spiritual waste of humanity. He awakened the sense of need, which the Redeemer satisfied.

(Φάραγξ, in Luke iii. 5, 6, = τάφρος, *hollow place, valley*. This is the only place where it is found in the New Testament. The opposites to it are βουνός and ὄρος. The first of these words, βουνός, is found also in Luke xxiii. 30. The LXX. use it for גִּבְעָה, *elevation, hill*. On σωτήριον τοῦ Θεοῦ, see Luke ii. 30; Acts xxviii. 28; σωτηρία is used in the same way, Luke i. 69. In the concluding formula, ὄψεται πᾶσα σάρξ κ. τ. λ., the Evangelist fol-

---

* On the passage, Mal. iii. 1, see further the observations on Matth. xi. 10; Luke vii. 27, where the same quotation is adduced with similar variations, evidently indicating the use of the same sources of information.

† Hengstenberg's supposition, in his Christology, vol. iii., p. 398, ff., 464, ff., that St. Mark quoted the passage out of Malachi as belonging to Isaiah, because the former borrowed it from the latter, and Malachi is, therefore, only the *auctor secundarius*, appears to me to be forced. They are still the words of Malachi.

lows the LXX., contrary to the Hebrew text, where the words σωτήριον τ. Θ. are wanting. On the other hand, the words ὀφθήσεται δόξα τοῦ κυρίου, which the LXX. have, agreeably to the original, are omitted by St. Luke. In the prophecy, the Saviour's work is represented, quite after the prevailing mode of Old Testament representation, as completed at once.)

Ver. 4-6.—The Baptist's dress and manner of life quite agree with the portrait of Elijah, (2 Kings i. 8, compared with Zech. xiii. 4.) John lived and laboured in an austere and strictly ascetic manner. ('Ακρίς is the well-known large oriental locust, used as food by the poor; Lev. xi. 22.) It was precisely by means of this strict form of life, and the reproving severity of his whole course, that the prophet roused the slumberers; an apparition from past times seemed to have entered the spiritless present. The φωνή βοῶντος echoed loudly through the wilderness; those who were awakened gathered round the prophet, to gain ease for their consciences. The βαπτισμός and ἐξομολόγησις are specified as the forms which John's work assumed. Confession is to be viewed as the condition of baptism, since it was intended to be, as it were, a type of the coming forgiveness to be completed by the Messiah, which required genuine μετάνοια; so that where confession was wanting, baptism also was refused. (See ver. 7, ff., the rejection of the Pharisees.) The confession, however, is not necessarily a special confession of individual facts, (though that is not to be excluded in particular cases,) but a genuine expression and manifestation of a sense of destitution, cognizable as such to John's searching, prophetic spirit.

Ver. 7.—Those whom St. Luke comprehends under the term ὄχλοι, excluding the few sincere-minded, St. Matthew describes more particularly as Pharisees and Sadducees. These Jewish sects, so thoroughly known from the history of the Church, appear in the New Testament as the representatives of hypocritical superstition and carnal unbelief. Phariseeism, however, had a deeper foundation; it was based on the ground of the Divine Word, only that traditional precepts had been associated with it. Although, therefore, the Pharisees (taken collectively) are constantly opposed in the New Testament, and particularly in the Gospels, because, by confounding things external with things internal, they had sunk into hypocrisy, and pursued godliness as a trade; yet there were individual believers among them. But Sadduceeism was utterly devoid of any deeper foundation, or any higher principle of life; pure worldliness shews itself in it, often, however, as it would seem, united with a degree of kindness of disposition. This tendency was therefore insignificant, while Phariseeism, embodying, as it did, something positive, was both more dangerous in its corruption, and, in its nobler manifestation, was more adapted to fall in with the Gospel. The New Testament does not speak of the *Essenes*, partly because they did not come in contact with the public life of the Jewish people in general—partly because their aim, though noble on the whole, was, on the other hand, deformed by subtle errors, which rendered it too dangerous to be recommended as a pattern for imitation. Besides which, it is the nature of the Gospel to set up nothing for imitation but the Saviour himself, in whom the fulness of all that is desirable is included. There was no call for anything positively polemical against the Essenes, since their exclusiveness as a sect rendered them unknown, except in narrow circles, and because the best antidote to the errors of the sect lay in the principles of the Christian truth itself.*

The Baptist's exhortation to the multitude, who were under Pharisaic or Sadducean influence, and shared in the insincerity of these sects, bears the stamp of the strict legal spirit which John represents. In his spirit the Baptist contrasts the kingdom of the prince of this world with the kingdom of God, proclaimed by him, and takes the insincere minds, who hypocritically pretended to sincerity of heart, as types of this evil kingdom. (The language γεννήματα ἐχιδνῶν = שֹׁרֶשׁ נָחָשׁ, Isa. xiv. 29, *generation of vipers*, is certainly harsh; but it is in the nature of love plainly to call evil evil, and, agreeably with the truth, to refer it to its origin. The serpent denotes what is devilish; and

---

* A correct view of the Essenaic sect, which had all the faults common among Separatists, particularly secret arrogance and dependence on good works, is a sufficient refutation of the notion that Jesus had been brought up in their schools. That our Lord knew them, is beyond a doubt, since Galilee was their stronghold; that their existence may have had a stimulating effect on Him, is likewise highly probable: only we must never forget that the development of the Saviour's character was purely internal, influenced only by spiritual streams from above; that therefore nothing can have been adopted by Him from the Essenes. Christ brought down into the world a principle of spiritual life, different as heaven and earth from Essenism, and every other human form of religious life,—a principle which invariably exercised a positive influence on what surrounded it.

that Jesus himself means it to be thus viewed, is seen by a comparison of Matth. xii. 34; xxiii. 33, with John viii. 44; Rev. xx. 2.) But their coming under the condemnation of God is not to be regarded as absolute, (see note on Acts xiii. 10, 11;) the exhortation that follows in ver. 8 shews evidently the wish, that they may cease to be what they are. But, *as such*, they necessarily come under the Divine condemnation. The passage, therefore, involves the doctrine of the possibility of the generation of vipers being transformed into children of God by repentance and faith. ('Οργὴ μέλλουσα, for which ὀργὴ ἐρχομένη is put in 1 Thess. i. 10, expresses the idea of God's punitive justice; hence the ἀποκάλυψις τῆς ὀργῆς = κρίσις. See Rom. i. 18. In John's exhortation, agreeably to the Old Testament form of conception, the last judgment [ἐσχάτη κρίσις] is considered as concurrent with the appearance of the Messiah, as His first and second coming are not here separated. On ὀργὴ τ. Θ., see note on Matth. xviii. 34.)

Ver. 8.—These words of reproof in John's discourse are followed by words of exhortation, which insist upon the necessity of the actual manifestation of true repentance in practice. Luke iii. 11, ff., contain the comment on the ἔργα, such as the Baptist, from his point of view, demanded. (The phrase, καρπὸς τῆς μετανοίας ἄξιος, occurs once more, with some variation, in Acts xxvi. 20. The reading καρπούς in St. Matthew is spurious; it was probably derived from the parallel passage in St. Luke.

Ver. 9.—John contrasts the boasting of external advantages with the practical evidencing of a sincerely repentant disposition required by him. (Μὴ δόξητε in St. Matthew is no more superfluous than μὴ ἄρξησθε in St. Luke. The former is to be understood of the fancied right, which the Pharisees imagined they possessed, to boast of their descent from Abraham; the latter, of their beginning with self-sufficiency and vanity to plume themselves on that right, both aloud in the presence of men and in their own minds.) Being a child of Abraham, is spoken of as the centre of all the advantages belonging to the theocracy. In its true meaning, this descent was not so much an advantage in itself, as it was a stronger obligation to a godly life and walk. Where this obligation was left unfulfilled, the supposed advantage was turned to a disadvantage. (See Rom. ii. 28, 29; iv. 16, on the ideal conception of being a child of Abraham, and sharing in the advantages of the theocracy.) In order to teach them properly to estimate the value of natural descent, the Baptist refers to the free grace of God. As it was purely of grace to have been born in the bosom of the theocracy, so the Almighty can reject those who shew themselves unworthy of such grace, and call others who were far from His promises. (Ἐγεῖραι, viewed in relation to those who were born children of Abraham, involves their rejection.) The words: δύναται ὁ Θεὸς ἐκ τῶν λίθων τούτων ἐγεῖραι τέκνα τῷ Ἀβραάμ, do certainly admit of being understood figuratively of the heathen; just as in the passage before us the "*trees*" denote the Jews in their Pharisaical tendency, who were going onwards to destruction. But the word τούτων being added, compels us to understand them of the stones lying on the banks of Jordan, in which case the parallel with the history of the creation must not be overlooked. As God formed man out of the dust of the earth, so He can even now form men out of stones.

Ver. 10.—In order to enforce the exhortation, the time is represented as a decisive one. In the Old Testament, the parallel is drawn between the moral world and the physical in the same way as here, (Psalm i. 3; Isa. vi. 13;) in the New Testament the same comparison is very frequent. (Matth. vii. 19; Rom. xi. 17.) The time of harvest is that of κρίσις, when the fruit is the chief concern. The fruit required here was δικαιοσύνη, and genuine inward μετάνοια. (Ἐκκόπτεσθαι, εἰς πῦρ βάλλεσθαι, are emblems of the ὀργή, ver. 7.) In Luke iii. 11-15, there follows an expansion of John's address peculiar to that Evangelist. It reveals plainly the Baptist's legal standing. He recommends a faithful fulfilment of the law; "the voice of one crying in the wilderness" does not enter upon the domain of faith and love. He directed to *doing* only, as those who asked for instruction put only the question, What shall we do?*
(Πράσσειν in ver. 13, = בגשׂ *exigere* scil. φόρον.—Διασείω, *to frighten, to exact by terror.*—Συκοφαντέω denotes properly "to perform the part of a petty and false informer;" then "to be greedy," "avaricious," see Luke xix. 8.) As a peculiar trait in the character of the Baptist, his childlike humility is also prominent, which is intimated in the following verses, but which St. John, in the early chapters of his Gospel, portrays carefully for

---

* Compare the New Testament answer to the question, What shall we do? in Acts ii. 37.

special reasons. Even in John's lifetime, his disciples would have him to be the Christ; but he himself humbly acknowledged his inferiority, and pointed his followers to the Saviour. Against his own will, his later self-willed disciples (the Sabeans) made him afterwards serve as the historical prop of their sect.

Ver. 11.—Disclaiming for himself the dignity of the Messiah, the Baptist points to Him to whom it belongs. He calls Him: ὀπίσω μου ἐρχόμενος, leaving the time of His appearance undetermined. The Evangelist John, who had special reason to be more circumstantial regarding the declarations of the Baptist as to his relation to the Saviour, (see on this point notes on John i. 19, ff.; iii. 27, ff.,) mentions facts, which prove that John had a deep and true knowledge of the Saviour and His work. St. Matthew notices particularly this point only in the Baptist's words, that Jesus possessed a greater power of the Spirit, (ἰσχυρότερός μου ἐστίν.) He therefore represents John's relation to the Saviour as that of a servant to his master. (The phrase ὑποδήματα λῦσαι, or βαστάζειν, is put for the performance of menial services in general.) But the Baptist gives especial prominence to the superiority of the Messiah, in reference to His baptism. (See note on John i. 25, ff.) He contrasts the ἐν ὕδατι βαπτίζειν with the βαπτίζειν ἐν πνεύματι ἁγίῳ καὶ πυρί. We might feel tempted here to join πῦρ with πνεῦμα; so that πῦρ should appear as a concomitant, (as if the baptism of the Spirit would be accompanied by fiery appearances, as on the day of Pentecost;) or that πνεῦμα should be taken as qualifying πῦρ, (= πῦρ πνευματικόν,) πῦρ, as the more powerful element, being contrasted with ὕδωρ. But the passages, Matth. xx. 22; Luke xii. 50, appear to me to favour the ancient distinction of a threefold baptism, (*fluminis, flaminis, sanguinis.*)* In this the Saviour appears as the type of believers, who, like himself, if not outwardly, yet inwardly, must all pass through the consummating baptism of blood. In the triple elements of baptism,—viz., water, spirit, and fire, a gradation in the development of the spiritual life, and in the element from which it results, is intimated. While the lowest gradation, baptism with water, implies external purification from sin, and repentance, baptism

---

* *De Wette* is altogether wrong in taking πῦρ to denote punishment; for the idea of baptism does not admit of any reference to punishment. It is always subservient to salvation.

with the Spirit refers to the inward cleansing in faith, (the Holy Spirit being conceived of as the regenerating principle, John iii. 1, ff.; Acts i. 5;) and lastly, baptism with fire expresses the glorification of the regenerated higher life into its own peculiar nature.

Ver. 12.—The exhortation concludes, very appropriately, with a renewed admonition of the nearness of κρίσις, (ver. 10,) the execution of which belonged to the Messiah's office. The act of judging is here represented under the figure of the winnowing of chaff and wheat. The same figure occurs in Jer. xv. 7; Luke xxii. 31. (οὗ ἐν τῇ χειρὶ αὐτοῦ = אֲשֶׁר בְּיָדוֹ. Πτύον = vannus, ventilabrum. Ἄχυρον = מֹץ, Psalm i. 4. On πῦρ ἄσβεστον, see note on Mark ix. 44.) In the concluding verses in Luke iii. 18-20, the Evangelist calls these addresses of the second Elijah a εὐαγγελίζεσθαι, (ver. 18,) inasmuch as they treated of the coming of the Messiah, and even of His presence. (John i. 26.) St. Luke's incidental observations on the Baptist's imprisonment may, perhaps, have been occasioned by a document used by St. Luke, in which the further progress of John's fortunes was narrated. St. Luke mentions, by anticipation, in this place, what occurred long after. (See note on Matth. xiv. 1, ff., for a fuller discussion.)

§ 2. THE BAPTISM OF CHRIST.

(Matth. iii. 13-17; Mark i. 9-11; Luke iii. 21-23; John i. 32-34.)

The fact of the baptism of Christ by John is somewhat surprising, as it is undeniable, that the less is blessed by the better, (Heb. vii. 7;) but in this case the reverse takes place. As before observed, the prominent distinction in baptism, in which it differs from mere lustrations, is, that one party appears as the baptizer, the other as the baptized; and the baptizer, so to speak, elevates the baptized to his own element of life. Now, it is not clear how the weaker can raise the stronger to his standing. John himself was penetrated with a sense of the inappropriateness of Christ's being baptized by him, (ver. 14,) and acknowledged that he rather stood in need of a higher baptism from Jesus. Objectively viewed, this was quite right; but by the divine dispensation, which assigns the limit to everything, and thus also to each individual's course of life, (without prejudice to liberty, which has its expansion within the assigned limits,) John was not called for the New Testament; he formed the top-stone of the Old; and, like Simeon, (Luke ii. 25, ff.,) beheld the Messiah without experiencing His regenerating efficacy in himself; he was saved, like the saints of the Old Testament, through faith in the coming Saviour. For though John beheld Christ, yet redemption was still future to him, since Christ's work was not completed till after the death of the Baptist. It was, therefore, part of John's humility, that, taking his stand purely and simply, he baptized Jesus; a formal refusal to baptize Him would have been false humility,—that is, a want of obedience to the divine will, which had appointed this relation between John and Christ. The words of Jesus: οὕτω πρέπον ἐστὶν ἡμῖν πληρῶσαι πᾶσαν δικαιοσύνην, (Matth. iii. 15,) give the key to the understanding of it. The term δικαιοσύνη, the meanings of which will be treated connectedly in note on Rom. iii. 21, denotes here δίκαιον, *what the law demands*. The words contain, therefore, the general principle on which the Saviour proceeded, and which John, too, had to follow on this occasion,—viz., to observe all legal ordinances as divine institutions. This was not, indeed, the consequence of any inward necessity, (for which reason πρέπον ἐστί is used, and not δεῖ or χρείαν ἔχω,) but a propriety, and a propriety in the highest and noblest sense; the opposite would have been a disturbing of the harmony of life. As, therefore, Jesus was in all things γενόμενος ὑπὸ νόμον, (Gal. iv. 4,) He must submit to John's baptism, thus establishing it as divine; by God's will that was to be also the moment of His being anointed with the Spirit,—His solemn inauguration as the Messiah King.* The baptism of Jesus stands, therefore, on a level with His undergoing circumcision and the purification. (See note on Luke ii. 21, 22.) The Mediator himself took part in the sacrifices and the other institutions of reconciliation ordained by God in the temple service, until, by His one sacrifice on the cross, He had made the repetition of all other sacrifices superfluous. Ac-

---

* It takes away the sinlessness of Christ, when *De Wette* says, "*Sin was latent in Him*. A possibility of sinning must be carefully distinguished from the germ of sin, such as sinful man has in himself. Christ, like Adam and the angels before their fall, had merely the possibility of sinning, without a shadow of disposition for it; to maintain the latter is to make God the author of sin.

cording to God's prediction, (John i. 33,) *the baptism with the Spirit* coincided with John's baptism with water, to which Jesus submitted; the former, of course, could not come through the medium of John, it was rather a sign (σημεῖον, אוֹת) for John himself, by which he might infallibly recognize the promised Messiah. By this anointing of the Spirit, the gradual development of the *human* consciousness in Jesus attained its height, and that fulness of power was imparted to Him which was requisite for the fulfilment of His office as a teacher. Even the pure offspring of the Spirit needed the anointing of the Spirit; it was not till His human nature (the ψυχή) was strengthened to bear the plenitude of the Spirit, that it was abidingly filled with power from above. The baptism, accordingly, was the sublime season, when the character of the Χριστός, מָשִׁיחַ, which was dormant (as it were, *potentiâ*) in the gradually developing child and youth, now (*actu*) came forth and expanded itself; the baptism is the inauguration of the Messiah, for himself and John in the first instance.*

Ver. 13.—According to St. Mark's account, (i. 9,) our Saviour appears to have continued at Nazareth till the time of His public appearance. The inner life in Him expanded, doubtless, quietly and without appearing. But when the hour was come, which the Spirit within gave Him to know with indubitable certainty,† He came to John at Jordan, (on the locality, see note on John i. 28, 29,) in order to be introduced by this messenger of God.

Ver. 14, 15.—The important conversation between Jesus and John, *before* the baptism, is narrated by St. Matthew only. It

---

* Compare the remarkable words in *Justin, dial. cum Tryph. Jud.*, p. 226. Χριστὸς δὲ εἰ καὶ γεγέννηται καὶ ἔστι που, ἄγνωστός ἐστι καὶ οὐδὲ αὐτός πω ἑαυτὸν ἐπίσταται, οὐδὲ ἔχει δύναμίν τινα, μέχρις ἂν ἐλθὼν Ἠλίας χρίσῃ αὐτὸν καὶ φανερὸν πᾶσι ποιήσῃ. (See note on Matth. xvii. 10, ff.) At the close of Christ's ministry, (see note on John xii. 28,) a similar public approval of Him took place by a voice from heaven; so that the same event forms alike the commencement and the close of His public life.

† It is quite an erroneous notion, that Jesus made His public appearance in consequence of an exactly calculated and carefully formed plan. His inward life obeyed only the direction of His heavenly Father; what He saw Him do, that the Son also did. There was, indeed, at the same time, the clearest consciousness of what He did; but all calculation and human forming of plans must be conceived as excluded, because it trenches upon Christ's direct oneness of life with God.

is of the highest importance for an insight into John's relation to the Saviour; and St. Matthew gives, even in this communication, a proof of the importance and originality of the accounts, (contained particularly in the discourses,) which are peculiar to him.

Ver. 16, 17.—The form of John's baptism is not further described; whether the Baptist uttered any words, or what words, over Jesus, is left unnoticed. We are told only what took place after the baptism was over,—that is, *at* the emersion out of the water, (ἀνέβη ἀπὸ τοῦ ὕδατος.) That the outpouring of the Spirit did not take place *before* the submersion, perfectly accords with the symbolical character of the action, (see Rom. vi. 1, ff.,) which is not indeed in itself applicable to John's baptism, but which the Saviour typically imparted to the action by His baptism. The one part of the action—the submersion—represents the negative aspect,—viz., the taking away of the old man, (Rom. vi. 4;) in the other part—the emersion—the positive aspect,—viz., the appearance of the new man, is denoted; the communication of the Holy Ghost must therefore have been connected with the latter. St. Luke adds, (iii. 21,) that Jesus prayed, which must naturally be understood only of being inwardly absorbed with devotion.—After the emersion, these three circumstances constitute the progress of the action,—the opening of the heavens, the descent of the Spirit, the sounding of the voice. But that all this did not pass as a spectacle before the assembled multitude, but was seen by Christ and John alone, is clearly implied in Matth. iii. 16, (ἀνεῴχθησαν αὐτῷ οἱ οὐρανοί,) and in John i. 32. Spiritual eyes are needful for the contemplation of spiritual transactions; he only who possessed such, was in a condition to behold the working of the Spirit. An unconscious surmise, roused by the mighty working of the Spirit, may have crossed the minds of the multitude at the sublime instant, when the flower of heaven descended to earth; but the transaction itself was not seen by them. (Compare the analogous case in the conversion of the Apostle Paul, Acts ix. 7.) If we thus transfer the occurrence into the region of the Spirit, we do not need to have recourse either to the historical interpretation, (which calls to its aid the Jewish notions of a brazen vault of heaven, and the supposition of birds accidentally directing their flight to the place of the baptism,) or to the mythical interpretation of it. The Spirit—the invisible cause of all that is visible—contains in himself the ground of all things; the revelation and bestowment of himself is a quality of His nature. The opening of heaven—the region of the Spirit—is, consequently, nothing but the revealing of the world of spirits to the spirit. Every revelation is a rending of the heavens,—a descent of the Spirit. (Isa. lxiv. 1; Ezek. i. 1; Acts vii. 55.) Far as we ought to be from viewing the opening of the heavens materially, we should be just as far from considering it as imaginary; it is a real operation of the Spirit for the spirit. For the person of the Saviour, this opening of heaven was an abiding one; the flow of His inner life towards the eternal home of the Spirit, and the stream thence down to Him, never again ceased. Gradually during their intercourse with our Lord, the disciples had their spiritual eye opened to this relation; they then beheld heaven constantly open, and the angels of God ascending and descending upon the Son of Man. (John i. 52.) The descent of the Spirit is therefore nothing but His bestowment, which is His very nature. As love, God descends, in His Spirit, into the hearts of His people. So also the sound of the voice is a necessary operation of the Spirit. The Spirit—the author of language—speaks for the spirit; His operation is nothing but *word*. *What* He speaks, the spirit understands immediately; not by the intervention of the physical ear, but by the spiritual ear,—that is, by its spiritual susceptibility to spiritual operations.*

---

* It is not intended by these remarks to assert, that, in the whole occurrence, there was not also something visible and audible to all. The Gospel according to the Hebrews (see the author's History of the Gospels, p. 81) mentioned an additional circumstance,—viz., the visible appearance of fire at the baptism. As all revelations of the divine take place with light and splendour, the idea is not incorrect; only, it is viewed materially. Just so with the voice, (see John xii. 29,) there may have been something audible to *all*. Only we must not fancy it to have been what is called the בַּת קוֹל, *daughter of the voice*. The Rabbins maintain, indeed, that it has been heard from the time of the second temple; or, what is the same thing, since the gift of prophecy became extinct in Israel. But, as a historical statement, we can the less pay any regard to this, as the whole matter is so much exposed to misconception and abuse, that it is impossible to believe that Providence meant to bestow this as a compensation for the silence of the prophets. The voices from heaven mentioned in the New Testament are divested of the peculiarity frequently felt to attach to them, if we consider that the idea of divine speaking, which is equivalent to revelation, occurs throughout the Scriptures, and the same manifestation presents itself in all divine appearances. In the case of God's appearing, the voice is forgotten in the

With regard to the comparison of the Holy Ghost to a *dove*, the word ὡσεί, used by all the four Evangelists, shews that it was meant to be regarded only *as a comparison*. The reality of the appearance is, indeed, expressly signified, (σωματικῷ εἴδει, Luke iii. 22 ;) but, as a real spiritual appearance, it was not visible to physical eyes, and, consequently, the impression could only be described by a comparison with things of a visible nature. According to the symbolism of the Bible, certain mental characters appear expressed in several animals, as in the lion, the lamb, the eagle, and the ox. In this system of natural hieroglyphics, the dove denotes purity and sincerity, and hence the spirit of purity may be most fittingly compared with the dove.* The coming of the Spirit like a dove denotes, consequently, that the fulness of the spirit of purity and sincerity was imparted to Jesus, whereby He became the purifier of mankind. He was therefore sealed, so to speak, as the Son of God; on which account the declaration of the voice from heaven is, οὗτός ἐστιν ὁ υἱός μου κ. τ. λ. That the term υἱὸς Θεοῦ refers here to the divine eternal nature of the Son, is shewn by John i. 34. In the baptism of the Spirit, the Saviour himself was assured of His being perfected in that nature, and was manifested first of all to John. (Ἀγαπητός = יָחִיד. Εὐδοκεῖν ἔν τινι = רָצָה בְ. Nothing but His own image is well-pleasing to God, and, consequently, only those who are in Christ, Ephes. i. 6.) There are two other points in the account of the baptism, according to the Evangelist John, (i. 32,) peculiar to him. First, the words : πνεῦμα ἔμεινε ἐπ' αὐτόν,—i. e., ἦλθεν ἐπ' αὐτὸν καὶ ἔμεινε. In these words the Evangelist notices, in the Saviour's case, what he usually insists upon as the peculiar aspect of the Spirit's operations under the New Testament. While in the Old Testament form of His operation He reveals himself at

---

appearance; but when the voice alone is perceived, we do not bear in mind that the same Being is present, though, on that occasion, invisibly. But, in the direct operation of the Spirit, the senses penetrate each other so as to attain to a unity of perception. The name "Daughter of the voice," is correctly explained by *Buxtorf* in *lex. talm.* p. 310, in the words, *filia,*—i. e., *vox secundaria, cœlestis vocis partus.* The earthly words were viewed as the echo of the heavenly words, and were, therefore, applied as prophecy to present relations.

* The comparison of the Spirit with the dove is found in the Samaritan and Rabbinical writers also. In the tract *Chagigah*, it is said on Gen. i. 2: "Spiritus Dei ferebatur super aqua, ut columba." The Christian sects probably derived the comparison from the New Testament.

particular moments, He appears, in the New, as statedly and uniformly efficient. In the life of Jesus we find this uniformity in His consciousness of God represented perfectly; while, in the developments of life in Old Testament saints, there was an alternation of elevated, and, as it were, spiritless seasons. Besides this, the words: οὐκ ᾔδειν αὐτόν, (John i. 33,) are remarkable. They appear to be at variance, on the one hand, with the passage Matth. iii. 14, which supposes an acquaintance between Jesus and John; and, on the other, with the nature of the circumstances, which, from the intimacy of the mothers, involves the knowledge of the one by the other. But ᾔδειν evidently does not stand opposed to the supposition that John knew Jesus *externally*, and cherished anticipations of His exalted destination. But to gain divine *indubitable* certainty, that it was in the person of Jesus that the hopes of mankind were to be fulfilled, express confirmations were necessary, of such a kind as to be raised above all subjective impressions, and the deceptions to which they are exposed. Such a miraculous sign was appointed him in the outpouring of the Spirit, and this sign he had at the baptism. (John i. 33.)

St. Luke (iii. 23) connects with his account of the baptism, the genealogy, in which, agreeably to the popular notion, (ὢν ὡς ἐνομίζετο,) he commences with Joseph, Mary's husband. With this transition, St. Luke connects the important observation, that Jesus was thirty years old at the beginning of His ministry. Ὡσεί being added, seems indeed to make the date uncertain; but as the age of the Levites' entrance on office was fixed by Numb. iv. 3, 47, at thirty years, and as the Saviour invariably adopted the existing ordinances of the Old Testament, we may conclude with probability that the Saviour was *not less* than thirty years of age. Yet there is no reason to suppose that He exceeded the fixed number; in the Saviour's life all is disposed according to number and measure, and it is therefore best to adhere to the age assigned. The only remaining uncertainty is, whether His public appearance falls at the beginning or the end of the year. (With respect to the construction of the sentence, it is best to supply the verb διδάσκειν with ἀρχόμενος. It is not conformable to the connexion to construe the participle with ἦν, or ὤν with ἀρχόμενος.)

§ 3. CHRIST'S TEMPTATION.

(Matth. iv. 1-11; Mark i. 11, 12; Luke iv. 1-13.)

The Saviour's endowment with the fulness of the Spirit is most appropriately followed by His stedfastness in the contest with the evil one. It is part of the idea of the Messiah, that He is appointed to destroy the kingdom of darkness; His whole life on earth, therefore, appears as a conflict with its prince. The Gospel-history, however, particularizes two periods in the life of Jesus, in which He opposed the full and united power of the evil one, and overcame. These periods form the commencement and the close of His public labours, and each possesses its peculiar character. In the first temptation, just at the commencement of His ministry,* temptation approached the Saviour by the avenue of *desire;* in the other, at the close of His earthly labours, by that of the *fear* of suffering and death. Every temptation appears in the one or the other of these forms; by the conquest of both alike, our Lord stands as the *ideal* of perfect righteousness—as victor in the war with sin. The narrative before us of the temptation of Jesus through the medium of desire, makes it approach the Saviour in the three principal forms by which the world uniformly works,—viz., the lust of the eyes, the lust of the flesh, and the pride of life. (1 John ii. 16.) This narrative, consequently, exhibits the comprehensiveness and sufficiency of His victory over sin, and thus forms a suitable introduction to the description of the labours of the Saviour, who was in all points tempted like as we are, yet without sin. (Heb. iv. 15.) The same temptations of desire, which on this occasion met Jesus concentrated, and were repelled by Him in that form, followed Him individually through the whole period of His earthly ministry, assuming various forms at various times. In a similar manner, temptations of aversion offered themselves to the Saviour throughout His whole life, till, at the close of His earthly course, they presented themselves in their full concentration.

---

* Even in Jewish theology the conception had been formed from the general idea of the Messiah, that He would have to be tempted by Satan just at the commencement of His office. See *Schöttgen, Jesus der wahre Messias; aus der jüdischen Theologie dargestellt.* Leipzig, 1748. 8vo., S. 754, ff.

The view taken of the evangelical narrative of the temptation of Christ is necessarily qualified by the expositor's views regarding the doctrine of the devil and the bad angels in general. Reserving fuller explanations on this point for the note on Matth. viii. 28, we simply remark, that it is only by the most arbitrary procedure, that exegesis can set aside the doctrine of the existence of evil spirits, since even in the Old Testament the doctrine, though for wise reasons veiled, is taught, that man did not produce evil from himself, (by which the idea of salvation, which supposes a bondage under a foreign force, would be destroyed,) but that he was led away by a wicked power, and thereby exposed to its influence. (See Gen. iii. 1; Lev. xv. 8; Deut. xxxii. 17; Psalm cvi. 37; Job i. 6; Isa. liv. 16; Zech. iii. 1.) In the New Testament, Christ confirms this doctrine, partly by His universally taking it for granted, as appears times without number in His discourses, that there is a kingdom of evil in opposition to the kingdom of good, (see Matth. xii. 26, ff.,) and partly by express assertions respecting this doctrine, (Matth. xiii. 39; John viii. 44; xiv. 30,) which admit no other explanation by unprejudiced exposition. If, then, the expositor feels himself compelled to include the doctrine of the existence of the devil among those which Christ and the Apostles taught, he will be the less in a situation to give his sanction to explanations of the temptation, which understand the term διάβολος in St. Matthew and St. Luke (for which St. Mark has σατανᾶς) of some kind of human enemies or tempters, since, in the idea of Christ, the idea of His contest with evil in its centralization is necessarily included. The whole doctrine of the Bible concerning Christ's relation to the kingdom of evil, even though we did not possess the narrative of the temptation, would lead to the same idea which is there stated. But if we cannot adopt these explanations, this is the case in an incomparably higher degree with those which regard Christ's temptations spoken of in the Gospel-history as arising from within the Saviour. *Schleiermacher* is not wrong in saying: "If Jesus ever harboured any such thoughts, (as the tempter suggested to Him,) even in the most evanescent manner, He would no longer be Christ; and this explanation appears to me the worst neological outrage that has been committed against Him." (*Versuch über den Lucas*, S. 54.) The absolute purity of Jesus does not in any way admit of an impure thought coming *from* himself; as the first Adam, according to the profound narrative in Genesis, was tempted *from without*, so was the second Adam also, (1 Cor. xv. 47,) only, with this difference, that the latter came off victorious.* *Schleiermacher's* own view, however, that the temptation is merely a parabolical narrative, which was afterwards misunderstood,—which view *Ullmann* also (Studien, H. 1, S. 59, ff.) approves,—is sufficiently refuted by *Usteri*, (Studien 1832, H. 4.) Undoubtedly we possess here a pure fact, undistorted by any mythical elements, (*Blätter für höhere Wahrheit*, B. v., S. 247, ff.;) but in a purely biblical point of view it may be doubted, whether we are to conceive of an external appearance of Satan standing, as it were corporeally, before Christ. It may be denied for various reasons. In the first place, there is no proof of any analogous fact either in the Old Testament or the New; for the narrative in Gen. iii. 1, let it be taken as it may, cannot, at least, be called an *appearance* of the devil. But then the fact would not be explained even on the supposition of an outward appearance of the prince of darkness; for, if it were assumed that Jesus was physically transported through the air, yet it would still be inconceivable how all the kingdoms of the world could be surveyed from a mountain. Besides, the words which the tempter uttered outwardly, must be conceived to have been united with an inward effect, because, without this there would have been no temptation; this would, therefore, be the essential point, even on the supposition of an outward appearance. It is, therefore, doubtless most fitting to lay the scene of the occurrence, as being an internal one, in the sphere of the soul; all that is essential will then be preserved, as well as a true conception of the event obtained. The temptation consisted in this, that the ψυχή of Jesus was exposed to the full influence of the kingdom of darkness. This kingdom, in the person of its representative, first displayed to the Saviour its bright

---

* The hypothesis started by *Meyer* (in *Ullmann* and *Umbreit's Studien*, 1831, II. 2,) does not differ essentially from this view. He supposes that the temptation was a *dream*, and compares with it Solomon's dream, 1 Kings iii. 5, ff. For if those seductive thoughts could have arisen in Christ's heart, though only in dream, His purity would have been sullied. But if any one chose to refer the excitement of the thoughts in a dream to a hostile power, the opinion would not indeed be offensive; but then, there appears no reason why the whole occurrence should not have taken place in a waking state, as the narrative implies.

side, and endeavoured thus to seduce Him from the narrow path marked out for Him on earth.

We meet with analogous appearances in the Old Testament as well as the New. (See Ezek. viii. 3; xi. 1; Rev. i. 10; xvii. 3.) And if we are disposed to connect 2 Cor. xi. 14, "Satan is transformed into an angel of light," with the temptation, that expression does not by any means require us to imagine an outward appearance; but it can be taken to mean an inward revelation of Satan, as a good angel, in order to be more sure of success in deceiving.

Matth. iv. 1.—Immediately after the baptism, the Saviour left the Jordan, (see Luke iv. 1,) and withdrew into solitude, quietly to prepare for His lofty calling. That the wilderness is here meant in its literal sense, is seen by Mark i. 13. Tradition speaks of Quarantaria as the scene, which lies near Jericho. (*Joseph. Antiq.*, xvi. 1. *Bell. Jud.*, iv. 82.) Inasmuch as this quiet preparation, and the temptation connected with it, was based on God's plan itself, it is said: ἀνήχθη ὑπὸ πνεύματος εἰς τὴν ἔρημον. That this πνεῦμα was that good spirit who filled Jesus at the baptism, is seen from Luke iv. 1, in the words: Ἰησοῦς πνεύματος ἁγίου πλήρης κ. τ. λ. But in that case it seems inexplicable how we can speak of the Saviour, who was armed with the fulness of the Spirit, as being tempted, (πειρασθῆναι.) (The meaning of the word is always one and the same; only, it is modified according to the object or subject of temptation. Used of the evil one, it denotes *to test*, in order to be able to destroy. In this sense it is said of God, πειράζει οὐδένα, James i. 13. God, on the contrary, tempts in order to purify and to perfect, Gen. xxii. 1. Used of men in reference to God, it is always the product of unbelief and presumption, since it involves the contrary of humble waiting for indications from God, Heb. iii. 9.) But we must include the possibility of a fall (like Adam's *posse non peccare*) in the very idea of a Saviour; because, without this, no merit is conceivable.* It is true, this possibility must be viewed as purely objective; for inasmuch as God became man in the person of Christ, we must ascribe to Him the impossibility

---

* The consolation, too, that is afforded to unhappy man, struggling against sin, in the fact that the Saviour himself tasted the bitterness of that struggle in all its forms, (Heb. ii. 17, 18,) would be destroyed, if the objective possibility of Christ's falling were denied.

of sinning, (*non posse peccare*.) This blending of the possibility of falling with the necessity of a victory over evil, is a mystery, which is one with the idea of the God-man itself. It is only by distinguishing between ψυχή and πνεῦμα that we can attain to a clear idea of the relation. His liability to temptation was attached to His human ψυχή; the necessity of a victory, to the fulness of the πνεῦμα. By the former, He is made like us, and set for a pattern; by the latter, He is above all that is human, and assists individuals to become like himself, by the power of the same Spirit. In His last great temptation, by the sufferings at the close of His life, the Saviour himself announced His being deserted of the fulness of the divine Spirit, (Matth. xxvii. 46;) this destitution, in which the humanity of the Saviour stood as it were isolated, affords a view of the nature of His conflict at that time. In this case nothing is expressly said about such a desertion; but it must be supposed, particularly as the Saviour does not at once recognize the Tempter. The outward fasting in the wilderness was an emblem, as it were, of His inward forsaken condition; and it is not till this is supposed, that the temptation acquires real importance. In full possession of the divine Spirit, temptation is inconceivable; it is only as divested of that fulness that the ψυχή of Jesus could humanly fight and struggle. According to this, the scene should be conceived in the following form:—After the effusion of the Spirit on our Lord, He went, under the impulse of that Spirit, into the wilderness, in order to begin His great work in the seclusion of His inner life. There, as in the garden of Gethsemane, and on Golgotha, the fulness of the Spirit was withdrawn from Him, and He was left to the power of darkness, (Luke xxii. 53;) pleasure, in its most seductive forms, tempted His soul. But, in perfect innocence, the Saviour passed through the conflict; and, when the temptation was repelled, the fulness of heavenly powers returned to Him, (Matth iv. 11.) If it were said, that John i. 32: πνεῦμα ἔμεινεν ἐπ' αὐτόν, is contradictory to this view, the same might be said of Matth. xxvii. 46, where such a state of spiritual desertion must certainly be supposed. By whatever method the difficulty is solved in that case, the same must be applied here. My idea of this obscure relation is this: In the Saviour there was an alternation of states; He had seasons of the richest spiritual fulness, and of desertion; but, in the *first place*, these states were not so variable as they are wont to be in sinful men; and, *next,* they did not penetrate to the inmost sanctuary of His being. His ψυχή itself was holy and pure; and, from its being most intimately pervaded by the πνεῦμα, so entirely a ψυχή πνευματική, that even at the moments of complete desertion, by the overflowing fulness of the Spirit, (as we must suppose in Matth. xxvii. 46,) His soul acted in the might of the divine Spirit. This unalterable repose in the depths of His holy soul—this perfect freedom, in the inmost seat of life, from the agitations of trouble, which the Redeemer bore for our good, as He did all the other consequences of sin—are denoted by the μένειν τοῦ πνεύματος, which is contrasted with the alternating states of Old Testament saints, which might be immediately overpowered by sin whenever dark hours arrived.

Ver. 2.—In Christ's fasting for forty days, there is evidently a parallel with the fasting of Moses (Deut. ix. 9, 18) and Elijah, (1 Kings xix. 8.) We are, therefore, the less justified in taking νηστεύειν in a wider sense,—viz., "abstaining from *ordinary* nourishment," since it is said of Moses, that he ate no bread, and drank no water, which coincides with Luke iv. 2: "He did eat nothing." The intention of the Evangelists is to place Jesus in comparison with the great prophets of earlier days, (according to Deut. xviii. 15: "A prophet *like unto me,*" says Moses, "will the Lord thy God raise up;") He could not, therefore, do anything less than they did. The number forty was certainly a sacred number with the Jews; but it does not follow thence that it is not to be taken exactly; but rather that the idea entertained by the Jews of the sacredness of certain numbers has itself a deeper foundation, which, taken as a general proposition, may be thus expressed:—"According to divine arrangement, which is pure harmony, every development proceeds by definite measure and number." The forty days of the temptation form an interesting parallel with Israel's forty years' journey through the wilderness.* All the passages quoted in the

---

* Such parallels are acknowledged by the advocates of the mythical character of the Gospel-history, *Strauss* and *De Wette;* but in such a way, that precisely because of those parallels they deny the historical reality, both of the typical event in the Old Testament, and of the antitype in the New. But in this way they are degraded into mere puerilities. For a serious person they can have no import, unless they be founded on real transactions, by which God speaks to men in the language of fact.

history of Christ's temptation are taken from the narrative of that journey.

Ver. 3, 4.—The point of the first temptation is very justly regarded as lying in the thought of employing the higher powers bestowed upon Him for satisfying His own wants. The principle here established,—that, namely, of using His miraculous powers only for the good of others,—the Saviour followed out with self-denying love through the whole time of His ministry. Jesus repulsed the powerful solicitation of sensual appetite by faith in God's power, with a reference to Deut. viii. 3, where the LXX. translate כָּל־מוֹצָא פִי יְהֹוָה by ῥῆμα ἐκπορευόμενον διὰ στόματος Θεοῦ. In this passage the manna, viewed as an extraordinary heavenly aliment, (Psalm lxxviii. 25,) is contrasted with earthly means of subsistence, and just so Jesus contrasts the earthly ἄρτος with the heavenly. According to the connexion, therefore, another kind of earthly food cannot be meant. The ῥῆμα Θεοῦ is to be conceived of here as the effectual creative cause of *all* nourishment. As everything was made by God's word, and by the breath of His mouth, (Psalm xxxiii. 6,) so that same word also preserves all things, since the preservation is nothing but a continued creation. Jesus is stayed by faith in this power of God; so long as the Spirit did not release Him from the wilderness, He was fed by the hidden word of God, which strengthened soul and body, without His providing anything for himself by the miraculous gift granted to Him. (On ῥῆμα Θεοῦ, see note on Matth. iii. 2.)

Ver. 5.—St. Luke has placed the second temptation last; evidently with less propriety.* The first two thoughts the Tempter suggests to Jesus we can, for a moment, imagine as coming from a good being; the temptation is more hidden, and Satan, consequently, does not display himself as he is; but in the last requirement his dark origin is openly revealed, so that it is properly followed in St. Matthew's account by ὕπαγε. (Ἁγία πόλις = עִיר הַקֹּדֶשׁ, a designation of Jerusalem as the centre of the Old Testament theocracy. Πτερύγιον = כָּנָף, a wing of the temple, in the shape of a tower, with a flat roof. The conducting Him thither took place ἐν πνεύματι, Rev. xvii. 3.)

---

* [See *Greswell's* Dissertations on the Gospels, vol. ii., p. 192, ff, *second edition.*]—*Tr.*

Ver. 6.—The point of the second temptation lies in the thought of *parading* the gift of working miracles; this thought, being clothed in the words of Scripture,* is suggested to our Lord in a dazzling form. In this respect Jesus acted constantly on the principle here approved,—His miracles always had reference to the moral and spiritual world. The quoting of the Scripture words was intended to excite His vanity from the consciousness of His being the Son of God, through the medium of the raptures inspired by the miraculous powers residing in Him. Humble obedience, laying aside all one's own will, can alone secure the victory in such a case. The passage is quoted from Psalm xci. 11, according to the LXX., but in an abbreviated form. In the context, the words apply to all the pious in general, and represent them as under God's protection. But the pious part of mankind, conceived as a whole, has its representative in the Messiah as the second Adam; and therefore it is quite right to *refer* the passage to the Messiah, only, the *application* of it to cases of our own making is wrong. The angels appear here as "ministering spirits, sent forth to minister for them who shall be heirs of salvation." (See note on Heb. i. 14.) The entire fulness of the heavenly powers is present for those that fear God, as Paul says, "All things are yours." (1 Cor. iii. 21, 22.)

Ver. 7.—Jesus meets the Tempter, who plants himself on the temple, and makes free use of the word of God, with that same Word. In the words of the passage (Deut. vi. 16) this thought is expressed, that the perverse application of a correct principle is a tempting of God. The words are quoted according to the LXX. ('Ἐκπειράζειν is used in Luke x. 25; 1 Cor. x. 9, in a bad sense only; and not, therefore, of God's temptations.)

Ver. 8, 9.—This passage, as has been already observed, is particularly to the point, as proof that the temptation is to be conceived as an inward fact. A view of all the kingdoms of the world is of course impossible from any physical elevation; even on the hypothesis of physical changes of place, we must still bring to our assistance a spiritual ecstacy.† The mountain from

---

* Concerning the use of the words of Scripture on the part of angels, see remarks on Luke i. 17.

† According to our view, we avoid the question altogether whether the ὄρος ὑψηλὸν λίαν was Tabor, or some other mountain,—a question we are utterly destitute of data for answering.

which Jesus viewed all the kingdoms of the earth, was the inward elevation of spirit on which He stood, and in which position the consciousness was given that it was possible for Him to rule over the world. But in His holy humility and self-abasement, He chose the cross instead of the crown. But that we are not to think of a dominion over the Jews merely, but of universal monarchy, is evident even from the Jewish notion of a Messiah, which maintained it to be one of His prerogatives to rule over all nations. (See *Bertholdt, Christol. jud.*, p. 188.) The idea, rightly conceived, is also perfectly correct and true. In this last temptation, proud lust of dominion appears to be the point. Satan is here manifested as the "prince of this world," (John xii. 31; xiv. 30; xvi. 11,) and as desirous of making Jesus his instrument, (that is, Christ Antichrist,) since he aims to delude Him by the promise of dominion over the world, and by the revelation of its glory. As payment, the Tempter demands worship from Him. (Προςκυνεῖν, taken as an outward rite, such as kneeling or prostration, is to be conceived of here merely as a symbolical expression of the inward spiritual act, at which the temptation was aimed,—*i. e.*, acquiescing in Satan's will, permitting him to rule in the soul, and submitting to become his instrument.) It was just this which disclosed to the Saviour the dark nature of the being that suggested to Him the thoughts which He dismissed; and Jesus, therefore, bids the creature of the night depart, with the word ὕπαγε.—St. Luke's narrative contains some peculiar traits. On occasion of the view of the kingdoms of the earth from the mountain, he adds: ἐν στιγμῇ χρόνου, = ἐν ῥιπῇ ὀφθαλμοῦ, 1 Cor. xv. 22, which is still more in favour of the interpretation of this scene as a spiritual vision. St. Luke next adds in his account of this temptation the following words to what the devil said: ὅτι ἐμοὶ παραδέδοται, καὶ ᾧ ἐὰν θέλω, δίδωμι αὐτήν. Παραδίδοται conveys a hint worthy of notice, as opposing the doctrine of an original evil principle; the prince of this world has *received* all from God, to whom alone, as the everlasting παντοκράτωρ, dominion is due. The confession of having received all, forms the strangest contrast with the demand of worship. What the Tempter here says of himself, is true of the Saviour in the purest and deepest sense. (See John xvii. 22; Rev. xi. 15.)

Ver. 10.—In answer to this last temptation, the Saviour put forward the first commandment, (Deut. vi. 13,) which contains all the rest in itself. Only the One, the Eternal, the True God of heaven and of earth, ought to be the object of worship. Where the assumption of this divine prerogative shews itself, the spirit of the devil is displayed. (See 2 Thess. ii. 4.) Through this maintenance of the honour of God, not only *this* world, but the *other* also, became the possession of Jesus; to Him all power in heaven and earth was given. ($\Lambda \alpha \tau \rho \varepsilon \acute{u} \omega =$ עָבַד is stronger than $\pi \rho o \varsigma \varkappa v \nu \varepsilon \tilde{\imath} \nu$; the latter is used also of subordination to man, the former refers only to God.)

Ver. 11.—The temptation of Jesus stands as one of those decisive events, such as are met with in a lower degree in common life also, and which, by the determination which we take in them, give a direction to the whole after-life: As, after Adam's first transgression, all subsequent sin was nothing but the unfolding of original sin; so this, the Saviour's first victory, appears as the foundation of all those that follow after. The Saviour here appears as standing between the two worlds of light and darkness. As the hostile powers fled, heavenly powers surrounded Him, and joined in celebrating the victory of good.* The Tempter wished Christ to serve him, instead of which the angels minister to Jesus, and announce that He is King of the kingdom of light. The circumstance mentioned in Mark i. 13: $\tilde{\eta}\nu \;\mu \varepsilon \tau \grave{\alpha} \;\tau \tilde{\omega}\nu \;\theta \eta \rho \iota \omega \nu$, has also, as *Usteri* (*ut. sup.*) strikingly observes, a typical meaning, because it is meant to represent Jesus as the restorer of Paradise. Adam fell in Paradise, and made it a wilderness; Jesus conquered in the wilderness, and made it a paradise, where the beasts lost their wildness, and angels took up their abode. But that the Redeemer's great conflict with the kingdom of darkness was not over for ever, is expressly noticed in Luke iv. 13, in the words: $\dot{o}\; \delta \iota \acute{\alpha} \beta o \lambda o \varsigma\; \mathring{\alpha} \pi \acute{\varepsilon} \sigma \tau \eta\; \mathring{\alpha} \pi'\; \alpha \mathring{v} \tau o \tilde{v}\; \mathring{\alpha} \chi \rho \iota\; \varkappa \alpha \iota \rho o \tilde{v}$, which close the history of the temptation.

Since, according to the view given above, the temptation of Jesus took place in the depth of His inward life without witnesses, we must regard the narration of Jesus as the only source of information, and testimony to its reality. This, and similar events, probably formed the subject of Jesus' discourses

---

* After our Lord's second great temptation in Gethsemane, there appeared to Him an angel to strengthen Him, Luke xxii. 43. We may suppose something of the same sort in this case.

with the disciples after the resurrection, when He spoke to them of the things pertaining to the kingdom of God. (Acts i. 3.) In order to become acquainted with the nature of that kingdom, it was needful that they should behold it in its establishment, and into that, the temptation afforded the deepest insight. The accurate agreement in the narratives of St. Matthew and St. Luke, though writing quite independently of each other, both as to the event itself, and its place in the Gospel-history, is an *external* testimony to the event not easily invalidated. It carries its *internal* testimony within itself, and in the close connexion in which it stands with the person and work of the Saviour.

THIRD PART.

OF

CHRIST'S WORKS AND DISCOURSES,

PARTICULARLY IN GALILEE.

Matth. iv. 12—xviii. 35; Mark i. 14—ix. 50; Luke iv. 14—ix. 50.

§ 1. JESUS APPEARS AS A TEACHER.

(Matth. iv. 12-17; Mark i. 14, 15; Luke iv. 14, 15.)

VER. 12.—Were it not that we are accurately instructed by the accounts of the Evangelist John as to the many events which intervened between the public appearance of Jesus and the imprisonment of John, (see John iii. 24,) we should have been led to conclude from Matth. iv. 12, and Mark i. 14, that the incarceration followed close upon the temptation of Jesus. This fact confirms the view detailed above, (Introduction, § 7,) that in this part of the Gospel-history, a chronological arrangement of the individual events is impracticable, since it is evidently by accident only that a comparison of John's narrative enables us to demonstrate, that the events thus connected in the narrative are separated in point of time.* For even though St. Luke does not mention John in this place, (see, however, Luke iii. 19, 20,) yet he begins his narrative (iv. 15) with the general statement, that Jesus " taught in their synagogues, being glorified of all;" by which this section is deprived of its chronological character. St. Matthew (iv. 23) applies similar general formulas, which is a *primâ facie* evidence that he likewise renounces all pretensions to an exact chronological arrangement of the several events. Such of the accounts of the first three Evangelists as may be, with a certain amount of

---

* That this does not warrant any conclusion unfavourable to St. Matthew as an author, is shewn by *Sieffert, ut sup.*, S. 72.

probability, incorporated in the earliest history of Christ's public ministry, cannot be arranged except by the help of the Gospel of St. John. The references to *place* are as indefinite as those to time; particularly in St. Matthew. At the very beginning of this section (iv. 12) this Evangelist does indeed lay the scene in Galilee and Capernaum; but when the attempt is made to infer thence, that St. Matthew knew nothing of Christ's extending His labours beyond the limits of Galilee, till His last journey to Jerusalem, this conclusion is unwarranted; for this reason, that it cannot possibly be demonstrated where the separate events recorded by St. Matthew took place, since this Evangelist, paying very inferior regard to matters of time and place, arranged them all according to certain general features.* Though it is probable, therefore, that St. Matthew, as a Galilean, narrates especially what took place in Galilee, yet his narrative assumes so general a form, (see from ix. 35 onwards; x. 1; xi. 1, 2, 7; xii. 1-9.; xv. 22,) that it may refer to events in Judea quite as well as in Galilee.

Ver. 13.—After having intimated, in general terms, that the Saviour selected Galilee as the chief scene of his ministry, St. Matthew informs us that not Nazareth, the dwelling-place of His parents, but Capernaum, became the centre of His labours. (Καπερναούμ, more correctly Καφαρναούμ, = כְּפַר נָחוּם, *vicus consolationis*. It lay on the lake of Gennesaret, [hence called παραθαλασσία, see John vi. 17,] on the border of the tribes of Zebulun and Naphtali, in the neighbourhood of Bethsaida, not far from the mouth of the river Jordan.) There is no apparent reason assigned here for His leaving Nazareth; but, according to Luke iv. 16-30, it was the unbelief of its inhabitants that constrained our Lord to withdraw His blessed influence from these ungrateful people. The parallels to this narrative in St. Luke do not occur till Matth. xiii. 54, ff.; Mark vi. 1, ff.; and the same cure, which St. Luke places immediately subsequent to the occurrence at Nazareth, St. Mark (i. 21) transposes quite to the commencement. Although we think it highly probable, therefore, that St. Luke has placed the occurrence at Nazareth in a more correct chronological order, still we have preferred to postpone the exposition of that passage till we

---

* For a more complete discussion of this subject, see the author's programmes on the authenticity of St. Matthew.

come to Matth. xiii. 54, ff. For we should not think ourselves justified in departing from our plan of following St. Matthew in this part of the Gospel-history, unless it could be proved (as it certainly cannot) that Luke iv. 16, ff., is to be understood of a much earlier, and Matth. xiii. 54, ff., of a second, and much later, visit of Jesus to Nazareth.

Ver. 14-16.—The Evangelist St. Matthew does not regard the choice of just these districts as something accidental, but recognizes in it the fulfilment of a prophecy of Isaiah, (viii. 22, ix. 1.) The passage quoted contains the prediction, that the light of the Messiah will be manifested with the greatest splendour in the most despised regions of Palestine. (Micah v. 1 is similar.) Moreover, St. Matthew gives the passage abbreviated, and specifies only the names of the tribes of Naphtali and Zebulun, and the neighbourhood of the lake of Gennesaret, which latter part experienced most richly the blessing of our Lord's presence, and witnessed the majority of His miracles. (The expression ὁδὸς θαλάσσης = דֶּרֶךְ הַיָּם denotes, undoubtedly, the western shore of the lake of Gennesaret, here called יָם, as πέραν τοῦ Ἰορδάνου = עֵבֶר הַיַּרְדֵּן denotes the eastern shore of the same lake. The two expressions, therefore, taken together, include all its circumjacent parts; and, according to the Gospel-history, the Saviour is known to have visited both shores of the lake of Gennesaret.) Of the inhabitants of these northern border provinces, it might be said most emphatically, that they lived in spiritual darkness; in part, because they were far distant from the theocratic centre,—Jerusalem and the temple, in which the true knowledge of God, so far as it existed among the people, was collected; in part also, because they had not kept themselves free from much that was impure, through continual contact with their heathen neighbours. But, at the same time, these very inhabitants of Galilee, whom the rigid Jews despised as half heathen, were most fitted to receive the new doctrine of the kingdom of God; since they were freed from their gross exclusiveness by intercourse with people of the neighbouring states, while, at the same time, their degraded condition made their need of salvation very prominent. As, therefore, the sinner (as a penitent) is nearer to the kingdom of God than the righteous, (Matth. ix. 13,) so our Lord manifested himself to the poor Galileans in preference to the other inhabitants of Palestine. (On the opposition of φῶς and σκότος, see further in note on John i. 3, 4. Σκιὰ θανάτου is after the Hebrew צַלְמָוֶת, which is commonly used as synonymous with חֹשֶׁךְ. The LXX. derived it from צֵל and מָוֶת.)

Ver. 17.—After this notice of the locality, St. Matthew mentions briefly the matter of the Saviour's preaching. He confines himself to the same points which he had spoken of in John's preaching, (iii. 2)—repentance, urged by the near approach of the kingdom of God. The Saviour's proclamation was at first naturally connected with that of John; yet the remark in Mark i. 15, is certainly not to be overlooked, that πίστις was connected immediately with μετάνοια,* and that, not merely a general πίστις, such as formed the groundwork even of the Old Testament, but a πιστεύειν ἐν τῷ εὐαγγελίῳ. (On πίστις, see notes on Matth. viii. 1; ix. 2; xiii. 58; xvii. 20.) The εὐαγγέλιον implies here the βασιλεία τῶν οὐρανῶν, as actually present and represented in the living person of the Messiah, foretold by the prophets, and so long desired. Jesus announced that thus all that was ever foretold and desired was fulfilled in Him, and that the new principle of life bestowed by Him demands only to be received. The phrase: ὁ καιρὸς πεπλήρωται, (Mark i. 15,) evidently points, like Gal. iv. 4, to an established order of development, and internal regularity in it. The time of the Saviour's incarnation, as well as His public appearance among the people, were necessary epochs fixed by divine appointment.

§ 2. JESUS CHOOSES DISCIPLES.

(Matth. iv. 18-22; Mark i. 16-20.)

The calling of the brothers, Peter and Andrew, and afterwards of James and John, (of whom a fuller account will be

---

* *Schleiermacher* remarks beautifully in his *Festpredigten*, ii., S. 93,—"When Christ commands repentance, He does it with a powerful word, to which the act is not lacking. This word, which commands repentance, and which, properly speaking, creates the new spiritual world, since every one comes into existence there through repentance alone, is just as powerful and effectual as the commanding word, which summoned into existence the external world around us." Christ's preaching of repentance is, therefore, quite different from John's; the former was accompanied by the Spirit, who creates it: it is itself a Gospel; the latter, like the Old Testament in general, demands without giving. Even repentance is a gift of God.

found in note on Matth. x. 1, ff.,) is left, in this place, without either an explanation of the motives for it, or a full description of the circumstances. It is certain from St. John, (chap. i.,) that these disciples became known to Christ immediately after His baptism; and this passage refers, therefore, only to their being received to a more intimate companionship with the Saviour. St. Matthew, whom St. Mark here follows, means to make a passing allusion to the calling of the Apostles, in order immediately to pass to the discourses of Jesus, which were, to him, the most important subject.

(On ποιήσω ὑμᾶς ἁλιεῖς ἀνθρώπων, see note on Luke v. 10, where the thought stands in a more definite connexion.—Ἀμφίβληστρον, from ἀμφιβάλλω, does not occur elsewhere in the New Testament. It signifies a double net of considerable size, while δίκτυον means a net of smaller size, used either for hunting or fishing. On θάλασσα τῆς Γαλιλαίας, see note on Luke v. 1.)

§ 3. CHRIST'S SERMON ON THE MOUNT.

(Matth. iv. 23—vii. 29.)

The Evangelist first sketches, in its general features, the work of the Saviour who had appeared—the same words occur Matth. ix. 35—in order afterwards to portray fully His labours as a teacher. He diffused blessings on all sides, and went about to do good; like the sun, quietly and majestically pursuing His course. He did not *demand* like the Law, but *poured blessings* on men; He shewed by actions that the kingdom of God was come; teaching and healing, restoring soul and body, were His great business. (Synagogues [συναγωγή = בֵּית הַכְּנֶסֶת] are not mentioned till after the captivity. See *Joseph. Antiq.* xix. 6, 3, *de Bell. Jud.* vii. 3, 3. In the time of Jesus they were spread all over Palestine, as well as among the dispersed Jews, [διασπορά;] in Jerusalem there are said to have been 480 of them. Smaller places of meeting in villages, or for smaller congregations, were called προσευχαί; [Acts xvi. 13.] They served, like the synagogues, for the daily meetings for prayer; doctors of the law, even if they were not exactly priests or Levites, could speak in them.—Νόσος and μαλακία are related as sthenic and asthenic disorders, while βάσανος denotes especially such diseases as are accompanied with excruciating pains.)

Ver. 24.—The fame of Christ's healing power (the effects of which are not particularly narrated till viii. 1*) spread through the whole land as far as the borders of Syria, and all the sick people came to Him in crowds. (Ἀκοή = שְׁמוּעָה; Luke iv. 37 has ἦχος.—Συρία denotes the regions of Palestine bordering on Syria, and the border districts of Syria itself, which the Saviour touched in His journeys.—St. Mark has in the parallel passage, i. 28 : εἰς τὴν περίχωρον τῆς Γαλιλαίας. We shall afterwards speak particularly of the different forms of disease.—On the δαιμονιζόμενοι, see note on Matth. viii. 28.—Σεληνιάζεσθαι is not found elsewhere in the New Testament, except in Matth. xvii. 15.—Συνέχειν = עָצַר, *to bind, to fetter;* the disease is conceived as some power that restrains the free action of the organization.)

Ver. 25.—People from all parts of the Jewish land, stimulated by the mighty manifestations of His healing power, joined our Lord, and accompanied Him (some distance) in His journeys, in order to enjoy His society the longer.

(Δεκάπολις, Mark v. 20 ; vii. 31. In *Plin.* H. N. V. 16, *regio decapolitana,* a district of ten towns, which cannot, however, be named with certainty, on the further side of the Jordan, in the tribe of Manasseh. See note on Matth. viii. 28.)

Chap. v. ver. 1.—After this preliminary description of the cures wrought by Jesus, and the impression they made upon the people, St. Matthew immediately introduces his readers to the long discourse of Jesus, which, from the locality on which it was delivered, is usually called *The Sermon on the Mount.* But before we consider minutely this first larger division in the Gospel by St. Matthew, we shall prefix some general observations.†

The SERMON ON THE MOUNT, in the form in which it is given us by St. Matthew, cannot possibly have formed a whole when delivered by Jesus. For the connexion of the sentences is such as to make it appear extremely improbable that the Saviour should, in speaking, have thus passed from one thought to another; such an arrangement cannot be justified, except for a

---

* Compare also the explanations on the cures by Jesus and His Apostles in general, given in the note on Matth. viii. 1.

† This important section, the antitype of the giving of the Law on Mount Sinai, has been frequently the subject of special treatises ; particularly by *Pott*, (Helmstadt, 1789 ;) *Rau*, (Erlangen, 1805 ;) *Grosze*, (Göttingen, 1819 ;) best of all, by *Tholuck*, (Hamburg, 1833. The third edition appeared in 1845.) Among the Fathers, Augustine has left a separate work on the Sermon on the Mount.

written composition, and the special objects of the Evangelist. But a comparison of St. Luke is decisive in favour of this opinion.* We do indeed find in that Gospel (vi. 17, ff.) a discourse of Jesus, evidently very nearly related to the Sermon on the Mount in St. Matthew, and at the beginning and end apparently identical with it; but it is much shorter than that in St. Matthew. If it should be said, St. Luke gives an epitome of the full discourse in St. Matthew, it is true, that in St. Luke there are only two verses (vi. 39, 40) which St. Matthew has in a different connexion, (xv. 14; x. 24;) as, however, these verses are both conceived in a proverbial form, they might have been uttered on more than one occasion. But those parts, which St. Matthew only has in the Sermon on the Mount, are placed, for the most part, in quite a different connexion in St. Luke, and that connexion, too, so accurately fixed, that we are compelled to regard them as preserved by St. Luke in their original connexion.† In addition to this, there evidently prevails, in St. Luke's Gospel, an accuracy of historical combination, which is wanting in that of St. Matthew. If, therefore, we wish to maintain the unity of the Sermon on the Mount, we are driven to the hypothesis, that those parts of it which stand in St. Luke in a different and distinctly specified connexion, (*e. g.*, the Lord's Prayer, Luke xi. 1, ff., compared with Matth. vi. 7, ff.,) were spoken *twice*. But as this hypothesis will scarcely find supporters now, there is no alternative left but to adopt the opinion, that the unity of the Sermon on the Mount has not descended to us from the Saviour himself, but from St. Matthew. St. Matthew attached parts of kindred discourses to one actually delivered by Jesus under definite circumstances. These circumstances, under which Jesus spake, are exactly detailed by St. Luke. According to Luke vi. 12, ff., Jesus

---

* *Tholuck* has decided that the discourse in St. Matthew is the original, laying particular stress on the circumstance, that our Lord might have repeated many things twice. Granting this, however, the place of the Lord's Prayer in St. Matthew cannot but be pronounced less appropriate than that which it occupies in St. Luke. That which Tholuck (Clark's Biblical Cabinet, No. xx., p. 134) says,—viz., that our Lord may have repeated the prayer to one of His disciples, according to Luke xi. 1, is possible indeed, but not probable.

† On the connexion of the single passages in St. Luke, which are parallel with passages in the Sermon on the Mount, see the Commentary on St. Luke, from ix. 51, onward.

had gone up to a mountain* for the purpose of prayer. In the morning after the prayer, He completed the number of the twelve disciples, (see note on Matth. x. 2,) and, descending to the level ground, (καταβὰς ἔστη ἐπὶ τόπου πεδινοῦ, Luke vi. 17,) taught the people who pressed upon Him. The circumstance that Jesus, according to St. Luke, descended from the mountain, while, according to St. Matthew, (v. 1,) He went up to it, may be thus reconciled,—either St. Matthew connects the previous ascent with the teaching, without mentioning the subsequent descent; or the pressure of the people, eager to be healed, caused Jesus, after His descent, to retire up the hill, so as to be able thence to address a greater multitude. This appears to have been one of the first public and solemn discourses of Jesus addressed to vast multitudes. (Hence ἀνοίξας τὸ στόμα αὐτοῦ, [ver. 2,] which Tholuck correctly regards as denoting the solemn and silently expected commencement of the discourse.) As such, St. Matthew made use of it to attach to it all those parts of other discourses, which might appear appropriate for the purpose of giving a general view of the peculiarities of the Gospel, in relation to the Old Testament. Neither the oral discourse of the Saviour, nor St. Matthew's written one, could have been intended as an initiatory discourse *for the disciples.* Both were intended as much for the multitudes as for the disciples, (Matth. v. 1; Luke vi. 17, 20;) but it certainly was intended to supply to all a view into the nature of the kingdom of God. According to St. Matthew, the discourse appears like a second giving of the law, which is distinguished from that on Sinai, because, in the first place, it teaches the freest spiritual interpretation of the commandments, and, in the second, presupposes μετάνοια, (as an effect of the law of Moses, Rom. iii. 20,) and, with the law, proclaims, at the same time, the grace which accomplishes its fulfilment. This placing of the New Testament lawgiving† at the commence-

---

* On the situation of the mountain, it is impossible to come to a definite opinion. Tabor has been thought of by some, probably incorrectly. Tradition speaks of a hill near Saphet (Bethulia) under the name "Hill of the Beatitudes," as that from which our Lord pronounced this discourse.

† The assertion, that Christ was not a lawgiver, contains a truth which I by no means wish to deny by my view of the Sermon on the Mount. The specific end of the Saviour's work was not to bring any new law, but to deliver from the yoke of all law. But in so far as He taught us to view the law of the Old Testa-

ment of the Messiah's work, is designed for the members of the Old Testament theocracy, who, on the authority of Deuteronomy xviii. 15, ff., looked upon the Messiah as a second Moses.

In both Evangelists, St. Matthew as well as St. Luke, a connexion may be traced in the discourses. It is, indeed, more close in St. Luke, as he gives the discourse in an abbreviated form.* For as, in the first part, four woes exactly correspond to the four beatitudes, (ver. 21-26,) so, again, the exhortations to pure, disinterested love (ver. 27-31) correspond to the descriptions of natural interested love, which does not come up to the Gospel, (ver. 32-34,) and is followed, by way of conclusion, (ver. 35-38,) and with a reference to ver. 27, by the renewed exhortation to the disciples of the New Testament to live in pure, sincere love. The whole, therefore, forms a delineation of the nature of the Gospel, in contrast with the stern law; only, that this contrast is presented more at length and in a stronger light in St. Matthew. At ver. 39, St. Luke breaks off in the discourse with the remark, that the Saviour continued His address in parables. (On παραβολή, see note on Matth. xiii. 3.) The words: ἀλλ' ὑμῖν λέγω, probably indicate an abbreviation of the discourse, as St. Luke has omitted here the more pointed contrast between the Old and New Testaments, furnished by St. Matthew (v. 13-43.) The parabolical parts are also incorporated by St. Matthew, only in quite a different order. We may, therefore, conclude, with probability, that they formed an integral part of Christ's address. This arrangement of the parables, as given by St. Luke, is thoroughly natural. For in all of them this thought is presented to the disciples, that, so far as they desired to gain credit in the world for the new higher principle of life, (before described,) they must first fully adopt it

---

ment, in its spirituality, as it had not till then been viewed, He reiterated, as it were, the law of Sinai, and perfected it. Moreover, as Son of God, the Sinaitic law is His also. Moses was but the μεσίτης at its proclamation; and it was not simply law for others, but for *himself* also. See *Schleiermacher's* beautiful explanation of this point in the *Festpredigten*, B. ii., S. 66.

* I cannot coincide with *Schleiermacher's* view of the discourse in St. Luke, (Ueber die Schriften des Lucas, S. 89, ff.,) who thinks unfavourably of it. The discourse is, indeed, abridged, (the "woes" only appear to be explanatory additions, see note on Matth. v. 8,) but still, in the main, it is accurately and connectedly epitomized.

as their own, and live according to it. Accordingly, they must first be cured of their spiritual blindness—have the motes removed out of their eyes—themselves bring forth good fruit, and build their house on the eternal foundation of God's word, (in opposition to pharisaical human doctrine,) and then they may help others. The only passage which does not seem to fit in with this course of thought, is ver. 40, on which see the remarks on Matth. x. 24. On closer consideration of the context, however, this thought also appears to be inserted in its appropriate place. The previous expression, "Can the blind lead the blind?" (ver. 39,) as well as the subsequent parable of the mote, (ver. 41, ff.,) evidently points to the Pharisees, as exercising a determining influence on the Old Testament life, in the form which it had taken among the Jews at that time. For these Pharisees were occupied with the hypocritical work of seeking to produce in others what was lacking in themselves; and against this our Lord intends to warn in His parables. The thought that "the disciple is not above his master," fits thus very properly into the train of thought: "Break loose from all attachment to your old teacher; the law and Pharisees cannot guide you farther than they themselves have reached, and the perfect scholar is only equal to the teacher; choose me rather as your new teacher, with decision and earnestness; then you will not remain blind leaders of the blind, but will walk in the light of the living."

As in St. Luke, so also in the Sermon on the Mount, as given by St. Matthew, a connexion may be traced.* For though we must suppose that St. Matthew has connected kindred thoughts uttered by the Saviour on other occasions with those uttered at this time, yet out of them the Spirit of God in him formed a new connected whole. The beginning and the end, according to St. Matthew's narrative, agree perfectly with the discourse in St. Luke, which circumstance sufficiently proves their identity. Only in the fifth chapter St. Matthew carries out the contrast between the Old and New Testaments much more carefully, since he accurately expounds the nature of both in a series of propositions. In this form the discourse appears more expressly as the giving of a new and more spiritual law; but, at the same time, with the law grace is brought into view, since the increased

---

* See *R. Stier*, in his "*Andeutungen*," Th. i., S. 104, f. The connexion is more minutely considered at the individual passages.

strictnesss of the commandments follows on the blessing of the poor and the sorrowing. Hence true repentance, which necessarily includes faith, is presupposed, in order to receive the law of love. By means of this, really to receive the higher principle of life into oneself, and to preserve it, and thus properly to conceive of the relation of Gospel and Law, is the connecting thought between the beatitudes and our Lord's new commandments. (See Matth. v. 13-20.) Of the new commandments, six forms are specified by way of example, (ver. 21-47;) in which, however, the spirit of the New Testament was sufficiently unfolded, so that the general proposition in ver. 48, "Be ye therefore perfect, even as your Father which is in heaven is perfect," might conclude this comparison. Then, in the sixth chapter, the Evangelist, with a reference to chap. v. 20, proceeds further in the comparison of Old and New Testament piety, viewing the Pharisees as the representatives of the Old Testament,—impure representatives indeed, but at that time exercising a potent influence on the popular religious character. The sincerity and reality of the spiritual life form a contrast to the external show and pretence of pharisaic piety. The usual forms in which such piety exhibited itself,—viz., alms-giving, (ver. 2,) praying, (ver. 5,) and fasting, (ver. 16,) form the points in which the Saviour unfolds the contrast of the New Testament with the Old. The giving of the Lord's Prayer forms here the centre, since, in the first half of it, the spirituality of aim in the members of the New Testament, and, in the second half, a state of repentance, is set forth as essential for the members of the kingdom of God, and, at the same time, as the deficiency of the Pharisees. The close of the chapter (ver. 19-34) is occupied with a discussion on the relation of the children of the kingdom to the necessities of their life on earth, particularly food (ver. 25) and clothing, (ver. 28;) and this concludes the contrast between the New and the Old Testaments, which prevails through the whole discourse. The Pharisees, in their eagerness to gather earthly treasure, (see Luke xvi. 13, 14,) served two masters, (Matth. vi. 24,) and thus corrupted the singleness of their spiritual eye, (ver. 22, 23;) but instead of that, childlike faith in the fatherly love of God, and consequently an entire separation from all care for earthly things, are insisted on as the marks of the children of God, which places our Lord's Prayer in a more striking light, as embodying all the wishes and cares of the children of the kingdom. The thoughts, which are connected in the seventh chapter more loosely, are gathered up by the concluding exhortation, and placed in connexion with what precedes. After the contrast between the piety of the Old and New Testaments, the whole is appropriately concluded by an exhortation to the hearers, in everything to exemplify the character of the higher life in the kingdom of God. The first condition insisted upon is to have a constant regard to our own sins, with true repentance, and a warning is given against that regard to others which diverts us from the true aim, (ver. 1-5;) still, a reckless casting of what is good before men unnecessarily is forbidden, (ver. 6.) With this negative view, the positive one (ver. 7-14) is conjoined,—viz., the exhortation to serious prayer and striving, as necessary conditions of the perfecting of a life in God. A call to a searching examination of all to whose influence they resigned themselves, forms the close, (ver. 15-23,) while the last verses (24-27) present, in figurative language, the consequences of a faithful application of the word of God, heard by us, as well as of a careless use of such a blessing.

In the form thus given by the Evangelist to the discourse of Jesus from the Mount, it constitutes a magnificent porch by which the reader of the Gospel is conducted into the temple of Jesus' ministry. It may be said, that His whole subsequent life, all His discourses and conversations, form a commentary on the Sermon on the Mount, in which the quintessence of all that is peculiar to the kingdom of our Lord is contained.

Ver. 3.—St. Matthew opens the Sermon on the Mount with a grand collection of the main features in the character of the children of the kingdom of God, and the children of the world. It is true, that the features of the latter are not expressly mentioned, but they are implied in the description by contrast; woes not uttered on the latter, are opposed to the blessings pronounced on the former. St. Luke, who has chosen the second person as more appropriate to a discourse than the third, makes this contrast distinctly prominent, (vi. 24-26;) but as he abridges the number of the beatitudes, it is not improbable that he has expressly enunciated this contrast only for the sake of greater plainness. The discourse would have been too long and uniform, if there were a οὐαί to answer to each of St. Matthew's sentences. But if we were inclined to regard St. Matthew's fuller record as an amplification of our Lord's shorter discourse, that opinion would be refuted by the peculiarity of the sentences found in St. Matthew alone; a supplementary amplification of the fundamental thought would have been of a less profound and original character. Besides, nothing essential is wanting in St. Luke's abridged form; the first and last blessings he has preserved, and omitted nothing but the rich amplification. In St. Matthew, the arrangement of the separate sentences is such, that ver. 3 corresponds with ver. 10, where the words, "theirs is the kingdom of heaven," with which the discourse commenced, recur. Consequently, there are only seven beatitudes to be reckoned, for ver. 10-12 do not add any new thought; they merely form the transition to what follows, since they characterize the relation which the children of God bear to the world, the description of their subjective character being completed. In all the beatitudes, the one thought is expressed, that, according to God's law of eternal recompense, he who here thirsts for divine things shall obtain full satisfaction in the kingdom of God; but, on the contrary, he who is satisfied with passing vanities, shall hereafter experience, as his punishment, the longing for that which is eternal. There is, therefore, here no contrast between virtue and vice; even the Old Testament punishes crime; but the sensible need of salvation is placed in contrast with the deadness of the natural man, who, without a deeper craving for eternal things, can find his rest in what is transitory. Over them a woe is pronounced, because, when the passing things in which they rest, shew their true character, disquietude will thence arise. The position which Christ thus takes up, is therefore one above the law; this last is seen to have fulfilled its office, a sense of the need of salvation is awakened (Rom. iii. 20)—the matter is now to satisfy it. The only circumstance that occasions surprise is, that several of the points particularized by the Saviour : μακάριοι οἱ πραεῖς, οἱ ἐλεήμονες, καθαροί, εἰρηνοποιοί, appear to rise above this condition of awakened need of salvation, inasmuch as they express an inward state of moral excellence. But this feature is easily accounted for, if we remember how frequently, in the language of Christ and His Apostles, the germ of the new higher life is viewed as coincident with its consummation. True poverty of spirit, as the necessary condition of every development of the higher life, includes it; and in this very unity Christ views it here. Thus understood, the first sentences of the Sermon on the Mount contain a description of the character of God's children, which is true for all gradations of development, for the highest as well as the lowest. For as in the lowest, purity of heart exists in its germ, so also in the highest, poverty of spirit is still maintained.

The first word of instruction which St. Matthew puts into the Saviour's mouth is, μακάριοι οἱ πτωχοί, with the addition of τῷ πνεύματι, which must be supplied in St. Luke, where it is wanting.* The term πτωχός corresponds to the Hebrew עָנִי, which so frequently occurs in the Psalms with a kindred meaning. It comes near to ταπεινός = שָׁפָל, (Prov. xxix. 23, שְׁפַל רוּחַ,) yet it is not synonymous with it, because even he who is endowed with the fulness of the Divine Spirit may be called ταπεινός, (Jesus calls himself so, Matth. xi. 29,) but not πτωχός. The word denotes here (as the hungering and thirsting in ver. 6) the state of spiritual need, the sincere repentance of the soul.—Πνεῦμα must not, by any means, be applied to ingenuity, mental capacity (νοῦς;) for the most ingenious, as well as the weak, must become poor; but to the whole higher, yet natural, vital principle in man. A sense of the insufficiency of this principle for attaining true righteousness and holiness, and a desire for a higher principle that can lead thither,—*i. e.*, the Holy Spirit, are the conditions of the βασιλεία entering the heart; it is even the presence of the kingdom itself; for the strict sense of the present tense should be retained here, as in verse 10, since the true πτωχεία includes the kingdom of heaven in its germ, because it is the noblest fruit of preparatory grace in the soul. The πλούσιοι form the contrast, (Luke vi. 24,) who, filled with what is present and vain, have no longing for the world to come. ("Ye have received your consolation," Matth. vi. 2.) Hence the βασιλεία is not an object of their desire, and consequently they receive it not. But the kingdom of God is here presented to us throughout as purely inward and spiritual; it seeks for nothing dazzling—nothing pleasing to the eye of man; but, on the contrary, it stoops to what is despised and

---

* *Strauss* takes the beatitudes in St. Luke in quite a different—an Ebionitic— sense,—viz., that of outward poverty and distress. Such an idea is very foreign to the New Testament. According to its representation, external poverty, apart from internal, is of no value. But in so far as external wealth is wont *ordinarily* to be associated with a clinging of spirit to worldly possessions, the term πτωχοί may include a reference to the poor of this world.

unworthy. In the view of those Jews whose senses were dazzled with brilliant pictures of the Messiah's kingdom, this commencement of His discourse contrasted strongly with the whole circle of their ideas; but to those in whom the law had fulfilled its office, and who were broken-hearted, such language was a balm. But that we are not to forget the outward, while making the inward aspect prominent, is manifest from ver. 5.

Ver. 4.—The second sentence merely adds an additional trait to the fundamental disposition just pronounced blessed. Mourning (πενθεῖν) joins to the feeling of poverty a consciousness of suffering, which is to be regarded as arising from sin. (St. Luke uses κλαίειν, *to weep*, with the same reference; only he has placed those who hunger before those who weep.) Hence παρακαλεῖσθαι here involves the idea of forgiveness, which is conceived only in its beneficial *result*, expressed in St. Luke by γελᾶν, used in a noble, sacred sense. Wherefore the Messiah, the author of consolation, is called παράκλητος = מְנַחֵם, *comforter*, (John xiv. 16.)

Ver. 5, 6.—It appears as if ver. 6 must be connected immediately with the first two sentences, as in St. Luke, because in it physical appetite after sustenance of the body is employed to express spiritual appetite. (On this comparison see Psalm xlii. 1; Isa. lxv. 13; Amos viii. 11.) This thought differs from ver. 3, 4, only in the object of desire; this last appears to be righteousness, no longer regarded as outward, but the inward New Testament δικαιοσύνη Θεοῦ, (see note on Rom. iii. 21.) The insertion of ver. 5 is explicable on this ground, that the desire of the children of the kingdom is meant to be described in its progress. Πραότης is to be viewed as the first fruit of the πενθεῖν. A sense of our own guilt—complete repentance—renders us gentle in judging of others. He who has actually received forgiveness carries a forgiving principle within. Thereby not only is the kingdom of God in him, but he also will be in the kingdom of God.—In this place the Future retains its full import, because the κληρονομεῖν τὴν γῆν is not synonymous with: ἡ βασιλεία ἔστιν αὐτῶν, (ver. 3, 10.) The phrase corresponds to the Hebrew formula יָרַשׁ אֶרֶץ, (Deut. xix. 14; Psalm xxv. 13; xxxvii. 9,) and may be traced to the Old Testament view of the land of Canaan, as the earthly object of the divine promises. The possession of this land is therefore the symbol of all and every divine blessing. That possession is viewed *ideally* in Heb. iv. In this place, in connexion with the kingdom of heaven, which is viewed in the πτωχοί as *spiritually* present, the phrase denotes the full realization of the kingdom of God, even in its *external* manifestation. Thus viewed, the land of Palestine stands as a symbol of the earth in general, conceived as restored and sanctified to God. The Saviour connects participation in the kingdom of God thus realized, with πραότης, because that kingdom, being a fellowship of brotherly love and union, is opposed to the disunion prevailing in the world, and in its perfected harmony only that which is akin to itself can find a place there.

Ver. 7.—In the following verses the consummation of the inward life, originating from a moral craving, appears in more distinct traits. First, with respect to the term ἐλεήμονες, it differs from πραεῖς (ver. 5) in this, that while the latter bear their brother's *guilt* with love, the former kindly assists him in his *distresses*. So far as distresses and guilt are connected, the two terms are quite identical. This declaration, therefore, follows the hunger and thirst after righteousness very appropriately; the sense of our own distresses awakens sympathy for those of others. It is, however, remarkable, that mercy is promised as something *future*, even to those who shew mercy; while it would appear as if, contrariwise, the experience of the divine mercy towards ourselves would first awaken compassion. The thought is rendered clear at once, if we consider that the character of the ἐλεήμων must always be taken relatively. Every one in whose heart compassionate love has been stirred up by the experience of mercy, still stands in need of divine forbearance, because the life of love in him is, after all, only in its infancy, and is mixed with all the imperfections of the old man.*

Ver. 8.—The two following declarations must also be taken with the same restriction; for absolute inward purity would necessarily be one with the present seeing of God, which is here connected with καθαρότης as something yet future. Καθαρὸς τῇ καρδίᾳ = בַּר לֵבָב, (Psalm xxiv. 4,) forms the contrast to moral ῥυπαρία, (James i. 21.) Καθαρότης is not specifically different from δικαιοσύνη, (ver. 6.) In the two expressions the same condi-

---

* See remarks on the interesting parallel passage in James ii. 13.

tion of the soul is viewed, only in different lights. But what is stated in ver. 6, as to be desired, is here represented to have been (relatively) attained; and, consequently, the life of the children of the kingdom is again conceived in its inward progress. Although all relative purity of heart is necessarily accompanied by an inward seeing of God, since nothing but the presence of the Divine Spirit in the heart can produce purity, yet that is not to be compared with the perfected vision of the divine glory, which is, therefore, here spoken of as future. (Ὀπτεσθαι Θεόν = רָאָה פְּנֵי אֱלֹהִים, [Psalm xlii. 3,] involves, of course, the idea of the highest blessedness; but is not, by any means, to be taken as an empty figure. The expression involves rather the capacity, though marred by sin, of the human soul really to recognize its eternal source—the highest good. This capacity presupposes close relationship to the divine, for it is only *like* that can receive its *like*. Wherever, therefore, a divine nature is born in the soul, from the craving for the divine, the capacity of knowing God's eternal nature is revealed; which knowledge, conceived as complete, is subsequent to our life on earth.* On this point see notes on Matth. xi. 27; John xvii. 3.)

Ver. 9.—In the last stage of moral perfection, the idea of εἰρήνη is put forward. It is represented as realized by the members of the βασιλεία. Εἰρηνοποιός is very distinct from εἰρηνεύων. The latter signifies one who *maintains* peace already existing; the former, one who *makes* it when wanting. Hence, in the εἰρηνοποιός, a (relative) purity is supposed, because the element of strife, sin, must be banished from his heart, and that of peace must be active there, if his labours are to have any effect. That the being a child of God is viewed as connected with the εἰρηνοποιός, is explained by the fact, that in the term υἱὸς Θεοῦ, the greatest blessing is implied which can be promised to man. For in the υἱός, the idea of spiritual relationship appears; agreeably with which the true son is the image of the Father. The God of peace (2 Cor. xiii. 11) begets children of peace, whose actions are peace. This (perfected) character of sonship to God is represented as future, or, at most, as present

---

* When we read in John i. 18, "No man hath seen God at any time," where the idea is implied, "No man *can* see God—He is invisible to the creature," (1 Tim. vi. 16.) This refers to the foundation of the divine essence—the Father God can be seen only in the Son. See the fuller discussion in note on John i. 18.

in its germ. (Καλεῖσθαι = εἶναι, with the meaning of "being essentially," see note on Luke i. 35.) The same thought is expressed Matth. v. 45. This implies, that all the gradations of moral perfection must be viewed relatively here on earth. The state of perfection hereafter is identical with sonship to God. Accordingly, men in their sinful nature are *not* children of God. They need first a higher principle of life, that must be imparted by Him who is Son of God in the full sense—a principle which is received in the desire for the divine, (in penitent faith,) and is gradually unfolded till it attains that point.

Ver. 10.—After having completed the description of the inward state of the true children of God, our Lord passes on to portray their relation to the world of ἀδικία. In so doing, He connects ver. 3 by repeating in this verse the words: "Theirs is the kingdom of heaven." The righteousness is here conceived as complete in the children of the kingdom, as they are viewed purely in contrast with the world.

Ver. 11, 12.—These two verses are merely an expansion of the thought in ver. 10. Under the reign of ἀδικία, δικαιοσύνη must necessarily suffer. The different forms of persecution by word and by deed are then more particularly specified.* (Ὀνειδίζειν is persecution by word, διώκειν by act. Luke vi. 22 has added ἀφορίζειν, *to separate*, to exclude from ecclesiastical and political communion. At the head of them all is put slander, [πονηρὸν ῥῆμα εἰπεῖν ψευδόμενος,] such as the charges of murder and licentious habits brought against the first Christians. St. Luke has given the thought somewhat modified: τὸ ὄνομα ὡς πονηρὸν ἐκβάλλειν = ἀφορίζειν, only a stronger expression.) But our Lord adds, as the peculiar feature of the persecution, which is endured because of the truth, that it is ἕνεκεν ἐμοῦ. By this weighty expression, we first learn the true import of the doctrine of Christian patience, which is much akin to self-denial, which also is to be exercised only ἕνεκεν τοῦ κυρίου. (See note on Matth. x. 39.) Since Jesus is himself the truth and the righteousness, and that, too, manifested in a living person,

---

* According to John xvi. 4, the Saviour did not at first speak to His disciples of the persecutions that awaited them. It is not improbable, therefore, that the mention of them in this place is among the parts taken from later discourses. Yet they are found mentioned as early as Luke vi. 22.

pure suffering for what is good requires faith in Him to be exercised by the members of the kingdom of God. Where selfishness prevails, there cannot be such suffering as bestows happiness. But where such suffering is incurred for the faith's sake, and is borne in faith, it perfects the inward life, and awakens the desire for eternity. This last circumstance is very prominent in ver. 12, since we are there called upon even to rejoice in opposition to the sufferings. ('Αγαλλιάω = גִּיל. It is a stronger term than χαίρειν. Luke vi. 23 uses σκιρτᾷν.) This joy, with respect to ourselves, does not exclude sorrow in reference to the persecutors. In the former respect, the suffering is only a testimony to the believer that He is God's. In the "woe" (vi. 26) St. Luke presents the other aspect. The exciting of human applause presupposes a worldly spirit. Where that is given, it is to be feared that the applauded one belongs to the community of the wicked, and of the false teachers, (ψευδοπροφῆται,) just as the persecuted one is thereby numbered with the company of persecuted prophets. (The reference to the prophets gives greater prominence to that aspect of the discourse, which shews it to have been addressed principally to the actual μαθηταί, ver. 1.) The mention of the μισθός, ver. 12, appears remarkable, as it seems to reconduct to a legal standing. In the kingdom of God, the motive for actions is not the reward in itself. The term was, perhaps, chosen with immediate reference to the standing of the disciples, as Christ's earlier discourses do often still bear a legal colouring; but there is, too, a reward for pure love—a reward which is pure in proportion as the love itself is; for the reward of love consists in being appreciated, and in moving in its own atmosphere.

Ver. 13.—It has been already observed, in the general survey of the connexion in the Sermon on the Mount, according to St. Matthew, that the giving of a new (stricter) law is connected with the beatitudes, in the course of the chapter, by the supposition of a power of the Holy Spirit being received in true repentance, which teaches us to observe such new commands. But the relation which the mention of ἅλας τῆς γῆς bears to what immediately precedes, and to the whole, is obscure. The most natural connexion is undoubtedly the following:— The idea of persecution presupposes a power of higher life in the persecuted disciples, by which sin feels itself aroused; but this very power, which awakens enmity among the opponents of what is good, is the condition under which it works effectually in susceptible minds. It must, therefore, be preserved and cherished notwithstanding persecutions. *First of all,* Jesus calls the disciples ἅλας τῆς γῆς. (Γῆ is here = κόσμος, ver. 14, and denotes mankind generally with the additional notion of being corruptible, and requiring to be preserved by salt.) In the general system of natural symbols, which suggested itself in all profound research, salt always held an important place; Pythagoras regarded it as the emblem of the δίκαιον. Its use at sacrifices was also full of meaning. (Comp. Lev. ii. 13. This subject is more fully discussed in note on Mark ix. 50.) The point of comparison between the disciples and the salt lies in the power possessed by the latter of preventing corruption and imparting life.* The intimation that, without this power, the salt is wholly useless, was to excite the disciples to a careful preservation of the sacred power entrusted to them. (Instead of μωρανθῇ, some Codd. read μαρανθῇ, from μαραίνεσθαι, *to waste away,* which is less preferable. Μωρός, used of salt, corresponds to תָּפֵל, [Job vi. 6,] *insipidus, fatuus.* St. Mark [ix. 50] uses ἄναλος instead of it. St. Luke [xiv. 34] reminds us of the practice of applying salt as manure, [κοπρία;] but savourless salt is useless even for that purpose,—nothing remains for it but the ἔξω βάλλειν,—a figure of the spiritual ἀπώλεια of the backsliders.—On the parallel passages, Mark ix. 50; Luke xiv. 34, 35; and for what follows, Mark iv. 21; Luke viii. 16, see those passages in their connexion.)

Ver. 14, 15.—The *second* comparison conveys the same general meaning. According to it the world appears as σκότος, (John i. 5,) which the children of the kingdom are to illuminate. The disciples form the rays of Him who is himself the φῶς. (John i. 4; Phil. ii. 15.) In what follows, the circumstance is not specified, that the illuminating power may be lost, as was done with the salt; there is only the exhortation to let the light shine. But, indirectly, this exhortation involves the same warning which was given above; for to him who covers his light, it is extinguished. In order to give vividness to the exhortation

---

* *De Wette* compares 2 Kings ii. 20, according to which passage, Elisha heals water with salt.

which He had uttered, the Saviour makes use of two more comparisons. First, that of an elevated city, which strikes the eyes of all. Thus divine things have a loftiness in themselves, and, where they reveal themselves, they are seen, unless concealed for fear of persecution. Then comes the second comparison of a λύχνος, the intention of which is to give light to those who are in the house; this intention *ought* not be frustrated. (In the parallel passages the same figure is employed, only that in Luke viii. 16, instead of μόδιος, first σκεῦος, and then κλίνη, are used. But in Luke xi. 33, we have κρυπτή.)

Ver. 16.—An application of these comparisons is made; from which it is evident, that φῶς has reference not merely to doctrine and knowledge, but must be taken as the inward principle of life generally,—as the source of καλὰ ἔργα. (These are opposed not merely to πονηρὰ ἔργα, but also to νεκρά, such as do not grow from the life of faith.) As a mark of the genuineness of the good works, it is noticed, that they must call forth praise, not for man, but for God; it must be visible in them, that man is only the *organ* for the flowing forth of divine power from him to others.

Ver. 17.—The more undeniable it must have been to every one, that in Christ something entirely new appeared; and the more expressly our Lord himself acknowledged this, and, in the sequel, contrasts himself as a new Lawgiver with the old lawgiver,—the more important was it to prevent the mistake of imagining, that the manifestation of what was new in Him was detached from its historical foundation. Hence Christ here declares the intimate connexion between the Old and New Testament, in a manner which must have excluded all mistake on the point, if preconceived opinions on the subject had not been allowed to exercise an influence on the exposition. First of all, the Old Testament is described as inviolable in itself; then the New Testament is regarded as the completion of the Old; and lastly, in this completion the law is declared to be of divine and eternal authority.

The words: μὴ νομίσητε, intimate a thought very likely to arise on the part of the disciples, that by the New, the Old Testament was abrogated. The Saviour distinctly excludes such an effect from His intention, (οὐκ ἦλθον.) (Νόμος καὶ προφῆται = תּוֹרָה וּנְבִיאִים, is a general denomination for the entire writings of the Old Testament, and more fully still, Luke xxiv.

44. But the writings themselves are not to be regarded in their dead external character, but in the vital principle, from which they proceed, and which is discovered in them.) The opposition of καταλῦσαι and πληρῶσαι, is here of greatest importance. Used of law, καταλύω means "to do away with," "to repeal." (John x. 35.) But πληρῶσαι does not seem to be in contrast with that meaning; κυροῦν,—*to establish, to confirm*, ought rather to be put. It is most appropriate to look upon it as a figure taken from a building whose foundations have been loosened, but which can still be completed on them. Accordingly, the Old Testament is the foundation on which the building of the New Testament is to be placed, in order to complete it. In this comparison the Old Testament contains the outline, (μόρφωσις, Rom. ii. 20,*) and the New its filling up; the two are in organic connexion, like bud and blossom. The fulfilment is therefore to be regarded as a comprehensive one; Christ fulfils not only the prophecies and types of the Old Testament, but the moral law also He fulfils perfectly in himself and His people.

Ver. 18.—With strong emphasis the Saviour represents the impossibility of destroying (καταλύειν) the law from its very nature. ('Αμήν = אָמֵן, is always used in our Lord's words, to direct attention to a thought, and to give it emphasis.) The Old Testament, as God's word, is eternal and unchangeable, (1 Peter i. 25;) hence it stands in contrast to created things. Οὐρανὸς καὶ γῆ (Gen. i. 1) are put for the universe, creation in general. While this latter vanishes altogether, the former remains, even in its apparently unessential parts. (Ἰῶτα is mentioned as the smallest letter of the Hebrew alphabet. Κεραία means "*apex*," "points," by which some letters, e. g., ד and ר, are distinguished.† Moreover, as the first ἕως ἂν fixes a limit to the universe, so the second does to the law. In the phrase ἕως ἂν πάντα γένηται, scil. τὰ ἐν τῷ νόμῳ γεγραμμένα, the γίνεσθαι is = πληροῦσθαι. See Luke

---

* The Apostle Paul gives the same explanation about the relation of the Old Testament to the New, as the Epistle to the Galatians, in particular, shews. In Gal. ii. 18, the contrast of καταλύειν and οἰκοδομεῖν is also found. It is only in appearance that such passages as Ephes. ii. 15, contain a different view of the law.

† In like manner the Rabbins say : *Si quis Daleth in Deut*. vi. 4, *mutaret, concuteret totum mundum*. It would change אֶחָד into אַחֵר—the true God into an idol. See *Wetstein* on the passage.

xxi. 32.) This thought involves no difficulty relatively to the typical character of the Old Testament. In the universality in which it is here laid down, it must, however, be applied to the law in all points. But then it seems that what is moral in it, must be conceived as eternal, which can have no limit set to it. That is true; but in the world of perfection the law will be done away with, in so far as it will have become the inmost life of all beings; there is no longer need of any established law, for every one himself ordains what is right. As, then, there is no law for God, so there is none for the perfected world; for, like God, it also is law itself.

Ver. 19.—The following words point, perhaps, to some particular occurrences; as some of the disciples, under a false conception of their freedom, may have attacked the edifice of the old theocracy.* The passage has not, at any rate, a reference to the Jewish doctors' division of the law into great and small commandments, since such a depreciation of the moral part, (as the small commandments,) and over-estimation of the ceremonial part, (as the great commandments,) being false pharisaical doctrine, necessarily excluded from the kingdom of heaven. But the expressions: ἐλάχιστος εἶναι ἐν τῇ βασιλείᾳ, and οὐκ εἰσέρχεσθαι εἰς τὴν βασιλείαν, cannot possibly be synonymous. Our Lord speaks rather in general of a state influenced by Christian principle, but in which man proceeds without proper reverence for God's word, and teaches so to proceed, and does away with many apparently non-essential ordinances of the law. With a *false liberty* like this, a man may indeed be of the kingdom of God in

---

* *Tholuck* combats this assertion, and thinks that λύειν and ποιεῖν should be understood spiritually, so that the law may be broken precisely by an apparent fulfilment of it. But I cannot see how the sense allowed by Tholuck to the expression: ἐλάχιστος εἶναι ἐν τῇ βασιλείᾳ, can be reconciled with it. He who does not truly fulfil a command,—that is, without love, is a debtor to the whole law, and cannot, therefore, enter the kingdom of God at all. Thus there are only two ways of explaining this difficult passage; either we must take ἐλάχιστος εἶναι ἐν τῇ βασιλείᾳ, as synonymous with οὐκ εἰσέρχεσθαι, and then Tholuck's view may commend itself; or we take them as different, (and to my mind the identity of the two phrases is utterly improbable,) and then we are shut up to the exposition which I have adopted. That we have no definite information, that antinomian error prevailed so early, is not a reason against the opinion, because it is too probable, in the nature of the case, that as soon as the subordinate place held by the Old Testament law was understood, men would be led to suppose they might dispense with the fulfilment of its minor commandments.

his inmost soul, but he does not belong to it with all his powers; and for that reason, too, he is unfit to teach. The terms μέγας and ἐλάχιστος, denote, therefore, different gradations of development in the principle of the Christian life. The Scriptures often speak of different gradations like these, especially under the names of "children," "young men," and "men." (1 John ii. 13, 14; 1 Peter ii. 2; Ephes. iv. 13; Col. ii. 19.) The whole passage is, therefore, a warning to the disciples not to damage the cause of the kingdom of God and their own progress in it, by premature interference.

Ver. 20.—In what follows, Jesus contrasts with the arbitrary destruction of the Old Testament the equally arbitrary retention of it in its external form; this was seen in the Pharisees, and totally excluded them from the kingdom. In itself, indeed, what belongs to the Old Testament can never be *unchristian*; it is only *prechristian*, and, as type, includes what is Christian. It may, however, be represented as unchristian and antichristian, if it is retained in its germ-like form, and its free development is impeded. Such was the standing of the Pharisees; they confined the commandments of the Old Testament to their literal meaning, without penetrating to their spiritual contents. They had, therefore, a righteousness, but it was merely outward; they *seemed* to keep the law, but this appearance was only a means for them the more certainly to break it in its most sacred forms. And as they had, too, the law written in their hearts, (Rom. ii. 15,) they desecrated God's sanctuary within them, and closed the kingdom of heaven against themselves by *their* δικαιοσύνη, which never brought them to poverty of spirit. How the righteousness of the people of the kingdom was to stand related to that of the Pharisees, forms the main thought in the grand comparative view of Old and New Testament laws, to which the discourse now passes; only that Christ gives nothing new;[*] He merely seizes the Old Testament in its deepest root of life. The Pharisees, on the contrary, confound the form with the essence, and insist on the former instead of the latter.

Ver. 21.—First of all, the precept of the Mosaic law: οὐ φονεύσεις, is discussed. The words ἐρρέθη τοῖς ἀρχαίοις, are evidently not meant of the contemporaries of Moses, as if the meaning

---

[*] See 1 John ii. 7, 8, where what is *new* in the Gospel is called the *old* which was from the beginning.

were, "the law was given to *those* of old."* For the same law was given to the contemporaries of Jesus, and to all times. If it were taken in this way, the inappropriate meaning would be elicited, that Jesus set himself and His doctrine (ἐγὼ δὲ λέγω ὑμῖν, ver. 22) in opposition to the Mosaic, which He had just (ver. 18) described as eternal, divine truth. For the same reasons, it is not admissible to supply χρόνοις with ἀρχαίοις; the Saviour is not arguing against something antiquated, but against the active errors of the present time. The words ἐρρέθη τοῖς ἀρχαίοις, must, therefore, be explained by the construction of the passive with the dative. On this construction, see *Winer*, Gr. of the New Testament, p. 172, (Amer. Tr.;) and as to the Hebrew, *Gesenius' Lehrgebäude*, p. 821—so that the meaning is, "the ancients have said." ('Αρχαῖοι = זְקֵנִים or רִאשֹׁנִים, like πρεσβύτεροι, denotes the Rabbinical and pharisaical representatives of the Old Testament theocracy.) The connexion thus assumes a very appropriate form. To the external conception of the Mosaic commandments on the part of the Pharisees, our Lord opposes the inward one, and observes, that it is only this which introduces to the true, full meaning of the law. The whole argument against the Pharisees is, therefore, a defence of Moses, whose law was only given in a form which was adapted immediately to the wants of the inferior standing of the people, but, at the same time, did not prevent, but promote the highest and purest development in spiritual life. It was only the pharisaical Rabbins that checked the development, by retaining on principle the undeveloped form. The command: οὐ φονεύσεις, (Exod. xx. 13,) they interpreted simply of ordinary murder, and referred crimes of that sort to the inferior courts. All shortening of a neighbour's life by vexation, or in whatever way it might take place, they set aside, as not included under

---

* *Tholuck* has again defended this view, on the ground that in connexion with ἐρρέθη the dative must denote the person, and that ἀρχαῖοι is not elsewhere used for the authors of the pharisaical tradition. But the manner in which Tholuck endeavours to gather a reference to tradition out of ἐρρέθη and ἠκούσατε, is so harsh, that I prefer the other exposition, according to which the dative is taken as an ablative, because it suggests much more readily a reference to tradition, which is absolutely required by the connexion. Though ἀρχαῖοι does not elsewhere occur, as used of the authors of tradition, yet it may be so applied without hesitation; and Tholuck himself acknowledges that the dative is wont to be used as an ablative with εἴρηται.

this commandment. The Mosaic command is, therefore, here connected with the doctrinal interpretation of the Pharisees. From ver. 22, it is plain that κρίσις = מִשְׁפָּט, is not the judgment of the sanhedrim. While this latter denotes the last court of appeal in judicial affairs in Jerusalem itself, (see observation on Matth. xxvi. 57,) κρίσις refers to the inferior courts in the provincial towns, which were constituted in conformity with Deut. xvi. 18, and consisted of seven persons.

Ver. 22.—In opposition to this pharisaical explanation, in conformity with which murder was understood only outwardly, and reckoned among minor crimes, the Saviour unfolds the comprehensive meaning of the commandment, "Thou shalt not kill;" according to which, not only the outward act, but also the inward disposition of hatred, is forbidden. Our Lord thus conceives the action in its spiritual origin, and in that way attacks sin in its source, which the Pharisees hypocritically spared. Hatred is spiritual murder. (1 John iii. 15.) The Saviour evidently intends, therefore, to forbid hatred in general, and the reading, εἰκῆ = לַשָׁוְא, should be regarded as nothing but a correction, (*Fritzsche* on the passage justly removes it from the text,) which arose from the idea that there may even be good reason for anger. But this anger ought to be directed against the *sin* only, not against our *brother;* against the person (in which God's creature is ever to be honoured) there is no pure anger.—The one main thought, that the fellow-subject of the kingdom admits no hatred into his heart, is expressed in a threefold gradation. As no certain data can be obtained, either by means of history or grammar, to distinguish between these gradations, this can only be accomplished by means of the thought. Ὀργίζεσθαι denotes, in general, the rising of wrath in the soul, the admission of the murderous spirit into the mind. In εἰπεῖν ῥακά, the inward emotion is conceived in its external manifestation against the brother; but Jesus does not go beyond the mental action—the word—purposely in order to make the contrast more striking with the pharisaical spirit, which laid stress upon the outward act only. But the words of the angry man may attack human dignity itself: this latter is expressed by εἰπεῖν μωρέ. According to Tholuck's investigations, ῥακά is to be derived from רָקַק, *to be thin;* whence רִיק, רֵיקָא was formed, and used among the inhabitants of Palestine as a gentle term of reproach. Μωρός = נָבָל, is linguistically not easily distinguished from ἐκά; but the thought is clear; an increase of anger is intended to be conveyed in this utterance, such as cannot, however, of course be measured. The parallel gradation in the punishment, κρίσις, συνέδριον, γέεννα πυρός, is further remarkable in the passage. We should expect that Christ would oppose a judgment altogether *spiritual* to the *external* one of the Pharisees, (ver. 21;) but here human and divine judgment are mixed. Γέεννα, however, does not perhaps mean the place of punishment in the life to come, but the severest earthly punishment—death by burning. (See *Tholuck* in his commentary on the place.) This interpretation is not, however, altogether free from objection; for, in the first place, γέεννα does not occur elsewhere with that meaning, and then κρίσις and συνέδριον, as being two tribunals, should be followed by a third, and not by a punishment which the sanhedrim or council itself could order. But, in any case, the earthly transactions must be viewed here as denoting divine punishment in its different degrees. The domain of the laws of Jesus is the inward world of the Spirit, to which the punishments for transgressors of them belong.* The ὀργίζεσθαι cannot in itself be *a matter on which a human tribunal would pass judgment; for this reason, that the fact can never be proved.* Hence Gehenna denotes divine punishment in its severest form. (Γέεννα = גֵּיא הִנֹּם, means, primarily, the Valley of Hinnom. [2 Kings xxiii. 10.] The prophets use תֹּפֶת for it, which is from תּוּף, *a place spit upon*, Jer. vii. 31; xix. 6.) The place for bodily filth became the symbol of the spiritual slough, where all that is estranged from God is gathered together. As regards the relation of Gehenna to Hades, see note on Luke xvi. 23.

Ver. 23, 24.—From the negative view, the not admitting hatred and the spirit of murder into the soul, our Lord passes on to the positive one, and teaches that the believer should quench the flame of wrath in his brother's heart also, as becomes an εἰρηνοποιός, (ver. 9.) In this the purity of love is

---

* That this command of our Lord's, as well as all that follow, ought not to be understood literally, is plain from the passages, Matth. xxiii. 17, 19; Luke xxiv. 25, in which Jesus himself calls men "fools," (μωροί,) and in the last passage, even the disciples. This whole interpretation of the Old Testament necessarily requires a separating of the internal and external Church; in the latter, the words of Jesus do not apply literally, they are calculated only for the former.

manifested in its greatest splendour. This precept does not apply merely to those cases where the anger of our brother is excited by injury on our part. The expression ἔχειν τι κατά σου, is intentionally kept general. Even when any one hates without cause, we are to quench the flame in his heart,—that is, not merely be placable, but also not allow our brother to hate. The thought of bringing the expression of this pure love into connexion with the act of offering sacrifice, is uncommonly profound. In that act man approaches the eternal love in order to claim its compassion for himself. That is the most befitting moment for exercising it on others. But when these words of the Saviour are made to imply a sanction of sacrifices in the New Testament, there is an error at bottom. Christ evidently speaks here merely of the existing Jewish worship, which He left untouched. (On the supposed difference between καταλλάσσω and διαλλάσσω, see *Tholuck*.)

Ver. 25, 26.—The following verses were undoubtedly spoken originally in a totally different connexion, as is seen from Luke xii. 58, 59, where the question is more fully discussed. But St. Matthew has interwoven the thought in a peculiar manner in our Saviour's discourse. The circumstance of a debtor, who does well to free himself from his creditor at the right time, that he may not be cast into prison by him, is employed by the Evangelist for a further illustration of the foregoing principle. He conceives of our relation to an angry brother, whom we have injured, as a relation of debt. The ἀντίδικος is, therefore, any one who can prefer legal claims.* Such an one the Saviour advises us to satisfy by humble, childlike submission, that the hatred may not continue, and so draw perdition upon us. In order to strengthen the exhortation, ταχύ is subjoined, with an admonition of the transitoriness of life, (ὁδός = דֶּרֶךְ.) That which is not reduced to harmony here below, continues its destructive course hereafter.—Ἴσθι εὐνοῶν, *be gentle, ready to forgive,*—i. e., "offer thou the hand." The idea of the hatred continuing its effects, is particularly difficult, expressed, as it is, under the figure of being accused and cast into prison. (The κριτής is God, and the ὑπηρέται His angels. But the φυλακή is Sheol, not to be confounded with Gehenna, [see note on Luke

---

* On the principle "Owe no man anything, but to love one another," each is debtor to another in love.

xvi. 24.] The term has too definite an import in the New Testament to be interpreted agreeably to *Tholuck's* opinion, merely of a constrained uncomfortable condition.) As the kingdom of love forms a united whole, and by its power extends beyond life; so also the accusing principle (Rev. xii. 10) constitutes a mighty power, which demands its right, till a reconciliation has been made. The debt must be cancelled according to the *jus talionis* here or there. Love, such as the New Testament teaches, gives room for the adjustment of every jar by humiliation, a ready taking of the fault on oneself, in order to leave no room for the accusing spirit. That we are not to understand eternal punishment under μὴ ἐξέρχεσθαι, ἕως ἂν ἀποδῷ ἔσχατον κοδράντην (= *quandrans;*) but only a transition state, is shewn first by φυλακή, which never denotes the place of eternal punishment, and also by ἕως ἄν, which points to a definite limit. (See more fully in note on Matth. xviii. 34.) The general idea, too, forces us to this way of understanding the passage, since it is not unbelievers that are spoken of, as in ver. 22; but believers, who will indeed be saved for their faith's sake, (1 Cor. iii. 15,) yet are excluded from the kingdom of God on earth, from their having been deficient in sanctification.*

Ver. 27, 28.—The command οὐ μοιχεύσεις, is adduced as the *second* out of the Old Testament, which Jesus teaches us to regard more profoundly than the pharisaical teachers had been accustomed to do. That which they applied merely to the external act, the Saviour extends to the spiritual act, to the desire, (ἐπιθυμία,) and the tolerating of it in the soul. The desire in itself is an element in the sinfulness of human nature in general. It is not to be looked upon as actual sin when resisted with sincere earnestness; but the tolerating of it, and, consequently, the entering into it inwardly with the will, (precisely what βλέπειν πρὸς τὸ ἐπιθυμῆσαι denotes,) is the act itself, unless it may happen that external circumstances, independent of the man's will, hinder its execution.

Ver. 29, 30.—With these thoughts St. Matthew connects words which were uttered originally on another occasion, as the context of Matth. xviii. 6, ff.; Mark ix. 43, ff., shews; but

---

* It seems to me inadmissible to take the expression, "till the last farthing be paid," proverbially merely, as *Tholuck* does, to denote the extreme rigour of the law particularly on account of Matth. xviii. 34. 35.

here also the Evangelist has, with profound truth, collected different elements into a whole.* It is most fitting that the observation—that the command, "Thou shalt not commit adultery," which teaches inward modesty, as well as outward, should be followed by the exhortation to preserve that purity by the greatest moral strictness, and by the greatest resoluteness in self-denial, which does not spare even the most sensitive pain and privation. Eyes and hand are regarded here as organs of sense, which become the inlets of temptation, and, in turn, the means by which sin displays itself outwardly. To sacrifice these organs, in themselves useful and valuable, for the ends of sanctification,—that is, to abstain from the use of them, or to limit it, is the immediate lesson conveyed in this thought. (For the critical minutiæ, see note on Matth. xviii. 6, ff.)

Ver. 31, 32.—As the *third* example, our Lord specifies divorce. According to Deut. xxiv. 1, it was allowable for the husband to put away his wife, but he must give her a letter of divorcement, ἀποστάσιον = סֵפֶר כְּרִיתֻת. (On all that respects this subject, and particularly the Rabbinical explanations of the Mosaic ordinances, see fully in note on Matth. xix. 3, ff.) According to the express assertion of Jesus, (Matth. xix. 8,) this regulation was made only on account of the Jews' hardness of heart, σκληροκαρδία. The right view of marriage, as an indissoluble union of soul, is the basis of the Old Testament also. But the Pharisees did not regard this indulgence as such, and considered it as belonging to the essence of marriage, that a husband can dismiss his wife when he pleases, in order to marry another. To this vulgar notion the Saviour opposes the *ideal* conception of marriage, and sketches the evil consequences of divorce. *First*, the divorced woman, (ἀπολελυμένη,) who must still be conceived as bound by the marriage-tie, is exposed to the temptation of entering on another connexion. He therefore occasions her to sin, ποιεῖ αὐτὴν μοιχᾶσθαι. *Next*, he brings another man into the danger of forming an adulterous connexion with the ἀπολελυμένη. Nothing is said of his own sin if he marries another, because that is self-evident; and the case of infidelity is excepted, because then the ἀπολύειν, as a fact, has preceded the outward divorce. (See note on Matth. xix. 9.)

---

* Considering the sententious form of the passage, it may, however, be allowable to agree with *Tholuck* in regarding the words as original in both places.

(Παρεκτὸς λόγου πορνείας, where πορνεία denotes "adultery" as well as "fornication;" and λόγος, like דָּבָר, denotes here αἰτία, πρᾶγμα, *cause*.) The thought is in itself so easy of comprehension, that there can be no division of opinion on that point. The Saviour evidently forbids *all* divorces except in the case of infidelity, where that is itself the separation, and regards fresh connexions, formed by the divorced, as adultery. But the question as to our Lord's intention in the *application* of this principle in His Church, is more difficult. Just as in the case of oaths,* (ver. 33, ff.,) that intention can only be gathered from a general view of the position of the Church. The external Church, as a visible institution, cannot possibly be regarded as the expressed *ideal* of the kingdom of God. It is rather the covering merely, in which the communion of all the faithful is enveloped, than the kernel in the shell. Hence the regulations of the external Church cannot answer to the *ideal* requirements of the βασιλεία; but as it occupies the Old Testament standing in the majority of its members, it must also order its regulations in conformity to the Old Testament. As, then, in the Old Testament, God permitted† not only divorces, but also the re-marriage of the separate parties, (see *Michaelis'* Commentaries on the laws of Moses, translated by Smith, bk. ii., and Deut. xxiv. 2,) so the Church *may* admit modifications of our Lord's *law*, as expressed in this passage, for the mass of its members. Indeed, the Church *must* do so, because the application of the New Testament condition to unconverted and

---

* Consult the decision of the theological faculty at Bonn on the re-marriage of divorced parties, reprinted in the *Allgemeine Kirchenzeitung*, 1836, Nos. 148, 149, and afterwards published separately. In the main, I agree with this decision. The Church of the present day, grown up with the State, and filled with unbelieving members, cannot possibly be put on a par with the apostolical Church. The Fathers of the Church felt it necessary early to permit modifications in practice. (See the history of the exposition of the passage in *Tholuck's* Commentary.) Obstinate desertion and attempts to murder, early constituted valid grounds of divorce.

† God nowhere permitted murder in the Old Testament, nowhere allowed fornication; but He did expressly allow divorce. Those, therefore, who insist on Christ's command being literally applied in the Church, as it now exists, should ponder well what they do. The subsequent commands respecting the cloak, and the smiting on the cheek, show plainly enough that a literal fulfilment cannot be intended in the external Church. The passage Matth. xix. 9, ff., is also evidently not a precept given to be exalted to a universal external law. The Saviour there speaks for those only who are able to receive it.

unregenerate persons cannot but have injurious consequences. The Romish Church is, therefore, wrong in putting the words of Jesus authoritatively into practice in the visible Church, which has become subject to the authority of the law.* It is true, a spirit of severity must pervade the legislation of the Church, and everywhere the effort must be made to elevate the members more and more to a comprehension of the New Testament spirit. The case is quite different with those members of the Church who belong also to the Saviour's inward spiritual communion; because these latter are in a position both to recognize the Saviour's requirements, and, by His power, to satisfy them. This command is in full force for them and among them, just like the command not to hate, to give to every one that asketh, &c. But since, as such, they are under the Gospel, and not under the law, there is no constraint on them. To their Lord they stand and fall. (On the whole question, consult also the observations on Matth. xix. 3, ff., and 1 Cor. vii. 15, 16.†)

Ver. 33-37.—*Fourth* observation—on oaths. The plain requirement of the Old Testament in Lev. xix. 12, οὐκ ἐπιορκήσεις, was distorted by the Rabbins from a comparison of Numb. xxx. 3; Deut. xxiii. 21, (where vows, [ὅρκοι = נְדָרִים] which were, for the most part, accompanied by oaths, are the subject,) so that they taught the evasion of their fulfilment towards men

---

* Indeed, the Romish Church even increases the severity of the command on its own authority, since it does not permit divorce *quoad vinculum*, even in case of adultery.

† (The above discussion may seem strange to those who are unacquainted with the opinions and practices respecting divorce prevalent in Germany. Divorce is much more common than in England, and is granted for many other causes than that of unfaithfulness. The question has been much debated, and some of the pastors have felt strong scruples in solemnizing marriages, where one or both of the parties may be persons who have been divorced The defence offered above is very inadequate. The distinction between an external and internal Church results only from laxity of discipline, conjoined with the absorption of the Church in the State, which prevails in the German Governments. The external Church is, in fact, those who have the name of Christians, and nothing more, and are not, therefore, of Christ's Church, and would not be in visible communion, if a right state of things, as to discipline, were restored. It can never be admitted, that there is any power on earth that can assume authority to relax Christ's plain command. In the Church, His command is law, and, so far as marriage and divorce come under secular jurisdiction, the government of a Christian country is bound to follow the precepts of Christian morals.)—*Tr.*

through a hypocritical reference of them to God. To this hypocritical behaviour the Saviour opposes that of the children of God. The command of Moses, "Thou shalt not swear *falsely*," Jesus converts into, "Thou shalt *not* swear *at all;*" because He sees in swearing, just as in the case of divorce above, nothing but a permission rendered necessary by sin. But in order to combine the expression of this *ideal* principle in the kingdom of God, with a refutation of the hypocritical Rabbinical interpretation of the law of Moses, Jesus specifies four forms of swearing familiar to the Jews; and demonstrates, *first,* that all of them refer to God, and that it is only in their being referred to Him that they mean anything; *next,* that they are, one and all, inadmissible in the kingdom of God. The subjoined clauses, "For it is God's throne," &c., refer to that Rabbinical interpretation, that a man need not perform oaths that do not refer to God himself. For this reason, in the case of each form of swearing, its reference to God is demonstrated by our Lord; and it is implied, that it is only by virtue of this reference that it can have any meaning. (See more fully in note on Matth. xxiii. 16, ff.)—The conceiving of heaven and earth as throne and footstool of God (Isa. lxvi. 1) is, of course, figurative; but the figure is founded on the true thought, that to the Omnipresent Being heaven and earth stand in different relations. He who is everywhere present, is yet everywhere different. Jerusalem, as the seat of the visible theocracy, is called God's city, (Psalm xlviii. 3;) and an oath by the city acquires its meaning from this peculiar relation. The reason subjoined to the oath: "by the head,"* is obscure. That oath is similar to the Mohammedan swearing by the beard. It is explained, however, if we take, in this case negatively, what, in the other cases, was expressed positively. What impotent man cannot accomplish,—make one hair white or black,—*i. e.,* produce the slightest change in himself,—the Almighty can accomplish. Dost thou swear, then, by thyself? thy oath cannot have any meaning, except as thou intendest Him who wills that thou thyself existest. Hence every oath, if it is to have

---

* The construction of ὀμόσαι with the accusative, (James v. 12,) or with κατά and the genitive, (as in Heb. vi. 16,) is pure Greek. In the New Testament it is generally construed with ἐν or εἰς after the analogy of נִשְׁבַּע בְּ in Hebrew.

any meaning, refers to God, since He only, the Eternal, can give surety for the security of what is transitory.—But as the entire prohibition of *all* swearing is joined to this thought, it is evident that we may not draw this conclusion : " Since all objects of adjuration have a reference to God, by which they first acquire their import, we are to swear *only* by God ;" but, on the contrary, "Since we are not to swear at all—and all oaths refer originally to God, the eternal and true—we are not to employ *any* oath; the simplest statement of opinion is sufficient, anything further has sprung from the source of evil, and become necessary only by reason of sin." The idea, that only the *abuse* of oaths is forbidden, can never be defended by a true interpretation.* In the passage, James v. 12, a different view might, for a moment, commend itself, on account of the different position of the words; but even there, on a closer examination, the connexion requires the sense of prohibiting oaths in general. This absolute prohibition of our Lord cannot occasion any difficulty, if the difference of position under the Law and the Gospel is attended to in this case. An oath is, in and of itself, a result of sin; on the part of him who demands it, a want of confidence in his brother is implied; and on the part of him who tenders it without being required, it presupposes a consciousness that he is not to be depended on, or that sin prevails in those for whose sake he swears. In the world of falsehood it is a necessary requisite for attaining anything like security of intercourse. Nay, God himself condescends and swears by himself, the Unchangeable, because changeable man is prone to imagine the Unchangeable himself to be changeable.† But in the world of truth, the oath has no place, nor can it have, since neither distrust demands, nor a sense of unworthiness of confidence tenders, it. For this kingdom of truth the command of our

---

* *De Wette* properly interprets the passage as an unconditional prohibition of oaths. *Tholuck* also confesses that the words cannot be taken grammatically, otherwise than as an absolute prohibition; but is of opinion, that the analogy of the other commands (*e. g.*, give to him that asketh) makes a restriction necessary in this case also. But by that means these commands, one and all, evidently acquire a vacillating character. In the kingdom of God *all* have their full meaning without restriction ; out of that kingdom *no one* of them is literally applicable. On *Tholuck's* shewing, Christ's command would amount to nothing more than the old one, "Swear not falsely."

† See Gen. xxii. 16; xxvi. 3; Numb. xiv. 23, &c. In the New Testament the Apostles use forms of swearing. See Heb. vi. 16; 1 Tim. ii. 7.

Lord is valid. But as this kingdom yet only blossoms in secret in the Christian world,—as our political institutions are still on Old Testament principles, and, because of sin, *must* be so,* the believer must still be a Jew to the Jews in this respect also. (1 Cor. ix. 20.) The Quakers are wrong, therefore, and confound the dispensations, in desiring the abrogation of oaths in the world of falsehood, since Christ himself, who uttered the command, took an oath before the sanhedrim. (Matth. xxvi. 63.) But among the true children of God this command also must be fulfilled in its strict form; only, in the case of oaths, the relation of the individual to the political community also enters into the question, for which reason the believer does not find it possible to follow perfectly the higher standard, as he can in reference to marriage, where, in case they are believers, the relation of husband and wife alone is concerned. Belonging to the two spheres of life, he must satisfy the claims of both, according to the necessary conditions of their existence; he may, therefore, with strict propriety, fulfil Christ's command to the letter among his brethren, and yet, at the desire of the constituted authorities, take an oath.

Ver. 38-42.—The *fifth* instance comprises the nature of the law in a general maxim, and opposes the evangelical *principle* to the pharisaical conception of the former. The idea of retaliation, (*jus talionis*,) which is the foundation of the law in general, is expressed in ὀφθαλμὸν ἀντὶ ὀφθαλμοῦ scil. δώσεις κ. τ. λ. Exod. xxi. 24. But the Pharisees made such a use of retaliation, that it could not but become a cloak for revenge and uncharitableness. Christ, on the contrary, conceives the idea in the spirit of the purest love, and derives thence the command of self-denial and resignation. "Eye for eye, tooth for tooth," is an eternal law in the government of the world; but love takes the brother's fault on itself, and, by thus becoming like him, causes him to become like it. Thus, out of the *jus talionis*, love procures salvation and *forgiveness*, which is nothing but retaliation reversed, and cannot, therefore, exist without the Saviour's suffering. This conquering by succumbing is the essence of the

---

* No times can be more fitted than our own to dissipate all philanthropic dreams about the spiritual standing of the masses in Christian states. Eye for eye, tooth for tooth, is the only law by which the licentiousness can be restrained, which rebels against all order.

Gospel; the law is founded on the ἀντιστῆναι τῷ πονηρῷ, repelling force by force.* The manifestations of love in contrast with the coarse character of retaliation, are then presented in four instances, arranged in an anti-climax. Outrage on the person is the most grievous, (ῥαπίζειν is of kindred meaning with κολαφίζειν, the latter, however, denoting rather blows with the fist;) next to this in order comes the *demanding* of property, (κρίνεσθαι, *to claim before a tribunal;*) *asking*, as the mildest form of presenting a request, forms the close. Between the two latter forms, ἀγγαρεύειν is placed, as partaking of both. (The term is of Persian origin, but was adopted into the prevalent languages of antiquity; the Aramaic language also adopted it. See *Buxtorf. Lex. talm.* s. v. אנגריה.) In Luke vi. 30, the words καὶ ἀπὸ τοῦ αἴροντος τὰ σὰ μὴ ἀπαίτει, are added—the general thought for the particular instances in St. Matthew. (Ἀπαιτέω = נגה, *to collect, to call in.*)

The preceding observations on marriage and oaths apply likewise to the carrying out of this command. The Saviour does not intend by His precept for the βασιλεία to invalidate the truth of the maxim, "An eye for an eye," for the legal standing; he who takes up that standing cannot, and must not, be treated otherwise than according to the law.† But for him who is seized with the spirit of the Gospel, without having as yet overcome the power of sin, the conduct indicated by the Saviour is suitable. Where the mind is still too rough and harsh, there it would not be love, but unkindness, to shew unappreciated love. What, for instance, could be more unkind than a literal use of the precept, παντὶ τῷ αἰτοῦντί σε δίδου, *give* TO EVERY MAN *that asketh of thee?* That would be to educate begging vagabonds.

---

* We cannot very well take πονηρῷ as neuter here; for it is our duty, under all circumstances, to oppose what is evil in itself. But here the evil is viewed in its effects in an individual, in whom there is, at the same time, a susceptibility for good. In reference to this mixture of good and bad, the Saviour may say, that the member of the kingdom of God does not resist the manifestations of sin, in order to accomplish for the good a perfect conquest in the heart of his brother, by the manifestation of forbearing love, which is expressed thereby.

† Thus the Saviour himself answers the rude servant who struck Him on the face: If I have spoken evil, prove that it is evil; but if I have spoken right, why smitest thou me? John xviii. 23. To turn to him the other cheek would have been an infraction of love, as it would have brought the man into the temptation of increasing his sin by increased turpitude. Paul behaves similarly, Acts xxiii. 3.

Hence the application and exercise of the laws of love cannot be reduced to fixed rules; love alone teaches us to apply them properly, and enables the scribe, instructed to the kingdom of heaven, to bring out of his treasure things *new* and *old*. For *this* order of things, before the full manifestation of the kingdom of God, the law still retains its application; yet the Gospel has ts sphere, in which it is ever gradually unfolding its nature more perfectly.

Ver. 43-45.—At last Jesus comes to what is highest and final—to *love* itself. The command, וְאָהַבְתָּ לְרֵעֲךָ, *Thou shalt love thy neighbour*, (Lev. xix. 18,) applied, it is true, *immediately*, as the context shews, to the nation of Israel, which, from the undeveloped views of the people, represented the collective whole, to which רֵעַ in its profoundest sense referred. But the hypocritical Pharisees drew the inference from this command, that we were at liberty to hate our enemy. (Ἐχθρός, like *hostis*, primarily "one not of the same people." See the passages quoted in *Wetstein* and *Schöttgen, ad loc*.) They not only *tolerated* hatred of enemies, as something at the time not quite conquerable, but they *cherished* it as something allowable, nay, included (by implication) in the command. To this outrageous interpretation of the Old Testament, Jesus opposes His own, which unfolds the undeveloped truth from its inward nature and principle. The fulness of love, as Jesus teaches it, and imparts it to His people out of His fulness, extends not only to the narrow circle of a nation's ties, but makes what is opposite, as well as what is akin to it, the object of its exercise. The different manifestations of love (ἀγαπᾶν, εὐλογεῖν, καλῶς ποιεῖν, προσεύχεσθαι,) form a climax, and are in contrast with the forms of hatred; these latter, indeed, as such, cannot and ought not to be loved; but the individuals are, in whom they are seen, since there is in them the latent germ of a higher existence, which is to be stimulated by the power of love. But with respect to the love thus enjoined, it is not any passive love, residing merely in the region of feeling; for that cannot possibly be stimulated by the manifestations of hatred; only something akin inflames it; but rather love as a *power of the will*, which is in a condition to overcome all (opposing) feelings. For this reason, too, assimilation to God is assigned as the end of the manifestation of love to enemies. (In υἱός, the representation of the image, existing in the Father, is expressed.) As God abhors *evil*, and commands us to abhor *it*, (Rom. xii. 9,) but blesses the evil *man;* so does he, too, who lives in pure, divine love. The Spirit of God in him teaches him to separate the evil from the man; and while he hates the former, to love the latter. But such love man cannot obtain for himself by a determination of will or by any effort, for it is divine; he can receive it only by spiritual communication in faith. But this does not, by any means, exclude the effort to exercise it before it is possessed, as it is through that very effort that the consciousness is first awakened how much man needs it. ('Επηρεάζειν occurs, besides in this passage, only in Luke vi. 28; 1 Peter iii. 16. According to *Pollux*, it is a law term, meaning "to drag before a judge with ignominy and insult;" then, in general, "to injure," "to insult.") St. Luke adds another trait, δανείζετε, μηδὲν ἀπελπίζοντες, (vi. 35,) where, likewise, sincere, disinterested love is expressed. St. Luke has expanded this thought afterwards, when he comes to portray the forms in which natural love manifests itself. On the whole, with the exception of one unessential transposition, St. Luke has the same thoughts here, and they must, therefore, certainly be regarded as original, integral parts of the Sermon on the Mount.

Ver. 46, 47.—As a parallel to this sacred love, which includes even what is hostile in the sphere of its exercise, and which is bestowed in regeneration alone, Jesus brings forward natural love, which loves only what is akin to it, and, in that, itself essentially. (Ephes. v. 28, "He that loveth his wife, loveth himself.") This love is that which is seen to prevail in the Old Testament, a few traces of love to enemies excepted, which stand as the commencing notes of a higher gradation in religious life to come,—*e. g.*, David's conduct. (1 Sam. xxvi.) As such it does not stand *opposed* to the higher love of Christ, but *beneath*, as something subordinate, which has its analogy even in the animal world. The τελῶναι and ἐθνικοί in St. Matthew, the ἁμαρτωλοί (πόρναι, Matth. xxi. 31) in St. Luke, are mentioned as emblems, familiar to the Pharisees, of what is despised. In the publican, in particular, the prominent characteristic is being involved by the calls of his station in the lowest worldly connexions; for which reason the taxgatherers are used as a symbol of worldliness and its temptations. ('Ασπάζεσθαι is a general term for tokens of love of all kinds.)—In these verses, moreover, the idea of μισθός appears again. (See note on ver. 12.) Natural love is represented as being accompanied by a less reward than pure love. There is evidently a condescension here to the legal standing, for it is just the nature of sincere love to seek no other reward than that which is in itself. But as, in fact, the possession of it involves all that constitutes blessedness, because God is love, (1 John iv. 8,) and no one can love but he in whom God dwells; it is certainly true, also, that its reward is great. But a *distinction* between love and its reward, and of an effort to attain the former for the sake of the latter, cannot exist but in a legal point of view; pure love seeks itself on its own account, for it includes in itself all that can be desired.

Ver. 48.—The last words contained in this verse are, as it were, the key-stone which completes the whole. The general result not merely of our Lord's last commands, but of all that precedes, is: Let *perfection* be your aim. ("Εσεσθε οὖν is parallel with ὅπως γένησθε above, ver. 45.) For the observation of but *one* of these commands, as here laid down by our Lord, nothing short of perfection is sufficient. It does not, therefore, alter the thought, if, instead of τέλειοι, as it is in St. Matthew, we read οἰκτίρμονες, as it is in Luke vi. 36. For neither pure love nor mercy can be conceived *alone* in the human soul, without the other qualities involved in perfection; so that all must necessarily be conceived as joined with the one. But to refine upon the idea of τέλειος, and to understand it of a relative perfection, is evidently forbidden by the words subjoined: ὥσπερ ὁ πατὴρ ὑμῶν, which, as compared with ver. 45, cannot mean anything else than that the image of God is to be represented in men, as the υἱοὶ τοῦ ὑψίστου. Accordingly, the passage is parallel with that in the Old Testament, וִהְיִיתֶם קְדֹשִׁים כִּי קָדוֹשׁ אָנִי, (Lev. xi. 44,) which St. Peter adopts: ἅγιοι γένεσθε, ὅτι ἐγὼ ἅγιός εἰμι, (1 Pet. i. 16,) and is explained by it. That is, as in that passage the requirement of holiness on man's part is *founded* on the holiness of God, so here also in relation to perfection; so that this passage may be interpreted, "Be ye perfect, *because* God is perfect." The perfection of man, as well as his holiness, is not separate from that of God, such as man might possibly attain of himself, but *that* perfection *itself;* God himself designs to be the perfect and holy One in man. In this way the passage must be interpreted, on the principle that every speaker is the expositor of his own words, even though we should regard the notion itself as false. Jesus teaches throughout (particularly in John xiv. 23; xv. 5, 7; xvii. 23, 26) the doctrine of an indwelling of the Divinity in men; and in conformity with this profound fundamental idea of Christianity, which annihilates all righteousness and holiness of our own, the present passage must be interpreted.

Matth. vi. 1-6.—After this prefatory comparison of the holy in the doctrine of Jesus with the unholy in the teaching of the doctors of the law, the thought of v. 20 is resumed. The reality is opposed to the appearance; the latter has what is visible and transitory for its object and proper end, (ὅπως δοξασθῶσιν ὑπὸ τῶν ἀνθρώπων;) the former has what is invisible and eternal; God in heaven is placed in contrast with men on earth. Δικαιοσύνη* conveys again, as in ver. 20, the general idea of a proper relation to God, viewed in the light both of the Old and the New Testament. This contrast is viewed in reference to alms (ver. 2) and prayer (ver. 5) as the prominent manifestations of the religious life. (Σαλπίζειν is not to be taken literally, but figuratively, "to do anything with ostentation." Μισθὸν ἀπέχειν is spoken of in reference to the time of the future general reward, when only what is eternal finds its reward, because it was accomplished by the working of God's eternal Spirit.) The figure in ver. 3 cannot mean total unconsciousness, which ought not to exist in any case, but only the absence of self-appropriation of the act; every good deed must be referred to its origin, —to the spiritual source from which it springs; there it has even now its hidden reward, and hereafter its open one. To the outward proclamation of works of love by the Pharisees, the inward humble ignorance of one's doings is opposed. (Ταμιεῖον = עֲלִיָּה = ὑπερῷον, a chamber, to which they could retire for prayer, in quiet, Acts x. 9; see also Isa. xxvi. 20. The term ὑποκριτής occurs very frequently in the Gospels,—e. g., in this chap., ver. 5, 16; vii. 5; xv. 7; xvi. 3; xxiii. 13, and frequently in St. Matthew; again in Luke vi. 42; xi. 44, &c. The verb ὑποκρίνεσθαι occurs only in Luke xx. 20. It is properly originally = ἀποκρίνεσθαι, to answer, then particularly, "to answer as a

---

* The reading ἐλεημοσύνη, which is supported by very many Codd., is, probably, only an explanation of δικαιοσύνη, which, in later Greek, is used for "alms," like the Hebrew צְדָקָה. St. Paul uses it in 2 Cor. ix. 9, for "kindness," "charitableness."

character in a play,"—*i. e.*, "to act on the stage." Then, in general, "to assume a form not one's own,"—"to represent." In the New Testament it is always used of religious *form*, with which the inward *nature* does not correspond.)

Ver. 7-13.—These verses bring out the last remark in a special manner. In Phariseeism, not only is there an air of hypocrisy manifest in prayer, but also the heathen notion, which is always reproduced from the heathenism that dwells in human nature, that prayer avails as *opus operatum*, and, consequently, from length and copiousness of words. From the pure idea of God, the Saviour derives the doctrine, to regard the inward disposition and the purity of thought resulting thence as that which is well-pleasing to God. St. Matthew also presents, as a pattern, a prayer given by Jesus, which is pervaded by simplicity, depth, and humility. St. Luke (xi. 1) records the circumstances which occasioned our Lord to give such an injunction. The disciples felt their spiritual poverty, and supplicated His rich grace to teach them to pray. Hence, too, it is said, οὕτως προσεύχεσθε ὑμεῖς; for it is a prayer calculated for the position of sinful men, not for Him who knew no sin. (Βαττολογεῖν* is not from בָּטָא, *effutivit;* but according to *Suidas* it is derived ἀπὸ Βάττου τινὸς μακροὺς καὶ πολυστίχους ὑμνους ποιήσαντος. Hence βαττολογία = πολυλογία.) *Superstition* places the reason of the hearing of prayer not in the grace of God, but in its own godless work. *Unbelief* deduces the uselessness of prayer from the omniscience of God, in whom it does not itself believe. *Faith* rests its poor prayer precisely on this holy, gracious, divine knowledge. Thus our Lord teaches us to pray in faith, *because* God knows, before the petition, what we need, (χρεία taken both bodily and spiritually,) and, consequently, can himself prompt the acceptable prayer, and fulfil it accordingly. The words οἶδε γὰρ, are to be taken as the reason which prevents the Christians from praying after the heathen manner. The believer does not pray for God's sake, (to do Him a service,) but for his own sake; that God knows, affords to him the consolation that he cannot ask wrong; for he is concerned only for God's will, not for his own. The prayer of the believer is therefore nothing less than the

---

* See the copious discussion on this rare term, which is nowhere used but by *Simplicius* in one passage (in Epict. enchir., c. 37) in *Tholuck's* Comm. (Clark's Biblical Cab., No. xx., p. 114.)

divine will itself becoming manifest among mankind; thus the Lord's Prayer is conceived. It is an expression of the highest, final, divine plans in the government of the world, both as to the whole and the individual.

With reference, first, to the state of the text of THE LORD'S PRAYER,* the doxology at the close is undoubtedly of later origin, and is added for liturgical purposes. In the *Const. Apost.,* vii. 24, it appears in the process of formation; it reads, ὅτι σου ἔστιν ἡ βασιλεία εἰς αἰῶνας. Ἀμήν. But the contents are profound and agreeable to the spirit of the prayer, and, therefore, certainly belonging to a period when pure Christian feeling prevailed in the Church. It is wanting in Codd., B. D. L., and in many others, as *Griesbach's* New Testament shews. Still it is found as early as the Peshito, where, however, it may be an interpolation. So also the petitions, "Thy will be done in earth as it is in heaven;" and, "But deliver us from evil," are wanting in the text of St. Luke. They are wanting not only in B. L., but also in the earliest Fathers, as in *Origen,* (de Orat., p. 226, edit. de la Rue, vol. ii.,) who expressly notices the omission. But it does not follow from this that they are spurious in the prayer; St. Luke rather appears to have abridged here, in the same manner as we noticed on Matth. v. 1. These petitions do not, indeed, form an essential part of the prayer, since they are included in those immediately preceding; but for an unfolding of the meaning they are an integral part.† The question, *Whether Christ meant to lay down a stated formula in this prayer?* may be best answered to this effect, that the Saviour certainly had in view, as His primary object, to teach the disciples to pray in spirit; but in so far as there was in His view the arising of an outward Church that should require liturgical formulas, He might intend its permanent use also; and the Church has done right to retain it. But that no value is to be ascribed to the letter, is shewn by the variation with which the

---

* We possess separate expositions of this prayer by *Origen, Tertullian,* and *Cyprian.*

† On the form of the Lord's Prayer found in St. Luke, see the more copious remarks in note on Luke xi. 3, ff. On the omission of the doxology, see *Rödiger's* dissertation at the end of the synopsis, p. 231, ff. A transposition of the second and third petitions in *Tertullian* is discussed by Nitzsch, in the "Studien und Kritiken," published by *Ullmann* and *Umbreit,* 1830. H. 4, S. 846, ff. *Meyer's* "Blätter für höhere Wahrheit," Th. v., S. 10, ff., give an exposition of the prayer.

Evangelists themselves record the prayer. In Rabbinical and Talmudical writings (according to *Wetstein, Schöttgen, Lightfoot,* in their notes on this passage) there are very many thoughts akin to the individual petitions. We learn thence how much of what is spiritual and true is contained in the Jewish writings; only it is generally mixed with error by the pedantic Rabbins. But it is very perverse to infer from this relationship of the prayer to Rabbinical passages, that Jesus compiled His prayer by reflection from such elements of Jewish prayers. Even the noble and true element presented in the national culture had only a stimulating effect on His inward development; and what He gathered thence He reproduced, in a new form, out of the creative power of His inner life. But the exposition has not only to unfold the thought contained in the single sentences, but also to regard them in their connexion. Regarded as a whole, the Lord's Prayer contains but *one* thought—the desire for the kingdom of God*—in which all the prayers of God's children (and, as such, Christ here teaches us to pray) are contained. This one thought is conceived in two relations; *first*, in reference to God's relation to man—thus in the first three petitions, which represent the kingdom of God as advancing to completion—the highest purpose of God expressed as a wish; *next*, in reference to man's relation to God—thus in the last four petitions, in which the impediments to God's kingdom are noticed. The *first* part commences, therefore, with speaking of the riches of God:—

> THY name be hallowed;
> THY kingdom come to us;
> THY will be done.

The *second* part, on the other hand, speaks of the poverty of man:—

> To us give daily bread;
> To us forgive sins;
> Us lead not into temptation;
> Us deliver from evil.

In the significant doxology, the certain hope is expressed of

---

* *Luther* is right, therefore, in saying, "the true Christian prays an *everlasting* Lord's Prayer," inasmuch as his whole desire centres in God's kingdom.

the prayer being heard,—a hope founded in the nature of the unchangeable God himself, who, as the chief good, will cause the good to be realized in a manifest form, (the kingdom of God.) At the same time, this prayer admits of an application to the individual, who is compelled, however, in the constantly recurring plural, to regard himself in connexion with all, as well as to the collective human race; for this very reason, that being uttered from the inmost soul of mankind, and seizing the relation of God to the sinful race in its deepest root, it meets the wants of the whole and of the individual equally, provided always that he is living in faith. Every prayer which has not for its object transitory particulars, but eternal things, is included in the Lord's Prayer.

In the invocation: Πάτερ ἡμῶν ὁ ἐν τοῖς οὐρανοῖς, there is implied, *first*, an elevation above what is earthly and transitory to what is eternal and enduring; and, *next*, the consciousness of our relationship to the eternal. The name Πάτερ presupposes the consciousness of υἱοθεσία, (Rom. viii. 15;) still, of an imperfect one, since otherwise the divine would, with less strong expression, have been removed to heaven. This sentiment marks the prayer as belonging to the New Testament; for though Isaiah exclaims, כִּי אַתָּה אָבִינוּ, (Isa. lxiii. 16,) yet that must be viewed as a momentary illumination of the higher spirit of the New Testament; in general, the relation of servant to master (in which relationship is subordinate) prevails in the Old Testament. The *first* petition: ἁγιασθήτω τὸ ὄνομά σου, is closely connected with the two following. Ἁγιάζεσθαι, used of what is unholy, means "to be made holy;"* but, used of what is holy, it means "to be recognized as such," = הִקְדִּישׁ. The spread of the pure worship of God is, therefore, the subject of this petition. Only, as *Augustine* (de Corr. et Grat. c. 6) very truly remarks, this is not here to be viewed as the outward spread, but the inward; so that the meaning is, "sanctificetur nomen tuum *in nobis*." A knowledge of what is holy, (not in idea only, but experimentally,) presupposes inward holiness; for only kindred minds know what is akin, (Psalm xxxvi. 10.) The meaning of ἁγιάζεσθαι, in this place, is therefore much like

---

* *Tholuck* gives it the signification, "to treat as holy," "to keep holy," which supposes, however, "a being holy," if it is to be real. It seems, therefore, more natural to understand it in this place as denoting the cause, rather than the consequence.

that of δοξάζεσθαι, as employed by St. John (John xiii. 31; xiv. 13; xv. 8, and frequently) in the sense of being glorified. The divine name (ὄνομα = שם) is put for the divine essence itself, inasmuch as it expresses and reveals the latter in its nature. (See the *locus classicus*, Exod. xxiii. 21.) The divine must therefore, first of all, glorify itself in human nature, and by that means become known to man in its true nature; not till then can the kingdom of God come. The *second* petition: ἐλθέτω ἡ βασιλεία σου, regards the divine power exerting itself *within*, which is supposed, in the first petition, as appearing *outwardly*; but, in so far as the kingdom of God appears still as displaying and developing itself, Christ subjoins, in the *third* petition, γενηθήτω τὸ θέλημά σου κ. τ. λ., in order to express the consummation of the kingdom of God, which consists in the unlimited fulfilment of God's will; so that the three petitions stand related to each other as beginning, middle, and end. The words "as in heaven, so in earth," express the *unqualified* fulfilment of the will, which now appertains to the heavenly state only, but which, in the consummation, is to extend to earthly things also.

In the *second* half of the Lord's Prayer, the subjective distance from the kingdom of God, and the steps of approach to it, are apprehended and described with the supplementary thought, "That it may be so, give us daily the bread of life." That ἄρτος does not denote bodily food merely, is seen from the context; it stands among purely spiritual petitions, and supposes spiritually-disposed petitioners. It is true, he who prays should set out from his physical existence, and ascend to what is higher; for which reason the reference to bodily nourishment, on which the existence of the whole man depends, should not be excluded, nay, it may even be regarded as the immediate one; but the spiritual food must still be looked upon as included, since otherwise the important petition for the Spirit of God would be entirely wanting in the prayer. (On ἄρτος, as spiritual food to man, as a spirit, see Matth. iv. 4; John vi. 32, compared with 41, 48, 50, 51.—The word ἐπιούσιος, which occurs nowhere else, is difficult.* *Some* derive it from

---

* *Origen* (de Orat., p. 94) regards it as a word coined by the Evangelist himself, without giving an etymology. The derivation from the participle is admissible after the analogy of περιούσιος, ἐθελούσιος. But it may be derived from the participle of εἶναι as well as from that of ἰέναι. See *Tholuck* in his comm. on the passage.

the participle ἐπιοῦσα, which is used like *sequens*, [Acts vii. 26; xvi. 11; xxi. 18; xxiii. 11,] particularly in the phrase ἡμέρα ἐπιοῦσα = מָחָר, which, according to *Jerome*, was used in this passage in the *Ev. sec. Hebr.* [Comm. in Matth. *ad loc.*] But this interpretation, which Dr. *Paulus* extends even to the future in general, is in contradiction to Matth. vi. 34, where care for the morrow is forbidden. In that case the connexion of σήμερον with ἐπιούσιος is inappropriate. *Others* more correctly derive it from οὐσία, either in the sense of *substantialis*,—so that the term is meant to define the bread more accurately in its nature, nourishment for the true being of man,—or what is sufficient for existence—what is enough. Thus *Tholuck*.)

In the consciousness of the dependence of spiritual and bodily life on God and His preserving power, the consciousness of *guilt* is implied, which is expressed in the *fifth* petition, and from which the desire proceeds to see all hindrances arising thence taken away by forgiving love. That the prayer is that of a believer, is evident from ὡς καὶ ἡμεῖς ἀφίεμεν; in which words forgiveness is again (see v. 7) made dependent on the forgiving love in the heart, which alone permits us to believe in forgiveness, without denying that this love itself is the gift of grace.* The idea of ὀφείλημα is taken very widely, comprehending sin in general, which, even in believers, contracts new debts, that need continual forgiveness,—*i. e.*, blotting out. See the similes, v. 25, and Luke vii. 41, ff.; and in ver. 14, immediately below. A lively perception of sin is accompanied by a sense of weakness, such as may not only disobey God's command

---

* The words, "as we also forgive," must not be understood as determining the *measure* of forgiveness; for if God did not forgive men in a higher degree than they themselves shew forgiveness, no one would be forgiven. God always forgives completely and absolutely; while man oftentimes, even when honestly struggling, can forgive partially only,—that is, so as that something yet remains in the mind. The words are rather to be taken as a *proof* how much God is forgiving love, since He not only forgives the believer his own sin, but also enables him to forgive others. *Being able* to forgive others, is accordingly a *token* to the believer of his being in a state of grace; and the petition may therefore be thus paraphrased: "Forgive us our sins,—that is, reveal the entire fulness of Thy forgiving love unto us, as Thou givest us to taste it in this, that in Thy power we can forgive." Moreover, we must not overlook, that forgiving *sins toward man* is alone spoken of; for we cannot and ought not to forgive *sins against God*. Thus David forgives Shimei's sin *against himself*, but on his deathbed he retains the sin *against the Lord*; and thus does the Apostle Paul also, according to 2 Tim. iv. 14-16.

occasionally, but even fall from it altogether. This is the view taken in the *sixth* petition. (On πειράζειν, see note on Matth. iv. 1.) The dangerous nature of temptation, from which the children of God beg to be delivered, lies in the disproportion between the power of the new life, and that of evil. The fear of God, therefore, in the believer begs for the removal of the cup. The Saviour, after having been already led into one temptation at the beginning of His ministry, and after having overcome it to the saving of men,* prays himself, (for He became in all things like us, only He was without sin,) in the second temptation, at the close of His ministry: "If it be possible, let this cup pass from me." (Matth. xxvi. 39.) In this petition, therefore, the assurance is not implied, that no temptation shall happen to the believer,—rather, as our Lord drank the cup, so every follower *must* drink *his* cup also. (Matth. xx. 23.)

As the two previous petitions referred to salvation in particular points, so the *seventh* petition, in conclusion, takes up salvation in its comprehensive idea.† As the whole prayer is uttered in the spirit of the communion of all the faithful, so, at the close, good appears in contrast with evil itself; by the overcoming of which the consummation of the kingdom of God is attained, and the impossibility of any temptation whatever is secured. Hence, the ἀλλά is used in contrast with the previous petition. Whether we take τοῦ πονηροῦ as masculine or as neuter, is indifferent, provided the neuter is regarded as including all that is wicked and evil, according to which notion it is Satan's very element. The masculine is, however, more agreeable to Bible usage. (Matth. xiii. 19, compared with ver. 38; Ephes. vi. 16; 2 Thess. iii. 3.) The petition for the consummation of the work of salvation connects itself with the beginning, since that is the

---

* See in the Epistle to the Hebrews ii. 18: "For in that He himself hath suffered *being tempted*, He is able to succour *them that are tempted*." And again, 1 Cor. x. 13, where πειρασμὸς ἀνθρώπινος seems to be placed in contrast with another,—namely, θεῖος, in which God himself, as in the cases of Abraham, Job, and other distinguished believers, and particularly in that of the Saviour, led into temptation; at such trials nature shudders. To *be* led into temptation must, however, be carefully distinguished from presumptuous, determined *entering* into it, which is one with tempting God.

† *Chrysostome*, the theologians of the Reformed Church, the Arminians, the Socinians, and others, recognize only six petitions, as they join the sixth and seventh.

kingdom of God; and the doxology, though not uttered by our Lord, but added by the Church in the Christian spirit, assures the fulfilment of all that has been asked by the consciousness that all is God's; and, consequently, by means of this highest and only good, all good is as certain of triumph as the evil is of destruction. At first sight, however, it looks as if the δύναμις should have been mentioned *before* βασιλεία, as being the more general idea, by the instrumentality of which that kingdom is realized. But this order was probably chosen for this reason, that it is not the divine omnipotence in an absolute sense that is meant, but its manifestation in the establishment of the kingdom of God, which the whole prayer presupposes. Hence, the doxology being, as it were, an assurance of the certain fulfilment of the prayer, declares very appropriately, first, that the kingdom is the object of *God's* desire,—that is, its realization is *willed* by God; and connected with this is the idea, that He himself *completes* it, and, accordingly, will assuredly bring all to a *consummation*.

Ver. 14, 15.—The subsequent thoughts are in St. Luke (xi. 4, ff.) more immediately connected with the prayer. St. Matthew expands the thought in ver. 12, respecting the exercise of forgiveness, in order to the receiving of forgiveness, with which the closing petition also stands connected, inasmuch as salvation is just a comprehensive forgiveness, of which only the forgiving mind is a fit subject. A similar thought occurs in a different connexion in Matth. xi. 25, 26. There is a difficulty in this thought, since forgiveness seems to be made dependent on the existence of love, while it is forgiveness received that first produces love; see note on Luke vii. 47. But it is not the first kindling of love proceeding from forgiveness, that is meant, (although the very reception of forgiveness supposes receptive love;) but the exercise of enkindled love in particular instances. (Παράπτωμα a single manifestation of the general ἁμαρτία. It is = ἁμάρτημα, Mark iii. 28. The expression, πατὴρ οὐράνιος, like βασιλεία τῶν οὐρανῶν, is peculiar to St. Matthew; see Matth. vi. 26, 32; xv. 13.)

Ver. 16-18.—The following verses are parallel with ver. 2 and 5—a renewed exhortation to seek for the reality instead of the appearance. After prayer and almsgiving, *fasting* is taken up as another manifestation of the religious life. ('Ἀφανίζω denotes primarily "to make invisible," thence "to spoil," "to destroy," as ver. 19. Here, "to disfigure"—the Latin, *squalere*. To mournful negligence in externals, joyful attire, denoted by ἀλείψαι, and νίψαι, is opposed.) In that (apparently open) exhibition of the religious life, therefore, hypocrisy is manifest, which might be erroneously looked for in this (apparently not open) concealment of it; for the essence of piety is the most inward reference of our life to God. All stealthy glances towards the external are the fruit of hypocrisy. (Ἐν τῷ κρυπτῷ is opposed to being open before men. It is, therefore, equivalent to the inward man, to whom God reveals himself.) This fundamental thought, that God himself must be the end of man's aim, extends to the close of the chapter. It is the thread by which the different thoughts hang, which, in St. Luke, stand in a different relation to Christ's discourses.

Ver. 19-21.—Earthly possessions are placed in contrast with heavenly ones in their indestructible nature, and the spirit is directed thither—to the source of all truth. (Σής, *tinea* = סס, Isa. li. 8. Βρῶσις denotes "being consumed" in general, to which all earthly things are subject. The meaning "rust" does not suit; for gold and silver do not rust.* In Mal. iii. 11, it is used also for a kind of worm.) The union of the heart with the treasure is assigned as the reason of this admonition to store up heavenly possessions. The θησαυρός is regarded as the aim of the longing and desire which proceed from the καρδία. The concentrating of them on created things must produce misery, since the soul is destined for what is eternal.

Ver. 22-24.—Seeking after earthly treasure (which is so very contrary to man's inward spiritual nature) implies, therefore, inward impurity. The connexion with the preceding context is not altogether simple, though not to be mistaken. This circumstance indicates, doubtless, a different original position of the thought. (See Luke xi. 34, 35.) The inward relations of spiritual life are illustrated by physical ones. It is remarkable that the eye should be called λύχνος. It seems to be merely the capacity of receiving light. But capacity to receive light implies a partaking in the nature of light. "Were not thine eye sunny," says Göthe, with great depth and truth, "how could it ever behold the sun?" (See Psalm xxxvi. 10.) Thus the eye, with the light which flows to it, is that which itself

---

* See, however, note on James v. 3.

illuminates, which makes light,—a view which is optically true.* The condition of the bodily eye, however, modifies its action; ἁπλοῦς—πονηρός = διπλοῦς, *double-sighted*, as it were, (ver. 24,) or even totally blind, to which σκοτεινόν refers. Just in the same way the Saviour views the spirit's inward eye—the reason—the power of receiving divine things.† Its capacity for the higher light implies the nature of light in it, whence φῶς ἐν σοί = λύχνος, ver. 22. Jesus accordingly does not teach the absolute moral depravity of man. That noble power destined for divine things, when drawn away to what is sensual, becomes blindness. The inward light is wasted, and the power of sight destroyed. The state of spiritual darkness is then more fearful than that of bodily blindness. But in Luke xi. 36, the other aspect is also brought into notice,—that is, the entire inward illumination of our being, by which the very last traces of darkness (μὴ ἔχον τι μέρος σκοτεινόν) vanish. (On the special difficulties in the passage, see note on Luke xi. 36.) This is followed immediately by the mention of *two masters*, in which comparison the double-sightedness—glancing stealthily from God to the world—is expressed in another way. The appropriateness of the contrast lies in the strictness with which the one excludes the other. The relation of the masters to each other does not allow of *indifference* among the servants. Μισεῖν, therefore, stands opposed to ἀγαπᾶν, and καταφρονεῖν to ἀντέχεσθαι. (Ἀντέχεσθαί τινος, properly "to seize anything," "to hold it fast," = הֶחֱזִיק, thence "to pursue anything with diligence and interest," 1 Thess. v. 14; Titus i. 9.) Μαμᾶνας, or Μαμμωνᾶς, (according to Luke xvi. 9,) from מָמוֹן, on the authority of *Buxtorf*, (lex. talm., p. 1217,) is so used in the Targums for the Hebrew בֶּצַע, כֶּסֶף, that the term may be taken as equivalent to the Greek πλοῦτος. *Augustine* observes on the passage: "Con-

---

* *Philo* expresses the same thought (de vit. theor. ii. 482, edit. Mangey) when he says: ἡ θεοφιλὴς ψυχὴ ἀθάνατα ἔκγονα τίκτει, σπείραντος εἰς αὐτὴν ἀκτῖνας νοητὰς τοῦ πατρὸς, αἷς δυνήσεται θεωρεῖν τὰ σοφίας δόγματα. (See also *Gesenius* in the Lexicon, s. v., שָׁוֶה, Job xx. 9.)

† The *Reason*, provided it has been made clear and pure, can receive divine things. It has a receptive faculty; but it cannot originate anything divine out of itself. It is carefully to be distinguished from the *understanding*—the faculty of ideas. In the New Testament the former is νοῦς, the latter φρόνησις. (See the *author's* Opuscula, p. 152, sq.) *Philo* de cond. mundi, t. i., p. 12, says: ὅπερ νοῦς ἐν ψυχῇ, τοῦτο ὀφθαλμός ἐν σώματι.

gruit et punicum nomen, nam lucrum punice Mammon dicitur." In opposition to God, money, when personified, appears as an idol, after the manner of Plutus, without our being able to shew that an idol of this name was outwardly worshipped. In the Saviour's meaning, the name Mammon applies to the author of evil, which consists precisely in confounding what is not divine with what is. Evil we *must* hate (Rom. xii. 9) if we are to love good. The natural man, from the fear of encountering the world, where good and evil are found mixed, endeavours to avoid this alternative; but Christ compels a decision of the heart to pure love, which gives at once sincere *hatred* against sin, never against the person of the sinner.

Ver. 25-34.—The Saviour raises man, involved in the common wants of earthly necessity, and wasting his poor existence in the anxious satisfying of them, from subjection to the prince of this world, who retains his hold on his slaves by such cares, to faith in God, by which a holy care is created, which dispels those vexations of the earthly everyday life. The passage, Phil. iv. 6, is a commentary on these words. In it the Apostle puts the command: μηδὲν μεριμνᾶτε, in contrast with the direction to ask of God what is needful. *Prayer* is, therefore, the opposite of *anxious care*, because in prayer man commits the care to God. The *natural* man cares without praying. The brute, and the man who has become as the brute, care as little as they pray.— Ver. 25. The discourse turns on the double meaning of ψυχή, = נֶפֶשׁ, which denotes, 1, *life*; 2, *soul*. Viewed in their essence, the two meanings involve each other; but the carnal man places the principle of life in the flesh, and regards eating and drinking as its chief requirements. For the believer, the life of man, as such, is in the soul, and the soul alone is to him the principle of life, (that is, the ψυχή viewed as ψυχή πνευματική,) and, consequently, he provides for it chiefly. The words: μεριμνᾶν τῇ ψυχῇ, are not, therefore, equivalent to ἐν τῇ ψυχῇ = καρδίᾳ; but ψυχή is the object of care—the psychical life. —Ver. 26. Faith in God's fatherly care for the nourishing of the body is awakened by a view of His procedure in nature. (Πετεινὰ τοῦ οὐρανοῦ = עוֹף הַשָּׁמָיִם. The general expression is, in Luke xii. 24, made special: κατανοήσατε τοὺς κόρακας.) Man stands connected with physical nature by his body, and may, therefore, trust himself to fatherly love in reference to that, as unreservedly as the birds of heaven. But since a divine principle of life reigns in his physical being, it bears him to a higher region of life.

Ver. 27.—The helplessness of the creature in all that is external is viewed in contrast with the fulness of the Creator's power, who daily nourishes all beings. Man cannot make a single blade grow, nay, he cannot make any physical change in himself. ('Hλικία is primarily, "size of body," "stature," [Luke xix. 3,] then "age," [John ix. 21.]) To add a cubit to the stature would be something monstrous in proportion to the body, which does not exceed three cubits in height. From the connexion, something small is intended here. It is better, therefore, to interpret it, "to add a little to the age." The care for eating and drinking—the conditions of physical life— is in agreement with this.—Ver. 28. The same applies to raiment. (Κρίνον = שׁוֹשָׁן, Song of Sol. ii. 1, *lily*. Νέω, *neo, filum ducere*.)—Ver. 29. The formations of nature exceed in beauty all the formations of art. Art, therefore, can only try to imitate nature,—a powerful motive to unreserved confidence in the wondrous Framer of the universe, in whose kingdom the greatest and the least appear clothed in the most splendid dress.

Ver. 30.—If God thus cares for what is most perishable, how much more for the heirs of His eternal kingdom! (In regions where wood is scarce, as is mostly the case in the East, the use of other substances, as grass and brushwood, for burning, is the natural result of circumstances. 'Ολιγόπιστος = אֱמוּנָה קְטוֹן, Matth. viii. 26; xiv. 31; xvi. 8.)—Ver. 32. Hence is deduced the prohibition of care for the physical necessities of life; and that care is represented as rooted in heathenism, where, instead of the living God who *knows*, (ver. 8,) we meet with a blind fate (εἱμαρμένη) which compels man to be his own god.—Ver. 33 and 34 qualify the noble and freely expressed thought, that the believing child of God is not careful, in order to prevent misconception, as if the prohibition of care was to destroy all exertion for earthly things. Ζητεῖν is contrasted with μεριμνᾶν, so that the latter signifies anxiously caring *without* God,[*] the

---

[*] St. Luke (xii. 29) subjoins the admonition: μὴ μετεωρίζεσθε, which word does not occur elsewhere in the New Testament. In the Old Testament it is often found, as well as μετέωρος, and the derivatives, μετεωρισμός, μετεωρότης, in the sense of being lofty, proud. (Psalm cxxxi. 1; Ezek. x. 16, 17; 2 Macc.

former striving in faith *in* God and *with* God. St. Luke, however, (xii. 29,) uses ζητεῖν as synonymous with μεριμνᾶν. Πρῶτον, *first*, gives the first rank to striving for the kingdom of God, to which the striving for earthly things is subordinate. For God's fatherly care is manifested by the believer himself; he does not expect, in a spirit of tempting God, to be supported on air. The βασιλεία τοῦ Θεοῦ must be taken again, in undefined generality, as comprehending what is external and internal, (see note on Matth. iii. 2,) just as the δικαιοσύνη, which, though in itself an essential part of the kingdom of God, (Rom. xiv. 17,) is yet specified, in order to direct attention to the nature of the kingdom of God, whether inwardly or outwardly manifested, and to guard against false conceptions. The term προστεθήσεται, points out the divine as the immediate and proper object of all man's endeavours, with which bodily concerns are associated *by the way*, and *necessarily*, if the endeavour after God be pure. Hence the exhortation closes with the words with which it began: μὴ μεριμνήσητε, ver. 25. The words εἰς τὴν αὔριον, do indeed seem to limit the universality of the exhortation, and to describe the care for the present as well founded. But in the idea of care a reference to the future is always included, and the present appears as provided for, as is seen in the succeeding context; consequently the requirement *not* to care, should be maintained to its full extent, (see 1 Peter v. 7;) but, as was observed, without thereby excluding truly believing exertion. The words immediately following: ἡ γὰρ αὔριον μεριμνήσει τὰ ἑαυτῆς, confirm this view; for in them God is represented as He who takes thought, since time itself, to which taking thought is ascribed, must be viewed in its dependence on Him, by whom every need is supplied for every circumstance. Lastly, the Saviour notices that, even apart from lading himself with care for the future, the life of the believer in the present retains its burden because of the sin of the world; so that the *taking no thought* urged upon us, cannot be *exemption from suffering*. (Κακία is purposely used, as it expresses physical ills, but in their moral origin. Ἀρκετός occurs also Matth. x. 25; 1 Peter iv. 3.) As regards the critical state of the verse, the Codd. vary in the words: ἡ γὰρ αὔριον

---

v. 17; vii. 34.) In the sense of *suspenso esse animo*, "filled with hope and fear," —a sense not uncommon in profane writers,—it occurs only in this passage. The βεβαιότης of πίστις stands opposed to the μετεωρισμός of μέριμνα.

μεριμνήσει τὰ ἑαυτῆς, as some omit τὰ ἑαυτῆς; others only τά; while some give περὶ ἑαυτῆς or ἑαυτῇ. The *various readings* do not alter the meaning essentially; but the usual construction of μεριμνᾶν is with the accusative;—we might, therefore, be led to prefer ἑαυτῆς as the less common. It is more important to notice a *punctuation* different from the ordinary one, which *Fritzsche* (comment. in Matth. p. 284) has adopted in the text: μὴ οὖν μεριμνήσητε εἰς τὴν αὔριον ἡ γὰρ αὔριον μεριμνήσει. Τὰ ἑαυτῆς ἀρκετὸν τῇ ἡμέρᾳ, ἡ κακία αὐτῆς. 'Η κακία αὐτῆς is then taken as in opposition with τὰ ἑαυτῆς. This punctuation seems to me worthy of regard; only the words: ἡ γὰρ αὔριον μεριμνήσει, produce, perhaps, the impression of something defective; the words subjoined give more completeness to the thought. The thought, however, is not essentially altered by this punctuation.

The series of normal sentences (*Gnomes*) that follows in the Sermon on the Mount, (ch. vii.,) was manifestly not originally uttered in connexion, since it is entirely contrary to the character of such sentences to be multiplied in a *discourse*; it is only when isolated that they exert their full effect. In *writing*, where the reader can reflect in quiet on the depth of the sentiment, the matter is different; and St. Matthew has, therefore, done well to form this collection of aphorisms, where he wished to present, in a connected view, the peculiar character of Christ's teaching. The connecting thought throughout is this,—to contrast the peculiar character of the Messiah's disciples with the prevailing popular conceptions, in order to present vividly what was new in the manifestation of the Gospel.

Ver. 1, 2.—This thought is expressed more fully in Luke vi. 37, 38; there is something similar in Mark iv. 24. Κρίνειν, κρίμα, in the normal sentences in St. Matthew must evidently be taken = κατακρίνειν, κατάκριμα, in which sense they occur, Rom. ii. 1; xiv. 3, 4; 1 Cor. v. 12, and frequently. This is seen from the parallel word, καταδικάζειν, used by St. Luke, which defines κρίνειν, and from the contrast between ἀπολύειν and διδόναι in Luke vi. 37; the former of which expressions denotes "acquittal by the court," (*absolvere reum;*) the latter, the "remission of what might legally be demanded." *Judging*, therefore, so far as it is *testing*, is not here forbidden; that is always *required* by Scripture. (1 Thess. v. 21.) But the connecting of the evil with the accusing of the individual in whom it is seen, is entirely prohibited to compassionate love; where the person is attacked, love is wanting; where love is wanting, the rigid law, and with it the *jus talionis*, prevails. Hence it is a repetition of the thought in v. 7: "The merciful shall obtain mercy." The phrase: "With what measure ye mete, it shall be measured to you again," is equivalent to: "An eye for an eye," Matth. v. 38. The nature of overflowing, forgiving love, which makes us in turn ready to receive forgiveness, is described by figure in Luke vi. 38.—(Μέτρον καλόν = ἱκανόν, *a just measure, not falsified;* πιέζω, *to press together;* σαλεύω, *to shake and move to and fro,* in order to force as much as possible into the measure; ὑπερεκχύνομαι = הֵשִׁיק, Joel ii. 24, the *overflowing* of the filled-up measure,—all in contrast to giving without love, which is done only to avoid a direct violation of the law. Κόλπος = חֵיק, *sinus,* the lap of the flowing dress for receiving anything,—a figure frequent in the Old Testament. Ἀνταποδοῦναι εἰς τὸν κόλπον, Jer. xxxii. 18; Psalm lxxix. 12, for "to recompense.")

Ver. 3-5.—The next verses carry out, in particulars, the same thought which had just been viewed in its relation to the whole character. Uncharitableness sees the faults of others, while it overlooks its own; pure love overlooks those of others, and watches its own keenly. The same figure is found in the tract *Baba Bathra:—Cum diceret quis alicui, ejice festucam ex oculo tuo, respondit ille: ejice et tu trabem ex oculo tuo.*

Ver. 6.—These exhortations to gentleness are followed very appropriately by the command to beware of the other extreme, —that is, an indiscriminate pouring out of holy things from want of judgment. He who forbids our judging, by which a man's *culpability* is determined, commands us to form an opinion, which marks only the *state*. This latter is absolutely necessary for the child of God, in order to be able to distinguish the false from the true. (Κύνες, χοῖροι, denote the common natural condition, which shows itself in shamelessness, carnality, and lust; these things the Christian must know as such, and not bring what is holy into contact with them;* for the condition of their

---

* *Tholuck* (Clark's Bibl. Cab., No. xx., p. 278) is of opinion that the Gospel should be preached even to the most abandoned. This ought, certainly, to be done in public preaching, where there cannot be a judging of the standing of the individuals. But here personal exertions for individuals is the subject, just

inmost nature does not admit of their receiving it, and it has an injurious reaction on himself. Ἅγιον, μαργαρῖται denote the holy doctrines of the kingdom of God. [Matth. xiii. 45.] For such men the law alone is fit; the Gospel they misunderstand to the injury of those who proclaim it to them. In dog-like natures, holy things excite rage, and swinish natures tread them without thought in the mire, which is their element.)

Ver. 7-12.—Prayer for the Holy Ghost alone leads to the passing of such a life of love as does not condemn, and yet carefully judges. The general maxim: "Ask, and it shall be given you," repeated in different circumstances, is exemplified by a similitude, which draws its conclusion *a minori ad majus*. —Ver. 8 proves ver. 7, from the general thought: "Every one that asketh, receiveth." The demonstrative force lies in the nature of Him to whom the prayer is addressed. Every prayer, which is really such,—that is, which flows from the inward necessity of the soul, God answers. The human relation between the father and the supplicating child forms an argument κατ' ἄνθρωπον. St. Luke (xi. 12) adds a third case: "Instead of an egg, a scorpion." The notion of something disgusting is here added to that of mere uselessness. The transition: ἢ τίς ἐστιν, gives emphasis to the opposition: "or does it ever happen otherwise?" In comparison with God, the eternal good, men, in their sinful alienation, appear as evil, (πονηροί;) in the relation of parental love, kindness still manifests itself in the midst of sin, how much more in the eternal God! St. Luke (xi. 13) calls the gift, which includes all other gifts, expressly the πνεῦμα ἅγιον, who must be understood there as the creative principle of holiness in man. In this Spirit we exercise pure love.—The maxim in ver. 12 is also based on proverbs current among the Jewish people. In the Talmud: "*Quod exosum est tibi, alteri ne feceris,*" stands as one of *Hillel's* sayings. Love for ourselves should give the rule of our self-sacrificing love for our neighbour, (Matth. xix. 19;) only God is to be loved *above* ourselves. Instead of οὗτός ἐστιν ὁ νόμος, as *Griesbach* reads, *Fritzsche* would read οὕτως; but, apart from critical reasons, οὗτος should be preferred on account of the deeper

---

as in the prohibition of judging, and then the wise householder must bring things old or new out of the treasure of his heart, according to the standing of the persons with whom he has to deal.

thought which it expresses, that in this command of love toward our neighbour, the *essential* import of the Old Testament is included. (Mark xii. 29, ff.; Matth. xxii. 40.)

Ver. 13, 14.—From what has been said, the difficulty of a walk in self-denying love naturally follows, being represented under the figure of a narrow path, which conducts through a narrow gate into the strong citadel of eternal life. The figure is so natural, so true, that it is repeated in every earnest attempt, even in subordinate stages of religious life. *Cebetis tab.*, c. 12, οὐκοῦν ὁρᾷς θύραν τινὰ μικράν, καὶ ὁδὸν τινὰ πρὸ τῆς θύρας, ἥτις οὐ πολὺ ὀχλεῖται, ἀλλὰ πάνυ ὀλίγοι πορεύονται, αὕτη ἐστὶν ἡ ὁδὸς, ἡ ἄγουσα πρὸς τὴν ἀληθινὴν παιδείαν. (The parallel passage, Luke xiii. 24, will subsequently receive a special explanation. For ὅτι, ver. 14, we should undoubtedly read τί; it corresponds to the Hebrew מָה.)

Ver. 15-20.—Yet is the way of the pure life in God not merely narrow in itself, it is rendered still more difficult by what the false prophets teach. Here we are required to try the spirits. The *fruits* are assigned as the test. In 1 John iv. 1, 2, pure doctrine is mentioned as the criterion. Is this meant here, too, under the term καρποί? I doubt it; though Tholuck has defended that view with specious reasons. The doctrines are of chief importance; they might well be compared to the root, but not to the fruits. The fruits are necessarily of a moral nature. It is certainly difficult to distinguish between the real fruits, and the counterfeits of hypocrisy and fanaticism; but the Saviour supposes in His people a simple sense of truth, that makes them separate the true and the false with certainty. The sheep's clothing is not to be understood as the actual prophetic dress, (Matth. iii. 4,) but denotes, figuratively, the outward show, in opposition to the true nature,—sayings and doings apparently full of love, which are the offspring of a selfish heart. The wolf's nature seeks its own, and soon discovers itself to child-like sense. By the physical processes in the vegetable world, we are shewn how the fruit characterizes the nature of that which produces it. The figure is similar in James iii. 11. ("Ἄκανθα, *thorn-bush.* Virg. *Ecl.,* iv. 29: "*Incultisne rubens pendebit sentibus uva?*"—See Matth. xii. 33 for the same figure rather differently carried out, as also Luke vi. 45, which passage will be explained with the former. On ver. 19, 20, see note on Matth. iii. 10; Luke iii. 9.

Ver. 21-23.—These verses make a special application of what

was observed of all false prophets generally, to those who are connected with Christ, among whom insincerity may creep in. Λέγειν is opposed to ποιῆ, as λόγος to ἔργον, or δύναμις. (1 John iii. 18; Col. ii. 23; 1 Thess. i. 5; James i. 22:) Λέγειν κυριε, κύριε, signifies pretending to an attachment which is not felt in reality. According to ver. 22, the foundation of this attachment appears to be spiritual vanity, which was nourished by the conspicuous exhibitions of the Spirit's power, which were imparted even to a Judas, along with his confession of Jesus as the Messiah. To prophesy—to cast out devils—to do wonderful works, are the most common operations of the Spirit's power, which, in the lifetime of Jesus, was so powerfully exerted;— their nature we shall afterwards consider more precisely in their several manifestations.* By the words: τῷ σῷ ὀνόματι, we must understand not merely a superstitious pronouncing of the name, as was the case with the sons of Sceva, (Acts xix. 13, ff.;) but a receiving of the power of the Lord,—only, an insincere one. (On ὄνομα, see note on Luke i. 49; and again on Matth. x. 41; xxviii. 19.) By the words: ἐν τῇ ἡμέρᾳ ἐκείνῃ, the revealing of the hypocrisy, unperceived by human eyes, is postponed to the time of the general judgment, when every secret must be made manifest. (Rom. ii. 16.) Hypocrisy, therefore, appears, in this place, as self-deception at the same time, in consequence of which a man persuades himself that he belongs to the Lord, till the discovery of the depths of the heart brings him to feel, that what he called his holy actions were a great violation of God's law, (ἀνομία,) because his final aim in them was constantly his own, not God's, glory. That we are not, however, to conceive of any exchange of words on the day of judgment, is self-evident. The situation here so vividly portrayed is the *language of fact;* the unbeliever will stand beseeching, but will be refused. (The words: ἀποχωρεῖτε, κ. τ. λ., are from Psalm vi. 8.) The solution of this psychological enigma—the possibility of such self-deception, is contained in the words: οὐδέποτε ἔγνων ὑμᾶς, ver. 22. Γινώσκειν, like יָדַע, is used in the Scriptures in a deep spiritual sense, particularly in the phrases: "God or Christ knows man or the soul." (Deut. xxxiv. 10; 1 Cor. viii. 3; xiii. 12; Gal. iv. 9.) Knowing God is connected with being known

---

* On these gifts, see the detailed remarks on 1 Cor. xii. and xiv.

by God as the consequence;—no one can know, without being known of, God. If we connect these expressions with the Christian doctrine of regeneration, the rich import of this contrast is evolved. The pure knowledge of God—not a merely *notional* knowledge, but that *essential* knowledge which is eternal life itself, (John xvii. 3)—becomes possible only by a revelation of the hidden God to the soul, (see note on Matth. xi. 27;) God's thus revealing himself is a knowing of the soul, (γινώσκειν τὴν ψυχήν.) The figure of a bridal relation of the soul to God, which is evident throughout the Scriptures, thus acquires its real import; the inward illumination of the soul is like a visit from the heavenly bridegroom, by whose agency the knowledge of God results in the soul, according to the Old Testament expression: "In His light we shall see light," Psalm xxxvi. 10. Those who say, "Lord, Lord," are, therefore, unregenerated men, who, with a false liberty, behave themselves as children of God, without having been born of Him. The phrase: πόθεν ἐστί, in Luke xiii. 25, is, therefore, very significant. It marks their foreign origin; they are not from above, (ἄνωθεν, John iii. 3;) they are σὰρξ ἐκ τῆς σαρκός, (John iii. 6.) In Luke xiii. 25-27, the elements of this passage are found in a different connexion, in which they will be considered hereafter.

Ver. 24-27.—The *epilogue* teaches the importance of applying a discourse like this, under the figure of a man who builds on a rocky foundation, and sets forth as the rock of salvation, the Word of eternal truth which was embodied in Christ's teaching. (Deut. xxxii. 15; Psalm xviii. 3; xlii. 10; Isa. xvii. 10.) Here the contrast is not between the bad man and the good, but between the fool and the wise man, (as in Matth. xxv. 1;) for all that hear are supposed to be well-intentioned; but in many, spiritual prudence for their being spiritually benefited was wanting. The similitude of a building is carried out in 1 Cor. iii. 9, ff., and there (ver. 11) Christ is called the foundation, on which the superstructure of the spiritual life must rest. In Luke vi. 48, the figure of laying a foundation is further carried out by digging deep. (Βροχή, "heavy torrent of rain," = נֶשֶׁם. In St. Luke, πλήμμυρα = πλημμυρίς is used, which means "the flowing tide," in contrast with ἄμπωτις or ἀνάρροια, *the ebb*. Here, where it is used in its more general sense, it denotes any overflowing, desolating flood, from streams or rain storms.)—Ver. 26. As a contrast to the building on the rocky foundation of the eternal Word of God, which defies all temptations and dangers, there follows the figure of a baseless building on the sand, to denote the founding of the inward life on transitory human dogmas, opinions, and fancies. This building on the sand evidently refers to a spiritual work, which has some affinity with the real work of the Spirit, even as born of faith, but which is destitute of the proper character of that work.

Ver. 28, 29.—The Evangelist concludes the whole with a reference to v. 1. St. Matthew, in conclusion, notices only the impression which Christ's words made on the hearers. 'Εκπλήττεσθαι is stronger than θαυμάζειν; it expresses "being inwardly affected." To this the words ἐξουσίαν ἔχειν point, which distinguished the discourses of Jesus from those of the Pharisees; the latter often uttered truths, but they were destitute of spiritual power; their discourses were pictures drawn in the air, without essential power and vital energy. These were breathed forth in the words of Jesus, and by them He moved the depths of men's hearts; wheresoever, therefore, anything in unison with these truths was latent within, it could not fail to be awakened by such a stimulus.

§ 4. HEALING OF A LEPER.

(Matth. viii. 1-4; Mark i. 40-45; Luke v. 12-16.)

After this portraiture of Jesus as a teacher, St. Matthew proceeds to describe Him as a *worker of miracles*, since the next two chapters contain nothing but narratives of the Saviour's wonderful works. In as far as such actions are generally viewed as manifestations of mighty power, they are called in the Scriptures, δυνάμεις, גְּבוּרוֹת. Regarded in their connexion with the divine purposes in relation to individuals or the whole, they are called σημεῖα, אוֹתוֹת. As events exciting astonishment or terror, they are called τέρατα, θαυμάσια, Matth. xxi. 15; מֹפְתִים, וְנִפְלָאוֹת. The most appropriate name for them, when used of our Lord's miracles, is ἔργα, (a word found in Matth. xi. 2, and very frequently in the Gospel of St. John.) In that name the miraculous character is, as it were, pointed out as the natural form of the Saviour's agency, since He, as possessor of divine power, must necessarily produce supernatural phenomena by means of it. *He himself* was the τέρας,

His wonderful works were but the natural ἔργα of His being. Hence it is evident that we cannot adopt that idea of a miracle, by which it is regarded as a suspension of the laws of nature. If we start from the scriptural view of the abiding presence of God in the world, the laws of nature do not admit of being conceived as mechanical arrangements, which would have to be altered by interpositions from without; but they have the character of being based, as a whole, in God's nature. All phenomena, therefore, which are not explicable from the known or unknown laws of the development of earthly life, ought not for that reason to be looked upon as violations of law and suspensions of the laws of nature; rather, they are themselves comprehended under a higher general law, for what is divine is truly according to law. That which is not divine, is against nature; the real miracle is natural, but in a higher sense. It is true, the cause of the miracle must not be sought within the sphere of created things; the cause of it exists rather in the immediate act of God. All God's doings are, to the creature, miracles, although, viewed in relation to the divine essence, they are purely law and order. To the believer, therefore, what is apparently natural,—*e. g.*, the preservation of the world—the growth of all its products,—is miraculous, because he is accustomed to refer everything to its first cause. *No miracle is therefore performed without a real power.* As we see human individuals working miracles, for the most part in the New Testament, we are taught the possibility of higher powers being imparted to men, which may exercise a commanding force over surrounding objects, whether nearer or more distant; unless we admit the presence of such a real element of power,—the Spirit in His gifts, (χαρίσματα, 1 Cor. xii. 10,)—there would be no connecting link between the miracle and the worker of it, and the former, consequently, would seem something magical or spectre-like. Animal magnetism may, if we choose, be regarded as something analogous to the presence of such an element of higher power; only, we must beware of confounding that obscure, dangerous power of the principle of sensuous life with the pure element of light, which wrought in the holy men of God, of whom the Bible speaks; this latter is God's nature in them; the former power is of the creature, and defiled by sin. But when fulness of spiritual might in great men of the Church in later days was *not* combined with the gift of working external miracles, this results from the course of mankind's development, and the varying necessities of the times, whereby only here and there bright seasons are ushered in, which call forth extraordinary phenomena of that sort, which, after surviving for a time, are gradually lost.

It is important to observe that the Scriptures assert not merely holy, but also evil,* power to be the cause of miracles. Two chains of miracles extend throughout Scripture history. As the works of the Egyptian magicians stand opposed to the miracles of Moses, (Exod. vii. ff.,) so in the New Testament the miracles of antichrist stand opposed to those of the Saviour. (Matth. xxiv. 24; 2 Thess. ii. 9; Rev. xiii. 15.) This distinction between the divine and the satanic miracles suggests the notion, that it cannot possibly be the end of miracles *to establish the truth of any affirmation.* In the sense of Scripture, too, this is by no means the intention of miracles. It was only the people that so viewed them, because they allowed themselves to be influenced in their judgment by the impression of power, or the excitement of the senses; for which reason they attached themselves to false prophets as willingly, and even more so, than to the true. The Saviour, therefore, severely rebukes this eagerness for sensible miracles. (John iv. 48.) But when our Lord in other places (*e. g.,* John x. 25; xiv. 10, 11) calls for faith in His works, and connects them with His dignity and His holy office, this is not done in order to establish the truth of His declarations; truth, as such, rather proclaims itself irresistibly to impressible minds by its inward nature. ("Every one that is of the truth heareth my voice," John xviii. 37.) They are intended rather to *demonstrate His character as a divine messenger*, for those in whom the impression of the truth, conveyed by the spirit and language of the Saviour, had wrought its effect. The proclamation of truths may be conceived, without the person who proclaims them bearing the character of a messenger from God. In such a case, the truths may predominate greatly both in word and power over what is erroneous; but error cannot be conceived as utterly excluded in the case of any human teacher. God, therefore, invested particular individuals as His instruments

---

* In so far as evil in general is merely a product of created powers, we may say that the satanic miracles are merely apparent miracles; since miracles can be performed by God's omnipotence alone.

with higher powers, in order to distinguish them from humanly excellent teachers, and to accredit them before mankind as infallible instruments of the Holy Spirit—as teachers of absolute truth. Hence the gift of miracles is one of the necessary characteristics of true prophets, and serves to witness their superior character—to prove that they are to be regarded as leaders and guides of the people, and freed from *all* error. For this reason, faith—that is, susceptibility to divine operations—is supposed in the case of miracles; and it is only the truth, *combined* with the testimony from miracles, that constitutes the character of a divine messenger; by virtue of which, things may also be established as true and certain, which cannot be known to be such by the indwelling susceptibility for truth. The reverse relation obtains with the representatives of the kingdom of darkness, whom the Scriptures call ψευδοπροφῆται, ψευδόχριστοι, because, notwithstanding a total inward diversity, they have an external similarity in appearance to the true messengers of God. Though these representatives of falsehood mix up much that is true in word and deed, and would fain appear as the messengers of the kingdom of light; yet to the sincere soul, fitted to receive the truth, the entire spirit of their doings discovers itself as unholy, and therefore all the miracles conceivable fail to induce that soul to surrender itself to them; the very association of miraculous powers with an unholy spirit is rather a proof to such a soul of their close connexion with the kingdom of darkness. When, therefore, the Saviour condemns the thirst for miracles, He rebukes the regard to externals involved in it, which is a sign of deadness for spiritual things, and exposes to the danger of doing homage to the operations of evil, when they are conjoined with miraculous appearances. But, on the other hand, our Lord commends the desire for miracles, as a confirmation of the inward certainty, that He, whose truth and purity of action at first touched the soul, is more than a human teacher—that He is a heavenly accredited messenger of God. Miraculous power in itself, and every separate manifestation of it, is accordingly without meaning; the main point is the connexion of that power with the general disposition of the person in whom it is seen. The *association* of miracles with what is holy, is the sublime testimony of God to His servants; the *association* of miracles with what is unholy, is a warning, meant to awaken horror at the emissaries of the abyss of woe; the knowledge of what is holy and what is unholy in itself, and in its true nature, is presupposed, in order to be capable of discriminating the nature of miracles; and this knowledge depends on sincerity and purity of heart. The insincere man persuades himself that God's true miracles might have been wrought by the evil spirit, and the false ones he regards as true; the sincere man views both in their true form, because he carries in himself the rule and criterion of truth.

If now we glance at the *history* of miracles, we do not find any miracles wrought by the intervention of human individuals *before* the time of Moses; for God's miracles, His revelations in the Son, and in angels, and so forth, are to be carefully distinguished from those in which miraculous gifts are attached to a human individual. It seems as if a ripeness of human nature were requisite, in order to be fit to serve as the vehicle of mighty spiritual energies. For this reason, Jesus wrought no miracles as a child; and the apocryphal books of the New Testament betray their senseless character in this, among other things, that they describe the child Jesus as working miracles. Again, *after* the time of Moses, we notice a difference between the miracles of the Old and New Testament. The miracles of the Old Testament bear not only a more colossal, but also a more external, character. They are more calculated to move the inferior powers of the soul, particularly the imagination. The miracles of the New Testament exhibit a more spiritual character. In them the reference to the moral world appears much more distinct. In particular, we find the Saviour, in His miraculous agency, following the maxims established in the temptation. He never wrought miracles to amaze—never for himself. The Father only wrought miracles in Him for His disciples, either in a narrower sphere, as at the transfiguration, or in a wider one, as at the resurrection, for the confirmation of their faith. In humble quiet Jesus employed the fulness of divine power and life dwelling in Him, to console the unhappy, and deliver them from the source of their sorrows; in this sense also to destroy the works of the devil, and to lay the foundations of the kingdom of God; since our Lord always knew how to apply outward help as a spiritual remedy. For the miraculous cures wrought by Jesus should be regarded as both physical and moral transactions, in which the fulness of divine life passed over to susceptible individuals, in order to evince the possibility of a spiritual harmonious life, together with the organic harmony of the vital processes. The cures effected by Jesus were also distinguished from those of His disciples in this, that the Redeemer performed them in His own name, by the perfection of His indwelling power. The disciples, on the other hand, wrought them only in the name of Jesus, by His power, as His instruments. Faith was, therefore, to them as much the medium of appropriating miraculous powers, as it was to others the means of healing; and, in this appropriation through the intervention of faith, we find them in a state of gradual progression. (Matth. x. 1, 8; xvii. 19, ff.) For a time the gift of miracles continued to be exercised after the removal of the Apostles, till, after the complete establishment of the Church in the world, it gradually disappeared. But, together with the Holy Spirit, there remained behind the inward miracle of regeneration, sanctification, hearing of prayer, which are greater than the outward ones. These outward miraculous gifts will not again appear till the last times, when the situation of the Church shall render necessary the sending of new prophets. The view held by the Romish Church of the necessity of an unbroken continuance of miraculous gifts, results from a confounding of external and internal miracles. It is only the latter of which a church cannot be conceived to be destitute; for the God whose every act is a miracle, dwells in it.

Matth. viii. 1.—With respect to the first of the cures narrated by St. Matthew, the connexion in which it stands, with reference to the chronology, is undetermined. (See Matth. viii. 1, 5, compared with Luke v. 11, 16, 17.) Still as, according to St. Luke, (vii. 1,) Christ heals the centurion's servant at the conclusion of the Sermon on the Mount, as St. Matthew likewise relates, (viii. 5, ff.,) the position given to this event by St. Matthew may be chronologically correct, and the healing of the leper may have happened immediately after the Sermon on the Mount, on the road to Capernaum. (St. Luke [v. 12] says, ἐν μιᾷ τῶν πόλεων.) The narrative begins with the observation, that, immediately on the Saviour's descending from the mountain, crowds gathered around Him. Among them a leper approached. (Καταβαίνειν ἀπὸ τοῦ ὄρους refers to ver. 1. The construction is remarkable for the repetition of αὐτῷ—a construction which occurs in this same chapter, verses 5, 23, 28, and frequently in St. Matthew. The first αὐτῷ looks like a dative absolute with καταβάντι. From this feeling, the various reading καταβάντος αὐτοῦ may be accounted for as a correction for the less usual dative.)

Ver. 2.—With respect to the λέπρα, it shewed itself in several forms,—some dangerous, others milder. The regulations of Moses respecting the צָרַעַת leave no doubt on that point. (Lev. xiii.; xiv.) The persons afflicted with the dangerous leprosy (see on the subject Winer's "Realwörterbuch," s. v.) were considered unclean according to the Mosaic law, and could not be received into the congregation again till their cure was ascertained. This leper, of whom St. Matthew tells us, might already have heard of Christ's cures, or have seen some of them. At any rate, he displays his faith in the person of Christ by prostrating himself, and by the express petition for healing, which he supposes Jesus able to accomplish for him also. (The word προσκυνεῖ = γονυπετῶν in St. Mark = πεσὼν ἐπὶ πρόσωπον in St. Luke, corresponds to the Hebrew הִשְׁתַּחֲוָה It is the general form of expressing respect in the East, and has not in itself any religious reference.) But, with respect to the *nature of the faith*,[*] which we must suppose to exist in the persons cured in this as in all similar cases, (see note on Matth. xiii. 58,) we must first of all lay it down that πίστις, viewed in its religious bearing, in every case retains but one and the same fundamental signification. This is modified only by the different objects of faith, which again are determined by the different degrees of its development. Now we must not make the essence of faith to consist in *knowledge* either of the divine in general in the Old Testament, or of the divine in Christ in particular in the New. For such knowledge, be it notionally confused or clear, may be conceived united with a state of the soul, which we must regard as the opposite of believing. Faith is rather rooted in a spiritual *susceptibility* to the divine, which has its seat in the *heart*, καρδία, (see Rom. x. 9, 10,) while knowledge (γνῶσις) depends upon the susceptibility to the divine in the *understanding*, (νοῦς.) Faith is also capable of inward gradation, according to the degree in which the divine is revealed. Particularly in the cures, where faith is made the negative requisite, which determines the ability to receive the Spirit's

---

[*] See remarks on Rom. iii. 21.

powers emanating from Christ, the faith demanded or exercised must not be looked upon as a holding certain doctrinal positions to be true, but a susceptibility, both spiritual and bodily, to the Saviour's agency. This susceptibility was undoubtedly uniformly accompanied by the notions that Christ was the Messiah, and that, as Messiah, He could work miracles. But we might also conceive these notions as existing apart from that fundamental disposition of the καρδία, which we have designated as susceptibility of the heart, and of the whole nature, for what is heavenly; and with such a separation they would not satisfy any condition of miraculous healing.* This is the view suggested by the description of all the cures wrought by Jesus. In no case does He ask after doctrinal positions as the objects of faith. In no case does He mention them as a necessary quality of faith. The Saviour leaves the mere profession of faith to speak for its quality, because demeanour and language at once proclaimed the general disposition of the soul, as being either open or closed to divine influences. Hence it is evident also, that the outward bodily healing was meant to be only a symbol of the *inward spiritual healing* really intended. (See note on John vii. 23.) For those same vital powers, by communicating which the bodily disorganization was removed, exercised an influence, in conformity with their nature, on the spiritual character of the person cured. They brought him into a real connexion with the world of good in general, and took possession of him on the position to which he had just attained, in order to raise him still higher.

Ver. 3.—At the sick man's request, our Lord lays His hand upon him, and heals him. In most cures wrought by Jesus there was a similar immediate touching; and there can be no hesitation in acknowledging a conducting medium of healing power (only not a necessary one) in the putting forth of the hand, just as in blessing with the solemn ἐπίθεσις τῶν χειρῶν. The analogy of animal magnetism strongly suggests itself, and it is certainly not accidental; only, as was hinted above, it must never be forgotten, that the power of Jesus Christ was divine,

---

* The ingenious mystic *Gerhard Tersteegen* calls faith, very appropriately, "the inwardly hungering desire of the spirit, which lays hold of not only the *form*, but also the *essence* of what is divine." (*Weg der Wahrheit*, S. 366.)

and magnetism cannot, therefore, be referred to, except to indicate a power presenting similar manifestations in an inferior region of existence. (Καθαρίζειν = טָהֵר may signify "to pronounce clean," inasmuch as the priest who pronounced the diseased man clean, restored him to society from which he had been cut off. [See Lev. xiii. 13, 17, in the LXX. translation.] But that an actual and instantaneous removal of the disease is intended in this case, is evident from the words εὐθέως ἀπῆλθεν ἡ λέπρα, [Mark i. 42,] which are explanatory of ἐκαθαρίσθη. In St. Matthew, too, the connecting of ἐκαθαρίσθη with ἡ λέπρα αὐτοῦ, requires that the verb should convey the idea of removing.)

Ver. 4.—All the narratives agree in recording, that the cure was followed by the command of our Lord to tell no one of the event. Similar prohibitions are often found in the Evangelical history. (See Matth. ix. 30; xii. 16; xvi. 20; xvii. 9; Mark iii. 12; v. 43; vii. 36; viii. 26, 30; ix. 9; Luke viii. 56; ix. 21.) The causes which induced the Saviour to give such commands, were certainly of various kinds. Sometimes He, doubtless, meant, in that way, to guard against popular tumults to make Him, the Messiah, king; at others, to abstract the people's attention from the transactions, and prevent their rendering Him external homage; or, as Luther observes, to give an example of humility. But often the Saviour may have forbidden the publishing abroad for the sake of those who were cured. If these persons were in danger of distraction by outward occupation, it might be the intention of Jesus to lead them thus to try themselves, and to turn their attention within. That this was sometimes the motive which influenced Him, is especially probable from the circumstance, that we meet with instances of an opposite character, where our Lord encourages them to declare what God had done by Him. (See Mark v. 19.) This appears to have been His practice towards those individuals who, being by nature reserved and lost in undue self-contemplation, needed prompting to outward activity for the prosperity of their inward life. The circumstance last noticed affords a glance into the profound wisdom of our Lord as a teacher, who understood how to treat every one according to his wants. In the present case, it appears, from St. Matthew's representation, most suitable to look for the reason of this prohibition in the person cured, since the cure was wrought in the presence of many, and yet the command to tell nothing of it was directed to the leper alone. It is true, St. Mark had not said anything of the multitudes; and from *his* representation, it is more probable that the command was intended to prevent popular tumults. His account is, (i. 45,) that the leper, notwithstanding the prohibition, published the miracle diligently, (πολλά often used in Mark—*e. g.*, iii. 12; v. 23; xv. 3—in the sense of "greatly," "zealously,") and that, by that means, such a commotion arose, "that Jesus could no more openly enter into the city,"—viz., without giving encouragement to the carnal hopes of the Messiah among the multitude. Perhaps St. Mark has also subjoined the words: καὶ ἐμβριμησάμενος αὐτῷ εὐθέως ἐξέβαλεν αὐτόν, to make the command more stringent. (Ἐμβριμάομαι has here the meaning of "to command with solemnity and emphasis," as in Matth. ix. 30. Ἐκβάλλειν = הוֹצִיא. See Matth. ix. 25.)

Not less important than this *prohibition* is the *command* to go to the priests and present the appointed offering. (See Lev. xiv. 2, ff.) In this command not only is there a wise care expressed not to interfere, in any respect, with the theocratic institutions, but also a tender cautiousness not to remove the subject of the cure from the standing he had attained, but to confirm him in a faithful discharge of the duties incumbent on him. We do not, by any means, find that Jesus sought, by awakening a higher feeling, to transport each individual He healed into the New Testament life by means of regeneration; very frequently He leaves the individuals, as happened in the case of John the Baptist, quietly to keep their legal standing, if they were called to be perfected in it, and only seeks to guide them to the true δικαιοσύνη, which, regarded in the Old Testament point of view, involved μετάνοια. All the Evangelists concur in specially subjoining the words: εἰς μαρτύριον αὐτοῖς. They intimate, that the command had reference to the priests also,—that is, by pronouncing the leper clean they were to testify to the reality of the cure, and thus, at the same time, condemn their own unbelief. (The antecedent ἱερεῖ, must be taken collectively on account of the αὐτοῖς, which follows. The word ὑποχωρέω, used in Luke v. 16, does not occur anywhere else, except in Luke ix. 10, with the meaning, *clam me subduco*.)

§ 5. HEALING OF THE SERVANT OF A CENTURION.

(Matth. viii. 5-13; Luke vii. 1-10.)

This narrative is one of the pearls among the many little episodes, complete in themselves, with which the Evangelical history is adorned. It exhibits to us a pious heart in the most amiable, childlike form, openly manifesting its life of faith without any doctrinal tinge whatsoever. The centurion, probably in the Roman garrison at Capernaum, having grown up in the principles of heathen life, was, from residing among the Jews, favourably disposed towards the Old Testament life. The miracles of the patriarchal times, of which he heard, he might often have longed after, without knowing that he was to see infinitely more than these. But his humility was as profound and sincere, as his faith was deep; he esteemed himself not worthy that the commander over spiritual powers should enter his house. In this character he recognized Jesus; but what was the precise view he entertained of Christ, it would be hard to determine, since it was, probably, as usually happens in childlike dispositions, undeveloped, though, in the main, correct. There was no effort on the part of the Saviour to extend his notions; only his desire is satisfied, and thereby his faith in the gracious manifestation of the divine, that had come near him, was strengthened, and an advance made towards perfection in his present standing.—With respect to the two accounts of St. Matthew and St. Luke, the latter undoubtedly possesses the superiority in point of vividness and exactness in external circumstances. Only St. Matthew gives greater prominence to that part (ver. 11, 12) in the address of Jesus, which refers to the Jews, whom that Evangelist everywhere chiefly regards. The circumstance that St. Luke makes the centurion send his friends to Jesus; while, according to St. Matthew, he goes himself to Jesus, cannot be regarded as a contradiction; for the latter representation is nothing but a shorter mode of expression, since, in the words of his friends, his own faith was made evident to our Lord. The occurrence mentioned in John iv. 46-53, *Semler* and others were inclined to regard as identical with this; but *Lücke* and *Tholuck* have convincingly proved the opposite. As the narrative of a cure, this transaction is so far remarkable, that, in this case, Christ, without personal contact, merely by the magic power of His will, (if I may use the expression,) exercises an active power at a distance,—a fact which again has its analogies in magnetism. On the circumstance of the centurion believing, while his servant is being healed, see note on Luke xvii. 14, ff.

Ver. 5, 6.—The locality of the occurrence is fully pointed out by both narrators. It took place as Christ was entering Capernaum. St. Matthew makes the centurion present the request for his sick servant in his own person. According to St. Luke, he presented it through the intervention of others,— viz., the presidents of the synagogue, to the erection of which he had contributed. This fact shews that the Roman warrior had been subdued by the power of the truth in the Old Testament life, and had united himself to the synagogue as one who feared God, (σεβόμενος τὸν θεόν,) probably only as a proselyte of the gate. As a heathen, the centurion might not dare to approach the Messiah at all, and would, therefore, seek His interposition through those representatives of the Old Covenant with whom he was intimate. (Παῖς = δοῦλος, Luke vii. 2, just as נַעַר = עֶבֶד. He was afflicted with paralysis, [παραλυτικός,] which is generally understood to imply a partial affection only; but as it had brought the sick man near to death, [ἤμελλε τελευτᾶν, Luke vii. 2,] it is probable the term is used for apoplexy. The Jewish πρεσβύτεροι made use of the centurion's good disposition towards the Jews as a motive to induce Christ, in whom they supposed the power of healing to exist, to exercise it in this case. Some Codd. read παρέξη for παρέξει, which, besides in this passage, is found also in Luke xxii. 42; Matth. xxii. 4; John xi. 40.)

Ver. 7, 8.—After Christ had expressed His willingness, and as He was approaching the centurion's house, (οὐ μακρὰν ἀπέχοντος ἀπὸ τῆς οἰκίας, Luke vii. 6,) the latter, according to St. Luke's more circumstantial account, sent some friends to meet our Lord, to prevent Him from giving himself personal trouble. (Σκύλλω occurs also Luke viii. 49; Mark v. 35, always with the meaning, "to trouble," "to put to inconvenience.") The idea, that the personal presence of the Saviour was not necessary for the healing of his servant, which he so much desired, but that the Saviour, as the Lord of spiritual powers, could help with a word, (λόγῳ,) is the expression of a faith both bold and free from what is sensible. But in the wish, that Jesus should not come under his roof, various emotions are involved. In the first place, it is certainly an expression of the deepest humility, which does not esteem itself worthy of a visit from a heavenly guest, (οὐδὲ ἐμαυτὸν ἠξίωσα πρός σε ἐλθεῖν, Luke vii. 7 ; οὐκ εἰμὶ ἱκανός, compare Matth. iii. 11.) Further, this humility may have been combined with fear of the presence of what is holy, as involving danger to what is unholy. (See note on Luke v. 8.)

Ver. 9.—The words in which the centurion assigns his reason for thinking, that it was not needful for the Saviour to trouble himself personally to come to the sick man, give us a deeper insight, than anything else, into his views of the person of Jesus. He compared Christ's relation to the world of spirits with his own military position. He derived thence, notwithstanding his subordinate rank, (εἰμὶ ὑπὸ ἐξουσίαν τασσόμενος,) absolute command over his inferiors. In like manner he imagined Christ commanding in the world of spiritual powers, which he probably conceived of as a host of angels, (στρατιὰ οὐράνιος = צְבָא.) But whether he conceived of Christ only as one of the superior princes among the angels, or as Lord of the entire host, cannot be determined. In any case his conceptions were probably dim. Heathenish ideas about sons of God (as in the case of the centurion at the cross, Matth. xxvii. 54) may have been mixed in his mind with notions which he had heard uttered about the Messiah. Notwithstanding this indefiniteness in his conceptions, he possessed in his heart a deep religious life, which excited the astonishment of the Son of God himself.

Ver. 10.—The Saviour's θαυμάζειν of the humble faith of the centurion (see note on Matth. xv. 21, ff., respecting the Canaanitish woman) points to a peculiar relation between divine and human things, intimated even in the Old Testament, (Gen. xxxii. 24, sq.) While what is lofty in man is abomination to the Lord, the lowly find favour before Him, so that He, the lofty One, dwells in the depths with the lowly, Psalm xxxiv. 19. The Saviour here makes use of the manifestation of that state of the soul, which is the main condition of the indwelling of the divine glory in man, as existing in a heathen individual, in order to arouse a sense of their proper destination in the Jews who accompanied Him. Israel was called not only to give birth to the Saviour from among them, but also to preserve a thorough susceptibility to His operations; and by means of those operations to erect the kingdom of God among themselves first. Jesus here censures the want of that spiritual susceptibility, and hints at the mystery of the transfer of the Gospel to the heathen, intimations of which even the Old Testament contains, (Isa. xix. 21, 22; lvi. 6, 7; Psalm lxxxvii. 4, ff.,) without, however, connecting the diffusion of the knowledge of the true God to the heathen with the rejection of Israel.

Ver. 11, 12.—The pious centurion stands in the sequel as the representative of those heathens in general, who, by their deep inward longing for what is divine, surpass the Jews, who were wedded with the stiffness of death to the mere form. Such spiritual members of Israel (Rom. ii. 14, 15; xi. 17, ff.) are conceived as scattered among all people and regions, but in Christ gathered together and united in the kingdom of God, John x. 16. (Ἀνατολαί, δυσμοί, to which in the parallel passage [Luke xiii. 29] βοῤῥᾶς and νότος are added, denote all the dimensions of the earth's extent, according to the sensible impression, —implying the whole of it. See Isa. xliii. 6.) The Jews, as υἱοὶ βασιλείας, are contrasted with the Heathen, so that the latter are viewed only in a more general relation to the divine kingdom. (In like manner, Rom. ix. 25: καλέσω τὸν οὐ λαόν μου, λαόν μου· καὶ τὴν οὐκ ἠγαπημένην, ἠγαπημένην, after Hos. ii. 23.) The abuse of their privileges on the part of the Jews, caused this relation to be exactly reversed. The privileges in which the Jews trusted, became the possession of the believing Heathen; the punishments they desired for the Heathen fell on their own heads. These privileges are comprised in the phrase: ἀνακλίνεσθαι ἐν τῇ βασιλείᾳ; only we are not at all warranted in regarding the expression as an empty picture of happiness. Jesus was addressing Jews, who had adopted into the circle of their Messianic conceptions the idea of a social meal, as a general expression for being and living together with the saints of old, raised from the dead, as the representatives of whom, "Abraham, Isaac, and Jacob," (and in Luke xiii. 28, "all the prophets,") are mentioned. (See *Bertholdt, Christol. jud.*, p. 196, seq.) Passages in the Old Testament (such as Isa. xxv. 6) might have contributed to the formation of this notion. Accordingly, the readiest supposition would be to regard the expressions in this passage as an accommodation to the Jewish conception of the opening of the kingdom of God with a banquet, if we could persuade ourselves to incorporate such a feature into our idea of the Saviour, as accommodation to popular superstition (which was just what He came to destroy) would add to His portrait. Moreover, as this one particular feature appears elsewhere in the New Testament, (see Luke xiv. 14, 15; Rev. xix. 9,) another interpretation of this passage offers itself, less at variance with the general tenor of Scripture doctrine on the closing events of the world, and with the idea of the Saviour. For the doctrine of a restoration of the world defiled by sin extends through the whole New Testament; and it is acknowledged in other passages—*e. g.*, Rom. viii. 19, ff.— by many expositors, who do not acknowledge it in the passage under discussion,—which doctrine is necessarily connected with the resurrection of the body, viewed, according to 1 Cor. xv., as a real restitution, not indeed of the corruptible body of death, but of the incorruptible one, growing up out of the elements of the former. To this restoration of the paradisaical condition of the earth, in which the acmé of Christ's power to overcome the power of sin will be manifested, the present passage refers, so that the kingdom is here the state of righteousness, outwardly and visibly attaining to power. The commencement of that state, combined with the resurrection of the Old Testament saints, is conceived as being celebrated by the Saviour visibly presenting himself in company with His people at a new covenant-banquet. As the Saviour, when about to depart, was united with His disciples for the last time at the Lord's Supper, so in the kingdom of God He will (according to Matth. xxvi. 29) again gather them, as the great family of God, at the supper of the Lamb. (Rev. xix. 9.) Hence the Jews' fundamental idea of a feast in the kingdom of God is undoubtedly correct, and likewise expressed in Christ's words in the New Testament, only that their carnal sense had, on the one hand, given it a gross material form, and on the other, viewed it isolated and without its spiritual conditions.* An external participation in the kingdom of God, realized outwardly and

---

* On account of such aberrations, Chiliasm has been condemned by the Church ever since the third century. But that the fundamental ideas of that system, apart from their materialized form, have their root in the Scriptures, has been acknowledged by many expositors in recent times, though with the intention of deriving arguments against the Bible. These fundamental ideas are no other than—victory of good over evil, even in outward things, and restoration of the original harmony in the visible creation also.

visibly, necessarily presupposes its inward establishment in the spirit.

Not less erroneous than this Jewish materialism is Gnostic idealism, which, in the place of a real resurrection of the body, which necessarily implies a glorified world, teaches a so-called pure life of the spirit, known, indeed, to Scripture, but only to be condemned as a worthless conception. (2 Tim. ii. 18.) The Bible teaches that the soul necessarily needs an organ; and that, consequently, the state after the dissolution of this terrestrial body till the resurrection is an imperfect, intermediate state. With the ἀνάστασις, the kingdom commences in its complete form, and to this the passage before us points.

While, then, the heathen are represented as being received into it, (the kingdom,) the Jews appear as excluded from it. (Ἔξω points to an ἔσω, since the kingdom is conceived as a limited region of existence into which nothing extraneous can make its way. On this point, see Matth. xxv. 10.) Φῶς is viewed as the element of the kingdom, to which σκότος forms the contrast. In the epithet ἐξώτερον, the idea of distance from the element of life and joy is expressed. (Wisdom of Solomon xvii. 21; xviii. 1.) The κλαυθμὸς καὶ βρυγμὸς τῶν ὀδόντων in the kingdom of σκότος, is parallel with the happy enjoyment of the feast in the kingdom of God, in which former expression the idea of the most exquisite sense of pain, arising from a consciousness of having missed the end of life, is the eternal truth. Moreover, as little as the kingdom is here in itself identical with eternal happiness, so little is the "weeping and gnashing of teeth" identical with eternal punishment; but it must be granted, that kindred circumstances nearer at hand are frequently used to designate more distant analogous ones, and in so far it is correct to refer these contrasts to the final decision. We can only regard the state of suffering in Sheol, (a fuller discussion of which is found in note on Luke xvi. 24,) which the Scripture distinguishes from Gehenna, as the immediate reference in the description of the "weeping and gnashing of teeth." That every possibility of return ought not here to be denied to the rejected Israelites, is indicated, above all, by Rom. xi. 26, where the promise of salvation is given to *all* Israel.

Ver. 13.—In conclusion, both historians then relate that the Saviour, overcome by the bold faith of the warrior, immediately healed the sick man. (Ἑκατοντάρχης is another form for ἑκατόνταρχος, the one used in ver. 1. 'Υγιαίνω, Luke vii. 10, means "to *be* well;" so that, according to his narrative also, the cure appears to have been wrought suddenly.)

§ 6. RAISING OF THE YOUNG MAN AT NAIN.

(Luke vii. 11-17.)

This transaction, which St. Luke alone mentions, is distinctly connected with the foregoing context by the words ἐν τῇ ἑξῆς, ver. 11; we, therefore, proceed here with this paragraph, and the more so, because verses 16, 17, where we read of the fame of Jesus beginning to extend, assign it plainly to the earlier period.

But with respect to the fact of a raising from the dead in general, it is difficult of apprehension, on account of the uncertainty of the fact of death, and of its nature. For the separation of the soul from the body is not to be viewed as absolute, even where corruption is evidently going forward, because then the resurrection of the body (as described 1 Cor. xv.) would be impossible, and, at most, it could only be called a new creation of it. But if there remains, even in death, a bond between the higher vital principle and the elements of the body to be raised, and if medical men confess, that, even to go no farther than ordinary experience, the determination of the actual occurrence of death is, in the highest degree, difficult, we can see that no other assurance against the supposition of a trance in this and the other cases of raising from the dead recorded in the New Testament is *possible*, than that which the word of Christ and the Apostles affords. Where death is really in appearance only, as in the case of the daughter of Jairus, (Matth. ix. 24,) the mouth of truth expressly declared it, though she was thought by all to be dead; but, where death is actually present, it declares the fact with equal plainness. What the short-sighted eye of man can perceive but imperfectly, the Lord of the world of spirits saw through with indubitable certainty. The reality of His miraculous raisings from the dead rests upon the veracity of His person. But, at the same time, the view of death just given renders it easier to picture to ourselves the awakening. For, as at the resurrection it will take place in all through the Saviour's life-giving power; so, in the individual awakenings, He revived activity in the organ that was dead, but not destroyed ; so that the ψυχή which had escaped might again make use of it. Hence every raising from the dead is, so to speak, a full restoration of the entire relation between soul and body, which had been interrupted ; while, in partial restorations, it is the removal of only the disturbance in this or that function, with which the organism of soul and body was affected. But the same heavenly power, which is the life itself, (John i. 4,) effects the latter as well as the former. As the source of all individualized life, it can just as well recal to its organ that which had departed, and restore to harmony what was disordered, as it creates what did not exist. On questions such as these—where the departed soul of the person raised up dwelt in the meantime, and whether, in the meanwhile, it had consciousness or not—the Scriptures, for wise reasons, give no information; and it is sufficient for us to know, that, in this respect, as in general, the state of the dying influences their future condition. But it is the more important to conceive of the raising up of the dead as not unconnected with what is moral. The corporeal resurrection was to be a means of spiritual vivification, not merely for the relatives and for all who saw or heard of the event, but particularly for the person who was himself raised up.* So extraordinary an event could not but affect his inward life decisively, and render the man so raised up a living witness to our Lord's miraculous power.†

Ver. 11, 12.—The town where Jesus restored the son to his afflicted mother, was called Nain, (perhaps from נָעִים, *pleasant*,) a small town of Galilee not far from Capernaum. (On ἱκανός and πολύς, see Matth. viii. 30, compared with Luke viii. 32.) As He approached the town gate, (πύλη,) the Saviour saw a dead person carried out ; it was the only son of a widow. (Μονο-

---

* *Strauss* thinks a reference to the persons raised up improbable, (B. ii., S. 157, second ed.,) because it is not anywhere specially noticed. But this reference did not need to be particularly mentioned, because it was a matter of course. Jesus always wrought for the salvation of men, in every word, and in His most casual intercourse with them ; how much more, then, in an awakening from the dead !

† According to John xi. 41, 42, Lazarus was raised for the glory of God ; but that does not *exclude* a view to his own perfecting by his death and resurrection ; it *includes* it ; for a vivification of the whole man is precisely the highest glory of God.

γενής, as in Luke viii. 42 ; ix. 38 ; Heb. xi. 17, in the sense of "only." But in the idea of "only," as in the Hebrew יָחִיד, there is included also that of "dear," "valued.")

Ver. 13, 14.—The feeling of sympathy for the mother (on σπλαγχνίζεσθαι, see note on Luke i. 78) is specified as that from which the determination of Jesus to waken the dead man lying in the coffin arose. But that does not exclude a regard for the man himself in the transaction. Man, as a conscious being, can *never* be merely a means, as would be the case here, if we were to regard the mother's joy as the sole purpose of the raising of the young man. It is rather the immediate *result* of the action, noticeable by the bystanders, but the less essential; its concealed result was the *spiritual awakening* of the youth to a higher existence, by means of which the mother's joy first became true and lasting. (By σορός is not meant a closed receptacle, but an open bier. The Hebrews called it מִטָּה, *lectulus*.)

Ver. 15, 16.—The Saviour raised the dead man, without contact, by His mere word, (compare Elisha's raising the dead, 2 Kings iv. 34,) which should be viewed as the audible expression of the invisible agency of His Spirit, by which the ψυχή and σῶμα were restored to their true relation in the young man. In the neighbourhood, the bodily raising produced a beneficial spiritual excitement, and that, in the first instance, as was natural, under the form of φόβος τοῦ Θεοῦ. Penetrated by the holiness of Christ's work, they rightly conclude that such holiness, united to such power, indicated a definite mission of Christ from a higher world. They view the miracles quite agreeably to their appointment as an evidence of His prophetic dignity. (The expression: προφήτης μέγας, refers to the greatness of the miracle; raising from the dead was known to be peculiar to the princes of the prophetic order. On ἐπισκέπτεσθαι, see Luke i. 68.)

Ver. 17.—By individual flashes of His divine power like this, darting hither and thither, the Saviour aroused in the whole nation the consciousness that great things were before them. From the ardent anticipation connected with that consciousness, there arose a deep sense of misery and present distress, and a confident courage for the future,—spiritual elements which our Saviour understood how to guide and to employ for His purposes.

§ 7. HEALING OF PETER'S MOTHER-IN-LAW.

(Matth. viii. 14-17; Mark i. 29-34; Luke iv. 31-41.)

After having narrated (Luke iv. 31-37) the history of the cure of a demoniac in the synagogue at Capernaum, which, as it contains nothing peculiar, we passed over, referring the reader to Matth. viii. 28, ff., St. Luke immediately subjoins the healing of Peter's mother-in law with the words: ἀναστὰς ἐκ τῆς συναγωγῆς. St. Mark also (i. 29) introduces this narrative with the same words, while St. Matthew connects it loosely with the account of the cure of the centurion's servant. It is surprising that St. Luke here mentions Simon Peter as a well-known person, without having spoken of him before; this fact might be accounted for on the ground of St. Luke's being entitled to suppose Peter known to Theophilus. Still it can hardly be denied, that this circumstance does also suggest a consideration not unimportant in favour of the view, that St. Luke incorporated memoirs in his Gospel; and as Peter was mentioned in them, St. Luke also named him, without noticing that no allusion had been yet made to His connexion with Jesus. St. Matthew and St. Mark had already prefixed a short mention of Peter, Matth. iv. 18, ff.; Mark i. 16, ff. The fact itself does not contain anything particular; the general observations on the cures wrought by Jesus are applicable to this case also. (See note on Matth. viii. 1.)

Ver. 14, 15.—The mention of πενθερὰ Πέτρου, implies that that apostle was married. According to 1 Cor. ix. 5, Peter did not forsake his wife in the exercise of his apostolical calling, but had her to accompany him in his missionary journeys. (To attempt to explain the form of the disease from St. Luke's expression: πυρετῷ μεγάλῳ συνέχεσθαι, cannot but be unsatisfactory.) In this case, our Lord again wrought by immediate contact, (ἥψατο τῆς χειρός,) and restored her so perfectly that she was at once able to employ herself. The διακονεῖν αὐτοῖς must be viewed only as the *result* of the cure; the proper intention of the cure we must in this case also regard as a moral one.

Ver. 16.—The news of the miraculous cures wrought by Jesus, attracted multitudes to Him, supplicating help. They came after sunset, because the heat of day would have been too distressing to the sick. The Saviour, surrounded by crowds of such unfortunate individuals, who were bowed down by bodily pains, presents, in the healing agency by which He relieves external necessities, an emblem of the spiritual agency which He incessantly exercises within the hearts of men by the power of His salvation. Only we must suppose, that, even in the corporeal deliverance which He granted, He would constantly lead their minds beyond the crowd of earthly wants, to the malady of the soul and its cure. On the δαιμονιζόμενοι, as well as on the prohibition to the demons not to speak of Him, (Mark i. 34; Luke iv. 41,) see more fully in note on Matth. viii. 28, ff.

Ver. 17.—St. Matthew, who, as writing for Jews, takes pains to connect the manifestations in the life of Jesus with the Old Testament delineations of the Messiah, here quotes Isa. liii. 4, with the formula so familiar to him, ὅπως πληρωθῇ. (See note on Matth. i. 22.) The Evangelist, moreover, again departs from the text of the LXX., who thus translate the Hebrew text: οὗτος τὰς ἁμαρτίας ἡμῶν φέρει, καὶ περὶ ἡμῶν ὀδυνᾶται, in which form the words were altogether unsuitable for his purpose. He follows the original precisely, and translates חֳלִי by ἀσθένεια, and מַכְאוֹב by νόσος; the verbs נָשָׂא and סָבַל, used by the prophet, St. Matthew renders by λαμβάνειν and βαστάζειν. This independent treatment of the quotations from the Old Testament forbids us to regard the Greek text of St. Matthew in the light of an ordinary translation,—i. e., one in which the translator does not allow himself any free action. But the bringing forward of just this passage does not seem agreeable to the purpose designed by the context, particularly as in 1 Peter ii. 24, the same passage is explained of the vicarious satisfaction of our Saviour, and the whole 53d chapter of Isaiah is a description of the Messiah as suffering for sinful mankind. But the apparent difference in the exposition of the same passage by two writers in the New Testament disappears, if we keep in view, that physical sufferings (as the acmé of which we are to regard death, see Rom. vi. 23) are only the other aspect of the consequences of sin. The Saviour, who was called to restore the original state of mankind, removed external suffering no less than internal; and, indeed, ordinarily, the former first, because deliverance from it is wont to be a means of arousing a desire for deliverance from the miseries of the soul, and quickening the faith in the possibility of that deliverance. The referring of Christ's saving efficacy to bodily sufferings no more excludes the extending of it to spiritual sufferings, than, on the other hand, the referring of it to spiritual sufferings excludes its extension to such as are bodily. The *whole* man is the object of salvation, body as well as soul. The only point of difficulty is, that λαμβάνειν and βαστάζειν are used of Christ's relation to the ἀσθένειαι and νόσοι, as well as of His relation to the inward sufferings of mankind. (See John i. 29, where our Lord is called, ἀμνὸς τοῦ Θεοῦ ὁ αἴρων τὴν ἁμαρτίαν τοῦ κόσμου.) It seems as if the exercise of healing energy were by no means anything so difficult and productive of suffering, as that βαστάζειν would be an appropriate term to apply to it. Hence we are tempted to interpret λαμβάνειν and βαστάζειν as simply = ἀφαιρεῖν, which, however, is not at all in accordance with the context of the passage Isa. liii., where the Saviour appears in the character of a sufferer. This difficulty is solved, however, if we conceive the healing energy of the Saviour more in its essential character. Viewing the person of the Saviour, as we must, as truly human, as well as truly divine, we cannot but think, that the healing energy of our Lord consisted in a pouring and breathing forth of His vital fulness—that, moreover, His whole soul entered, with heartfelt sympathy, into the necessities of the sufferers—that He really suffered with them. As, therefore, physical exertion produced physical weariness, (John iv. 6,) so also spiritual exertion would exhaust Him spiritually. Hence we may say, that in respect to the ἀσθένειαι and νόσοι also, Jesus laboured in His soul, and bore the sin of the world.

§ 8. PETER'S DRAUGHT OF FISHES.

(Luke iv. 42-44; [Mark i. 35-39;] Luke v. 1-11.)

The idea just suggested receives confirmation from the succeeding verses in St. Luke and St. Mark. For early next morning the Saviour retired into solitude (εἰς ἔρημον τόπον) for prayer. St. Mark uses ἔννυχον λίαν instead of the more usual expression ἡμέρας γενομένης in St. Luke. Ἔννυχον, for which some Codd. read ἔννυχα, occurs only in this passage. We are frequently told that Jesus spent the night in silent prayer. (See Luke v. 16; vi. 12; ix. 28.) We must believe that this retirement for solitary prayer proceeded from a real necessity, unless our Lord is believed to have done something unmeaning, or merely apparent,—which would favour Docetic notions. According to the Scriptures, Jesus was in all things (κατὰ πάντα) like men, excepting in sin, that He might be merciful, (ἐλεήμων, Heb. ii. 17.) And it is just in this view of our Lord that rich consolation is afforded, and the possibility is provided of taking Christ for our example. Regarded in His character as man, the prayers of Jesus (which must, indeed, be conceived as uninterrupted, agreeably to His own command to us, [Luke xviii. 1,] but still as having their points of elevation in peculiarly consecrated moments) were, so to speak, seasons of heavenly refreshment and strengthening from above, in order to overcome the powers of darkness that incessantly bore down upon Him. But, at the same time, our Lord's moments of prayer are to be viewed as seasons when the Saviour was absorbed in the contemplation of the high purposes of the Father with Him, and in the depths of the divine love, in order to consecrate himself more and more to the completion of His work.

Ver. 43.—The people, however, touched with the impression which the demeanour of Jesus produced, hastened after Him into the wilderness; and St. Peter, who always appears the most energetic among the Apostles, goes to Jesus to inform Him that the multitude was seeking for Him. But our Lord withdraws, with the observation, that He must extend His ministry over the whole of Israel. The ministry of the Saviour, according to its entire constitution, was not calculated to be exercised continually at the same place, but to arouse the mass of the nation from the slumber of death. For this reason He never stayed long in a place, but journeyed hither and thither. Jesus limited His more special oversight of souls to the narrower and wider circles of His disciples, who so yielded themselves to His sanctifying influence, that they forsook all— came out from their previous connexions, and followed Him. (St. Mark [i. 38] uses the expression ἐχόμεναι κωμοπόλεις, which occurs only in this passage. By κωμοπόλεις, he means villages of some size, approaching towns in extent. The participle ἐχόμενος is to be taken as in ἡμέρα ἐχομένη, [Luke xiii. 33; Acts xiii. 44,] in the sense of "near," "neighbouring." The words in St. Mark: εἰς τοῦτο ἐξελήλυθα, which correspond to St. Luke's expression: εἰς τοῦτο ἀπέσταλμαι, are also remarkable. It is true, there is the various reading in St. Mark, ἐλήλυθα, which, as being the more common phrase, [ἔρχεσθαι sc. εἰς τὸν κόσμον,] must be regarded as inferior in value to the less common. Ἐξέρχεσθαι refers to the formula used by St. John: ἐξέρχεσθαι ἐκ τοῦ Θεοῦ, ἐκ τοῦ πατρός, with which ἐκ τῶν οὐρανῶν would be synonymous. [See John viii. 42; xiii. 3; xvi. 27, 28; xvii. 8.] In ἐξελήλυθα, a distinct reference is implied to the original relation of the Son to the Father; while ἀπέσταλμαι refers only to the appearance of Jesus as determined by God.)

Luke v. 1.—With an indefinite transition, the narrative of St. Peter's draught of fishes is appended; for the multitude, whose inconvenient proximity is here spoken of, (ἐπικεῖσθαι, *to crowd, to press upon*, a sign of eagerness indeed, but still an annoyance to Jesus,) is not the same as that mentioned in ver. 42, because the clause interposed, ἦν κηρύσσων ἐν ταῖς συναγωγαῖς τῆς Γαλιλαίας, resumes the indefinite character. It is, therefore, uncertain whether this narrative should be connected immediately with the preceding.

With respect to the narrative itself of St. Peter's draught of fishes, it has been already remarked, in the note on Matth. iv. 18, that in the mere outline there given of the calling of St. Peter, (on which event St. John alone sheds adequate light,) the mention of the circumstance, that St. Peter was called to become a fisher of men, was introduced into the picture merely as an individual feature, without our being able to maintain that this expression of our Lord's was uttered just at His first meeting with St. Peter. In this place St. Luke gives the more circumstantial historical narrative of the occurrence, in connexion with which our Lord designated St. Peter a fisher of men; but he takes for granted that Jesus had, on a former occasion, become acquainted with St. Peter, and only shews how, on this occasion, the exalted greatness of Jesus opened upon him with unsuspected splendour, and thus powerfully attached him to the person of Jesus. (The Lake of Gennesaret, on the shore of which Christ here appears as teaching, derives its name from the district Γεννησάρ. *Josephus* says, [B. J. iii. 10, 7:] Ἡ δὲ λίμνη Γεννησὰρ ἀπὸ τῆς προσεχοῦς χώρας καλεῖται. The lake is also called θάλασσα τῆς Γαλιλαίας, Matth. iv. 18. In the Old Testament it is called יָם כִּנֶּרֶת, *Sea of Chinnereth*, Josh. xiii. 27. The Chaldee spelling of the name has the various forms, גְּנוֹבָר, גִּינֵסַר, גְּנֶסַר. [See *Winer's* "Realwörterbuch," *s. v.*]

The extent of the lake is given by *Josephus* (*ut sup.*) as 120 stadia in length, and 40 in breadth.

Ver. 2, 3.—The pressure of the people caused Jesus to leave the land and enter one of the boats. This was drawn up on land, as was usually the case with small vessels; Jesus desired St. Peter, to whom the boat belonged, to push it off from the land into deep water, (ἀπὸ τῆς γῆς ἐπαναγαγεῖν,) and then taught from the ship, unmolested by the crowding of the multitude. This setting of the boat afloat is to be distinguished from the bringing it out into the midst of the sea, (ἐπαναγαγεῖν εἰς τὸ βάθος = *altum.*, ver. 4,) which was done for the purpose of fishing.

Ver. 4, 5.—After His discourse was finished, and the people, consequently, dismissed, our Lord orders St. Peter to cast out the net for a draught. (Χαλάζω, properly "to slacken," "let go,"—*e. g.*, a bow, then "to sink," "let down.") St. Peter, disheartened by a whole night's unsuccessful toil—a circumstance which shews, that at that time the Apostles still pursued their business, at times at least—complies, more out of deference to the dignity of Jesus, than from faith in a successful result. (St. Luke alone uses Ἐπιστάτης. See viii. 24, 45; ix. 33, 49; xvii. 13. He calls Jesus by that name, instead of the Hebrew "Rabbi," which he could not assume, as being known to his Greek readers. But he uses διδάσκαλος for it also,—*e. g.*, vii. 40.)

Ver. 6, 7.—St. Peter complies with the Saviour's desire, and they enclose a multitude of fishes in their net, so that it broke, and their companions were obliged to bring the other boat alongside, in order to take in the abundance bestowed. (Βυθίζεσθαι occurs only in this passage with the signification of "sinking deeper," "sinking." The word is used figuratively in 1 Tim. vi. 9.)

According to the intention of the historian, the abundant produce of this draught, which forms a contrast with the unsuccessful fishing through the night, when St. Peter toiled alone, are to be viewed as the *result* of Christ's presence, and the *effect* of His power. Christ is, therefore, here set forth as the Sovereign of nature, who, by the secret magic of His will, had power to direct even what is unconscious, according to His purposes; just as the same power of the unsearchable God, who governs the universe, year by year conducts the fish of the sea and the birds of the air in the courses of their migrations by invisible clues.* Phenomena, analogous to the great miracles of nature, appear around the person of our Lord, as if clustered around their centre; He rules in the extended kingdom of existences as a God visible, personally near; by invisible, mysterious ties, all is connected with the word of His mouth,—the expression of His holy will. And what are apparently unconscious movements and stirrings of nature, appear, when controlled by His will, as directed to the highest ends of the moral world.

Ver. 8, 9.—The feeling of a special divine energy, which proclaimed itself to them as emanating from Jesus, seized them all with astonishment ($θάμβος$) mixed with fear; but St. Peter, from his excitable temperament, at once gave expression to this feeling in act and word. His sinfulness appeared to him in such glaring contrast to the heavenly power displayed before him in the Saviour, that he fell down, partly adoring and partly praying: $ἔξελθε\ ἀπ'\ ἐμοῦ$. In all this the idea is evidently involved, that what is divine, and what is not so, are incompatible with each other. He who beholds God must die, (Judges vi. 23; xiii. 22; Dan. x. 17,)—an idea which is perfectly true of the revelation of the divine character according to the legal point of view —which we must conceive as being still that of Peter—in the thunders of Sinai, Exod. xix. 12. But in God's gracious revelation in the Saviour, God's nearness to sinful man is not only endurable, but even animating and refreshing; since, not on a sudden, but gradually, it makes old things pass away, and dreates things that are new. For this reason also our Lord quiets his anxiety, and calls upon him to be a fellow-worker for the kingdom which He had come to establish.

Ver. 10.—The words: $ἀπὸ\ τοῦ\ νῦν\ ἴσῃ\ ζωγρῶν\ ἀνθρώπους$, express the main point in the whole transaction, to which not only the draught of fishes, but also the strengthening of the Apostles in faith, were subordinate. We observe here, for the first time, a

---

* The conception of what are called *instincts*, by which the brutes are said to be guided to such orderly movements, is destructive of the profounder view of the life of nature. The same may be said of the instincts, which brutes are supposed to possess as something detached from the general life of nature, as must be said of the so-called *faculties of the soul*, or *powers of nature*, in so far as they are imagined to be complete organs, existing and acting of themselves. Just as the latter are functions of the one life of the soul, so the former are functions of the one great life of nature, which must be viewed, not as *out of* God, but *in* God.

characteristic of Christ's actions, which we shall have frequent occasion to notice in future. The Saviour *teaches by actions,*—He speaks by deeds to those around; penetrating with deep spiritual glance into the essence of things, He is enabled to deal with the formations of nature in such a manner as to use them as a rich system of symbols or hieroglyphics.* Something analogous may be observed even in the conduct of noble and exalted personages on earth. The ideas which inspire them are shadowed forth in their doings; and under their influence the most insignificant relations become ennobled. A system of symbolical actions of this kind is expressly seen in the ministry of the ancient prophets. (See Jerem. xiii. 1, ff.; Ezek. xii. 1, ff.; xxiv. 1, ff.) Of all the actions of Jesus, none presents this characteristic so undeniably as the cursing of the fig-tree, (Matth. xxi. 18, ff.,) which, without such a theory, involves inexplicable difficulties. The advantages of a language of fact like this, are self-evident; where fancy and feeling predominate, as is always the case wherever the mind has not risen above that state which is marked by the absence of reflection, a lively, concrete fact always produces infinitely more effect than an abstract argument. In reference to the question in what the import of this transaction consists, we are met by the circumstance, that an occurrence similar to this, which introduces the more intimate connexion of St. Peter with the Saviour, concludes it also. (John xxi.) A symbolical intimation of the subsequent spiritual ministry of St. Peter, who is regarded as the representative of the apostolical body, meets us at the beginning and the close of St. Peter's connexion with his Lord on earth. In the expression: ἔσῃ ζωγρῶν ἀνθρώπους—instead of which we find in Matth. iv. 19, and Mark i. 17, ποιήσω ὑμᾶς ἁλιεῖς ἀνθρώπων—that they are to gain over others to themselves, is not the only point of comparison with the spiritual

---

* Augustine observes appropriately on this point:—*Interrogemus ipsa miracula, quid nobis loquantur de Christo; habent enim, si intelligantur, linguam suam. Num quia ipse Christus verbum est, etiam factum verbi verbum nobis est.* (Tract xxiv. in Joann. Opp., vol. iii., p. 349, edit. Bened.) With these words a beautiful passage out of *Hamann's* works (pt. i., p. 50) may be compared, who, instructed by that Spirit, who always teaches the same truth in all places and at all times, writes quite independently of that Father, as follows:—" Every Bible-narrative bears the image of man,—a body, which is ashes and worthless,—that is, the outward letter; but besides that a soul,—the breath of God, the life and the light, which shines in the dark, and cannot be comprehended by the darkness."

work of the Apostles; other and more minute relations evidently present themselves. In the first place, the idea of catching includes the relation of the conscious agent to an unconscious subject, and the latter's being overcome by the former. This is precisely the relation that subsisted between the Apostles—as the representatives of the βασιλεία—and the κόσμος. While the former represent the higher principle of life, those who are in the κόσμος are in a state of ignorance as to the nature of the higher life. Next, the figure of catching fish refers to the transference of the convert from the old element of life, to the pure, holy element of the Gospel, on which import of the figure the hymn, ascribed to Clement of Alexandria, dwells in the following strain :—

Σῶτερ Ἰησοῦ	Saviour Jesus!
Ἁλιεῦ μερόπων	Fisher of men,
Τῶν σωζομένων	Even the saved!
Πελάγους κακίας	From the ocean of sin
Ἰχθῦς ἁγνοὺς	Winning pure fish,
Κύματος ἐχθροῦ	From the hostile wave
Γλυκερῇ ζωῇ δελεάζων	By a sweet life.

Allusions to this passing from the old element of life into the new one of Christianity, are often found in the early ages of Christianity in the use of the name ἰχθῦς of Christians. (See *Suiceri thes. eccl.*, s. v., ἁλιεύς.) Even in the Old Testament there exist the elements of this comparison. See Jerem. xvi. 16, where the first hemistich runs thus in the LXX.: Ἰδοὺ, ἐγὼ ἀποστέλλω τοὺς ἁλιεῖς τοὺς πολλοὺς, λέγει κύριος, καὶ ἁλιεύσουσιν αὐτούς. Parallel with this the second hemistich has—Ἀποστέλλω τοὺς πολλοὺς θηρευτὰς καὶ θηρεύσουσιν αὐτούς.

Ver. 11.—This miraculous event united the bond between the disciples and the Saviour more closely; they left their worldly employment, and, following Christ, espoused that spiritual calling which He pointed out to them in its analogy with their former external one. The ἀφιέναι and ἀκολουθεῖν are not, however, to be viewed as an outward act merely, but pre-eminently as an inward transaction, of which the external was but a visible expression. The power of the higher life in Christ, which seized them, liberated them spiritually from those earthly fetters, and joined them to their Lord by invisible bonds.

Externally they did, even at a later period, return to their craft. (See note on John xxi. 3, ff.)

§ 9. JESUS STILLS THE SEA.

(Matth. viii. 18-27; Mark iv. 35-41; Luke viii. 22-25.)

According to St. Matthew and St. Mark, the following event is placed immediately after the healing of St. Peter's mother-in-law (ἐν ἐκείνῃ τῇ ἡμέρᾳ;) in St. Luke, on the contrary, it stands in a totally different connexion, and is connected with the preceding context merely by the loose expression, ἐν μιᾷ τῶν ἡμερῶν. The first verses of this section in St. Matthew (viii. 19-22) are, moreover, parallel with a passage in St. Luke, (ix. 57, ff.,) separated from the first passage (viii. 22, ff.) by a great intervening space. Now, as we have seen above, (Luke iv. 42, ff.; v. 1, ff.,) that in St. Luke the several sections of his Gospel, which have just been explained, are connected with the healing of St. Peter's mother-in-law, as immediately as this narrative of the stilling of the sea is in St. Matthew and St. Mark; but that according to all the three Evangelists the healing of the Gergesene follows the stilling of the sea, the time being accurately noted, we have here another striking example of the uncertainty which attends every attempt to dispose the separate details of this section, as found in the different narratives of the Evangelists, in a complete chronological arrangement. The words Matth. viii. 19-22, are, moreover, rather an introduction, than an integral part of the narrative. St. Luke introduces them at a later period (ix. 57, ff.) in a more precise connexion, and in a more complete form. For the interpretation of them we refer, therefore, to that passage. St. Matthew seems to have inserted them here in the section which treats of the miracles of Jesus, to bring out the contrast with the all-commanding will of Jesus; and to make apparent, that the greatness of the requirement to follow Him who had not where to lay His head, is, on the other hand, modified by the fact, that He governs the elements. With respect to the fact itself, it exhibits Christ as the Lord of nature in a new aspect, and as calming and pacifying its throes and convulsions. Sin, which, in its fearful effects, disturbed even the physical part of existence, is thus represented as overcome by the Prince of

Peace in the most various forms of its manifestation. (Isa. ix. 6.) In so far as what is external is always a mirror of what is internal, this, and similar events in the evangelical history, express the analogous influence of the Saviour in the agitated region of the inward life. (See note on Matth. xiv. 21, 22.) The Saviour in a ship, accompanied by His disciples, tossed on the waves of the sea, is a natural antitype to the ark containing the representatives of the incipient human race, and a prefiguration of the Church in its relation to the πέλαγος κακίας in the κόσμος.

Ver. 23, 24.—Our Lord, intending to pass over to the eastern shore of the lake, (ver. 18,) entered the ship, and fell asleep. St. Mark, with his usual care, finishes the picture more minutely. On the one hand he observes, that in company with that one ship other smaller ones crossed, (iv. 36,) and on the other, he describes precisely the Saviour's position. (He was lying in the hinder part of the vessel, [πρύμνα, Acts xxvii. 29, 41,] resting His head. Προσκεφάλαιον is probably a support to lean against; in other cases, generally a "pillow.") While Jesus slept, a sudden hurricane arose. (Instead of λαῖλαψ, which St. Mark and St. Luke use, St. Matthew has σεισμός, which denotes properly "earthquakes," then "violent agitations" in general. The LXX. use it for סָעַר.)

Ver. 25, 26.—Though of *little* faith, because they feared being swallowed up together with the sleeping Saviour, (on ὀλιγόπιστος, see note on Matth. vi. 30,) yet the disciples are *believing*, since they ask deliverance from the Lord; and the Saviour, not to put their faith to shame, produced a perfect calm. (Γαλήνη = דְּמָמָה, Psalm cvii. 29, in Symmachus.) It is remarkable, that Jesus' word appears not merely as checking the lawless course of the elements, and reducing the scattered powers to oneness and harmony, but that, according to St. Mark, He quiets the waves of the sea by a direct address to it: σιώπα, πεφίμωσο. There is undoubtedly more implied in this than a mere oratorical personification. It indicates a view of nature, as of something living, which is affected by divine, as well as by hostile, influences. Our Lord, by viewing the commotions of nature as the echo of the general interruption of harmony, refers them to their original source. (On ἐπιτιμᾷν, expressing a command of divine power, see note on Matth. viii. 29.—Φιμόω, *to close the mouth*, 1 Tim. v. 18; φιμοῦσθαι, *to be dumb*, *silent*, κατάζω = ἡσυχάζω, used of the wind, Matth. xiv. 32; Mark vi. 51.)

Ver. 27.—The more colossal and externally striking the effects of the Saviour's power are, the more they impress the natural man. In themselves the hidden spiritual effects are infinitely mightier and more exalted; they go to the root of sin, while in the former, it is only its distant echoes that are affected.

§ 10. CURE OF THE GADARENE DEMONIAC.

(Matth. viii. 28-34; Mark v. 1-20; Luke viii. 26-39.)

We avail ourselves of this most important and difficult of the miraculous cures—the first, according to St. Matthew's arrangement, among the narratives of the treatment of what are called δαιμονιζόμενοι—to develope in a connected way, agreeably to the intimations contained in the Scriptures, the view which we entertain on the condition of such persons, and on the several phenomena which the Scriptures mention in connexion with them. The entire Scriptures are undeniably pervaded with this idea,* that what is holy and what is unholy in mankind,

---

* The vigorous opposition offered to the doctrine of the existence of the devil and bad angels, may, in part, arise from a pure intention,—viz., the desire to prevent the great abuses which have been made of the doctrine; but, in part, motives of a totally different kind prompt to this opposition,—viz., a laxity of morals, and an unwillingness to acknowledge to themselves, in all its deformity, the nature of that evil which men detect plainly enough in themselves. They ought to separate the abuses from the thing itself, and then it would be seen how, in this information respecting the relations of the world of spirits also, the Scriptures are perfectly adapted to the wants of men. Many a soul despairs in the conflict with evil thoughts, or yields itself up to them, which might be well able to overcome them, were it taught to distinguish itself from the Evil One, and to ascribe the fiery darts by which it is assailed, to the wicked being who directs them against it. (Ephes. v. 16.) If we carefully banish the devil and his angels, we retain a world full of devilish men, and for ourselves a heart full of devilish thoughts, as Göthe appositely remarks: "They got rid of the wicked *one*, but the wicked *ones* remain;" for evil itself, with its frightful manifestations, cannot possibly be removed; it stands engraved in history with indelible lines. Hence the doctrine, that the source of evil is in a higher region of life, is a blessing to mankind; it contains the key to the doctrine of redemption. On this account also, it is so deeply based in the teaching of Scripture, that it will never be possible to overthrow it in the Church, except, indeed, the Church should ever so far forget itself as to admit accommodation to evident errors into the idea of its Saviour, which would be equivalent to self-destruction. But, as truth in

has not its root in themselves, but in a higher region of existence, whence arise those influences of good and evil, which may be received or rejected on the part of men, according to the standing and the faithfulness of the individual. With a comprehensive glance, the doctrine of Scripture conceives the good as well as the evil in the universe as a connected whole,—only with this difference, that the good, being the divine itself, always appears likewise as the *absolute;* the unholy, on the contrary, is indeed represented as a real interruption of the harmony, but still only as something dependent on the will of the creature. The Scriptures know of no second principle, and the Church has invariably condemned the doctrine of Manicheism as incompatible with the idea of God. By removing the source of evil out of human nature, *redemption* is recognized as possible. For it is only the germ of good in man, viewed in its state of bondage under a hostile power, that can be redeemed; but the hostile power, as well as man himself, if he has consciously resigned himself to it altogether, and is, therefore, absorbed in it, is not an object of redeeming power. The kingdom of evil, then, regarded in its individuality, and

---

general will remain unconquered, so will also the truth respecting evil, which consists precisely in our knowing *that* it exists, and *how* it exists. For it is the real victory of evil not to be known. But with regard to the *use* to be made of the doctrine, great care is certainly commendable in this respect, as all deeply impressive ideas, like edge tools, must be applied prudently. The use made of the doctrine in Scripture supplies most excellent hints on this subject. *First,* we find that, in the earlier periods of the Old Testament, the doctrine appears only in obscure intimations; it is not till the times of the captivity, when the worship of the true God was firmly established among the people, that the germs were further unfolded. In this fact, we have a plain hint not to propound the doctrine either before children, or before minds so immature that they may be regarded as childish; before such, it is better, after the example of the Old Testament, to refer the manifestations of evil to the permission of God, without entering more minutely on the subject. The Saviour *teaches* concerning the devil only in the presence of His disciples. *Next,* the doctrine of the kingdom of darkness and its agency ought never to be brought forward in any other way than in connexion with the doctrine of redemption. The consciousness of grace which overcomes all, is the surest means to prevent all misconception of the doctrine. *Lastly,* the doctrine, in general, is not so much included among the subjects of the formal κήρυγμα τῆς ἀληθείας, just as it does not appear so in the New Testament, and in the Confessions of Faith; it is more particularly important in the private cure of souls. In the manifold enigmas of self-examination, we shall find that this doctrine has not only a deep psychological root, but that a beneficial effect may be expected from its being wisely employed.

conceived as the opposite (though only relatively) of the kingdom of good, is called in the Scriptures, διάβολος καὶ ἄγγελοι αὐτοῦ, (Matth. xxv. 41; Rev. xii. 9;) also, the βασιλεία τοῦ σατανᾶ, (Matth. xii. 26.) The terms, διάβολος, and σατανᾶς, (= שָׂטָן = κατήγωρ τῶν ἀδελφῶν, Rev. xii. 10,) are used only in the singular for the central power of evil, who is conceived as carrying in himself potentially the power of his kingdom. In one passage, (Matth. xii. 26,) it is true, Satan seems to be used as equivalent to δαιμόνιον; but even there, it is only in appearance. The subordinate spirits, corresponding to the ἄγγελοι τοῦ Θεοῦ, are called δαιμόνια, less frequently, δαίμονες; (Matth. viii. 31; Mark v. 12; Luke viii. 29;) more frequently, πνεύματα ἀκάθαρτα; and, (in Ephes. vi. 12,) πνευματικὰ τῆς πονηρίας. The signification of the word δαίμων = δαήμων, is, among ancient writers, more comprehensive; it denotes "one who is well informed, knows;" and because knowledge manifests itself as the essence of the spirit, it denotes spiritual existences in general. (The character of the knowledge is more accurately specified by adjuncts, as ἀγαθοδαίμων, κακοδαίμων.) In the same way as good is viewed in its different modifications in the angels of light, evil is individualized in the angels of darkness in its modifications. (On the classes among the demons, see note on Ephes. vi. 12.) The germs of this mode of viewing the subject are found in the very earliest writings of the Old Testament, and we may imagine a development of these germs in the popular mind by continued enlightenment through the spirit of truth, without calling to our aid the foreign influence, which some have thought to have been exercised over the Jews during the Babylonish captivity.* But then if we start from the mag-

---

* This view, which has become so current, is involved in considerable historical difficulties. For since those regions, to which Nebuchadnezzar removed the Jews, were under the dominion of the Chaldeans, by whose popular worship such an effect cannot be supposed to have been wrought upon the Jews, since they had no doctrine of evil spirits, (*Münter's* conjecture in his "*Religion der Babylonier*," S. 87, ff., that there was some instruction on the subject of demons in the Chaldean esoteric doctrines, is mere hypothesis;) the question arises,— Whether the system of the Zendavesta, to the influence of which it is ascribed that the Jews became acquainted with the doctrine of demons during the captivity, ever was prevalent in the Chaldee kingdom? There were Magi in Babylon, it is true, even before the capture of that city by Cyrus, (see *Bertholdt's* third Excursus to his commentary on Daniel;) but whether these Magi were worshippers of Ormuzd, and acquainted with Ahriman, is very doubtful, because

nificent conception of the unity of the kingdom of darkness, the question occurs,—What peculiar form of the influence of the powers of darkness do the Scriptures denote by the name δαιμονιζόμενοι? For although it likewise connects what is spiritually evil in mankind with the influence of the devil, (*e. g.*, St. John says of Judas Iscariot: ὁ σατανᾶς εἰςῆλθεν εἰς αὐτόν, chap. xiii. 27,) yet the representatives of evil among mankind (false prophets and antichrists) are never called δαιμονιζόμενοι. In the case of the latter, on the contrary, we always perceive appearances of sickness, generally convulsions of an epileptic nature, and a derangement or loss of personal consciousness. But still this state of sickness does not appear as the characteristic of demoniacs; for it is evident that the same maladies may, in one case, be of demoniacal origin, in another, not; for instance, one who is dumb in consequence of organic defect, perhaps an injury to the tongue, would never be called a demoniac, though we read in Luke xi. 14 of a demoniac who was dumb. Many demoniacs shew themselves to be maniacs, (*e. g.*, the Gadarene, whose history we are discussing;) but it does not, therefore, follow, that every madman, even such as were disordered by organic injuries of the brain, was considered by the Jews a demoniac.* All the descriptions of demoniacs indicate a

---

(see *Gesenius'* second appendix to his commentary on Isaiah) none of the Chaldee names of gods have the least similarity to the Persian. But if the religion of the Zendavesta had been esoteric only in the Chaldee empire, then, again, it is not easily conceivable how the poor Jewish exiles should have become acquainted with it, and that so far as to have received thence new doctrines into the circle of their ideas. The whole subject needs, as before observed, a more thorough historical investigation. But *that* idea is not less to be rejected, that the belief of the existence of evil spirits is a notion belonging to the infancy of mankind. The history of the development of demonology in the Scriptures, as well as the nature of the case, proves the contrary. The purer, the deeper, and the truer the conception of the divine, as the good, the more thoroughly does man know evil in its nature, and comprehend it in its development. The Scriptures represent the false prophets and false Christs as its most perfect forms, and place them at the end of the world's course. The fact that our most modern systematic theology, even since its restoration after its self-destruction, has been still so little able to adopt the doctrine of the kingdom of darkness, (as is seen in *Schleiermacher's System,* for instance,) proves, that the Christian consciousness has not allowed itself to be thoroughly penetrated with the light of Christian principle.

* *Josephus* (*Ant.* vii. 6, 3) pronounces the demons to be the souls of wicked men, and, on the same supposition, *Justin Martyr* explains the nature of the demoniacs. (Apol I. c. 16, p. 14, edit. *Braun.*) This view must, however, be

strange *mixture* of psychical and physical occurrences. In the *first* place, the condition of the demoniacs appears always to suppose a certain degree of moral delinquency; but yet so, that the sin which they practised manifests itself, not so much as wickedness, properly speaking, but more as predominant sensuality, (probably lasciviousness in particular,) which was indulged in opposition to their better self. In this manner, in such persons, the noble, deep-seated germ of life might be preserved, and out of it the desire for deliverance might be developed, if the consciousness of the frightful condition of knowing themselves to be bound under the power of sin was awakened within them. *Next*, in the demoniacs there appears, as a characteristic, a weakening of the bodily organization, particularly the nervous system, occasioned by the sin in which they indulged; and from the very intimate connexion of the nervous life with all mental activity, the enfeebling of the former must very easily produce derangement in the whole internal life. This derangement appears the more striking in such unfortunate beings, the more excitable their conscience seems to have been; testifying to them that their misery was the result of their own fault, without their being in a condition, by their own power, to extricate themselves from the fetters of sin and the kingdom of darkness, to the influence of which they had resigned themselves. On the other hand, one who, in his inmost life, had resigned himself to sin, and that more of a refined than a sensual kind, might be a πονηρός, but not a δαιμονιζόμενος. For in such persons there is still a kind of inward unity, which may in the end become despair, (as in the case of Judas,) but not madness, which presupposes a violent inward conflict between the better self and the power of darkness, by which it feels itself enthralled. It coincides with our view, *first*, that in all the descriptions of demoniacs we find mention made of physical sufferings. Convulsions, epilepsy, raving, and lunacy, (according to Matth. xvii. 14, ff.,) are particularly noticed—the kind of maladies which agree well with our hypothesis. This agreement appears to be less, where demoniacs are called dumb or deaf; but even such forms of

---

regarded merely as the private opinion of a few, and is not to be taken as the prevailing popular sentiment. *Josephus* (*Ant.* viii. 2, 3) narrates the cure of a demoniac. *Philostratus* (iv. 20, 25) records of Apollonius Tyaneus also that he exorcised evil spirits. Compare *Baur's* "Leben des Apollonius," S. 144.

physical suffering may be easily brought to harmonize with our general view, if only, as just observed, we do not conceive of organic destruction of hearing and speech in the case of demoniacal deafness and dumbness, but rather nervous paralysis, ascribed by the troubled conscience of the sufferers to the influence of the kingdom of darkness, which they were conscious they had permitted to enter their souls. Hence the common opinion, which pronounces the demoniacs to be sick people, is true in one aspect; but it takes a partial view, embracing only what is outward, while the representation of Scripture regards the phenomena in their moral origin. *Next,* it is equally in accordance with our view, that a desire for deliverance, a hope of being cured, is expressed by all the demoniacs. And though this longing is, as it were, but a *spark* of hope and faith, which yet glows within; still even this implies a susceptibility to the powers of the higher life which the Saviour presented to them. Accordingly, the demoniacs do not appear by any means as the most wicked, but only as very miserable men. The decidedly wicked man, who has admitted the hostile influence, undisturbed and unopposed, into the inmost recesses of his heart, cannot be healed. Faith—susceptibility for a higher principle of life—is wanting in the most secret depths of the soul. In the demoniacs, the contest against evil presents apparently a more hideous form; but that there is still a contest against it remaining, is just what speaks for the existence of a germ of noble life; so that in the case of the demoniacs also, *faith* is the necessary condition of their being healed. But *again,* our view is in accordance with the circumstance, that, in the descriptions of the demoniacs, we often find an absorption of the human individual consciousness in the influence of the hostile power of darkness. They speak in its character, or rather it speaks through them, but always in such a way, that, for a moment, the consciousness of their individuality again rises to the surface. This state is quite parallel with ἔκστασις, or ἐν πνεύματι εἶναι, and γλώσσαις λαλεῖν; that is, the effect produced in these latter states by the holy element of the πνεῦμα or φῶς—see 1 Cor. xiv., where the suppression of the consciousness (νοῦς) by the overpowering holy force manifestly appears—is, in the former case, produced by the unholy element of darkness (σκότος.) We are not, therefore, by any means, to conceive of the inward state of the demoniac, as if two or more persons were contained in the individual; but the suffering person appears with his own human consciousness suppressed, and a foreign (spiritual) life in vigorous action; but as there are alternating seasons in which the hostile power is ascendant, and in which it retreats, so, after a paroxysm, even in lucid intervals, the human self again shews itself with all the sense of its misery in a condition of such bondage. And, *lastly*, we discover also in the demoniacs an enhanced faculty of foreseeing, a kind of somnambulic *clairvoyance*, by which, in particular, they recognize the significance of the Saviour's person for the entire kingdom of spirits. This very circumstance agrees perfectly with the hypothesis, that nervous affections form the basis of such states, so far as they are corporeal; and how easily unnaturally increased nervous action is united with the gift of clairvoyance, is sufficiently familiar from the history of animal magnetism. It is thus that the contradictory language of the demoniacs is to be explained; at one time they manifest a deep insight into the truth; at another, coarse popular notions are mixed up in their words, so that the whole of their conversation has the fearfully vivid character of the mistaken and confused talk of madmen, who not unfrequently give utterance to striking thoughts, but put them in such a connexion with other elements, that the splendour of the thought is only a more melancholy testimony to the greatness of the derangement in the seat of life whence it issued.

On these grounds, we have still to explain why demoniacs are no longer to be found.* *First*, it is certainly undeniable, that the spirit of the Gospel has had a beneficial influence on mankind even in this respect, and that thus various of the manifestations of evil (particularly in its coarse forms) have been mitigated. It is a mistake when some have gone so far as to maintain, on the authority of 1 John iii. 8, that the devil has no more opportunity to exert his influence in the Church of Christ,

---

* I assume here, according to the prevalent opinion, that such is the fact, and that no demoniacs are now to be met with. But it must not be forgotten, that eminent medical men are of a different opinion,—*e. g.*, Esquirol in Paris, (compare the "Magazin für ausländische Heilkunde, von Gerson und Julius." Sept. 1828, S. 317.) *Kerner's* views on the subject are well known. The missionary *Rhenius* gives an account of a remarkable demoniac in the East Indies, in the year 1817. (In *Meyer's* "Blätter für höhere Wahrheit," B. 7, S. 199, ff.) Were the Apostles to visit our madhouses, it is questionable how they would designate many of the sufferers in them.

(least of all can the passage referred to supply any proof of that opinion.) It might be allowed of the *ideal*, invisible Church—the communion of saints; but the external Church evidently forms a mixed communion, in which the power of Christ's redeeming work is, indeed, in a state of advancing development, but has not yet, by any means, sanctified the whole; for which reason, the influences emanating from the kingdom of darkness must not be conceived as destroyed, but only as modified. *Next*, the fact in question may be accounted for from this, that the knowledge of evil spirits and their influence is not now so prevalent. In many maniacs or epileptic persons there may be a state very similar to that of the demoniacs, only the sufferer himself (as medical men commonly do) looks upon his state in a different light.* But it is evident that the circumstance of the unhappy being's knowing or not knowing of his state, is something purely accidental; it is but a reflection of the time in which it may happen to take place, just as the name is which the madman applies to his demon. At most, therefore, we can only say, that the cases have become much more rare; and this shews how the restorative power of the Saviour will, at some future period, harmonize all discords in the life of man, both of his body and of his soul.

---

* On the same grounds it is accounted for, that there is no mention made of demoniacs in the Old Testament. The doctrine of demons and their influence had but little currency among the people before the captivity; even if, therefore, the kingdom of darkness did produce similar manifestations, (as at the present day,) yet they were not *recognized* as such. After the captivity, forms quite analogous to those of the New Testament may have existed; but the prophetic writings of that period contain little historical matter, and hence it is easily explained how we meet with no references to the subject in them. At the time when the Apocryphal books were written, spiritual life in general was at a low ebb among the Israelitish people; and for that very reason the opposing principles were but little developed. For that *such frequent* manifestations of the hideous power of darkness appear in the New Testament side by side with the noblest manifestations of the divine, is, doubtless, to be accounted for from the excited character of the whole period, which caused all the opposing principles to come out more distinctly. But with respect to the cause of the Evangelist *St. John's* silence about demoniacs, that cause is to be sought only in his relation to the synoptic Evangelists; the latter had narrated a sufficient number of the cures of demoniacs; and for that reason St. John (to whom, in general, the actions of Jesus serve only as points of connexion for the discourses to be communicated) thought he might pass them over in silence. At least the view which St. John entertained of the devil (according to viii. 44; xiii. 27) was not, in any respect, different.

If, after these remarks, we turn to the history of the *Gadarene demoniac* before us, which has, moreover, special difficulties, we have to observe, in general, that St. Matthew speaks of *two* sufferers, while the other two Evangelists know of only *one*. A similar case of the number being doubled occurs in Matth. xx. 30, where he speaks of two blind men, though St. Mark (x. 46) and St. Luke (xviii. 35) make mention of one only. This difference belongs to the class discussed in the Introduction, (§ 8,) which we must take to be such as they manifestly are— as discrepancies—without seeking for explanations; as, for instance, that one carried on the conversation, and is, therefore, alone mentioned, and so forth. In this case it is extremely improbable that there should have been two persons afflicted in this manner. Probably St. Matthew has combined this occurrence with a kindred one, which might happen all the more easily, because he is wont uniformly to treat of the mere framework in the general outlines only. *Further*, there is an uncertainty about the spelling of the name of the place, after which the demoniac, of whom our narrative speaks, was called. In all the three Gospels there are the various readings, Γεργεσηνῶν, Γαδαρηνῶν, Γερασηνῶν; from which we may conclude, that they did not originally agree in the reading. The difference of the reading arose from the effort to establish uniformity. Then, too, it must be allowed, that the possibility of such a variation in the name of the place results from the character of the locality itself. In Decapolis, (see note on Matth. iv. 25,) where, according to Mark v. 20, the occurrence took place, lay the well-known town of Gadara, the capital of Perea, sixty stadia distant from Tiberias, and renowned for its warm baths. Farther to the north lay Gerasa, a place on the eastern boundary of Perea; at some distance from the sea indeed, but yet so that the territory of the town extended down to it; and hence the "countries" (χῶραι) of the two towns might easily be confounded. (On the two places, see *Winer's* "Reallexicon," s. v.) *Origen* (Opp. vol. iv., p. 140) does indeed report, that in his day the precipice was shewn down which the swine were said to have cast themselves, and calls the neighbouring town Gergesa.* But the entire account speaks only of a tradition, and,

---

* *Origen* speaks of the reading Γεργασηνῶν as the common one in the Codd. of his day. He says, that the reading Γαδαρηνῶν is found in only a few copies,

for that reason, the existence of any town of that name is rendered doubtful, since there are not any other traces of its existence at the time of Jesus that can be relied on. (On the ancient Gergesa, see Deut. vii. 1; Joshua xxiv. 11; *Joseph. Ant. I.* 6, 2.) In the text of St. Mark and St. Luke, the reading Γαδαρηνῶν is undoubtedly the correct one. In St. Matthew, on the other hand, that reading is certainly only taken from the other two Evangelists. But whether Γεργεσηνῶν or Γερασηνῶν is preferable in St. Matthew, it would be difficult to decide. In the edition of *Griesbach-Schulz*, the former reading is adopted on the authority of the Codd.; but yet it may be questionable, whether this reading was not introduced into the Codd. simply on the authority of *Origen*, and whether the original reading in St. Matthew was not Γερασηνῶν. *Fritzsche* is also against Γεργεσηνῶν, but decides in favour of Γαδαρηνῶν, in which case the original reading must have been the same in all the three Gospels, which is not probable on account of the many variations in the name.

Ver. 28.—The description of the demoniac, in the present narrative, is evidently of such a kind, that we must regard him as a maniac. The madness seized the unhappy man convulsively at separate moments; then, after such paroxysms, a period of quiet supervened. St. Mark depicts the poor man's state most vividly in his description, (v. 3-5.) He shewed tremendous muscular power, as is usual in cases of mania. In order to restrain him they had chained him, (πέδη = περισκελίς, *fetter for the foot*, is a species of the general term ἅλυσις;) but he broke the bonds, and would not even endure clothes on his body. The hostile power, to which he had allowed an entrance into his soul, drove him to solitary places, where he lived in the tombs, and his appearance terrified the passers-by. We are to imagine the μνήματα to have been at a distance from the town, as well as hewn in the rocks; for which reason St. Mark (v. 5) connects ἐν τοῖς μνήμασι καὶ ἐν τοῖς ὄρεσιν. But, from time to time, his better self awoke up within, and gave vent to itself in

---

and decides in favour of Γεργεσηνῶν, on the ground of the traditional report. The passage about Gergesa is as follows:—Γέργεσα, ἀφ' ἧς οἱ Γεργεσηνοί, πόλις ἀρχαία. περὶ τὴν νῦν καλουμένην Τιβεριάδος λίμνην, ἀφ' οὗ δείκνυται τοὺς χοίρους ὑπὸ τῶν δαιμόνων καταβεβλῆσθαι.

a doleful cry of anguish, and in self-inflicted torments, to which the consciousness of guilt drove him, (κράζων καὶ κατακόπτων ἑαυτὸν λίθοις, Mark v. 5.) The narratives of St. Mark and St. Luke only, supply a vivid picture of Jesus' meeting with this unhappy man, and the way in which the Saviour dealt with him. St. Matthew (ver. 29) begins at once with the exclamation: τί ἡμῖν καὶ σοί, which renders the picture of the action obscure. According to St. Mark and St. Luke, there was first a salutary emotion, which came over the poor man, who experienced the tumult of wild powers within, at the sight of the Prince of Peace. He hastened up to Jesus, and fell at His feet,—evidencing, in this act of homage, the obscure confession, that he expected help from Him. We should, indeed, utterly disarrange the connexion if we were to take the words κράξας μεγάλῃ φωνῇ, which St. Mark and St. Luke connect with the προσεκύνησε, as being contemporaneous with it. Then the worshipping could only be an action proceeding from the dominion of demoniacal power, and the object of the humble petition could not have been to be healed, but μή με βασανίσῃς.* But it is evident, that in that case the demoniac would not have hastened to meet Jesus; but would have fled from Him. And, moreover, this view does not accord with Mark v. 8: ἔλεγε γὰρ κ.τ.λ. (Luke viii. 29 has παρήγγειλε γὰρ κ.τ.λ.) The γὰρ is evidently intended to mark the reason of the exclamation: τί ἐμοὶ καὶ σοί; and the aorist is, therefore, to be construed as a pluperfect. See *Winer's* Grammar, § 41, 5.

Ver. 29.—The whole is then conceivable in the following form:—With a presentiment of help, the unhappy man, when he came within view of the Saviour, hastened towards Him, and fell at His feet; Jesus commanded the unclean spirit to depart from Him, and in an instant his condition was reversed. A violent paroxysm seized him, and, under its influence, he spake, with a suppression of the human consciousness, in the character of the demoniacal power, and cried, τί ἐμοὶ καὶ σοί, although he had just before sought the Lord with purely human feelings. (The common term for the command to the demons to come out, is ἐπιτιμᾶν = גָּעַר, in which the idea of severe reproof

---

* Similar expressions from demoniacs occur also in the exorcising of a devil by *Apollonius* of *Tyana*; but *Philostratus* probably had reference in them to the narratives of the New Testament. See *Baur ut sup.* S. 145.

is implied.) This change in the temper of the demoniac in connexion with the fact, that his healing was not contemporaneous with the command of Jesus to the spirit, is a very important circumstance for the comprehension of this narrative, and of the state of demoniacs in general. According to our general view detailed above, it is most simple to conceive of the matter thus. By the contraction of deep guilt, and long continuance in the practice of sin, the situation of this pitiable being had, probably, become so dangerous, that a forcible penetration of the holy power of Jesus into him might, indeed, have availed to repulse the power of darkness, but would, perhaps, have destroyed the bodily organization of the demoniac. Even Christ's first effort, expressed in the words, ἔξελθε ἐκ τοῦ ἀνθρώπου, was followed by a violent paroxysm, (although we must conceive of the Saviour's power as moderated,) and, under its influence, the unhappy man spoke in the character of the dominant power of darkness, absorbed in it as to his consciousness. To bring him out, again, from this state, and recover him to a consciousness of himself, Jesus, diverting him from the inventions of his fancy, inquired his name, which must necessarily bring him to reflections on himself. In the words of the demoniac, τί ἡμῖν (ἐμοί) καὶ σοί, (corresponding to מַה־לָּנוּ וָלָךְ, Joshua xxii. 24; 2 Sam. xvi. 10,) which are here intended to denote the consciousness of complete distinction of nature, as well as in the invocation "Son of God," we have a plain instance of the gift of *clairvoyance* common with persons of this kind. For although we are not to conceive of any doctrinal notion connected with the use of this name, yet it denotes a holy character, in whom the better self, in its enlightened seasons, surmised a helper, but in whom the hostile power, when it gained the predominance, saw the judge. Just because of this character of the confession, the Saviour often *forbids* it,—e. g., Mark i. 34; Luke iv. 41, οὐκ ἔφιε λαλεῖν τὰ δαιμόνια, ὅτι ᾔδεισαν αὐτόν. (See also Acts xvi. 17.) Believing confidence alone, and not knowledge associated with terror, makes the confession of His name desirable. That it was not forbidden in this case, was on account of the state of the unhappy man, who had to be treated with great care. According to two of the Evangelists, this confession was immediately followed by the petition, μή με βασανίσῃς. If we were to regard the man as the subject speaking, fear of suffering, which he imagines coming upon him from Jesus, would not agree with his previous approach to our Lord; from which it must be supposed that he expected good from Him. But if we suppose that it is the demon speaking through the man, the singular does not agree with the subsequent statement, that many evil spirits have possession of him. But that the latter view is the more correct, is shewn by πρὸ καιροῦ, Matth. viii. 29. For this suggests the idea, that a period of the victory of light is at hand, in which all the powers belonging to the kingdom of darkness shall be consigned to the ἄβυσσος. (See note on Luke x. 18.) But this idea, correct in itself, appears, in the language of the demoniac, in an insane connexion. First, confounding himself with the hostile power that ruled in him, he utters in *behalf* of it a prayer, which stands in contradiction with the inmost longing of his real self; then again, in the conversation carried on, for the most part, in the character of the kingdom of evil, there is a mixture of various things derived from the habits of the sufferer as a man, particularly the phrase ὁρκίζω σε τὸν Θεόν, (Mark v. 7,) which, of course, suits only his character as a man. But this very confusion in the talk of the demoniac evidences the truth of the narrative; just as evil is in itself contradictory, so the talk of the unfortunate subject of evil likewise appears self-contradictory.

As was hinted above, the Saviour did not desire to dispel the power of darkness suddenly, because, from the man's depressed state, that would not have cured him, but would have annihilated his organization by the too mighty conflict of powers; for this reason He wisely prepared for the complete cure. After the first paroxysm, therefore, Jesus asks, as was observed, (according to Mark v. 9; Luke viii. 30,) in order to recover him to a consciousness of his individuality, Τί σοι ὄνομα? But the insane man, persisting in his confusion of himself with the power which ruled over him, cries out, Λεγεών; and the Evangelists add, that this name was suggested by the impression, that more than one evil power was exerting its influence over him. In this trait, error and truth are combined with fearful vividness, just as they were interwoven in the unhappy man's mind. The impression was true, that not merely one part of his being was given over to the influence of the demoniacal world, but that his *whole inner man* was laid open to them, (see Matth. xiv. 9, where it is said of Mary Magdalene, that she had seven devils, —*i. e.*, was become the possession of the kingdom of sin in all the departments of her being.) But this correct idea the sufferer expresses in the form of calling himself Λεγεών; St. Mark (v. 9) adds, ὅτι πολλοί ἐσμεν,—very expressively choosing the first person. This name was evidently derived from the immediate experience of his senses. The view—which he might at some time have had the opportunity of taking of a compact Roman legion—that terrible instrument of the Roman dominion over the world, at the sight of which the Jew especially trembled—gives him the idea, that a compact host of Satanic powers was come down upon him. In his present state of mental aberration, he confounds himself with this host, conceives of it as a unity divided into many, and gives himself the name Λεγεών.* The utterance of this name is then followed (Mark v. 10; Luke viii. 31) by the repeated (see Matth. viii. 29) petition, in which the afflicted man again speaks in the character of the power that controlled him, not to deprive the devils of their power, and send them to the ἄβυσσος. (This term is used also in Rom. x. 7, and frequently in the Apocalypse, ix. 1, 2, 11; xi. 7; xvii. 8; xx. 1, 3. It is used like τάρταρος [2 Peter ii. 4] and γέεννα, and corresponds to the Hebrew תְּהוֹם, which, by the by, is not used in the Old Testament for the dwelling-place of evil spirits. In the Old Testament שְׁאוֹל comprehends, in its more general signification, what we find distinguished in the New. The ᾅδης or the φυλακή of the New Testament, as the assembling place of the dead, must be conceived as strictly separate from the ἄβυσσος. See note on Luke xvi. 28.) But again, popular notions are mingled in this petition, as the additional clause in St. Mark, ἔξω τῆς χώρας, shews. These words are, doubtless, connected with the popular Jewish opinion, that certain spheres of operation were assigned to the bad angels, as well as to the good. The demon desires not to be removed out of his. If a removal out of one χώρα into another was regarded as impossible, their being driven out of the χώρα assigned would be precisely equivalent to being sent down into the ἄβυσσος.

---

* A similar instance of diversity regarded as a divided unity, may be found in the Rabbinical language, in which לִגְיוֹן denotes "the commander of a legion." (See *Buxtorf, Lex. Talmud.*, p. 1123.) We might imagine, that the poor man had an indistinct idea of being possessed by an archfiend, (ἄρχων τῶν δαιμόνων,) so that *potentiâ*, the power also of the angels subject to him, was exercised upon him.

Ver. 30-32.—Thus far the evangelical narrative affords a most vivid picture of this occurrence, which, up to this point, presents a kindred appearance to all other narratives of this sort. But now a circumstance is subjoined, which is the more difficult, because the New Testament supplies nothing analogous to it; and for that reason it is a tempting subject for the mythical interpretation.* But it must be confessed, that, independently of the general reasons against that interpretation, it is opposed, in this case, by the exact accordance of all the three narratives, which is rarely demonstrable in mythical subjects. It is recorded that a great herd of swine (Mark v. 13, states the number as 2000) presented itself to the view of the demoniac,† who, speaking in the character of the hostile power, begged that the demons might be allowed to enter the animals. Jesus permits it, the demons enter the swine, and they precipitate themselves from the cliff (κρημνός) into the lake. The fact of the devils' passing into brute creatures, is here quite as difficult as the subsequent circumstances.‡ For although an influence of what is spiritual over what is physical, both on the part of righteousness and of sin, is recognized throughout the Scriptures, (see Gen. iii. 17, ff. compared with Rom. viii. 18, ff.,) yet the expression, εἰσέρχεσθαι εἰς τοὺς χοίρους, is particularly difficult; for this reason, because it stands contrasted with εἰσέρχεσθαι εἰς ἄνθρωπον, in such a way as too much to identify what is human

---

* As in the New Testament the swine of the Gadarenes, so in the Old, Balaam's ass, (Numb. xxii. 28, ff.) forms an offence and a stumbling-block. In both events spiritual effects are seen in connexion with the brute creation.

† The Evangelists seem not to agree exactly here, since St. Matthew says, the herd was μακρὰν ἀπ' αὐτῶν; but the other two, that they were ἐκεῖ. The idea of μακράν must be taken relatively; the herd was on the *same* plain, which extended down to the lake, (ἐκεῖ) but at a considerable distance (μακράν) from the scene of the dialogue.

‡ Dr. Strauss here, as everywhere, settles the matter at once, and cries, Myths, nothing but myths! He smiles when he sees any one taking pains to solve the difficulties which the case presents. And yet this great master of negation, in his review of *Kerner's* work on similar phenomena of the present day, is compelled to acknowledge that he is unable to devise any solution of them at all plausible. What presumption to deny that similar phenomena may have existed in the apostolic times, which his wisdom may not be able to understand! for he has no other reason whatever for his assertion, that these narratives of the New Testament are myths, than their extraordinary character. (See "Jahrbücher für wissenschaftliche Kritik." 1836, Dec. S. 111, ff.)

with the brute. Besides, it seems unaccountable why the Saviour should yield to a passing whim of the sufferer, as one might be inclined to regard his request, to which the Evangelists ascribe such real consequences; first, the entering into the animals, then, their destruction. To suppose the latter occasioned by a violent assault of the unhappy man, is as inappropriate, as it is contradictory to the narrative, to view the destruction of the animals as *accidentally* coinciding with the request of the afflicted man. But if we assume that, agreeably to the meaning of the narrators, the destruction of the animals was occasioned by the spirits, we do not see what reason can be conceived why the demons should have entered the swine in order themselves immediately to destroy these subjects of their power. On this obscure passage I beg leave only to offer a few hints and conjectures, which may lead to farther inquiry. The expression, εἰςέρχεσθαι εἰς τοὺς χοίρους, must, in any case, be taken to imply merely an *influence* on the crowd of animals; but this must have been immediately intended for their destruction, and that on account of their *possessors*. On the part of evil, the intention of their destruction might then have been to limit the Saviour's power in its salutary influence, just as the effect of it actually was (Matth. viii. 34) to prepossess the minds of the people against our Lord. On the part of Christ, the permission might appear sufficiently prompted, in the first place, relatively to the sufferer, because, by that acquiescence, the subsequent paroxysm was alleviated, and the cure made possible; next, relatively to the owners of the animals, since the worldly loss would be a trial for them, and might consequently lead them to a decision for or against God and His cause; or, if we suppose that the animals belonged to Jews, (which would not be impossible, since there was often a mixture of heathenism and Judaism in the border provinces,) it must have been a warning visitation, because a culpable love of gain led them to keep animals which, according to the law, were unclean. By such an interpretation, the *moral* aspect in this fact would be kept in view, which is no small advantage, since we thus avoid questions such as these:—How could Christ be so unjust as to destroy 2000 swine? Such a question is exactly parallel with the absurd remark, how God can be so unjust as to allow a murrain to take place in this or the other spot. The simple answer to the question is, that where cattle die, men are to be quickened, in order to learn that there is a God, and that all that He does is right.

Ver. 33, 34.—St. Matthew follows up the account of the destruction of the herd with a notice of the flight of the herdsmen, and the crowds of inhabitants coming out of the city. Of the state of the patient he gives no further account. But St. Mark and St. Luke describe him most vividly in his totally altered condition after his complete recovery, which was doubtless preceded by another violent paroxysm. He sat quietly and clothed at the feet of Jesus, and was an object of surprise and admiration to the inhabitants. They acknowledged, that nothing but supernatural holy power could have accomplished the cure of one so shattered. St. Matthew, in common with the other two Evangelists, records, that the inhabitants besought Jesus to leave that region.* This might have been an expression of the fear of God, (as in Luke v. 8;) but as the Saviour immediately leaves them, the anxiety lest they should suffer further loss of property from the Deliverer of souls, may have mingled in this request,—a meanness of disposition which must have taken from our Lord all hope of being able to sow the seed of eternal life with profit in hearts so overgrown with thorns and thistles. St. Mark, (v. 18-20,) and St. Luke, (viii. 38, 39,) give some particulars of the man's future course, which St. Matthew does not touch upon. He desired to accompany the Saviour; but the latter discouraged him, and sent him back to his friends, *charging* him to tell what God had done for him. The reason of this charge (see note on Matth. viii. 4) must be sought in the *man himself* who was healed. The deeper the malady had been rooted in him, the more advantageous it would be for him to take an active part in the duties of life, since being much occupied with himself might have drawn him back to his old sins. Moreover, such employments would form a salutary check on his undue partiality for solitude, which was, in all probability, closely connected with the vices that had laid the foundation of such a surrender to the evil powers. And, lastly, the telling of his being healed by the Messiah of Nazareth, naturally confirmed his faith in the person of his deliverer.

---

* The phrase ἐξέρχεσθαι εἰς συνάντησίν τινι, is not found anywhere else in the New Testament, except in Matth. viii. 34. In the Old Testament the LXX. use it several times,—*e. g.*, Gen. xiv. 17; Deut. i. 44.

§ 11. CURE OF A PARALYTIC.

(Matth. ix. 1-8; Mark v. 21; ii. 1-12; Luke v. 17-26.)

St. Matthew proceeds in his delineation of Jesus as a worker of miracles, without reflections and eulogies, merely by the simple narration of mighty acts that fill the soul with holy astonishment. His call by our Lord (ver. 9, ff.) does, indeed, seem interposed as something foreign to the subject; but it is manifestly narrated not on its own account, but for the sake of what stands connected with it, (ver. 11-13). The Evangelist means to exhibit the contradiction which existed between the judgment of the Pharisees, uttered at the feast in St. Matthew's house, and that of the people, as to the person of Christ, and, at the same time, to shew how our Lord fulfilled His high calling in such miraculous cures. It must be confessed, that the verses 14-17 have a less direct reference to the context of the ninth chapter. They seem to have been occasioned by the previous narrative of the feast, and to serve merely to complete the narrative of a day so important to St. Matthew.

If, too, we compare the *place* of the first event of this chapter in St. Matthew, with that which it occupies in St. Mark and St. Luke, we here again meet with a most surprising variation. According to Matth. ix. 1, 2, the cure of the paralytic is in immediate connexion with the account of the demoniac, as having taken place directly after arriving at the other side of the lake. St. Mark and St. Luke, on the other hand, assign this event to an earlier period. The former connects it with the history of the cure of the leper, (Mark i. 40, ff.). St. Luke does, indeed, likewise connect it with this event, (ver. 17;) but with the loose expression: ἐγένετο ἐν μιᾷ τῶν ἡμερῶν. The account of his call, and the circumstances connected with it, which, in St. Matthew, follow the cure of the paralytic, are, indeed, placed in the same sequence in St. Mark and St. Luke; but the narrative of the woman with the issue of blood, which comes next in St. Matthew, (ix. 18, ff.,) is recorded by St. Mark, (v. 22, ff.,) and St. Luke, (viii. 41, ff.,) much later. The difficulties arising hence as to the chronological arrangements of the several sections of the Gospels appear to us insuperable.

Matth. ix. 1.—St. Mark does indeed also mention the circumstance, that Jesus returned to the west coast of the lake after the cure of the demoniac; but his narrative becomes indefinite in the words: καὶ ἦν παρὰ τὴν θάλασσαν, and he then introduces the narrative of Jairus' daughter with the phrase: καὶ ἰδού. St. Matthew makes Him go immediately to Capernaum, (ἰδία πόλις,) which St. Mark (ii. 1) also mentions as the place where the paralytic was. St. Mark and St. Luke carefully describe the scene in the house where Jesus was. People filled the porch of the house, (τὰ πρὸς τὴν θύραν scil. μέρη = vestibulum,) so that the entrance was closed up. Among those present, St. Luke enumerates learned Jews, (νομοδιδάσκαλοι = γραμματεῖς, סֹפְרִים,) some of whom were even from Judea and Jerusalem; but that they were come to Capernaum purposely on account of Jesus, is a gratuitous conjecture. Our Lord is represented as being employed partly in teaching, (ἐλάλει αὐτοῖς τὸν λόγον scil. περὶ τῆς βασιλείας, Mark ii. 2,) and partly in healing.

The words in Luke v. 17, δύναμις κυρίου ἦν εἰς τὸ ἰᾶσθαι αὐτούς, are very obscure. There is no previous substantive to which the word αὐτούς refers; we might take it as an indication that St. Luke, in the narrative of this event, had incorporated a document with his gospel, without taking care to alter what in it had reference to some antecedent. But the words δύναμις κυρίου ἦν, are still more difficult. To refer κύριος to God, so that we should have to supply μετὰ Ἰησοῦ, in the sense of the power of God being with Him, so that he *could* heal, is unsuitable for this reason, that the ellipsis is too harsh. But as referred to Christ, the thought can be no other than this, that the power of healing that dwelt in Him *manifested itself;* so that ἦν would have to be interpreted with a pregnant meaning, perhaps with ἐργαζομένη supplied.

Ver 2.—On this occasion, among other sick people, they brought a paralytic (see note on Matth. viii. 6) to Christ, who could not, however, as he was laid upon a bed, be brought to Him in the usual way, because of the crowd. St. Mark and St. Luke relate in detail the manner in which those who carried the sick man made their way to Jesus. The whole description can be understood only from the oriental construction of houses, in consequence of which the flat roof might be reached either by a ladder from the outside, or from a neighbouring house.

Still the breaking up of the top-floor, which was generally laid with tiles, (διὰ τῶν κεράμων, in St. Luke,) appears rather strange; but perhaps the description is to be understood of their somewhat enlarging the entrance into the house from above. (Ἀποστεγάζω, Mark ii. 4, is a strong term to express the undertaking of the people, so strong in faith. Χαλάω = χαλάζω, used by St. Mark, is several times found in St. Luke also, v. 4, 5; Acts ix. 25; xxvii. 17. Κράββατος = *grabatus*, corresponds to κλινίδιον in St. Luke.) In this proceeding, though extraordinary, and in some measure even inconvenient, the compassionate Saviour saw only the faith of the parties concerned. (The faith of the sick man is viewed as one with that of the friends who assisted him; he doubtless encouraged them, and imparted to them his own lively emotions.) In this case, again, (see note on Matth. viii. 1,) definite doctrinal ideas do not form the substance of this faith, which consists rather in the inward need of help, that feels itself powerfully attracted to that quarter whence it expects help. That this sense of need was, in some of the cases of cures, only of an external kind, is seen from narratives such as that in Luke xvii. 12, ff., of the ten lepers. Usually, however, the *external* need was associated with the *internal*, and, in every instance, the latter was *intended* to be aroused by the former; and where that did not happen, reproof was administered. The words immediately addressed to the sick man by our Lord: ἀφέωνταί σοι αἱ ἁμαρτίαι σου, shew that in this case there was no want of inward susceptibility. Perhaps this address was occasioned by penitential expressions on the part of the paralytic, which the words (in St. Matthew) θάρσει τέκνον might suggest. His peculiar sin might have brought on the illness under which he was suffering, and thus have excited a sense of his sinfulness. But even if that was not the case, still Christ might have felt himself called to pass at once from the outward phenomenon to its moral source, in order to prepare for the inward cure by the outward one. The connexion of sin and disease, or suffering of any kind, is a necessary one. The Jews, like the unspiritual man in general, (see John ix. 2, 34,) erred only in this, that, from a case of affliction, they felt themselves warranted to criminate the patient *personally*, which could not but necessarily give rise to false and unrighteous judgments. The just conclusion is to regard the suffering of the individual as proof of the guilt of the whole race, and consequently of himself; that produces humility and meekness. (See note on Luke xiii. 4.) But in what light soever the condition of the patient may be viewed, Jesus announces to him the forgiveness of sins. This is to be viewed as the root of the new life that was to be awakened in the soul of the penitent, and, for that very reason, the expression implies not merely the annulling of the punishment of sin, but the removal of sin itself by the communication of a higher, holier power of life, which, however, could only gradually (as we see in the case of the apostles) transform the whole inner man; so that ἀφίωνται (the Doric form) is to be taken not as a wish, but as creative and effective: "Thy sins are forgiven; I forgive them thee even now." But in those words, the Saviour had regard not only to the good of the sufferer, but also to the spiritual excitement of the people, and even of the Pharisees, as the sequel of the conversation shews.

Ver. 3.—The Pharisees had a correct insight into the nature of forgiveness of sins; they recognized in it a prerogative of God;—that is, so far as it is intended to be not merely a kind wish or an empty declaration, but a *living effect*, it presupposes a knowledge of the secrets of the heart, and a divine power of life, which is capable of overcoming the sinful power, and of translating into the element of the spirit. Hence, so far as the Church forgives sins, (John xx. 23,) God is in it, and the persons who pronounce the forgiveness are only the organs of the forgiving power of God. But as Jesus here forgives sin, not in the name of another, but in His own, and in full inward power, their accusation would have been true, if, as they imagined, Jesus were a mere man. They regarded the forgiveness of sins as a sacred act of God, which no one could perform without robbing God of His honour; and in that they were perfectly right. (The profound sense which the Scriptures attach to βλασφημέω, βλασφημία, is unknown to the profane writers of antiquity; it there denotes primarily only "to speak injuriously of any one," then "to utter something of evil omen," the opposite of εὐφημεῖν. It is monotheism only that leads to the notion of blasphemy, [corresponding to the phrase נֹקֵב שֵׁם יְהֹוָה in the Old Testament,] which denotes not only cursing and blaspheming God, but also, in particular, the assumption of the honour of the Creator on the part of the creature, John x. 33.) But as the Redeemer is the only-begotten Son of the

Father, He exercised even this prerogative; and blessed was the man who believed in Him, for he experienced the saving power of the Lord in his heart. But we must allow, that thoughts like those of the Pharisees might have occurred to a mind, not indeed decidedly irreligious, but more prone to speculation; for faith in the revelation of God in Christ is something very great. Such genuine doubt, or, rather, such an uncertainty, would have exhibited itself very differently from what it did in the Pharisees; in them the Saviour reproves such thoughts severely, as sinful. The reason was probably the following:—The conspicuous elevation of Jesus, which was reflected purely in childlike minds, reached their hearts also; but they opposed themselves to these sacred impressions, from the feeling that, if they gave entrance to them, they must renounce altogether their principles and their practices. Standing thus in inward opposition to God, they were glad to make use of circumstances, which might be perplexing even to sincere minds, as a welcome means of enabling them to justify their conduct in their own eyes. (Εἰπεῖν ἐν ἑαυτῷ, ἐν καρδίᾳ = אָמַר בְּלִבּוֹ. St. Luke uses διαλογίζεσθαι, by which the activity of the λόγος = νοῦς is expressed. But the διαλογισμοί, according to the invariable use in Scripture, are referred to the καρδία, לֵב. See note on Luke ii. 35.)

Ver. 4, 5.—Jesus, penetrating their thoughts, (Mark ii. 8 rightly assigns the spirit as the principle of knowledge in Him,) reproves their sin, but does not deal with them as incorrigible persons. Knowing the insincerity of their hearts, and the difficulty of believing, our Lord endeavours, by an external fact, to aid in overcoming these difficulties. Accordingly, the miracle (see note on Matth. viii. 1) appears here in its proper intention of deepening the impression on the heart, presupposed by it, in order to bring to the conviction that the worker of miracles does not teach *what is true* in his own name, but the *truth* by commission from above. (Ἐνθυμεῖσθαι, Matth. i. 20; Acts x. 19, and ἐνθυμήσεις, Matth. xii. 25; Heb. iv. 12, are nearly related to διαλογίζεσθαι and διαλογισμός, like θυμός to καρδία. But the former terms have generally a bad meaning associated with them. We might denominate θυμός the disturbed κραδία, and the ἐνθυμήσεις the impure actions thence proceeding. The question of our Lord, τί ἐστιν εὐκοπώτερον; is accommodated to the external manner of conception, which the miracle was intended to assist. According to it, what is external is called greater, more difficult, than what is internal,—that is, the forgiveness of sins; the spiritual eye, indeed, takes the opposite view of them.)

Ver. 6, 7.—As Son of Man, Jesus expressly claims the ἐξουσία to forgive sins, in which the declaration of His higher nature is involved. In the expression: υἱὸς τοῦ ἀνθρώπου ἐπὶ τῆς γῆς, there is the implied contrast with Θεὸς ἐν τῷ οὐρανῷ; so that the Messiah appears as the representative of God upon earth. The idea of the Jews, that the forgiveness of sins would be among the prerogatives of the Messiah, (*Schöttgen*, "Jesus, der wahre Messias," Leipzig, 1744, S. 307. *Bertholdt Christol. Jud.*, p. 159, seqq.,) evidently expressed the recognition of His higher nature; hence Jesus desires to rouse to a conviction of the true nature of υἱὸς τοῦ ἀνθρώπου. (*Fritzsche* removes the difficulties in the construction of the clause, τότε λέγει τῷ παραλυτικῷ, [Matth. ix. 6,] by the ingenious conjecture τόδε; but, as the Codd. exhibit no various reading, he has properly refrained from introducing it into the text. According to the common reading, we must take the words as parenthetical, and interposed by the Evangelist.)

Ver. 8.—The narrative is silent as to the effect of the miracle on the Pharisees, because there was nothing pleasing to report; but it is observed of the simple people who were open to divine influence, that they proclaimed God's praise with wonder, quite in agreement with the Saviour's intention, blessing the Author of all good for the revelation of His glory in Him. (See Matth. v. 16.) The concluding clause in St. Matthew, τὸν δόντα ἐξουσίαν τοιαύτην τοῖς ἀνθρώποις, is not to be interpreted as if (ἐξουσία being taken as the cause for the effect) it was in praise of the blessings flowing from God to men through Jesus; ἄνθρωποι = γένος τῶν ἀνθρώπων rather includes Jesus himself, in whose gift of miracles the divine power was so gloriously manifested. Without being able to define doctrinally the view held by the multitude regarding the person of Jesus, we may say, that this thought has its full eternal truth. For, as certainly as the Word of the Father was revealed in the person of our Lord, so certainly was Jesus also truly man; and what of divine fulness was manifested in Him had been imparted to the human race in general in *His* humanity. (Instead of θαυμάζειν, used in St. Matthew, St. Mark has ἐξίστασθαι, and St. Luke ἔκστασις ἔλαβεν ἅπαντας. The latter expression is the stronger; it denotes being in transports. [See Mark v. 42; Acts iii. 10.] In other places this expression has a qualified signification, [see note on Acts x. 10,] and is used, like ἐν πνεύματι εἶναι, of a state of prophetic rapture. In Luke v. 26, παράδοξα = θαυμαστά, corresponds to the Hebrew נִפְלָאוֹת.)

END OF VOL. I.

www.ingramcontent.com/pod-product-compliance
Lightning Source LLC
Chambersburg PA
CBHW051735300426
44115CB00007B/576